Inroads to Software Quality

"How To" Guide and Toolkit

Alka Jarvis and Vern Crandall

To join a Prentice Hall PTR Internet mailing list, point to
http://www.prenhall.com/register

Prentice Hall PTR
Upper Saddle River, New Jersey 07458
http://www.prenhall.com

Library of Congress Cataloging-in-Publication Data

Jarvis, Alka.
    Inroads to software quality : "how to" guide and toolkit / Alka
Jarvis and Vern Crandall.
        p.   cm.
    Includes bibliographical references and index.
    ISBN 0-13-238403-5
    1. Computer software--Quality control. I. Crandall, Vern.
II. Title.
QA76.76.Q35J37   1997   96-29566
005.1'068'5--dc21   CIP

Editorial/production supervision: *Jane Bonnell*
Cover design director: *Jerry Votta*
Cover design: *Talar Agasyan*
Manufacturing manager: *Alexis R. Heydt*
Acquisitions editor: *Bernard M. Goodwin*
Editorial assistant: *Diane Spina*
Marketing manager: *Miles Williams*

 © 1997 by Prentice Hall PTR
Prentice-Hall, Inc.
A Simon & Schuster Company
Upper Saddle River, New Jersey 07458

The publisher offers discounts on this book when ordered in bulk quantities. For more
information, contact Corporate Sales Department, Prentice Hall PTR, One Lake Street,
Upper Saddle River, NJ 07458. Phone: 800-382-3419; FAX: 201- 236-7141;
email: corpsales@prenhall.com

Product names mentioned herein are the trademarks or registered trademarks
of their respective owners.

Printed in the United States of America
10   9   8   7   6   5   4   3   2

ISBN 0-13-238403-5

Prentice-Hall International (UK) Limited, *London*
Prentice-Hall of Australia Pty. Limited, *Sydney*
Prentice-Hall Canada Inc., *Toronto*
Prentice-Hall Hispanoamericana, S.A., *Mexico*
Prentice-Hall of India Private Limited, *New Delhi*
Prentice-Hall of Japan, Inc., *Tokyo*
Simon & Schuster Asia Pte. Ltd., *Singapore*
Editora Prentice-Hall do Brasil, Ltda., *Rio de Janeiro*

Dedication

To my husband, Steve Jarvis, for his constant love, support, and encouragement, without which this book would not have been completed.

Alka Jarvis

To my three sons, Lance, Shane, and Scott, who have been an inspiration to me since the day they were born.

Vern Crandall

We would both like to dedicate this book to the pioneer software developers who established the true principles of software design early in the computer era and changed our lives and careers forever.

Contents

2 PRODUCT ASSURANCE   29

3 SOFTWARE QUALITY ASSURANCE (SQA)   77

4   SOFTWARE QUALITY STANDARDS   105

5   OVERVIEW OF TEST CYCLES   141

9   PROCESS IMPROVEMENT ROAD MAP   241

10   STANDARDS AND EVALUATION OF PROCESS   263

11   SOFTWARE DEVELOPMENT, TOTAL QUALITY
MANAGEMENT, AND RISK MANAGEMENT   281

Foreword

*O*ne of the greatest challenges people face is making changes. The traditional seems safe and comforting, while change poses risks and the possibility of failure to the person implementing the change. On the other hand, without change there would be no hope, because things would never get better.

Alka Jarvis and Vern Crandall epitomize risk-takers. I have known and respected both for many years. I have watched them master the traditional, and then recognize the need to find a better way. This book is about a better way to improve the quality of software, lower software costs, reduce cycle time, and improve customer satisfaction. The book is easy to read, and the New Paradigm described within the book brings testing up to date—designing errors out (and quality in), eliminating dependencies and minimizing the number of states the system can take on, thus making it easier to test and maintain. Rather than approach software development in terms of life cycles, they approach software development in terms of a Product Development Process related to Deming's view of quality. Rather than addressing quality in terms of error rates, they emphasize behavioral testing relating to quality from a user's perspective. In doing so, they introduce a new view of User Profiles, which can make "usability," "trainability," "installability," and other quality concepts easier to define and manage. Through the use of filters rather than testing strategies and feedback rather than metrics, they provide strategies to make concepts such as "Six Sigma" and SEI CMM Level Five attainable for anyone willing to exercise discipline. Many checklists and filters are provided in the book to help you set and achieve your quality goals. Indeed, application of the techniques described in their book can save you many years of effort.

The concepts described in this new approach to software quality can help you produce better software—on time, within budget, and to whatever quality standards you wish to attain. What is more important is that the New Paradigm is not a theory. While it is a completely new way of looking at things, it is based on the work of many software pioneers over the past few decades. While it may appear that the authors attack conventional approaches, this is sometimes necessary to make great advances. This approach, while new, is a proven technology, but they encourage you to start small and let your workers learn on small projects before tackling bigger ones. The approach described in the book should go a long way toward helping many organizations make practical and lasting improvements in their software quality and development process.

Yet Jarvis and Crandall address the traditional approaches as well. They provide you with time-proven checklists to help you implement the traditional approaches, should you decide to begin there and move on to the new approach as you gain credibility with upper-level management.

The road that Alka and Vern have taken to develop these concepts has been filled with potholes. The road has taken them to different careers, experience with many companies in all parts of the industry, and radically different environments. While they have presented this book in a simple, easy-to-read manner, the concepts are based on an extensive amount of mathematical and statistical concepts.

To an outside observer, the results are worth the price they paid for their views. This book is exciting to an old warrior who built mainframe systems using the tried-and-true waterfall methodology. Their concepts are as different as their analogy: Stop picking grounds out of a pot of coffee and begin to pour it through filters that improve the quality as well as removing the grounds in an efficient manner.

As you read this book, keep an open mind. Put aside the traditional tapes that play in your mind that say, "The way I am currently doing things is the right way." Be prepared for a trip through uncharted software development waters that will lead you to the safe port of improved software quality and customer satisfaction—with a marketing-driven, Deming-oriented approach to continuous process improvement.

William E. Perry
Executive Director
Quality Assurance Institute, Orlando, Florida

Preface

Welcome to *Inroads to Software Quality*. As we compiled this book, we recognized that there are several traditions associated with software quality.

- The old-fashioned methods of building software, with various attempts to "fix things up" after the fact.

- The new quality-oriented methods, as characterized by total quality management, ISO 9000, SEI CMM levels, and the Malcolm Baldrige National Quality Awards, among others.

- A new shift of paradigm which radically changes how software is built and delivered, which eliminates the need to perform traditional functional testing, in terms of unit testing, integration- and system-level functional testing, and regression testing. This is based on a well-defined, disciplined quality process. As you might expect, it is a controversial approach. It allows more time for performing behavioral testing. Normally, testing experts refer to functional testing as being the same thing as black box testing, and often, these are referred to as behavioral testing. We will use behavioral testing to relate to how a software system performs, rather than what it does. The product delivery process which implements this paradigm is based on market-driven product development, using filters to build quality into deliverables, and designing quality into software products at the outset. The process is based on constant feedback and continuous process improvement.

Most companies are attempting to move from the first approach to the second. Almost all quality initiatives are based on the second approach, so we will present that approach as the basic method for improving the quality of products. In addition, we will present a preliminary view of the new paradigm and show why it works and what a tremendous positive impact it can have on software quality—and on cost and schedule. Although software development and testing concepts can quickly become very complex, we attempt to keep this book as an easy-to-follow training guide that offers traditional quality assurance activities and core elements of testing required to improve the quality of the products.

In addition, we will provide new definitions of software quality and show techniques for achieving a higher level of quality than has been previously possible for most companies. In order to keep these techniques simple, some of them may appear dated; others may have different names and definitions from the standard. We will try to state the pro's and con's of each of these and provide references to sources of the various approaches.

A lot of what we present will be in the spirit of the quality concepts of W. Edwards Deming as described by Hahn (1995). You may be surprised to find that when these concepts are actually laid alongside the traditional software quality practices, they become very controversial. They have a major impact on the concepts of inspections, application of statistical quality control, inferential statistics as opposed to analytical statistics (case studies), software development strategies, life cycle models, software delivery systems, and testing.

There is a temptation to take each of the traditional and new testing techniques and critique them in terms of our new paradigm, but that would go beyond the purpose of this book. This book is mainly about quality and quality processes and not about testing. Many of the testing concepts summarized in this book are considered to be dated. Newer concepts, such as those found in Beizer (1991, 1995), come from the current refereed literature. Unfortunately, they are also based on the fact that the code must be taken as it has been programmed and tested in that state.

Our approach shows that much of what the new test techniques test for can be designed out. Many of the new techniques do not test against interface standards such as Microsoft® Windows®, etc. Nor do they test for problems related to event-driven environments. With good design, it is possible to make an entire software system deterministic rather than stochastic. This makes it possible to predict and create whatever condition you want to examine.

Because of the extreme importance of management commitment and discipline within the framework of the new paradigm, the book will outline the importance of managing software development and provide a strategy for doing so. Apart from this, there will be no general discussions of personnel management, statistical quality control, or the concepts of code complexity or estimation. We will present a software development strategy which provides the basis for the new software development paradigm.

The book will present information in layers. Rather than trying to cover all aspects of a topic in one place, the book presents information in small, nonintimidating chapters. In addition, there is a chapter on the relationship among total quality management and our concepts of software quality, managing risks, and the use of the new paradigm to increase quality. The most important aspect of this book is that each chapter contains detailed instructions on how to conduct some of the activities discussed and each chapter can be read independently. This calls for some duplication of terms and ideas throughout the book.

An introductory chapter on the techniques for process assurance is followed by a chapter on product assurance, techniques for product assurance, and planning and organization. Chapters 3 through 6 cover software quality assurance, software quality standards, an overview of test cycles, and test planning. Chapter 6 gives details on how to develop a test plan and test cases. Samples, outlines, and templates for a test plan and a test case are included. The two chapters that follow discuss software quality assurance reviews and basic concepts of software measurement. Chapter 7 outlines objectives, techniques, and guidelines for conducting successful quality assurance reviews. Chapter 8 focuses on how to start a measurement program, important issues, and some of the most commonly used engineering measures in the software. Chapter 9 presents a seven-step process improvement road map, with details on activities to be performed and other considerations. Chapter 10 discusses standards and evaluation of the software development process in the context of ISO 9000-3 and SEI maturity model. The final chapter addresses the process of achieving total quality management and how to minimize the risks involved in developing quality products.

The Appendix provides various checklists that can be used in their present format or customized, depending on your needs and the size of your project. *If these checklists are enhanced by defining the "quality" and "accuracy" required for each item, then these checklists become filters.* The Appendix also includes a description of some frontend filters and an example of the Configuration Control Board Impact Assessment document, which can be extremely useful in helping manage change.

The accompanying DOS-format diskette duplicates the content of the Appendix for use on your Mac or PC in three word-processing programs: WordPerfect® 5.1 for Windows, Microsoft Word® 5.1 for Macintosh®, and Microsoft Word 2.0 for Windows. The files are separated in two portions: "Templates/Checklists" and "Descriptions of Front-End Filters for Product Delivery Process." The WordPerfect files have the extension .wp, the Microsoft Word for Windows files have the extension .msw, and the Word for Mac files have the extension .mac.

Inroads to Software Quality is based on our experience over many years and the input of a large number of individuals and organizations. We therefore have not attempted to tie all the concepts back to a particular person or reference. Where we think you might benefit from additional reading, we have provided references.

In summary, this book is intended to appeal to a broad range of readers, including:

- individuals with little computer background wanting to begin a quality assurance program
- those with testing backgrounds who want advice as to how to implement an effective testing program
- testing personnel who wish a quick overview of the testing field
- programmers who want to improve the quality of their code
- software developers and architects who want to improve the quality of their software architectures and designs

- software managers who wish to install a measurement program to help them evaluate their quality processes
- high-level managers, middle-level managers, and software managers who wish to implement an effective quality program wherein quality is defined from a marketability point of view and is designed in at the start

There should be no need for prerequisites to be able to read this book. But the reader should have an orientation or context based on software quality. Even in Chapter 2, where simple program structures are presented, the reader should be able to relate these to any process: cooking recipes, instructions for operating or building some device, directions for how to get from one place to another, etc.

A Software Glossary with Commentary is at the end of the book to help you understand the material better and to provide quick summaries of specific topics.

ACKNOWLEDGMENTS

Many people contributed to the ideas in this book. Others helped us evaluate the accuracy and readability of the various parts of the book. Still others read and disagreed with us, especially in the more "novel" concepts of the new paradigm, helping us make more precise the arguments and examples we have presented.

We would especially like to thank Digital Technology International, where our product development process and the frontend filters were implemented and validated. We would not have been able to validate the success of the new paradigm without their cooperation and support.

Our special thanks go to Linda Hayes for her input to the chapter on automated testing and to Nate Oldham for drawing most of the diagrams in Chapter 2.

We would also like to thank Karen Snow, Estella Weems, Cindy Snow of Intel, Shauna Frandsen and Tracy Weymouth of Digital Technology International, and Amy Buckwalter of *Utah County Journal*. Thanks also go to Connie Marchewka of Texas Instruments for providing us with information on TI's award-winning quality programs, Nancy Cadjun for technical writing, and Cem Kaner for reviewing and giving feedback on vendor-supplier legal issues.

Finally, we wish to acknowledge our publisher, Bernard Goodwin, and our production editor, Jane Bonnell, and to thank them for their patience and guidance.

CHAPTER 1

Process Assurance

*P*rocess assurance is very important for companies that either develop software or buy software. The purpose of this chapter is to give you an understanding of process assurance and the impact of verification and validation on software quality.

We will also give you some strategies for how to make verification and validation work within your company. These techniques must be closely aligned to the software development life cycle you plan to use. In addition, we will present a new product delivery process which makes process assurance a very straightforward activity and reflects the need we have today for efficiently building quality into our products and processes.

1.1 TECHNIQUES FOR PROCESS ASSURANCE

Process assurance consists of the collective activities carried out while developing a product to ensure that the methods and techniques used are integrated, consistent, and correctly applied. Emphasis is given to cost, time, technical requirements, testing measurements, and prototyping. Process assurance involves the interrelationships of several different components. Depending on how these are managed, they can have a major positive impact on the products. Once an effective process assurance program is put in place and shown to be beneficial, then emphasis can be placed in making verification and validation strategies effective and in improving the quality of the products.

Successful process assurance is based on planning and organization. There are several important aspects of planning and organization that must be considered before starting the project. (See Figure 1-1.)

The following is a discussion of the components of planning and organization.

1.1.1 Project Team

The project team is the project manager's only means of reaching the project goals. Selection of team members is a vital step to the success of the

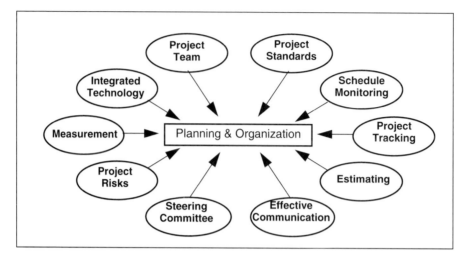

Figure 1-1   Components of planning and organization

project and the size of the team depends on the size and complexity of the project. It is important to identify the blend of the technical knowledge and the experience required for the successful completion of the project. Special attention should be paid to creating a team composition that fosters mutual respect among the team members and maintains good team morals.

1.1.2 Project Standards

Before the project is started, the team should establish standards for activities such as gathering requirements, developing design, and conducting unit tests. Standards or guidelines should also be established for quality control activities such as walk-throughs, reviews, and inspections. Many companies follow IEEE Software Engineering standards or they have their own internally developed standards. The standards should be flexible enough to be applied to large or small projects. Any deviations from the standards should be approved by the project team and the reason for such deviation should be noted in the minutes of the project meetings.

1.1.3 Schedule Monitoring

Stringent deadlines for the project are frequently established by management, end users, a project sponsor, or a client with no regard to the reality of achievement. The project manager is then designated to meet unrealistic expectations of the project completion date. For this reason, the project start date, milestones, and completion date should be negotiated upfront. If the unrealistic date is accepted and the project activities are then made to fit within this time frame, the quality of the project certainly will suffer. The key to an "on-time" project lies in the ability to identify the critical path before starting the project.

The critical path of a project is where problems that may affect the overall schedule are faced.

To define the critical path, you should develop systematic work breakdown structures which identify task groupings that consist of tasks that can be combined together, task sequences, and entrance/exit criteria for each task. To define tasks, follow the guidelines of the system development methodology used by your organization. In the absence of a development methodology, obtain copies of task lists and task dependencies from other projects and customize them to suit your needs of the current project. Clearly defined work breakdown structures will assist in selecting the correct skilled resources. At the same time, using the breakdown structures also ensures that no activity is forgotten. The technique of breaking down activities into smaller tasks takes an impossibly complex project and reorganizes it into manageable pieces under the direction of the project manager.

Once you have defined the critical path, review the tasks and schedule with the project team members and other significantly impacted individuals. Since these people are the stakeholders and are affected by the project in one or more of the following ways:

- their budget is charged for all or part of the project
- the department's resources are used by the project
- the department has either existing projects or ongoing projects that are affected by the new project

Avoid the most common mistake of adding another resource to shorten or meet the schedule. This usually results in increasing the overhead of the project and reducing the efficiency of the team members since additional communication and guidance are required for the new added resources. Overtime is often viewed as the alternative to meet the schedule. This can be effective for a short period. However, longer periods of overtime can exhaust the team, thus reducing the ability to function efficiently. The cost of overtime should also be considered to finish the project within budget.

You should note, however, the strategy we have proposed under project plans. It is possible to minimize the risk by how you manage your resources, especially your best programmers. *Never* put them on the critical path, nor the code they must develop.

1.1.4 Project Tracking

There are several project-tracking tools available on the market which give project progress information and provide a view of the total project schedule at a glance. Some of these tools have features to do task dependencies and estimations. These features allow the project manager to evaluate the impact of a delay in the completion of any individual activity within the project. Such tools are excellent vehicles in giving early warnings for project delays so there are no surprises at the end.

1.1.5 Estimation

The project manager must be capable of understanding any assumptions in the project, what is possible, and what is financially desirable. This will result in a fine-tuning of the schedule estimates, thus creating more realistic estimates. Realistic estimates allow you to discuss alternative approaches at the start of the project. Time estimates are not foolproof; activities are many times not clearly understood or defined and not all the situations can be predicted at the time of estimation. Allow time for resource management and unforeseen events like the illness of a team member. Such contingencies should be viewed as reserved time which may be required for the project. If unused, this time will result in early project completion. Evaluate the impact of unforeseen events so there are no catastrophes. Revise estimates at the end of each major phase and if there are any changes in scope, cost, or schedules encountered, notify management and obtain appropriate approvals.

1.1.6 Effective Communication

Two-way communication between the management and the project team is a critical interpersonal skill. An effective project manager must have the skills to listen, observe, and give guidance to the team. During a time constraint situation, the project manager should be able to delegate responsibilities to the team members but should also be able to give them guidance in order to control the stress level. The success of team harmony and good rapport between project team members, users, and integrated technology depends on the ability of the project manager to encourage open communication frequently and resolve any conflict thorough informal negotiations.

1.1.7 Steering Committee

A committee responsible for defining project policy, reviewing the project milestones, and evaluating risk factors must be established. Members of the committee should represent all the impacted areas of the business. They should be knowledgeable enough to make informed technological decisions and should not be just passive observers but should change the course, if need be. If the features of the project are changed or new features are added halfway through the project, the steering committee is responsible for evaluating the impact on the overall project and authorizing or rejecting the changes or deferring the changes to a later version. The steering committee should be in charge of the system management tasks such as

- estimating the time that will be required to maintain the system
- deciding on the type of support required from the operations for the running of the system
- deciding when the data will be available and how it will be managed, reported, and used

- forming a Configuration Control Board (CCB) that manages the impact of changes (see the DTI example in the Appendix)

1.1.8 Project Risks

It is a known fact that systems projects are risky if the project expectations are not controlled or if the outcome of the project was ill defined and misunderstood. While the risk of the project cannot be eliminated, many companies have opted to identify and address the risk factors upfront. All the risk factors are fully discussed with the project team, management and end users. These companies have evaluated the causes of the risks and implemented measurements to the risk element and have designed processes to minimize the risk by giving new projects additional management attention. Project risks can be assessed in three categories: (1) business risk, (2) technology risk, and (3) project size risk. The risks can be minimized by

- implementing controls from the initiation stage and by ensuring preestablished development standards are followed.
- providing project management training
- reducing the scope of the project by incremental development or phased development

Technical risk is encountered when the project team utilizes a new technology like new hardware or new development methodology for the first time. The technical risks can be controlled by

- appointing a qualified technical project leader
- implementing a strong, independent quality control group to evaluate the progress of the project and project deliverable
- getting additional technical expertise from outside consultants who have expertise and the knowledge to make a difference in the ultimate quality of the project

1.1.9 Measurement

Establishing measurement criteria, against which each phase of the project will be evaluated, is vital. When the exit criteria is well defined, it is sufficient to evaluate the outcome of each phase against the exit criteria and move forward. If the outcome of each phase does not meet the performance criteria, the project manager should be able to control the project by evaluating the problems, identifying the deviations, and implementing new processes to address the deviations. The preestablished quality goals for the project can also serve as criteria against which the project can be measured. In order to meet the goals, processes should be established to

- enable the organization to address customer complaints
- give the organization statistics regarding the types of customer calls

- incorporate reporting and handling of customer problems
- enable management to make staffing decisions based on the number of customer calls

It is important to know there are certain elements which cannot be controlled by project management, such as the selection of the wrong technology (wrong hardware or operating environment), the decision to go ahead with the project without understanding the needs of the business, the underestimation of the learning curve, and a lack of strategic plans for the future which means that the new project becomes obsolete without giving the full return on the investment.

1.1.10 Integrated Technology (IT)

Strategy for Integrated Technology (IT) should be considered by management in relation to the other business needs. This will empower the management to react to the operational needs of the business and, at the same time, take an inventory of the current status of various systems, projects, and the ability of technical staff to support any future projects. The IT trends, competitors, and demands of the customers should be visible to the management. When planning a project, the system architecture with its data groups, structures, processes, and dependencies must be considered. Parts of the new system that will be interfacing with existing systems should be identified so that the impact can be evaluated. If the technology is new and not well understood, allowances to incorporate experiments should be made in the overall project plan and schedule.

1.1.11 Final Comments

Lastly, before ending your planning and organizing phase, ensure that you have addressed the following items:

- Estimate the return on the investment.
- Estimate the corporate competitive advantage.
- Define and manage employee leverage (refer to Section 3.5 for details).
- Identify the sponsor and ensure the sponsor has the funds for the project.
- Identify the client for this project.
- Perform technical analysis:

    (a) Is the technology being reviewed for quality?

    (b) Is the technology being properly utilized?

    (c) Is the present system architecture given consideration?

    (d) Does the selected technology address business needs?

- Perform interface analysis:

    (a) Will the product interact with existing products?

(b) Will it take into consideration other products, if any, that are concurrently developed?

- Estimate hours for completion.
- Identify individuals responsible for various tasks, how these tasks are to be done, and their time frame.
- Monitor the project team's productivity:

(a) Will the product development team meet the requested time frame?

(b) Will the team have to make an unacceptable trade-off?

- Obtain all required resources.
- Determine application acceptability.
- Understand the user expectations and identify a strategy to meet them.
- Obtain user authorization (if applicable).
- Identify how the success of the project will be judged.

In addition to these items, you must answer the following questions before ending your planning and organizing phase:

- How will you monitor the project's progress against its original schedule?
- How are the project completion date and resource utilization estimated?
- How are the requirements to be traced through the various phases of development (i.e., design, construction, and implementation)?
- What will be the specific deliverable of each activity?
- What must be accomplished before entering the next phase of the project?
- How will you assess, improve, and verify the technology is being used correctly? (For example, conduct walk-throughs to ensure modeling and testing techniques are correctly applied.)
- What will be the activities you will establish to ensure continuous monitoring, feedback, and correction within each phase of the project?
- Are checkpoints established throughout the project?
- Are these checkpoints and deliverables well understood by the project team members?
- How will you establish, test, and assure communication protocols and interfaces to existing or concurrently developed products?
- How will you anticipate, measure, and if necessary, improve the performance of a system in order to make it acceptable?
- How will you ensure and monitor external compliance?
- What steps are in place, ensuring attainment of acceptable levels of quality for specific characteristics of the system?
- How will you assess and ensure that your techniques conform to your internal company standards?
- How will you ensure the operational integrity of the system?

Notice that much of what we discuss above appears in the new paradigm whose process model is shown in Figure 1-1.

In this section, we have provided a checklist for the project team to ensure that they have not missed items that are important for the success of the entire project. A majority of the items listed in this section are already covered in Sections 1.1 through 1.1.10. Any further details in this section are beyond the scope of this book. Most of the items would be addressed in a "project management" or "project planning" book.

1.2 CAUSES OF FAILURE IN PROCESS ASSURANCE

There are many reasons why process assurance efforts fail. Most of them are related to management failures rather than technical failures.

1.2.1 Lack of Management Support

Management very often assigns a project and then forgets about it. At other times management assigns it, feeling that it is important, but fails to allocate adequate resources for the project to be done correctly. This lack of project sponsorship leads to serious morale problems and lost resources. The project sponsor is usually a member of the senior management team on whose behalf the project is initiated. This person is responsible for researching and resolving regulatory issues, obtaining project funding, and managing the business implication for the project. Since the project sponsor is responsible for acting as the main advocate of the project and ensuring that the project is implemented as agreed upon, lack of such an individual is extremely serious to the process assurance activity.

1.2.2 Lack of User Involvement

When the end users of the project are not involved in the design and development phases of a project, lots of assumptions are made regarding the requirements. This is especially true where the requirements are ambiguous and user approval for the requirements is not obtained. The situation can be corrected by assigning a user liaison who is responsible for getting support for the project from within the end-user organization, providing detailed user requirements, providing feedback to the project team, managing user expectations, and identifying user acceptance criteria

1.2.3 Lack of Project Leadership

The single most important cause of failure is due to lack of project leadership. There are many consequences of not having a good leader such as

- IT and development staff members not understanding the business needs of the project.

- The project's scope and goals not being fully defined and the project team not being sure of the project's ultimate results. Often in this case, the solution is derived before the problem is identified and coding starts before any clarity of the project goals is obtained. The schedule is set before the full extent of the project is understood, thereby setting unrealistic schedule estimates.
- Performance not being controlled and checkpoint meetings not being conducted to monitor the progress.
- Improper selection of project team members and unavailability of potential team members during the project, resulting in the project manager being overburdened with various tasks.

Ensuring that the project is in the hands of a good project manager and that the project is progressing according to a preestablished schedule is vital for the success of the project. Selecting an individual who is goal-oriented, possessing the right traits with a positive attitude and competence for managing the project is a challenge.

However, even if an excellent project manager is located, the success or failure of a project may not have anything to do with the individual who is assigned to manage the project because other factors still influence the project's outcome. There are three attributes that must be treated equally:

1. The individual assigned to the project must have the responsibility to manage it (if an individual assigned to a project has no authority to make any decisions on the project, he or she will have very little control over the project).
2. The authority of that manager must be equal to the responsibility.
3. The manager must have access to the necessary resources for successfully completing the project.

There are projects whose outcome depends heavily on the project manager's performance and motivation. for example, information systems projects often have different characteristics and require a different management style than real-time systems. For this type of project, it is important to select a project manager who is most suitably matched in skills and personality to handle the requirements of the project and also the team members who are assigned to the project.

Although technical knowledge is necessary, the knowledge of human interaction and relationships is more important since it allows the project manager to deal with unexpected and adverse situations. The project manager should be flexible, responsive, and effective in coordinating day-to-day activities. For some reason, if the project schedule is sliding or if there are situations that need attention and decision making, the project manager should be competent enough to deal with them.

Careful planning and early process control can avoid pitfalls at the later stages of the project. Changing work environment and technology in the middle of the project can pose problems. In such situations, the project manager must be in a position to make effective decisions and implement them. The project manager should also be the content expert, thus allowing him or her to develop quick solutions and implement decisions and changes that are best for the success of the project. The project manager should be credible and respected by other team members to be able to orchestrate the strategies for the project and carry out negotiations. When under time constraints, the project manager should posses the skills to evaluate the schedule, risks, and resources and arrive at the conclusions that would be best for the project. If the goals of the project are unclear, the project manager should be able to work with the team members to go through the entire scope of the project, evaluate the benefits, and finalize the goals.

1.2.4 Lack of Measures of Success

In addition to the causes of failures listed above, another major contributor to failure is when you define the project success based on development efficiency measures only, such as on time and within budget. Effectiveness measures for the project are completely ignored, such as technical performance and quality. To evaluate the success of the project, objective measurements should be developed, for example the project is completed on time, within budget, and with all the required features. Successful companies enforce standards which require consensus to evaluate effectiveness and success criteria of the project. Each element of the success criteria must be defined and agreed upon prior to starting the project.

1.3 Verification versus Validation

Once the process assurance strategy has created a quality-oriented development environment with all of the aspects under control, it is possible to put a software verification and validation process in place. Verification and Validation (V&V) activities are rapidly becoming popular in software engineering. These activities indicate how well the software meets its stated requirements and performance criteria. The purpose of V&V is to ensure that the software is examined in many different ways before the actual testing begins. V&V also assists in measuring the reliability and consistency of the software. V&V is intended to be one more additional step to ensure the quality of the software.

Verification is a process-related activity. Walk-throughs, reviews, inspections, audits and official "sign-offs" are classified as verification activities. This is true regardless of what type of development life cycle model you are using (for example, waterfall, spiral, or parallel). At the end of each development phase, you should ensure that you have carried out all the activities that you said you would. At the same time, make sure any established standards, procedures, and processes for a given phase are adhered to prior to moving to the next phase. Throughout the software development life cycle, verification activities take place continuously to ensure that at any phase, a product is being built according to the standards. When you think of verification, ask yourself, "Did we follow the right procedures?"

Validation, on the other hand, is based on product-related activities such as testing. The validation activities, when carried out, assist you in ensuring you have built the product according to the requirements and as stated in the requirements document. *IEEE Standard Glossary of Software Engineering Terminology* defines validation as the process of evaluating a system or component during or at the end of the development process to determine whether it satisfies specified requirements. Validation takes place when the entire system is developed and validated against the requirements document. When you think of validation, ask yourself, "Did we build the right product?"

There are several benefits of conducting V&V activities:

- assist in deciding whether to proceed to the next phase of development
- highlight problems early in the development cycle
- provide early statistics of the software quality
- measure early on if the software does not meet stated requirements

Management plays a vital role in the success of V&V process by

- allowing time for evaluating the results of V&V activities
- supporting the technical staff in problem identification and process improvement
- providing support for proposed changes

If V&V is conducted by internal staff members, adequate time should be allocated for this activity. The staff should have training and experience on various software quality processes and in developing a Verification and Validation Plan (VVP). A VVP is a living document and its contents change as progress on the software project is made, additional information regarding the characteristics of the software is obtained, and problem areas are identified. In this process, the V&V activities are reviewed at each software checkpoint to identify deviations and to see if predefined activities are yielding desired quality results. As V&V activities are evaluated, it is important to ensure that strict discipline is adhered to confirm the integrity of results and to ensure the data is not corrupted.

Since no V&V activities can be effective without this VVP, we will present a section on VVP next.

1.3.1 Verification and Validation Plan (VVP)

At the minimum, a software VVP should consist of the following items:

1. Objective This section describes the purpose of the VVP. It indicates standards that need to be followed. It outlines the software project for which the VVP is being written and it highlights the goals for conducting the V&V process (such as meeting functional requirements, obtaining performance goals, satisfying acceptance criteria, meeting security objectives and operating needs, etc.).

2. Schedule   This section of the VVP indicates the time frame of individual V&V activities such as the requirements phase V&V, design phase V&V, implementation phase V&V, test phase V&V, and installation phase V&V. However, before you plan the schedule, you must consider which development life cycle you are going to follow. The schedule also contains the dates when the feedback of the V&V results is to be provided to either the sponsor of the project or the management.

Regardless of which life cycle model you use, the following V&V phases or some variations of them should be utilized. In the new paradigm, presented in Section 1.4, the requirements might be validated in terms of behavior of the system as well as the function of the system. For more discussion, see Chapter 5.

Requirements Phase V&V   This phase is designed to test requirements and consists of two activities: Requirements Validation Matrix (RVM) and requirements evaluation. The activity of validation is designed to test requirements. Complete coverage of requirements is ensured only when test cases are developed which test all functions.

The RVM is a cross-referenced method of ensuring that all requirements are covered by your tests. A matrix of this type should be prepared for each requirement as it is identified. Take an inventory of requirements identified in the requirements document and list them down the left side of the matrix. On the right side of the matrix, associated test case numbers are listed as you develop the test cases. You may want to create additional columns on the right side of the matrix to indicate the status of the test cases, program name, and number of any associated programs. The program name is the program identifier for the source code. Associated programs are the ones that are either called by the main program or to which data is passed, thereby creating a dependency between the main program and related program. The purpose of identifying any associated program is so that when there is a change to the main program, you will know that the change will also affect the related program. By knowing the "string of programs" as they are often called, you will be able to identify the "ripple" effect of a change or a bug in the main program. Table 1-1 illustrates a requirements validation matrix.

In Table 1-1, each test case may have a one-to-one relationship between the requirement and the test case or it may have one requirement and many test cases associated with that requirement. There are several benefits of using a RVM:

- It ensures that all requirements are listed.
- It ensures that there is a related test case for each listed requirement.
- It gives a quick overview of the progress of test cases when the "status" column is added.
- It makes it easy to identify the program when a change is introduced by adding the program name to the RVM.

Table 1-1 Requirements Validation Matrix

Description	Test Case Number	Status of Test Case	Program Name	Associated Program
Provide a capability to view YTD earnings of an employee	TC001	Open	PR023	PR021, PR022
Generate an automatic report of gross earnings at the end of each pay cycle	TC056	Closed	PR054	PR023, PR022, PR021
State tax to be deducted for all employees at the rate of 9.8%	TC003	Open	PR022	PR023, PR021
FICA to be deducted at the rate of 18.5%, until the deductions have reached total of $4,700	TC004	Open	PR021	PR023, PR022

- It makes it easy to review the test cases affected by a changed requirement so you can make appropriate changes to the original test cases.

Design Phase V&V This phase consists of an analysis of design interfaces, evaluation of design for completeness and accuracy, and design traceability analysis to the requirements document.

Implementation Phase V&V This phase consists of code interface analysis, code evaluation, and code traceability analysis to the design.

Test Phase V&V This phase identifies the inputs and outputs of each test, describes characteristics of anticipated problems, specific methods to be used to address these problems, and identification of specific criteria for evaluating test results.

Installation Phase V&V This phase consists of the final V&V report, description of how installation test cases will be selected, and how installation tests will be conducted.

3. Resources/Responsibilities This section identifies team members for the software project and lists the V&V activities for which each individual will be responsible.

4. Tools This section lists use of any automated tools for the V&V activities.

5. Control Procedures This section lists control procedures for the V&V activities. These procedures identify how the results of V&V activities will be collected, stored, and distributed. This sections elaborates on who sees the results and how the process improvement plan will be developed, implemented, and measured. The section also identifies how the data integrity of the results will be maintained.

6. Deviation Procedures   This section identifies the procedures to be followed in the event that there are any deviations from the predefined V&V activities. It also describes management escalation procedures for the deviations, who has to sign off, and who will have the ultimate say on whether the deviation should be permitted. It also describes the methods to resolve any deviation disagreements and identifies the reporting mechanism for such disagreements.

7. Documents   This section describes all deliverables from the V&V activities including the activity report which lists individual V&V activities and status of the activities and the V&V summary report which summarizes the results of each V&V activity and lists the assessment of software quality.

The minimum V&V tasks required by IEEE Standards for Software Verification and Validation Plans (SVVPs) for development phases are shown in Table 1-2. These requirements are applicable to all types of software and can be customized depending on the size and complexity of the project.

Table 1-2 Minimum V&V Recommended Tasks (IEEE Std. 1012-1986)

Phase	Task	Major Issues
Concepts	Evaluate concept document	- Meeting user satisfaction - Meeting project performance goals - Identification of interface systems - Identification of constraints
Requirements	Develop requirement traceability matrix Evaluate requirements for correctness, consistency, completeness, accuracy, and testability	- Assessing how well the Software Requirement Specification (SRS) satisfies software system objectives - Assess the criticality of requirements identifying key performance or critical areas of software - Evaluating SRS with hardware, user, operator, and software interface requirements documents for correctness, consistency, completeness, accuracy, and readability - Complying with all functional requirements as complete software end item in system environment - Complying with acceptance requirements

Table 1-2 Minimum V&V Recommended Tasks (IEEE Std. 1012-1986) (Continued)

Phase	Task	Major Issues
Design	- Trace software design description to software requirement specification - Analyze identified relationships for correctness, consistency, completeness, and accuracy	- Complying with established standards, practices, and conventions - Assessing design quality - Evaluating if software elements correctly implement component requirements - Assessing timing, sizing, and accuracy - Measuring test coverage and software reliability and maintainability - Planning integration test to determine if software correctly implements the software requirements and design - Measuring functional test coverage and software reliability
Test	- Develop test procedures for acceptance test - Perform integration testing in accordance with test procedures - Perform system testing - Perform acceptance testing	- Determining if software implements software requirements and design and the components function correctly together - Determining if the software satisfies system objectives - Determining if the software satisfies user acceptance criteria
Installation & Checkout	- Implement audit to determine if all necessary components are present - Generate final V&V report - Summarize all V&V activities and results	- Installed software corresponds to software subjected to V&V - Operations with site-dependent parameters or conditions

Adapted from Table 1 of IEEE Std. 1012-1986 (R1992) IEEE Standard for Software Verification and Validation Plans. Copyright © 1986 by the Institute of Electrical and Electronics Engineers, Inc. The IEEE disclaims any responsibility resulting from the placement and use in this publication. Information is adapted and printed with the permission of IEEE.

1.3.2 Who Conducts the V&V?

Who conducts the V&V is an important issue. There is a concern in the software industry regarding individual software project team members conducting V&V because these members may have vested interests and may not be objective regarding the quality. For this reason, many companies prefer to have consultants carry out the Independent V&V (IV&V) activities so that an unbiased assessment of the process can be accomplished. The individuals conducting an IV&V should have complete access to all the software development-related documentation, inputs as well as outputs. The IV&V individuals should have the freedom to publish an unedited version of all the findings.

When each of the above mentioned items is addressed carefully and the activities are carried out, the quality of the product increases so that there are fewer surprises at the end of the project.

1.4 THE PRODUCT DELIVERY PROCESS (A NEW PARADIGM)

In addition to the traditional quality assurance approach, we are presenting an approach based on a new paradigm. As with most other "new" approaches, it is based on the work of others, and while the approach seems only slightly different from traditional approaches, the results are radically different. At this point, we will discuss the new process, its verification and validation concepts, and definitions relating to its components.

An analogy might help illustrate the difference between this new approach and older, more traditional approaches. Traditional approaches to software development are similar to making a pot of coffee and then, after it has been brewed, attempting to remove the grounds one by one until they all have been removed—or at least as many as we can find. If you can get most of the grounds out, the coffee has "quality," no matter how it tastes. The new approach would be to pass the coffee through one or more "filters." If the filters have been constructed properly, no grounds should remain in the coffee after the coffee has passed through the final filter.

Using an "appropriate" filter has a massive influence on the efficiency and effectiveness of removing coffee grounds or, in software development, removing errors from a product. A nice byproduct of this analogy is that coffee is either "made" or "not made," and you have either "filtered out the grounds" or "not filtered out the grounds." Additionally, the filters are used to enhance the flavor or quality of the coffee. Similarly in software development, the filters allow us not only to improve the products but also increase the quality of the product. We will see that with the product delivery process, the control over development, development schedule, and error removal is highly predictable. Further, associated with every deliverable in the paradigm is a measure of quality. This is the major advantage of this approach.

In terms of how you use this paradigm, you can define your own measures of quality and the filters necessary to provide feedback to enhance them. This is a great benefit when you follow the area of continuous process improvement.

1.4.1 Basic Concepts

The product delivery process is based on several concepts which turn out to be very important if this entire process is to work effectively. However, these concepts can be adapted to your environment. They are

- market-oriented life cycles
- phased, parallel product development
- ad hoc development teams

- deliverables

- filters

- immediate feedback loops leading to an efficient, self-correcting system

The goal throughout this entire product delivery system is to design quality into the product at each stage of the delivery system. As you can see, this is the spirit of Deming's approach to quality. Filters do not filter out errors; they filter the quality.

As Deming says, "Cease dependence on inspection to achieve quality. The focus is on avoiding quality problems, in place of inspecting out defects after they have occurred." The idea, essentially, is that we build deliverables against a standard of the highest quality possible; then we filter them to make certain they meet that standard. If they do, we continue; if they do not, we fix them so they do. The feedback mechanism also allows us to fix the filters when they are broken and to continually factor in more and more quality standards, based on experience gained.

We do not use filters to add quality. Rather, we use them to verify that the quality designed in is really there. We filter, therefore, to ascertain quality. We filter the functionality to verify that it is correct and of high quality in both design and function. We test the behavior of the system to improve its quality and performance in all areas, not to remove errors.

A Market-Oriented Life Cycle   There are several different life cycles which have been published, and many more are being used as part of proprietary development strategies within various software companies. (We used a rather general one in our discussion of V&V.) What we are presenting here is a market-oriented life cycle that changes into a parallel life cycle when the specification and software architecture have been written and filtered and a project plan has been put in place.

The documents and filters from the marketing portions of the life cycle can be replaced by similar documents related to requests for proposals, business plans and corporate mission statements, contracts to build custom software, in-house cost/benefit analyses, and similar documents. We tend to base the justification for building a "commercial" product on leverage, which is defined to be the amount of profit or earnings projected, divided by the projected cost of the project. One problem we have found is that unless the product is very similar to some other one we have built, these two figures are very difficult to estimate accurately at the outset, especially the cost of building the product (see Sections 1.4.3 and 8.9.3). A reasonably good estimate of the potential sales is usually available fairly early—after the first sales filter has been passed. But, the estimate of the cost of building the product usually is not fairly accurate until the architecture and project plan are in place. One of the problems is estimating the schedule against the marketing window. An analogous situation exists in any product environment in terms of competitive advantage, lost sales or earnings on corporate commodities, or in terms of organizational inefficiency.

Whether you have a stable specification to start with and allow changes through an effective configuration management scheme, or whether you start with Rapid Application Development (RAD) and move through a spiral life cycle, you must keep your process under control. Our experience is that with an iterative life cycle, you may not lose control of the specification, but it is extremely difficult not to lose control of the software architecture and code quality.

Phased, Parallel Product Development   In the context of a parallel life cycle, as we describe it here, with a development process that is held tightly under control, managing the impact of changes through the use of a configuration control board, with a software architecture that is highly independent at the system level as well as the component level, it is possible to achieve the same results as those obtained through a spiral life cycle, but without giving up testability, maintainability, and other software quality issues. The question of efficiency in terms of RAD versus sequential/parallel development that we describe is more complex than it appears. These issues will be discussed later on in this chapter.

The parallel part of this life cycle comes from the fact that while the software components are being built, the documentation, training, sales, delivery, and support components can also be built. Changes may ripple across all these areas, but the hardest hit areas are usually documentation and training. Risk analysis, applied to the development sequence, can allow you to build the highest risk components first and write the documentation and training materials for them last.

Ad Hoc Teams   Effective problem solving involves the generation of a large number of alternatives (in terms of "ideal statement of the problem," "ideal solution to the problem," and "ideal implementation of the solution"). This approach to "real-world problem solving" is best implemented through use of teams of individuals rather than by one individual alone. In our experience at the various companies where we have worked and consulted, the use of ad hoc teams which come together for a short time, solve a problem, and then disperse to other activities, works best. Permanent teams and steering committees tend to become stagnant, ineffective, bureaucratic, and lean toward group think rather than consensus. Strong leadership, schedules, deliverables, accountability, and peer evaluations tend to keep the ad hoc teams efficient. Their main activity is to create or filter deliverables.

Deliverables   Deliverables are the outputs of the various phases of our product delivery process. They should be existing and measurable deliverables such as documents, brochures, code, interfaces, activities, or anything else you choose. Several critical ones, such as the marketing requirements definition and the product specification will later be outlined very specifically, as they seem to be the most important in software development—yet the least understood.

Filters   Filters are not entry/exit criteria. They are checklists, templates, outlines, or prototype documents. They allow deliverables to be evaluated for

- accuracy
- completeness
- quality

At every point in the life cycle, deliverables and their filters should have a quality measure defined and be evaluated against it.

Software quality should not mean a "lack of errors." To us, the basic definitions and measures of software quality are wrong. Attempting to find mean time to failure, accessibility, and error rates as a measure of quality is addressing the wrong problem and is not a measure of quality. We believe that software quality is related to the behavior of the software system and that this is what system testing should be all about, i.e., performance, usability, reliability. The analogy is like a automobile manufacturer stating that the mean time to failure (i.e., when the wheels fall off the car) is 10,000 miles plus or minus 1,000 miles. But the car corners terribly at 45 miles per hour and runs roughly over bumpy roads. What is quality? This behavior is based on user profiles, not mean time to failure, which is measured too late—if at all—during production and has little meaning. (Ideally, if one sticks to the same user profile, without deviation, a software product should have an infinite mean time to failure!)

The definition of quality depends on what the deliverable is; for example, a "quality" marketing document should describe the marketing potential and positioning of a software product in terms of its competition with an accurate assessment of who the users will be and how much they will pay. This should be in the context of the corporate mission statement and five-year marketing plan. Its assessment of leverage is expected to be in the ballpark, but precision of its estimates must be refined as the project progresses. Errors mean a filter is broken; quality means the deliverable is crisp, clean, and easy to understand, evaluate, use, and fix. Quality also means that the deliverable will safely "guide" those depending on it to the right decision, with the filters correcting any errors present. In Chapter 4, Figure 4-1 shows a filter for a marketing-oriented requirements definition document. A set of "frontend" filters with a description of some of their components are included in the Appendix.

Feedback Mechanism   If a filter shows that an error exists in a deliverable, then the error is immediately fixed by the person responsible for maintaining the deliverable. The error is also evaluated against all previous filters to see if it could have been caught earlier. If a problem with the filter is found, it is fixed immediately. If current products or parts of products are still in the delivery cycle, they are refiltered against the "broken" filters to see if errors slipped through them as well. This feedback mechanism is very powerful. We have found that it works quickly and harshly and that sometimes, when discipline has been lax, filters are fixed several times in a day. But comparing deliverables against filters is a very efficient process, since it is done through pattern matching against a standard, rather than reading or criticizing the deliverable, as with traditional inspection methods. If an error gets through to the customer, then usually it means that 18 or more filters have simultaneously broken (This might be compared to "root-cause" analysis, but it has a different orientation. See Chapter 11.)

1.4.2 Product Delivery Process

Figure 1-2 shows a sample product delivery process. It appears complex only because of the tentative inclusion of the individuals (by department or organization) who make up the various ad hoc teams.

In terms of the big picture, there are several stages that have been isolated in the product delivery system. Each deliverable has been followed by a filter or filtering activity. This allows for almost instantaneous feedback—to allow for correcting errors in the deliverables. The major stages are

- Marketing Business Plans
- Requirements
- Design
  - Architecture
  - Project Plan
- Development
- Testing
  - Behavioral Testing
  - User Profile Testing
- Delivery
- Maintenance

The last four phases basically define the time line for everything. While these graphic phases are being carried out, other activities are carried out in parallel. These are

- Final Marketing Promotional Plan
- Final Sales Plan
- Training Plan
- Product Documentation
- Delivery Plan
- Support Plan

These final two components are built around checklists that are specific to Digital Technology International. They involve how to install our software systems, complex databases, customize applications using AppleScript® and FaceSpan™, etc. DTI also performs sales audits to make sure a customer's network and system software are adequate.

Of course, these various components depend on your own environment and products. The major point is that you need a verifiable process with periodic deliverables which can be filtered. In addition, these deliverables must have associated with them measures of completeness, accuracy, and quality.

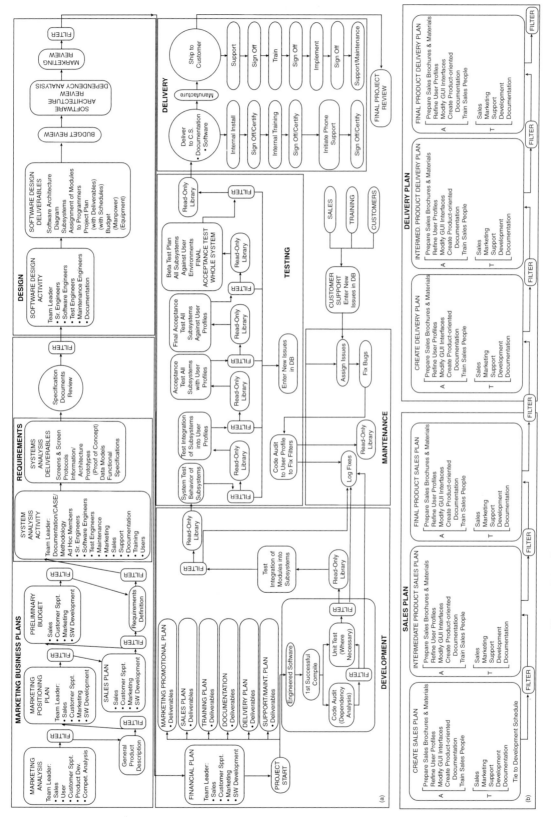

Figure 1-2 Product delivery process in use at Digital Technology International

1.4.3 The Importance of the Project Plan

Once the specification is complete and has been adequately filtered, the software architecture is produced. From this, the manpower is allocated to the project and either a Gantt chart, CPM chart, or PERT chart is created, showing exactly when and how each piece of the product will be built. This leads to a project plan that is realistically designed for the product. Thus, a project plan tells you exactly how you intend to build the product and what schedule you will follow. At this point, an actual budget can be created and most of the variables which have been estimated can be pinned down. It is the project plan, created against a software architecture made up of independent subsystems, that makes it possible for everyone to work together to deliver a final, high-quality product on time and within budget. When executive modules have been added to a software architecture, enormous versatility and predictability are added to the project plan (drivers merely add overhead to the software project).

When the project schedule, based on the project plan, is represented through use of Gantt charts, you can use the chart or charts to establish a series of weekly or biweekly deliverables, which are tied to the product specification through the software architecture. These deliverables are working modules or subsystems which can be executed and evaluated. They are not defined in terms of lines of code programmed or function points. For an alternative measure of amount of product produced, see Wilson (1995). They are not based on tasks, as Humphrey (1989) defines them or on entities. They are based on either events with accompanying triggers and responses, as McMenamin and Palmer (1984) define them or on assertions, which are another form of behavioral response. As we will see later, in Chapter 4, these behavior-oriented events will be combined into work flows and user profiles to allow us to create and test usability-oriented interfaces. These user profiles also allow for meaningful reliability testing. From this series of deliverables, you can predict relatively accurately the scheduled delivery date.

The question is often raised, "What if you have little or no idea how long programming a particular deliverable will take?" There are several possibilities. You can

- Establish early proof of concept prototypes for designs and code which are critical, but unknown. These can often be started before any formal specification has been established—at the point one knows parts of the software system will be based on a new technology—or whatever else leads to lack of information about time to design and program it.

- Put the development of high-risk code early in the development cycle. This way, you have a chance to recover if you have been unrealistic in your estimates.

- Realize that not everything lies along the critical path through the project plan. This allows for much leeway in reassigning key programmers to areas where you are behind schedule. It also allows for the possibility of having key programmers work on multiple projects at the same time without damaging either schedule.

- Put the code that is easy to develop, copied from other software, or for which the time to develop it is well known, at the end of the project, on the critical path.

There are some rather sophisticated estimation methods available. Many are discussed in Boehm (1981). Popular ones like fuzzy logic by Putnam, Function Points by Albrecht, PROBE by Humphrey, as well as others are discussed in Humphrey (1995). You may find them useful, but our experience is that the approach we propose is a good place to begin. Humphrey shows the error of the estimate for the regression formula but does not mention the impact on the error of estimating a project's "time to completion." Deming, as quoted by Hahn (1995), has indicated that "analytical" (case study-based) approaches are better than those based on statistical inference. We agree.

Most projects which are delivered late or have failed occur because an effective project plan has not been put in place. Many projects are programmed on schedule, but the integration takes two to three times as long as the basic programming—sometimes even more. This is usually due to excessive dependencies among the modules (at the system level) or to lack of definition of the module interfaces. Both of these are design issues related to the software architecture. Software should be incrementally built, implemented, and tested (reviewed/ audited and/or filtered).

1.4.4 Configuration Control Board

Because changes come during the development cycle—no matter how well thought-out a software system is—configuration management must also be put in place. Establishing baselines and versioning, important parts of configuration management practices, are usually not very critical activites when a stable specification has been built around marketing considerations and a high-quality software architecture and programming approach is in place. One of the major reasons a process goes "out of control" is because either there was no specification or little thought and marketing research went into the one that was created.

When changes are necessary, a Configuration Control Board meets to evaluate and manage the impact of change on the software development process. The impact of a change can be countered in only three ways:

- add more people to the project to reduce the impact of the change
- extend the time to completion
- cut out other nonessential or less essential functionality

In *The Mythical Man-Month* Brooks (1995) observed that the equation of adding people to offset time and schedule does not work because of the added communication involved. Brooks's observation about communication is only part of the issue; outside programmers must be brought up to speed or trained on the project and technology. The communication issue is resolved by an independence-based design (see Section 2.3.3). The people who are added must be experts in the areas to which they contribute and able to "hit the ground running," if they are to be effective.

The question may be asked, "Where do these expert programmers come from?" The answer is, that "They come from the noncritical paths in the same project or from a concurrent project." Note that these key programmers should be used for programming critical code, letting less experienced programmers program the functions on the critical path. The critical path is the path that takes the longest to do, not the path based on the code that is the riskiest to do.

If the changes are not managed properly, even a well-designed product succumbs to "creeping featurism" and the architecture crumbles into chaos. But if changes are not allowed, the product may not be marketable when it is ready to ship. Brooks (1995) said: "All repairs tend to destroy structure, to increase the entropy and disorder of a system. Even the most skillful program maintenance only delays the program's subsidence into unfixable chaos, from which there has to be a ground-up design." With an independence-based design, this does not need to be true. If a small amount of code is changed, it is redesigned into the old code; if a large amount is changed, a complete subsystem is redesigned as though it were a new product. Well-designed products should actually improve with time.

From a maintenance point of view, IBM used the following as a rule of thumb: "If 20% of the code must be modified, then the module should be redesigned and rewritten." This seems reasonable. At Digital Technology, a rule of thumb is 25%. How good are these rules? They are merely guidelines and should be tempered with common sense. There are strategies that attempt to estimate the best guidelines to do this (see Welker and Oman, 1995).

1.4.5 The Efficiency of a Software Development Strategy

If you are using a particular architecture or approach, you need to justify the efficiency in terms of other approaches against our new paradigm. This is important with respect to the evaluation of using RAD and other types of process architectures. Humphrey (1989) provides a description of the traditional approaches to process architectures and some ideas about how to proceed in an unstable environment.

The most important of these software development strategies or life cycles are probably the waterfall and the spiral. The waterfall life cycle, shown in Figure 1-3, is derived from IBM's old "snail curve." Its value is that it provides information to the developer as to what types of activities should be carried out at each stage. A variation on this, which comes closer to our new paradigm, is the life cycle proposed by Bruce and Pederson (1982). While it is a somewhat dated reference, it is one of the best books for showing parallelism in the processes to be accomplished at the various points, with descriptions of the deliverables involved. Another reference which provides a similar viewpoint is Metzger (1981).

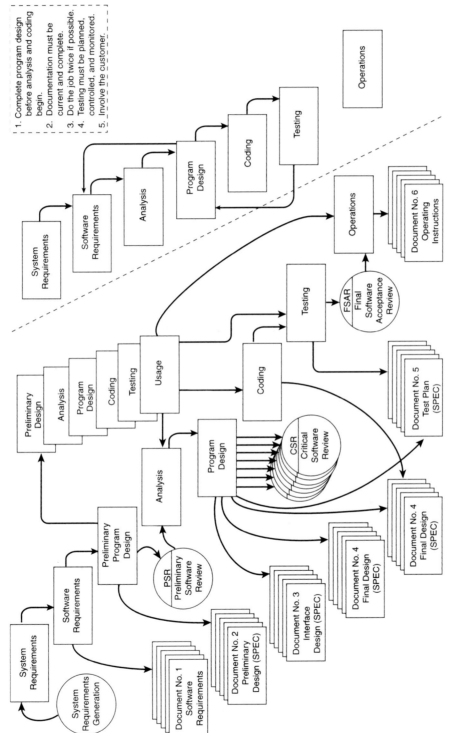

Figure 1-3 Waterfall life cycle. From Royce, "Managing the Development of Large Software Systems," Proceedings of IEEE WESCON, August 1970, © 1970 IEEE. Reproduced from Humphrey (1989), © 1989 Addison-Wesley Publishing Company Inc. Reprinted by permission of IEEE and Addison-Wesley Publishing Company, Inc.

As the rapid application development strategies become more popular, the spiral life cycle (Figure 1-4), proposed by Barry Boehm (1988), is becoming more and more applicable. While the spiral life cycle is extremely well thought-out and disciplined, much of the use of RAD is not. Our criticism is that usually the approach of using the new, easily defined interface generation tools to provide users with almost instant turnaround through use of rapid prototyping tools leads to complex products which end up with poor architectures which are almost impossible to maintain. Watts Humphrey (1989) does an excellent job of describing these life cycle approaches, along with some others.

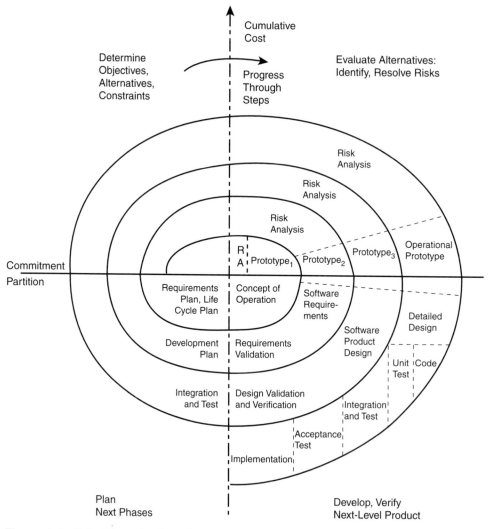

Figure 1-4   Spiral life cycle. From Boehm, "A Spiral Model of Software Development & Enhancement," IEEE Software Computer, © 1988 IEEE. Reproduced from Humphrey (1989), © 1989 Addison-Wesley Publishing Company Inc. Reprinted by permission of IEEE and Addison-Wesley Publishing Company, Inc.

Most of these, however, prove unnecessary if one uses the software architecture, with its accompanying process architecture (or delivery system) in the new paradigm. The unfortunate problem is that you cannot completely evaluate "process efficiency" until after you have finished developing the product, have a reasonable estimate of error rates, and have gathered the measurements which allow you to compare one approach against another. These are not available until long after the product is finished and delivered.

It is our experience that any efficient development methodology must be built against a baseline—no matter how unstable the specification or environment is. If you are building an imbedded system when neither the hardware nor software specification is known, we feel you are in an unresolvable mess. One of the two must be specified, held constant, and all dependencies isolated from the unstable specification. Then changes to the baseline specification—which we have found to be best identified in the software—can be iteratively changed using configuration control. When the hardware specification and product finally stabilize, you can modify the code which lies between the stable software and the unstable hardware. At some point, or subsystem, in a software product's architecture, the code and its specification will eventually be stable.

You may want to use other statements than those we have proposed below, depending on what is important for your organization, but we feel the following to be important considerations. These will be stated as assertions.

- The more time you spend designing a system, the less time it takes to program it. *Assertion*: Every week spent on design decreases the development time by a factor of 6. (This was an observation by Jean Dominique Warnier, 1974b.)
- Systems can have an unexpected impact on users and the users' environment. You may find that when the system is actually installed, it causes the users' environment to change in unexpected ways. As the data change, the changes may impact every place a data element or structure is. Humphrey states that relationships among data usages constitute dependencies and dependency trees must be created to catch all of these ripple effects. *Assertion*: If you design out dependencies at the system level, placing all pieces of knowledge where a dependency may occur in one place, there is no ripple effect and the system need only be changed in one place. (Later, when we discuss dependency analysis, we will describe how to accomplish this and show why it is true and why, therefore, dependency trees are unnecessary.)
- Given a change needs to be made due to
  - An error
  - A change in the specification
  - A change to the basic architecture

  How many changes need to be made to the code?

  In how many places within a module need the changes be made?

  In how many places within the system need the changes be made?

  How long does it take to make the changes (rework time)?

- Per fix
- Per error
- Aggregate

How does the aggregate of the time needed to make all the changes relate to the total design time for the software architecture? *Assertion*: Designing out dependencies makes it so that the rework time is negligible. No other development model seems to be as efficient.

How much testing is necessary to assure that the error rate (per lines of code) is below a certain value? *Assertion*: It is possible to pattern match code components and system components to remove errors rather than to perform exhaustive testing. This amount of time is predictable. Note: This is related to the time necessary to test, as related to such issues as those covered in Chapter 5, namely functional testing related to the:

- Module (Component) level (in terms of code coverage, branch coverage, path coverage, loop testing, domain testing, and others of the various black box techniques, etc.).
- Integration level
- Subsystem level
- System level

State testing related to the

- Subsystem level
- System level
- Regression testing

We will comment on the other types of testing in Chapter 5, when we talk about behavioral testing.

Product Assurance

*C*hapter 1 talked about process assurance which makes certain that the process for building and delivering software is robust and allows for the delivery and maintenance of the products. Assuming that the process is correct, what technology should you use to ensure a high quality product? Just as we indicated in Chapter 1 that we need to have goals on our quality process, we also need to have measures of quality to ensure a high quality product. Under the new paradigm, we will take issue with the classical concept of quality and open the door to higher standards.

Product assurance is the collective set of activities carried out to develop a product and ensure its quality, completeness, and recovery from potential disasters. It also involves building quality architecture which is free of dependencies. This makes it possible to respond to unexpected changes in the software environment, guaranteeing robustness and recovery. As the product is being developed, it is important to have established a set of quality standards and to make sure that they are integrated into the product assurance process.

A product, as referred to in this book, is (usually but not limited to) a system or a component of a system which may be a specific software unit, including such subsystems as code modules, documentation, and the like. The product may either be an entirely new development, a modification or enhancement to an existing system or subsystem(s), or a combination of both. Product assurance focuses on the methods used to assure that deliverables meet customer requirements, standards, and good development practices.

We feel that most of the classical software development methodologies tend to take a fairly narrow focus on software quality and do not address the product assurance issues adequately. Later in this chapter we will present, within the new paradigm, some extensions to the classical software development methodologies. We will show how these can introduce new levels of software quality and in addition, reduce or eliminate the need for traditional functional testing allowing you to focus more of your efforts on behavioral testing. In Chapter 5 we will provide you with definitions of many types of behavior testing you may want to conduct.

2.1 Techniques for Product Assurance

For each project, the team should evaluate what aspects of product quality are highly visible and important to successfully deliver the product. Product assurance techniques may be classified into two phases. First, identifying specific activities that have impact on product quality, such as

- Establishing standards for product quality
- Establishing standards for development technology
- Joint application development
- Prototyping
- Disaster recovery
- Configuration management

The second phase consists of implementing these activities to assure product quality.

2.1.1 Establishing Standards for Product Quality

One of the major problems in most companies, especially at the developer level, is the resistance to software quality standards. Software designers and developers tend to feel that standards impact their creativity and thought processes. Software quality standards relate to coding standards, design standards, etc. Just as users should be involved in creating specifications, developers must be involved in establishing meaningful standards and must be sold on the value of these standards to their company. The developers must have ownership and must develop acceptance to standards for them to be implemented effectively. In Section 2.3, we will provide some ideas of what software quality standards might be. In your company, the standards that are accepted by everyone will be the most effective. By measuring their effectiveness, you can usually prove their value to the company.

2.1.2 Establishing Standards for Development Technology

For some reason, developers very quickly learn and adopt new hardware, database, and operating system technology. They are quick to accept new compilers. But when it comes to standards on how to develop software, they tend to be very resistant. Your company needs to decide on the usage of development methodologies and support them with automated tools. Once this is decided, all developers should be required to adhere.

Note that contrary to what people believe, there is no perfect methodology. No one methodology is appropriate for all problems. To say, "We are a 'Yourdon' shop" or "We deal only with object-oriented methodologies" is a very shortsighted approach. Many managers feel that allowing multiple methodologies is inviting chaos into their development organization. Our belief is that regardless of the methodology used, there should be deliverables defined within each methodology and there should be standards for each deliverable. These deliverables should be filtered according to the concepts we mention in Chapter 1.

Is there a difference between project standards we mentioned in the previous section and the development methodology standards of this section? The answer is "yes." Regardless of the development methodology used, you must be able to trace each phase of building the product back to the original specification and to whatever quality standards are imposed on the software. We will discuss some possibilities under our new paradigm in Section 2.3.

2.1.3 Joint Application Development

In many instances, the traditional planning techniques have proved to be incomplete, ineffective, and inaccurate. Joint Application Development (JAD) is a technique developed by IBM in late 1970s. JAD is where key users and technology analysts get together in an intensive workshop with extensive user participation. The purpose of the workshop is to accelerate the requirements gathering and design processes. The traditional approach of gathering requirements through numerous interviews takes a long time to organize the meetings with appropriate individuals, document the minutes of these meetings, and come to a consensus.

There is a notable difference between this activity and the "market-driven" approach described elsewhere. This approach is the most appropriate one for a set of internal or external users and developers of a product within the same company. It can also be used if there is only a small number of customers. Most traditionally, it is used in Integrated Technology (IT) organizations. For widely marketable products, this approach is not as useful as effective marketing studies. Yet for groups of key users of widely marketed products, JAD is an extremely effective approach in building key interfaces, basic functionality specifications, and defining work flows and user profiles.

The JAD session is led by an impartial leader, with no vested interest in the end results of the project, to

- identify requirements
- define procedures
- define problems
- create a system proposal
- identify the outputs, including screens and reports

The foregoing parts of the JAD session are recorded to ensure nothing is missed. The session leader should have a thorough understanding of the problem the system is supposed to address along with each participant's concerns and ideas.

At the beginning of the session, the leader develops ground rules that need to be followed throughout the session, and ensures that these rules are well understood and followed. The session leader also ensures there is a thorough understanding of issues among the participants and that the views of each participant are heard. If any conflicts erupt, they are addressed right away so there is no impact on the progress. The leader is responsible for harmony throughout the session by handling the conflicts diplomatically so each participant is motivated to contribute and there is a "win-win" feeling. The leader also ensures that the outcome is complete, requiring no additional interviews or follow-up procedures.

The objectives of JAD session are documented prior to the workshop and the business perspective is provided during the workshop. The main benefit of JAD sessions is that users have a better understanding of the system. In addition, any constraints in the development of the system are brought to the forefront. Since there is constant user participation, the expectations of the users are managed and user ideas are also discussed upfront.

Ideally, the JAD participants are members of an internal audit team or project team and are technical specialists. There is a session leader, a sponsor, users, IT members, and a scribe. The JAD planning workshop is typically two to five days. It has structured approach where the design and proposals of end users are discussed, with the guidance from IT personnel. All the events and discussion of the session are documented by the scribe and distributed after the session.

IT and user management are not required in a JAD session; however their presence is strongly recommended when

- there are several interfaces required
- multiple user departments are involved in the system
- the project is large and the scope of requirements is huge

The important thing to remember regarding a JAD session is to establish a schedule upfront so that the individuals involved will know how much time they have for accomplishing any particular activity. All the deliverables of the activities should also be identified upfront. This discipline will eliminate continuous additions or changes to the requirements and will assure that the original JAD session schedule is adhered to. The typical JAD session agenda will consist of

- attendee introduction
- summary of the project by the sponsor
- gathering of the user requirements
- evaluation of the user requirements
- implementation strategy
- action items and responsibilities
- signoff

The output of the session is a document with project purpose, objectives, scope (including functions of the system and significantly impacted departments), any issues, assumptions, identification of interfaces, maintenance strategy, and future considerations.

2.1.4 Prototyping

Creation of screens and reports of a system are static and do not give users a true picture of the behavior of the system. Therefore prototyping is important. It gives a user true concepts of a system which the user can touch, feel, and play with in order to evaluate if the system is user friendly and if the system is consistent from one screen to another. A prototype is a mock-up, interactive model that is developed in less time with less expense in the requirements phase. The purpose is to determine how various functionalities and interfaces of the system would work and to show the users an early version of the system to get their feedback. Often the users' requirements will change after using the system for a while. Therefore, the idea is to revise the prototype until the users identify all their requirements and finalize them. It is important to remember that the language used for prototyping should be simple and easy to maintain. It should provide simple solution for screen development, report generation, data flow diagrams, and file maintenance.

Prototypes uncover little "glitches" and any user requirement that may have been left out. They are also used when little of the functionality of the system is understood by the developers. Unfortunately, in some cases, when the users have seen the prototype, they insist upon using it right away. After using the system for a few days, the users feel the system to be lacking in robustness and completeness. The key in prototyping is to help users understand upfront that it is a "sample" and should be used as such. Under the new paradigm, the use of executive modules will make prototypes much more realistic and fundamental. (See Section 2.3.3 for more information on Executive Modules.)

I. Sommerville (1985), in his book *Software Engineering*, cites that the prototype should be built and presented to the users who will experiment with it and then give any enhancement feedback. The feedback is then incorporated in the prototype. This feedback cycle, where the user continues to give the requirements to the prototype, continues until the users are satisfied with the product.

2.1.5 Disaster Recovery

Disaster recovery plans, often referred to as business contingency plans, have become necessary not only to minimize the adverse impact of a disaster, but also to reduce legal liabilities. The contingency plan should not only be for major disasters, but it should also address any loss of data or data center capabilities. A good plan is vital for the success and longevity of an organization (Jarvis, 1992).[1]

Developing the Disaster Recovery Plan (DRP) You must consider long-term recovery issues in your disaster planning. Management needs to justify new or continuing investment in contingency planning. In the times of poor eco-

---

1. The information presented here was originally presented in the *Journal of the QAI* in April 1992. It is reprinted here with permission from Quality Assurance Institute, Orlando, Florida.

nomic conditions when most companies are reducing their expenditures, some actually realize that adversity is not an excuse to lower their guard. The executives of these companies realize that the investment in contingency planning actually reduces their risks and liabilities. The DRP should address all of the critical business functions of the organization and should be flexible so that it can also be executed when the disasters are not always fatal to the business climate. It should indicate who will do what, how, and when. The following areas should be addressed in a DRP:

- hot site
- cold site
- electronic vaulting
- network recovery
- source code backup and availability (especially if outside vendors go bankrupt)
- evaluating team
- testing
- training
- communications
- approval

Selecting Backup Facilities: Hot Sites and Cold Sites   A hot site is an off-site computer center equipped with hardware where a company can move its operations, i.e. processors, peripherals, network, telecommunications, and personnel. Firms can operate on a contractual basis from a hot site for a short period of time until business is resumed in the usual location. The benefit of a hot site is that you can continue to conduct uninterrupted business. When looking for a hot site facility, pay special attention to

- length of time the company has been in business
- cost — especially review the daily cost to move to the hot site and use the facility
- number of customers the backup facility has (In a major disaster, when a number of businesses are affected, the facility should be in a position to accommodate every client.)
- whether the location of the facility is convenient for the current employees to be transported to this temporary location

A cold site is an empty room or building which does not have any hardware. When selecting the facility for a cold site, make sure the site has air-conditioning, water conduits, raised floors, power supplies, a security system, and generators. Usage of a cold site is less expensive than the hot site. In case of a disaster, you can have a system vendor ship and install the required hardware to the cold site. However, the time for shipment of the hardware from the vendor and time frame for installation should be taken into consideration when selecting a cold site.

Electronic Vaulting   Consider the option of using electronic vaulting. In the event of a disaster, electronic vaulting expedites the recovery process. It improves the reliability and performance of computers. Electronic vaulting reduces the labor-intensive process of off-site vaulting. To effectively use the electronic vaulting, copies are placed in the vault electronically after a scheduled backup and the information from the vault should be immediately available for retrieval.

Developing Strategies for Network Recovery   Network recovery is needed not only in case of a disaster, but also when there is a failure of a telephone system. When planning for the network recovery, you must first identify the requirements for a minimum number of lines to operate the business smoothly. Then you must ensure that the Public Broadcasting Exchange is in a separate safe site and make certain that a sufficient number of communication links are available in the PBX configuration for multiple terminals and important company activities. This will minimize the impact by reassigning links to accommodate individual terminals. In addition, avoid duplicating circuits, where possible. Installing a spare circuit to the recovery center for each circuit in day-to-day use is the safest method. Finally, develop a plan to route the lines to a hot or cold site so that in case of an emergency the users can directly dial the recovery site. This can be done by bridging the incoming circuits with a special switch on each line, which will enable the point-to-point and multipoint networks to send the transmission directly to the recovery site. The advantage of rerouting services is that they can be accomplished within a short time frame.

Selecting an Evaluation Team   Special attention should be given to identifying the evaluation team members. This team should be composed of influential individuals from the technical staff, senior management, quality assurance, and the DRP team. The evaluation team should be able to conduct a step-by-step analysis of each business component and should be responsible for

- analyzing the damage/risks
- communicating the findings precisely to management
- investigating any increase in expenses or decrease in customer service

Testing   The crucial factor in the success of a DRP is testing. Tests ensure the workability of the recovery strategies. The intent of the tests should be to develop working exercises that will cause the plan to be executed. These exercises can be considered test cases whose objective should be to cause different courses of action to be taken as specified in the DRP. The expected actions and the results should be outlined in advance for each test case. The test cases should be divided into groups according to the critical time frame. The frequency of disaster tests should vary with the size of a company and the objectives of testing. The DRP must be continuously updated to meet the new requirements of the critical business operations.

Training   Training also plays an important role. Disaster recovery training ensures a solid, zero-defect plan of action for developing, maintaining, and executing a company's contingency plan to restore business.

Communications   Continuous communication is the most effective measure of a successful DRP. An appropriate staff member should be designated as the spokesperson. The spokesperson should be a skilled individual who can get the message across and who knows how to address a variety of audiences. The message from the spokesperson should be clear. If the message is meant to assure the audience that the company is giving the highest priority to a given situation, the spokesperson should be able to emphasize this and be prepared to answer any type of questions regarding the situation. Consider having separate telephone lines which the employees can access in a disaster. These lines should be used to communicate the plan of action to the employees.

Approval   The test plan should be approved by the senior management and all the individuals who are involved in the preparation and decision making of the DRP. In summary, a well thought-out plan with concentrated actions of senior management and staff working together will reduce potential losses in case of a disaster. The results of being unprepared can be totally devastating in terms of liabilities, financial aspects, customer satisfaction, and company reputation.

2.1.6 Configuration Management

Daniel Hoffman and Paul Strooper (1995), in their book *Software Design, Automated Testing and Maintenance,* indicate that configuration management addresses the multiversion aspect of a software engineering project. In a commercial system, the code may be distributed over various files. The customer base may have various versions of the software customized to their own environment. With this scenario, the major problem that exists is to track the development and maintenance of the programs. As stated before, the main idea is to keep track of all the various components of a system, not only the product delivered to the customer but also any documentation and support code. Tom Gilb (1988) has indicated in his book *Principles of Software Engineering Management,* that the intent of configuration management is to analyze the interdependencies of modules and the effects of changes on unique configurations by knowing the contents of these configurations.

As we mentioned earlier, with effective architectural design and stable specifications built to marketing specifications, this should not be such a big problem, especially if the subsystems are independent. It is also possible, as we have mentioned, to isolate the user interfaces and their basic functionality from the rest of the software, so "one-off" versions, built for users who "bully" developers for their own view of the world, can be avoided. Usually if appropriate user profiles have been studied and designed around the products the users need to create with the software, developers and their sales people can convince most users that work flows built around already studied and well-designed user profiles are better than "one-off" versions. If they are designed around "true quality issues" such as trainability, usability, etc., users will ordinarily understand and accept a single version.

Issues such as

- how long to support a particular version of the software,
- what upgrade paths should be allowed, and
- how many variations (not versions) of the product should be produced and supported

should be examined and evaluated in terms of corporate return on investment and employee leverage. In our experience, allowing either users of an internal IT system or customers to demand and receive "one-off" versions is simply a good way of "shooting yourself in the foot." With good management and a lot of market research and planning software configuration management should be a minor problem. Code libraries built around effective software release strategies and well-designed software architectures should make most of these problems disappear.

Unfortunately, with today's complex systems and undisciplined software development, Software Configuration Management (SCM) is an essential component of software quality. The first and foremost objective of a configuration management system is to keep an inventory of your company's products with release numbers and associated documentation. The other objective is to help the developers manage the system entities such as design, code, test plans, problem reports, minutes of reviews, and so forth, as the system is being developed and released to the users. (This is also useful when you are attempting to qualify for ISO-9000 or other quality standards.) When a problem is found at a customer site, developers should

1. identify the version running at the customer site
2. analyze the problem and reproduce it
3. determine if there is already a "fix" that exists
4. if the answer to 3 is "no," identify the source code and environment used to develop and test the code
5. develop new code to fix the problem
6. test and release the new code to the customer

Imagine the horrendous task ahead of the developer to just identify the version of the code residing at the customer's site. Not only that, the developer must also identify the environment that was used to test that particular code. How many times have you encountered a situation where a developer had a question regarding the system and the only person who knew the answer no longer works in the company. SCM certainly assists in reducing errors caused by lack of communications. So do well-documented user profiles.

For commercial software where you customize different versions, it becomes extremely difficult to keep track of the different versions the customer base may have. If each of your customers has a different version, you will have to allocate resources to manage the SCM which could become a financial burden for your company. So if you plan on having a commercial marketing success through a large customer base, these "one-off" versions become an impossible nightmare.

The problem of multiple versions can be controlled if the user profile is tightened so that the users get one version and if there is a release mechanism in place.

Configuration Management Plan (CMP) The CMP should define the system entities that will reside under SCM. It should identify the resources that will manage the libraries, what type of methods will be used to control the project, status reporting plans, programs, documents, and other documentation that affect the system. The format of keeping all the developers abreast of changes to the source code may also be identified in the CMP.

2.1.7 Reusability

The concept of reusable code is becoming rapidly popular as it saves development time and money. James Martin (1990a), in his book *Information Engineering*, states that "information engineering makes possible a high degree of reusable design and code because it identifies common data and common processes across an enterprise." He continues by saying that it is easier to develop from designs that have been completed or to use modules of reusable code than starting from scratch. This is very much a part of the strategic data modeling and enterprisewide information management methodologies which are cataloged as part of Section 4.3.2.

Carma McClure mentioned at a recent conference that if companies get carried away with object-oriented code libraries and create too many, the whole concept collapses. Her suggestion was to have not more than 50 to 100 such libraries and have them tied to small sets of products. Ken Orr has made the same comment, and this has been our observation as well. As we mention later, often the fact that functionality is "collected" from a large number of small modules causes a whole software system to collapse under its own weight. This happened where one author consulted during the popularity of the higher order software approach to software design during the late 1970s and early 1980s.

The key in reusable code is to have an environment which makes it easy for a developer to access previously used code, modify, and use it again in other similar applications. The code has to be tested, debugged, and stored in a central location where it can be checked out by the developers. In this case, since some of the code is modified, you still will have to spend time to test it. The use of "massage modules" will give you the flexibility to reuse the modules from different points without rewriting or modifying the code. This results in time savings as it eliminates additional need of testing the modified code. (See Section 2.3.3 for additional information on massage modules.)

2.1.8 Code Management

In large applications, several developers many be working on a piece of the system. When each developer has completed his or her portion of the code, it is checked in the code library under configuration control. Entry criteria for checking the code in the SCM should be established, as developers usually do not maintain unit test cases with expected and actual results. For this reason, you need a certain comfort level that the unit test has adequate coverage before the code is checked in. When all pieces of code by various developers have been checked in, a designated test group checks the code out of the configuration management to conduct integration testing. The need for SCM becomes more severe in this case as a central location is needed to store the completed source code from each developer.

2.1.9 Software Changes

Once a product is shipped to a customer, depending on the maintenance agreement, you may provide weekly builds with fixes for critical bugs and send out a quarterly release of the product to the customers. Since the latest revised code always resides with the SCM, it provides a means to keep control on the code as the changes and fixes are applied. A developer may change the code several times in his or her personal library before the updated code is checked into the code library.

An effective archiving approach, especially during software maintenance, can allow you to re-create any version of the code from the day it was shipped, which makes it easy to regain control if your development process goes out of control for some product (it should *not* go out of control for all of them at the same time). This approach has been used effectively at Digital Technology International for many years during software development and is a fundamental part of their implementation of the new paradigm. In legacy code, dependencies still cause many problems, but as our competency with the new technology improves with each new product we build, we see these problems gradually disappearing.

If you can answer the following questions, you will know your SCM is rock solid.

What version does this program belong to?

What version does ABC customer have?

Who worked on the latest code changes?

What was the reason for the code changes?

What date were these changes made?

Before any product assurance activity is introduced, invite appropriate staff members to participate in the development of that activity. When individuals are requested to participate, the outcome of the participation becomes "their product" and it would be easier to obtain buy-in for the use. Respect each participant's feedback; let the participants analyze each idea and finalize the process.

2.1.10 Training

Many times, hesitation to accept a new procedure comes from lack of knowledge. For any new activity introduced, make sure the individuals are well trained. For example, if JAD is the methodology you are going to use, the appropriate staff should be put through thorough training of how to conduct JAD sessions.

2.1.11 Management Support

Identify the sponsor and management members from whom the support is essential. Invite them to the product assurance planning meetings. Keep management members abreast of all recommended activities and notify them of any roadblocks. When a new process is introduced, it takes additional time to accomplish the process. Management is the key to allowing this additional time until the staff becomes efficient in the use of the process. Management must also be informed of the fact that any time spend upfront in introducing activities that would improve the overall quality of the product will automatically save time and frustration at the end of the development.

2.1.12 Benchmarking

Benchmarking is a process of finding out what is vital to the success of your organization, learning about your organizations'processes, and identifying "Best In Class" companies that have implemented these processes with successful results. In addition, benchmarking is a process of learning from others regarding their experiences, what worked for them, and providing your organization the motivation it needs to embark upon a new process. Usually, true benchmarking involves exchange of management questions, answers, and visits to the "Best In Class" companies where team presentations are conducted.

Figure 2-1 indicates some of the essential steps of benchmarking. In short, it is a structured process for evaluating alternatives, indentifying proven strategies used by either competing or successful organizations, and implementing them.

2.2 ACTIVITIES TO ASSURE PRODUCT QUALITY

Ideas gained through benchmarking can be implemented within your company. Companies against which you benchmark do not always have to be in the same business as yours. Even if you are marketing software, sometimes a company that has an internal Management Information System (MIS) organization may have a lot of ideas from which you can benefit.

Measuring the defects and keeping track of trends is one way product quality can be analyzed. When tests are performed, defects are logged and categorized into the defect origin, for example, some of the defect origins may be poor requirements, incomplete design, poor coding, and inadequate tests. Each category is then evaluated to implement necessary steps to address and eliminate the problem from the root cause. Some of the common activities to assure product quality are to

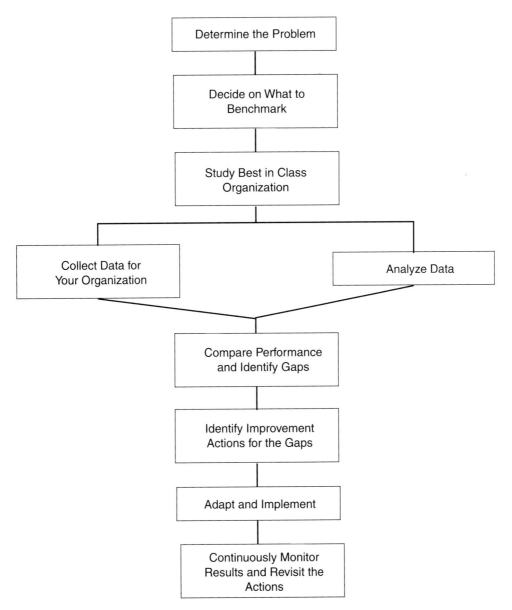

Figure 2-1 Some essential benchmarking steps

- Conduct peer and formal reviews and walk-throughs to identify problems and to evaluate the quality of the products (refer to Chapter 7).
- Run prototypes: Use functioning models to determine the workability of the product.

- Assign independent analysis and testing: Have individual testers and users from the project team test and analyze the product.

- Test product: Conduct unit, integration and systems tests. Log all the results of the tests and document all defects.

- Measure and analyze by gathering metrics and using data to improve the quality of the product and development efforts and to reduce the development cycle time.

Remember that from Deming's point of view, having to approach software quality in terms of what we have presented above is looking at quality after the fact. Ideally, we should design quality into a product upfront. The next section deals with the strategy for building in quality upfront.

2.3 A NEW PARADIGM FOR ASSURING QUALITY SOFTWARE DESIGN AND ARCHITECTURE

As has been mentioned, every deliverable in the product delivery system associated with this new paradigm—the product delivery process—has a measure of quality associated with it. Further, regardless of how "unstable" the environment, there is a baseline which is established. The instabilities—or areas for potential change—can be isolated from the software through dependency analysis and design. This makes it possible to minimize and control the impact of change.

This section may seem more complex and detailed than the previous ones, but the orientation here is toward how to design highly independent, high-quality software systems. At the module level, the "code" is often referred to as "formal logic." This term may frighten some readers, but the idea is simply that processes can be written with a minimal number of patterns. As we mention later on, a recipe for baking a cake could be considered "formal logic." The various structures from software design have their parallels in *any* kind of process, whether it be cooking recipes, directions for putting together a doll house, or anything else.

Boolean expressions may also seem overpowering, but they merely refer to relationships that are either *true* or *false*. For example, "a is less than b" is either true or false; "the person calling me on the phone is Mary" is either true or false; "either Bill or Sally will be at the PTA meeting" is either true or false; "Sam is going on vacation to either Hawaii or the Caribbean" is either true or false. That is all there is to it. Depending on whether an expression is true or false, some activity might take place.

Some common examples of process structures are: "stir the ingredients until they are thoroughly mixed" (an example of a "loop" structure called a DO WHILE or a REPEAT UNTIL, depending on its logic); "if you are making the frosting, do... (the following steps), else make the cake" (an example of a "branch" structure called an IF THEN ELSE). The use of other structures such as CASE simply relate to simple things like "make strawberry jello," "make raspberry jello," or "make lemon jello," depending on some condition (such as "who is coming to dinner").

We will be using computer-oriented examples to illustrate the impact of dependencies in which structures eliminate or minimize them. But these concepts relate to any process in the world. This is being stressed because dependencies create a large number of "states" the software system can take on. The problem is based on a mathematical concept called "combinatorics" which simply allows us to count the number of ways things occur. This might be all the different ways you can drive to Seattle or the number of different poker hands you can draw from a deck of cards. While the term might seem overwhelming, you tend to see examples of it all the time, *and they can cause problems which ARE overwhelming, since they lead to so many possibilities or ways something can happen.*

This condition makes some software difficult to test and maintain and detracts from its quality. This is true at both the code or module level and at the system level. Our examples illustrate that the software logic structures are "context-free" i.e., it does not matter what you are doing—baking a cake, driving from LA to Seattle, or sorting a list of names into alphabetical order—the appropriate logic structure will apply.

Some individuals feel that dependency analysis is the same as the object-oriented approach to software development. While there are similarities and while independence can be achieved with the techniques of the object-oriented approach, some approaches such as inheritance and instantiation can actually force dependencies. In the object-oriented paradigm, care must be taken to assure that this does not occur. We will approach dependency analysis independent of any particular methodology

Dependency analysis, the major activity that makes a software system conform to high quality standards, exists at the module or component level and also at the system level. This will be discussed before proceeding to the design measures, as their understanding is based on an understanding of dependencies. We will discuss the module-level approach first.

2.3.1 Dependency Analysis at the Module Level

At the module level, you must look at the structure of the logic of the code (the functionality of the logic does not matter.). Dependencies generally fall into two main types: logical dependencies and data dependencies. These may seem a bit difficult to understand in their general coverage, but some later examples will show a few of the concepts. We would like to spend more time giving you a lot of noncomputer-oriented examples, but space will not allow it. As you review code in a programming environment (which noncomputer-oriented clerks can easily be taught to do), it soon becomes obvious what we are cataloging below. (It is easier to learn to read good code than it is to learn to write or program it, if you have never programmed, since you only need to learn to "pattern match" a small number of patterns and relate it to an "English" version of what the program is supposed to do. But in our experience teaching hundreds of students to program is not a difficult task either if it is done right.)

Logical Dependencies Logical dependencies occur in several instances. The following describes five of these instances.

The Logic of One Segment Affects the Logic of Another These types of dependencies occur when the logic of one code segment affects the logic of another segment. A remedy for this is to repackage the two segments—or parts of segments—within the same structure. If a data dependency makes it necessary to include part of another segment in the repackaged segment, then it should be placed there as well—as long as it does not affect the logic or calculations of other parts of the segments. This would indicate another dependency. The goal is to eliminate the logical dependencies or, if you cannot, to package them together within the smallest structure necessary to contain the entire dependency or set of dependencies.

The Logic of One Segment Affects the Control Structure of Another Another time when logical dependencies occur is when the logic of one code segment affects the control structure of another segment. A remedy for this is to repackage the two segments—or parts of segments—within the same structure. (The same comments as those above apply here as well.) Also, try to set things up so that the code causing the dependency is "initialization" to the control structure in question.

The Code Structure of One Segment Affects the Code Structure of Another Logical dependencies also occur when the control structure of one code segment affects the control structure of another segment. A remedy for this is to repackage the two segments—or parts of segments—within the same structure. (The same comments as those in the first instance apply here as well.) In addition, attempt to create a "composite" control structure based on both dependencies.

The Control Structure of One Code Segment Affects the Logic of Another These logical dependencies also occur when the control structure of one code segment affects the logic of another segment. A remedy for this is to repackage the two segments—or parts of segments within the same structure. (The same comments as those in the first instance apply here as well.)

The Code Structure of One Segment Affects the Logic of Another Finally, logic dependencies occur when the control structure of one code segment affects the logic of the same segment. A remedy for this is to study the logic to see why the two structures (i.e., the values of a loop structure and the paths or calculations in various branches contained in the loop structure) are coupled or related. This usually indicates an error in thinking. If a different pair of structures will eliminate the dependency, then use them instead. If, for some reason, it is impossible to eliminate the dependency, then realize that the number of test cases necessary to test this dependency is practically infinite because you are dealing with a practically infinite number of states the system can take on. (See Figure 2-10 for an example and additional discussion.)

Boris Beizer (1995) discusses the concept of "states" in his excellent book *Black-Box Testing* as they relate to "state-transition testing." This is also true of Kaner et al. (1993). Most of what Beizer is talking about relates to how inputs generate states and he provides some "classical" approaches mostly as they pertain to system-level testing. While we agree with what Beizer says, a large percentage of these states can be removed through restrictions relating to input through user profiles, through the elimination of intermodule dependencies, and through use of transaction processors, as opposed to traditional state-transition approaches—especially when creating the information model of the system.

Almost all the testing strategies Beizer proposes in his book relate to what test engineers at the end of the "food chain" (software development chain) must do to create models from which to test. Most of the testing models Beizer proposes could be used by developers and designers to actually locate the potential problems and eliminate them in the design process. This is part of the design software development strategy which eliminates functional testing and constitutes a major shift of paradigm in the testing world. The system testing, transaction-tracking, and screen mapping strategies in Chapter 5 lend themselves to this approach.

In real time and imbedded systems, state-transition models are used in the design phase in a somewhat different manner than how we have presented them. For more information, see Ward and Mellor (1985a), Hatley and Pirbhai (1987), and others such as Ken Jackson (Mascot 3) and Ward and Jensen. The basic idea is to use dotted lines to connect bubbles that represent control in a data flow diagram. When these are leveled, they become state-transition models. Further leveling also produces state-transition diagrams or hierarchically nested state-transition diagrams.

Switches and other boolean expressions that are stuck open (stuck TRUE or FALSE) or stuck at some value representing a particular case in a CASE structure, can often show where logical dependencies occur. Most often, such anomalies force several control structures to process only the TRUE or FALSE part of an IF THEN ELSE structure or one particular value of a CASE statement, leaving the others to represent "dead code" (code that cannot be reached or cannot execute under any conditions). Often, fixing the logic around the boolean expression ripples through the succeeding control structures dependent on this value. This could be either a logical dependency or a data dependency, depending on how it is viewed. But fixing it is based on the logic it impacts. For example, correcting the logic can cause the "switch" or "boolean variable" to be stuck at a particular value, analyze the logic leading to—and processed in—the following control structures. If you can remove the dependency (usually by using multiple boolean variables or switches), then the various code segments will be independent; if not, then the structures related to the dependency must be packaged as close together as possible. If this is too much "new terminology," do not worry about it. Some of the later examples will show what we are talking about. If you do not see all of it even then, it is easy to see once you learn how to read code. Whether you feel you are "technically oriented" or not, if you are dealing with quality assurance in any form, you should learn to do it, as it is not difficult to learn.

Data Dependencies Data dependencies occur when two segments of code require a data element or structure to be processed in a certain order. There is always a dependency between the points where a variable is defined and where it is initialized and where it is used. To remedy this, a variable should be defined only in the module(s) where it is used. If it is a part of a data structure, it should be isolated from the data structure through use of an informational strength module (discussed in Section 2.3.5 which deals with dependency analysis at the system level) and only defined and used in each of the modules that require it.

When a variable is defined inside a module, it is usually not a dependency when it is initialized later in the module. This is because in most languages, variables are all defined in a special definition section at the beginning of the program or module. However, if a variable is repeatedly reinitialized within a loop structure, it normally indicates that it should have been initialized once outside the loop. If so, it should be as closely adjacent to the loop as possible. A variable should be initialized as close as possible to where it is used.

If you have trouble seeing this, write the logic of a process in English using the structures briefly defined above and defined and used more completely later on. Most programming is "common sense" if you program in English rather than C or COBOL or whatever. (Note that the process of "baking a cake" is a WHILE loop and the process is initialized by "setting the timer" and then successively "sticking a toothpick in it" to see if the timer accurately represents the time to bake the cake. This is called "updating the loop." You could also do it by noting that the timer advances, say, every second.)

If successive uses of a variable appear in different code segments, they are independent if their segments can be placed in either order. If order makes a difference, a dependency exists. To minimize the dependency, both segments should be placed adjacent to each other. If this is impossible because of other data dependencies, the nondependent segments should be separated from the dependent ones by placing them either before or after.

Examples of Intramodule Dependencies   We will try to use fairly simple examples to show first what dependencies look like and then how to get rid of them. Unfortunately, none of the testing strategies currently proposed in the typical testing references will uncover dependencies no matter what level of code coverage is achieved. First, we will show an example of a simple loop, which has a dependency relating to a three-case CASE statement which is contained within it. This is an example of a control structure having a dependency with the logic contained in three control structures. It could also be related to the control structures themselves. Either view does not affect the amount of testing that would need to be carried out to adequately test all the possible states that these control structures might be in. Note that this example is "context-independent"; therefore, it does not matter what the actual problem is; it only matters what the dependencies are. We will not look at a complete set of code—only the structure. The example is shown in Figure 2-2. (Note that "<" means "less than.")

In this example, we assume there is a dependency between the values of I and the code in each of the three CASE structures. If a dependency does exist, what must we test to assure that the entire loop structure processes correctly? Ordinarily, we would merely run the loop several times with logic such that each

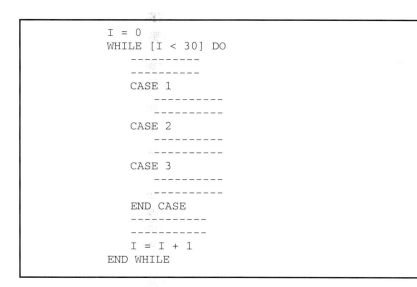

```
I = 0
WHILE [I < 30] DO
    ----------
    ----------
    CASE 1
        ----------
        ----------
    CASE 2
        ----------
        ----------
    CASE 3
        ----------
        ----------
    END CASE
    ----------
    ----------
    I = I + 1
END WHILE
```

Figure 2-2 Example of a code segment where I, the loop variable, causes a dependency on the three CASE structures

case structure was accessed at least once. This might vary from 30 times to 90 times. (Thirty times would execute the loop once, since it must execute for the entire count to be correct. Ninety times would be necessary to change the data in some way to make it so that each CASE executed completely for the various loop values of *I.*) On the other hand, if dependencies are present, each value of *I* must be evaluated for each case—for every time through the loop. If you figure this out, it turns out to be 3^{30}, or around 10^{14} (1,000,000,000,000,000). Using traditional testing techniques, this is more than can be tested in a lifetime. If those dependencies are there, it is probably an error. On the other hand, if they should be correct, then the loop is not the proper way to execute them, and the structures should be broken up to allow the dependencies to be contained in only one place.

Unless you are trained, it is not easy to tell what a dependency looks like. For example, if a variable, *A*, is calculated in one place and is used in a subsequent piece of code, is there a dependency between them or not? The answer is: "It depends on how it is used later." If *A* in the first piece of code is calculated incorrectly, what effect does it have on what happens to *A* in the second segment of code? If the second segment calculates the wrong value of *A* correctly, then they are independent. If the fact that *A* is wrong in the first segment impacts how *A* is evaluated, then they are dependent. The amount of testing necessary to prove that this structure works correctly would be exhaustive. Yet the efforts of a team of programmers to design out the dependencies would be only a matter of hours.

A second example is shown in Figure 2-3. If the first path of the first IF structure (called the IF part) is taken, it is impossible for the IF part of the sec-

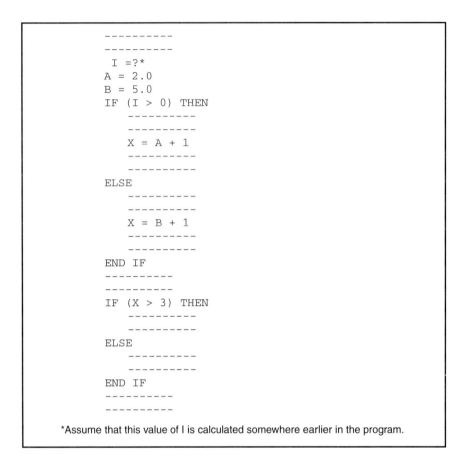

```
          - - - - - - - - - -
          - - - - - - - - - -
          I  = ? *
          A  =  2 . 0
          B  =  5 . 0
          IF  (I  >  0)  THEN
              - - - - - - - - - -
              - - - - - - - - - -
              X  =  A  +  1
              - - - - - - - - - -
              - - - - - - - - - -
          ELSE
              - - - - - - - - - -
              - - - - - - - - - -
              X  =  B  +  1
              - - - - - - - - - -
              - - - - - - - - - -
          END  IF
          - - - - - - - - - -
          - - - - - - - - - -
          IF  (X  >  3)  THEN
              - - - - - - - - - -
              - - - - - - - - - -
          ELSE
              - - - - - - - - - -
              - - - - - - - - - -
          END  IF
          - - - - - - - - - -
          - - - - - - - - - -
```
*Assume that this value of I is calculated somewhere earlier in the program.

Figure 2-3   An example of a dependency between a calculated value in one
structure and the control structure of another

ond IF structure to execute. The dependency can be seen to be between the value of A in the code of the first IF and the condition based on X in the second IF. But this is not the complete view of the dependency. It actually is related to the value of I, wherever it is calculated—and to the conditions and logic used to calculate that value. The way this type of dependency is eliminated (or minimized) is to find the code where I is calculated and attempt to package it adjacent—or as close as possible—to the place where I is used in the IF statement. Further, the fact that when $I > 0$, X takes on a particular value should be also packaged in the same place. If the rest of the code, represented by "----------," has nothing to do with X, then it can be left where it is in the various control structures. (The fact that we have represented the actual code with a dashed line merely indicates that it is context-independent and it does not matter what it is or what it does, as it relates to the dependency we are illustrating.) The second IF structure must also be evaluated for the impact of X on the calculations inside both the IF and the ELSE parts. If possible, these should also be repackaged to remove the impact of the dependency.

The impact of these dependencies on the testing effort will only show up if you are looking for a test that will cause both IF segments to execute in the same test case. If you do not do complete path analysis or path coverage, you may not find this dependency. The greatest impact this type of dependency will have is on software maintenance. When a maintenance programmer makes a fix to the code in either of the IF structures—or earlier where I is calculated—it may impact the code later at one of the other points. Test cases do not usually catch this impact during regression testing.

In these context-free examples, dependency analysis looks fairly simple; in many cases it is much more subtle. Once you start looking for dependencies, they become rather obvious. But, as was mentioned earlier, until you learn how to recognize them, it may be rather difficult.

Eliminating Dependencies at the Module Level   Regardless of which type of dependency you are dealing with, the basic strategy for minimizing their effect or eliminating them at the module level, could be one of the following.

Identify the Dependency and Its Impact   First you might identify the dependency and its impact. An effective way to do this is to draw a directed graph of the code structure. This is similar to a flow chart, but it does not contain any logic. It does not contain the symbols typically drawn in a flow chart; it merely shows the different structures that are present. You can use the directed graph against the code to help identify and map the effects of the dependencies through the code segments and code structures. When this has been taught at various companies where we have consulted, untrained clerical people can easily draw them from looking at the code—even though they are not programmers and thus have no programming experience. We emphasized this earlier.

Relocate the Code Segment   Another suggestion is to attempt to relocate the code segments and control structures as close to the initial dependency as possible. The goal is to get everything related to the dependency in one place. If you cannot move pieces of code to earlier places in the program because there are calculations which must be performed on them before they can be executed, then those pieces of code are also related to the dependency.

Check for a REPEAT UNTIL Structure   You also should check to see if a REPEAT UNTIL structure has been used. A REPEAT UNTIL structure is a loop where the test to see if it should be continued comes at the end of the code segment contained in it, rather than at the beginning, as in the logic of a DO WHILE loop structure. If a REPEAT UNTIL structure has been used, it always means that the logic condition on which the loop is based is dependent on the code in the loop structure, i.e., the code in the loop structure must be executed once at the outset before you know whether to loop back through or drop out. This constitutes two "states" of the loop. This type of dependency should be removed and the REPEAT UNTIL structure replaced with a DO WHILE structure. The dependency should be packaged in the initialization conditions and setup that come before the WHILE LOOP's first statement. WHILE loops are *always* the correct structure to use.

    Check for a WHILE LOOP Structure   Check also to see if a WHILE LOOP has been used. WHILE loops have four basic components: (1) initialization of loop condition, (2) WHILE (condition) DO, (3) update loop condition, and (4) END WHILE. Dependencies should always be evaluated in WHILE loops in the initialization code and in the update code—and that code should always come just before the WHILE statement (initialization) and just before the END WHILE statement (update). When a WHILE LOOP is implemented,

1. All conditions (code statements) relating to its initialization should be gathered from wherever they are found in the module and packaged in the code segment immediately preceding the WHILE loop.

2. All conditions (code statements) relating to its loop condition update should be gathered from the code segment(s) within the control structure and packaged immediately before the end of the WHILE loop.

This will allow all the code which impacts the loop condition to be packaged in one place—either where the loop condition is initialized or where the loop condition is updated.

    An example of a loop condition is the expression in parentheses in Figure 2-2: WHILE($I < 30$) DO (which is part of the logic of a count from $I = 1$ TO 30). Code inside loops is usually not dependent on which time through the loop—even if you are processing subscripts. (Subscripts are analogous to which person you are in a line waiting for a movie, i.e., the first person, the sixth person, etc. The subscript would be equal to "1" or "6," indicating where you are in the line.) The logic works the same way each time through the loop; it merely executes for a different subscript. The same thing holds true if one is searching a file, table, or database until a particular record is found. You do not drop prematurely out of the middle of the loop. You create an IF THEN ELSE structure which changes the condition of the loop and allows it to exit normally through the bottom, as is expected if you follow the criteria of structured programming.

    Even in textbooks—especially those on operating systems—you find examples of using code to branch out of the middle of a loop. This is supposedly justified in the name of efficiency and performance. In our experience, the 80/20 rule applies: 80 percent of the work is done by 20 percent of the functionality. Only in cases where you can prove inefficiency should you allow such violations of good programming practice. Global data structures are also frequently justified on the basis of performance. (Global data structures are structures like a "name and address" which can be accessed from all the modules in the software program; rather they should be restricted to only the modules that actually need them.) These data structures always cause dependencies and are never justified. Global data structures are among the worst examples of the deliberate construction of dependencies in software code. In some software systems—especially real-time, imbedded, and other complex systems—dependency analysis at the module level is not especially easy. Yet the time spent in the design phase will save hours and hours later on in terms of both testing the software effectively and during maintenance and regression testing. (Imbedded systems are software systems that run on a computer chip to manage a CD-player, the brake system in a car, etc.)

A comment on complex systems may be appropriate at this point. Individuals who routinely program for these environments, question whether it is possible to pattern match such complex code—especially for complex algorithms (within assignment statements or within loops). Our response continues to be: "If you cannot understand it well enough to pattern match it, how will you understand it well enough to write the test cases?" Of course, there is nothing in the software development model that prohibits traditional testing if you do not have confidence in the new approach. But you should compare the relative efficiency and effectiveness of the two.

2.3.2 Eliminating Functional Testing at the Module Level

When programming standards have been adhered to and dependencies have been eliminated, it is possible to do away with functional testing at the module level. This section will describe the conditions under which this is possible.

The Creation of Correct Software without Functional Testing   One of the major problem-solving techniques that people use is pattern matching. While we tend to use pattern matching while driving to and from work and performing certain tasks, we fail to apply it to software programs. Software programs can be pattern matched for correctness just as we pattern match whether we are on the correct route to or from work or correctly using any particular process.

The major breakthrough of this pattern-matching approach is that proper design—with the reuse of "previously correct, proven structures"—makes it possible to design out most of what traditional testing actually tests for. This, if it is implemented correctly and carefully, eliminates the need for functional testing at both the coding level and at the system level. As will be seen later in this section, the structure theorem of structured programming shows that all software systems, or any process, for that matter, can be built using a minimum number of differing structures. This makes it possible to recognize a logic structure and visibly determine whether it is correct without having to run test cases against it. This is similar to looking at a mathematical formula in a text book and recognizing what it represents without actually having to plug in numbers to see if it is correct.

You should also note that any usable software system is deterministic, meaning that given the same set of input values—regardless of the operating environment—the program will provide exactly the same outputs. This does not mean that the behavior will always be the same; only the functionality. There is often a question as to whether something is "behavior" or "function." An example might be a memory leak. (This is when a software system uses a piece of "memory" for some purpose and fails to "release it" for other software to use when it is through.) It usually does not occur each time you run it in exactly the same manner (unless your inputs are fairly simple); rather, it appears to occur "at random."

Since the system is deterministic, this cannot be. Therefore, it must occur only for certain combinations of software system states which are dependent on one another and on the operating system. These types of errors will not be found by pattern matching the system—but they usually can be designed out (often without realizing it) through effective dependency analysis. We call the type of testing that uncovers this type of problem "behavioral testing" (others call it "functional testing").

The Implications of "Well-designed," Dependency-Free Software on Maintenance (Regression) Testing   One of the problems with attempting to regression-test software during the maintenance phase relates to the number of states in which the software system can exist. During the work of one of the authors with maintenance programmers at IBM, we were made aware of the "push-and-pop syndrome." The observation was that when a maintenance fix occurred at one point in the program, it caused the system to break somewhere else. Fixing that bug caused it to break at still another point. The impact of these fixes rippled through the entire system. Sometimes they would even come around and break the code containing the originally fixed bug. Another observation was that bugs that are fixed sometimes do not remain fixed. We would go back and find that they were broken again—perhaps in a different way.

It was also pointed out to us—and we verified this through personal observation—that some regression tests were very sensitive to errors, while others would not detect an error even though they executed code in which a later-found error occurred. Sometimes during regression testing and even during unit testing, people encountered "coincidental correctness." Coincidental correctness is a situation where a test case—often occurring when numbers such as "0," "1," or "2" are used—leads to a test case which shows a correct answer when the code was actually wrong. An example might be: "The correct assignment statement is $X = A + B$, but it was either coded as $X = A \times B$ or as $X = A^{B}$." If the problem were tested using values such as $A = 2$ and $B = 2$, then the correct answer of $X = 2$ would be obtained for any of the three assignment statements—even though two of them are wrong.

But the most important concepts of regression testing are that

- There can be no "push-and-pop syndrome" if there are no dependencies.

- It is impossible for a maintenance programmer to "break another part of the system" if there are no dependencies.

- Contrary to what many testing experts believe, dependencies can cause an almost infinite number of states that need to be tested. This makes "traditional regression testing" practically worthless because of the low coverage obtained, due to the fact that the errors one is attempting to uncover tend to exist due to dependencies among variables or control structures among two or more states. This means—as we stated earlier— that it is easier and more cost-effective to design out the dependencies causing the "state-proliferation" (based on "combinatorics")—whether they occur in the user input or in the software architecture or in the module code.

- If there are no dependencies among different parts of the system, it is impossible to perform a maintenance fix at one point and have it impact code or functions at another point.
- The time necessary to even run an automated test suite—assuming you can establish a realistic, meaningful test oracle—large enough to adequately cover all the affected states usually takes longer than the maintenance programmer has available to fix the offending bug and get a working version of the program back to the user, even with today's exceptionally fast hardware.

Another observation was that in certain "regression test buckets" or databases, there were particular test cases that were very sensitive to errors. If there were an error condition, the test case would find it. Other test cases in the same "bucket" were completely insensitive to errors and would not uncover them even if they were to execute the exact code or path on which the error occurred. IBM asked Brigham Young University to determine why this was the case and what to do. The results indicated an appropriate method to efficiently access the database to extract a minimal set of appropriate test cases to test a particular maintenance fix to the code, but we could never find what the criteria were for a "sensitive test." Now, the answer is very obvious in terms of dependencies and pattern matching.

The Structure Theorem   One way to solve this problem is to approach it through the structure theorem. The structure theorem is based on the concept of a proper program. A proper program is one which satisfies the following three conditions:

1. *Single Entry / Single Exit* (no branching into or out of control structures).
2. *No Eternal Loops.* Loops should all be finite. In the REXX™ programming language, there is a construct called "Do Forever." In C one can achieve the same thing with WHILE (1) DO. People who should know better insist that this is "efficient." It never is.
3. *No Dead Code* (code that cannot be reached). Years ago, in the days of "spaghetti programming," this came about through poor design practices. With the excessive use of GO TOs, you end up "not able to reach a segment of code." (This was ordinarily found using compiler tools that "counted the number of times a code segment was accessed.") Sometimes it occurred because some maintenance programmer didn't dare remove a piece of code because he or she did not know if it was being used elsewhere. Another way in which this occurs is when the code actually executes, but its results are never used anywhere.

The structure theorem essentially states that: "If P is a proper program, then no matter how much spaghetti code is contained therein, it can be equivalently written using only the three canonical forms," which we will define below.

Since this theorem fits any program—or process—it applies universally to any process in the world. Most programming books never refer to this—and they tend to violate it without realizing its implications. Other than Harlan Mills's publications within IBM, the only text we are familiar with that covers this is Linger, Mills, and Witt (1979). There is actually more to the structure theorem than this, but this simplified version is all that we are really concerned about.

The Impact of the Structure Theorem   There are several concepts that make this "no more functional testing" concept work. The first comes from the structure theorem of structured programming defined above. Basically, it states that under certain conditions, all processes in the world can be implemented using only three basic structures (known as canonical forms). These are

- loops
- branches
- simple sequences of instructions

This is actually very powerful. It applies to directions for how to get from one place to another, how to build something or how to do something, basic algorithms of science, cooking recipes, and computer programs. Since any computer algorithm can be built using only these control structures, if a computer programmer uses discipline in programming a module, there are only a limited number of patterns that solve the problem correctly. Further, of the different logic constructs relating to loops and branches, it turns out that the most stable in terms of dependencies are DO WHILE loops and CASE statements.

A mention should be made here about FOR loops. FOR loops are very popular and indeed are encouraged in many programming texts. If you use them at all, they should only be used for counting. Using them—especially in C—can cause unreadable code. Once you have the template, it is just as easy to use a WHILE-loop structure.

Another byproduct of this is that there is an extremely efficient way to reverse-engineer legacy code. It is based on pattern matching using "directed graphs." Experience at IBM showed that normal approaches, i.e., simply "playing computer" and "learning what the program did," took around two weeks per 5,000 lines of PL/S code. Using the structured programming approach, it was possible to accomplish the same thing in one to two days. If you should attempt to accomplish the same thing using "formal, mathematical proofs," it takes around six weeks (and is not any more accurate or correct).

There is also a trade-off and a misconception with structured programming. Changing from spaghetti code to structured code usually adds from 50 percent to 150 percent more lines of code to the program. Parallel coding tends to show that this rarely adds to the runtime of the program. This is because the simplicity of the structured program provides efficiency, while the complexity inherent in the spaghetti code almost always adds inefficiency to the code. Yet there are certain control structures that tend to be more efficient than others even though both may be structured programming constructs. An example is that the dependency-laden nested IF THEN ELSE constructs tend to be more efficient than the equivalent, but more independent SELECT/CASE constructs.

Analysis of Conditions   There are issues relating to the CASE structure that space constraints will not allow us to get into in more detail. Some programmers resist the use of CASE structures, as they are not effectively implemented in some programming languages. Still other languages do not allow them—especially some Fourth Generation Language (4GL)-type languages. While IF THEN ELSE structures, such as we show in Figure 2-3, are in common use, they tend to be used incorrectly.

For example, one problem comes in using the ELSE as a default condition without defining the complete set which the IF and the ELSE logical conditions cover. Two different sets often get mixed together. For example, "males," "females," "blondes," and "brunettes" would be two sets mixed together and would not have meaning. An additional comment relating to this is: "What if one needs to look at multiple sets in the same CASE structure?" The answer is to either double up the boolean expression to take into account all the sets and their combinations or set up each one separately and use a function call to the appropriate CASE structure.

The basic idea that a set of conditions, either for an IF THEN ELSE or a CASE structure, might be illustrated by the following:

```
(X < 0)
(0 < X < 100)
(X >100)
```

In this example, the three boolean expressions cover the complete set of values X can take on. In other words, it covers from "minus infinity" to "plus infinity," with the middle expression covering from 0 to 100. Not all boolean expressions need to cover such a wide range. Some sets might just be

```
MALE
FEMALE
```

which are still evaluated using TRUE or FALSE. But it is important to make sure that you have examined the entire set, even if the default is "everything else."

The conditions which make up the control structures for WHILE loops and IF THEN ELSEs are always boolean expressions, (except in CASE structures, where they tend to represent states or elements of sets.) While this term might be confusing to some of you, all it means is that the expression can only take on the values TRUE or FALSE. We saw an example of this in Figures 2-2 and 2-3. While they can be quite complex, easy examples to remember might be

```
(A + B) > (C - D)
EOF (End of File)
T (where the variable T has been defined to be either "TRUE"
or "FALSE")
(A < B).OR.(C > D).AND.(X = Y)
E < 0.0001 (where E is the difference between 2 passes
through a loop).
```

We gave some "English" examples of such expressions earlier.

Sentinel values work in exactly the same way except that they require a user to enter the data—and then terminate the loop by typing a "sentinel value" in either the initialization or the update components of the loop. An example of a sentinel value might be the word QUIT. An example of the requisite program structure is

```
PROMPT USER
READ USER RESPONSE (DATA OR "QUIT")
WHILE (NOT. QUIT) DO
      ____

      ____

      PROMPT USER
      READ USER RESPONSE (DATA OR "QUIT")
END WHILE
```

Thus, the boolean expressions are merely ways of showing that a "condition" is either TRUE or FALSE regardless of how complex the expression may appear. In loops, we must "update" the condition so that the loop will terminate; otherwise we have an "eternal loop" that is impossible to exit from.

Since this is a thought process as much as a design activity, you look at the alternative solutions in terms of which will be simplest, least error-prone, and least dependency-related. This might be further reviewed during the code audit and the filter modified should a major piece of insight break forth as a result of the audit, especially if you see how an error could get through your pattern matching.

The other problem tends to come when there are several branching conditions which must be implemented. When sequential processing is appropriate, then the only structure that is appropriate is to nest IF THEN ELSEs. But when all the conditions are known in advance and one is using alternative processing, then the only appropriate structure is the CASE structure—using a complex boolean expression based on a SELECT structure. The SELECT structure is necessary because CASE structures are based on numbers, characters, or character strings. Most of the time, when the CASE structure is used to replace nested IF THEN ELSEs, you are using interval-type data. In this situation, you must convert the interval data to CASE numbers such as "1," "2," etc. An example of a SELECT structure might look like this:

```
SELECT
    IF (0 < X 20) KASE = 1
    IF (20 < X 40) KASE = 2
    IF (40 < X 60) KASE = 3
       Etc.
CASE OF KASE
    CASE 1
        ____

        ____

    CASE 2
        ____

        ____

Etc.
```

Of course, the basic coding implementation of this might look somewhat different, depending on the syntax of the programming language being used. But it should be noted that if these must run in a particular order, the decisions must be dependent on the order. Thus you have a dependency, among the boolean expressions of the IF statements, which you should try to eliminate, if possible.

Of course the major reason to go to the trouble to eliminate nested IF THEN ELSEs for alternative processing is that it tends to lead to dependencies among the parts of the code not included in each of the structures. For example, the code inside of one IF THEN ELSE which comes before or after the nested IF THEN ELSE may be dependent on the first IF. If you are reconstructing a CASE structure to replace a nested IF THEN ELSE, this common code—between the various nested IF THEN ELSEs—is replaced in the CASE statements by CALLS to subprograms containing the duplicate code. This eliminates the dependencies by "packaging" them in one place. If something in the common code changes, then one only needs to change it in one place. This is shown in Figures 2-4 and 2-5.

Note that these nested IF THEN ELSEs tend to create a maintenance nightmare. But they tend to run faster than the comparable SELECT/CASE structure. Normally the CASE implementation in Pascal and C tends to allow only for integer and character implementations, though Pascal will also allow for character strings. But the SELECT construct allows not only for complex boolean expressions; it also allows for interval data It can be seen that the SELECT/CASE construct makes visible the relationships between the boolean expressions and the CASEs and where the common functionality occurs within the CASEs. Note also that in languages such as Pascal and C, this could also be easily implemented by inserting the code for the various CASEs inside the IFs of the SELECT structure [using BEGIN/END and {with)], but CASE is a more general structure.

The other structure we considered for nested IF THEN ELSEs was for sequential processing. Figure 2-6 shows an example of what this type structure looks like and how one exits a loop should this be "error processing." While this might be an easy-to-read structure for error processing, the fact that the errors occur in sequence means there is a dependency. While in some cases this might be correct, it means that each IF structure creates a "state" which must be analyzed before proceeding to the next error condition. This has the potential of being very complex and error-prone.

Note that this also could be implemented as a SELECT/CASE structure. It would not work as well nor be as easy to read as Figure 2-6. Another argument for this structure is that normal processing will always occur at the bottom of the sequence—and each error condition causes an immediate exit from the WHILE loop, eliminating the need to branch out of a control structure—in violation of structured programming conventions.

Another benefit of this error-processing structure is that when an error occurs, the code necessary to process the error is found at the point in the program where the error is identified. This is not true if you exit from the middle of the loop. In fact, the code indicating where you go and how to get there tends to

```
                Initialize WHILE Loop
                WHILE (Condition_1) DO
                        /xxxxxxxxx
                    F1 < xxxxxxxxx
                        \xxxxxxxxx
                    IF (Condition_2) THEN
                            /xxxxxxxxx
                        F2 <xxxxxxxxx
                            \xxxxxxxxx
                        IF (Condition_3) THEN
                                /xxxxxxxxx
                            F3 <xxxxxxxxx
                                \xxxxxxxxx
                        ELSE
                                /xxxxxxxxx
                            F4 <xxxxxxxxx
                                \xxxxxxxxx
                        END IF
                            /xxxxxxxxx
                        F5 <xxxxxxxxx
                            \xxxxxxxxx
                    ELSE
                            /xxxxxxxxx
                        F6 <xxxxxxxxx
                            \xxxxxxxxx
                        IF (Condition_4) THEN
                                /xxxxxxxxx
                            F7 <xxxxxxxxx
                                \xxxxxxxxx
                        ELSE
                                /xxxxxxxxx
                            F8 <xxxxxxxxx
                                \xxxxxxxxx
                        END IF
                            /xxxxxxxxx
                        F9 <xxxxxxxxx
                            \xxxxxxxxx
                    END IF
                        /xxxxxxxxx
                    F10 <xxxxxxxxx
                        \xxxxxxxxx
                Update WHILE Loop
                END WHILE
```

Figure 2-4   Nested IF THEN ELSE for alternative processing

be very messy and hard to follow. A large percentage of the errors found in programs tend to occur in the exception handing routines.

If a large amount of code is necessary to process an error, it can be placed in a subprogram and called from the error handling routine in the nested IF THEN ELSE structure. Similar calls can be used when the error routines use the same

```
              Initialize WHILE Loop
              WHILE (Condition_1) DO
                  F1
                  SELECT STRUCTURE
                      IF (Condition_2 + Condition_3) KASE = 1
                      IF (Condition_2 + NOT Condition_3) KASE = 2
                      IF (NOT Condition_2 + Condition_4) KASE = 3
                      IF (NOT Condition_2 + NOT Condition_4) KASE = 4
                  END SELECT
                  SWITCH (KASE)
                  {
                  CASE 1:
                      CALL F2
                      F3
                      CALL F5
                      BREAK
                  CASE 2:
                      CALL F2
                      F4
                      CALL F5
                      BREAK
                  CASE 3:
                      CALL F6
                      F7
                      CALL F9
                      BREAK
                  CASE 4:
                      CALL F6
                      F8
                      CALL F9
                      BREAK
                  END CASE
                  }
                  F10
                  Update WHILE Loop
              END WHILE
```

Figure 2-5 Equivalent CASE statement for alternative processing

code. It should be noted that the logic of the CASE structure—or the nested IF THEN ELSE structure—if multiple CASE or IF THEN ELSE values need to be accessed as a part of the error routine—requires a loop. This is also true of any CASE structure; one must make multiple accesses by looping back through the CASE structure for each access. A variation on this is to name each of the error conditions in a meaningful way and put each of them in the boolean expression of the WHILE statement. (Each would be defined as FALSE in the setup for the WHILE structure and would be changed to TRUE in the logic of the IF THEN ELSEs.) You should note that if the error processing is required to run in a particular sequence, it indicates that there are dependencies based on the order of

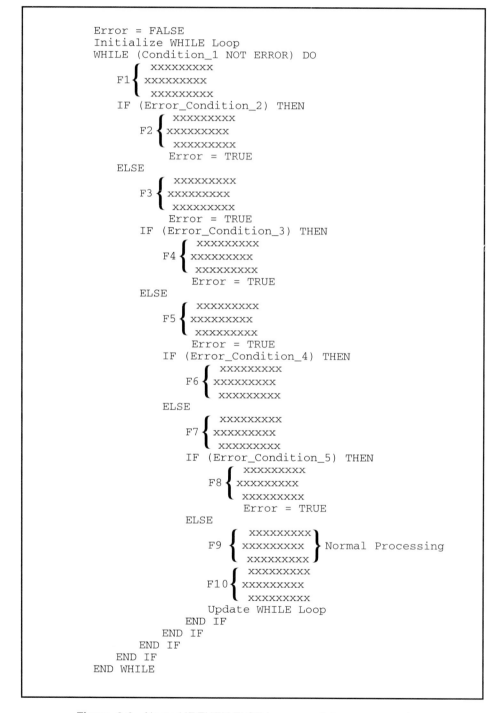

```
Error = FALSE
Initialize WHILE Loop
WHILE (Condition_1 NOT ERROR) DO
        ⎧ xxxxxxxxx
    F1 ⎨ xxxxxxxxx
        ⎩ xxxxxxxxx
    IF (Error_Condition_2) THEN
            ⎧ xxxxxxxxx
        F2 ⎨ xxxxxxxxx
            ⎩ xxxxxxxxx
             Error = TRUE
    ELSE
            ⎧ xxxxxxxxx
        F3 ⎨ xxxxxxxxx
            ⎩ xxxxxxxxx
             Error = TRUE
        IF (Error_Condition_3) THEN
                ⎧ xxxxxxxxx
            F4 ⎨ xxxxxxxxx
                ⎩ xxxxxxxxx
                 Error = TRUE
        ELSE
                ⎧ xxxxxxxxx
            F5 ⎨ xxxxxxxxx
                ⎩ xxxxxxxxx
                 Error = TRUE
            IF (Error_Condition_4) THEN
                    ⎧ xxxxxxxxx
                F6 ⎨ xxxxxxxxx
                    ⎩ xxxxxxxxx
            ELSE
                    ⎧ xxxxxxxxx
                F7 ⎨ xxxxxxxxx
                    ⎩ xxxxxxxxx
                IF (Error_Condition_5) THEN
                        ⎧ xxxxxxxxx
                    F8 ⎨ xxxxxxxxx
                        ⎩ xxxxxxxxx
                         Error = TRUE
                ELSE
                        ⎧ xxxxxxxxx ⎫
                    F9 ⎨ xxxxxxxxx ⎬ Normal Processing
                        ⎩ xxxxxxxxx ⎭
                        ⎧ xxxxxxxxx
                   F10 ⎨ xxxxxxxxx
                        ⎩ xxxxxxxxx
                         Update WHILE Loop
                    END IF
                END IF
            END IF
        END IF
END WHILE
```

Figure 2-6   Nested IF THEN ELSE for sequential error processing

processing. This should be evaluated very seriously to determine why this is the case.

A problem with using the SELECT/CASE structure sometimes occurs when the condition causing the branch is not determined until one is inside the code occurring in the segment following the preceding condition. If this occurs, one cannot determine whether the next condition is TRUE or FALSE until the preceding code has executed. Then the only viable structure is the nested IF THEN ELSE. For example, in the nested version in Figure 2-6, F2 might need to execute before Condition_3 can be determined. But this leads to a lot of "functional dependencies"—which are extremely hard to test and maintain and are very error-prone. Such types of problems should be rethought and reprogrammed. If you recognize that only a limited number of logic constructs are appropriate, then it follows that there are only a limited number of ways an algorithm can be implemented and have it be correct. Another serious point is that if you do not know until a piece of code has executed what its condition will be, you might be dealing with a stochastic program rather than a deterministic program.

For example, if you have figured out a correct implementation of a WHILE loop for a particular problem, it will be correct each time you reuse it—regardless of context. The reuse of correct algorithms—even though they may not be complete programs or functions—greatly enhances the ability of a programmer to program quickly, efficiently, and correctly. It also makes it easy for those auditing the code to pattern match and see that the constructs are correct implementations of the algorithm.

Another related concept is that each programmer makes certain to program things the same way each time something is implemented. Creativity by doing things in an obscure way defeats the purpose of both good programming and the ability to show correctness through pattern matching. Further, experience has shown that only a small number of ways can be incorrect. This is a very powerful observation—it means that it is easier to design out errors than to test them out. This is why it is practical to replace traditional unit and integration testing with pattern matching and filters.

2.3.3 Dependency Analysis at the System Level

Having looked at dependency analysis at the module level, we will now address the same question in terms of the intermodule relationships that exist in building a complete software system. Dependency analysis at the system level has a far greater impact on the quality of a software product than dependency analysis does at the module level. You can usually survive bad coding practices, as they tend to be limited to a small amount of code, but you cannot survive bad design and architectural practices, as they often involve massive amounts of code.

Dependency Analysis Strategies at the System Level   As was the case at the module level, there are only a small number of ways that dependencies can occur. And if software architects are disciplined in how they design the software system, there are only a small number of patterns that are correct and a small number that are incorrect. However, in an undisciplined environment, there are potentially an infinite number of patterns. It should be noted that dependency analysis at the system level—especially for some problems—can be very complex and time-consuming, but it is still cost-effective in making the software easy to build, test, and maintain.

Note that there are other system-level dependencies. These are not as easy to design out. Some examples are listed here.

Operating System Dependencies   These dependencies are related to how the software interacts with the operating system. This may not be easy to determine. It requires an in-depth knowledge of the components of the operating system and how to isolate them and cause your software to interact with them in an independent manner. Sometimes these are accessible through vendor-published Application Programming Interfaces (APIs); at other times, they are part of the description of how to use the operating system. Some compilers provide events such as Apple events. These events often manage how the software must be implemented. Usually, these interactions do not interfere with the goals of intersystem independence.

Hardware-Level Dependencies   Hardware dependencies are related to how the various drivers allow software to interface with and command a piece of hardware. Usually these can be controlled through informational strength modules that know both the data required from the interface as well as how to obtain it from the specific piece of hardware. How hardware operates has a tremendous impact on software design—especially in terms of performance and other behavioral issues.

Compiler-Level Dependencies   These dependencies relate to how a compiler compiles program code. Usually, the low-level compilers conform to ASCII standards and are easy to work with though sometimes new versions are somewhat flaky. Other compilers, especially those for 4GLs, tend to be written to solve a specific programmer problem, with little attention given to quality of the software to be compiled. Because they are easy to use and allow for fast software development, they become popular and are marketed, but they are never redesigned to make them more applicable to high-quality software development. Often poor quality is a "given" in spiral life cycle-oriented, specification-less rapid application development based on 4GLs. People tend to forget that even these products must be maintained.

These products lend themselves to the creation of dependencies. But the major design issue in this environment is to make the software independent of the idiosyncrasies of the compilers with which a software system must be compiled across various hardware platforms.

These types of dependencies must be evaluated as well as other software dependencies described in this book. But the strategies which are effective must be based on the idiosyncrasies of the individual operating systems, hardware interfaces, and compilers.

2.3.4 Eliminating Common System-Level Dependencies

Analyzing just what dependencies are present and the best way to eliminate them can be very time-consuming. Many of the dependencies encountered at the system level are inherent in the specification. If possible, the specification should be modified so that dependencies based on how it is written are eliminated first. Dependencies in the specification tend to have a negative impact on software usability. Listed below are several examples of actual dependencies we have encountered at various companies with whom we have consulted and at Digital Technology.

The Sort Routine Example   In the following example of a payroll program, a management report was created as a part of the process section in which the payroll records were sorted into sequence by alphabetical order within department. In the output section, the payroll checks and stubs were also printed out in alphabetical order within department (see Figure 2-7).

There are several different ways these two parts of the payroll system can be implemented.

- Sort the file into sequence twice—once for the management report and again for the payroll checks. *Problem*: You are performing the same function twice when one is all that is necessary. Even with an efficient sorting algorithm, this is not a good solution as it is still inefficient. Yet the two are independent.

- Sort the file into sequence once—at the point of the management report. *Problem*: This is efficient, but it introduces a dependency that is hard to document. The management report tends to be unstable, i.e., management may change at any point and decide to print out the management report from highest salary to lowest within department. This would cause the payroll check part of the program to crash, because it would print out the checks in the wrong sequence. There is no direct link between the two dependencies; they are related only by the state of the system at the two points. Do you insert a note in the code that states: "If you change the key for sorting this management report, you must insert a sort routine at the point the payroll checks are printed out"? Doing this sort of thing throughout the program would lead to a lot of unnecessary changes any time the management report should change. The same thing holds true if the sequence of the payroll checks should change and the management report remain the same.

- Sort the file into sequence once at the point of the management report, but set a switch that is passed along with the array indicating TRUE if it is in the proper sequence for the payroll checks and FALSE if it is not. *Problem*: This is an instance of control coupling (see Section 11.3.4), where the management subsystem knows what is happening in the paycheck subsystem. There is still a dependency. If it is the paycheck subsystem that changes, one must remember to change the management subsystem to

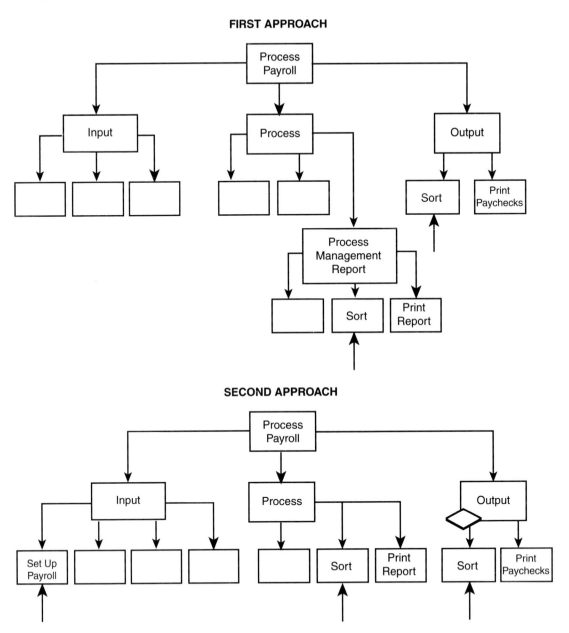

Figure 2-7   The sort routine example. Arrows at the bottom of each chart represent critical modules.

reflect the change. Further, it is a piece of information that should be unnecessary to the paycheck subsystem.

- Recognize the problem is that there is a part of the two subsystems that relates to the dependency between the two. *Solution*: Create a special module at the beginning of the program wherein both pieces of knowledge can be packaged. Set it up so it can be called when the program is initiated, should the user desire to change either of the sorting keys. Inside the module, create an IF THEN ELSE structure that sets a switch in the paycheck subsystem so that the SORT routine executes whenever the two keys are different—with whatever key is defined by the user as the appropriate key. Similarly, it is in this setup module that the key is changed for the management subsystem, as well. There is still a dependency, but it is automatically taken care of at a place in the program where all the facts are known.

This example may seem long and drawn out, but it illustrates the type of thought process that should go on as one attempts to eliminate dependencies. Note that this does not involve the creation of executive modules, modules to "fan into," massage modules, or informational strength modules. Those are only some of the tools available to help you eliminate dependencies.

The "Stuck Switch" Example This example (see Figure 2-8) shows where excessive use of global variables can impact a subsystem when one must fix a "bug" in one of the modules. In this example, a subsystem was found to contain an error. When the maintenance programmer located the bug, it turned out to be a switch in one of the modules of the subsystem that was "stuck TRUE." It caused three successive IF THEN ELSE structures to only execute the IF path. The ELSE path in each segment represented "dead code," i.e., it was "unreachable." It was easy to change the logic of the module to fix the error, but when a code analyzer was run against the code, it was found that the switch was "global," and there were 35 other modules that made use of the exit value of the switch. Further, it was found that under certain input conditions, any one of the modules could execute before any of the others. This meant that there were 36! (36 factorial) different combinations under which the modules could execute! This amounts to 3.72×10^{41} combinations that would need to be evaluated to be sure the system works correctly.

The first question was: "Were these other modules working correctly when the error in the offending module existed, or were they 'broken' and an input condition which would have 'uncovered' the fact that they were also broken simply had not been run?" There was no way of knowing. The maintenance programmer merely fixed the offending program and "crossed his fingers." Under the time constraints of the maintenance environment, he did not have time to completely analyze the situation. The question could also be raised: "What regression test data could there be that could test for even a part of these dependency conditions?"

How should this be programmed to be correct? First of all, that many dependencies—based on the order of execution—could not be correct. No problem

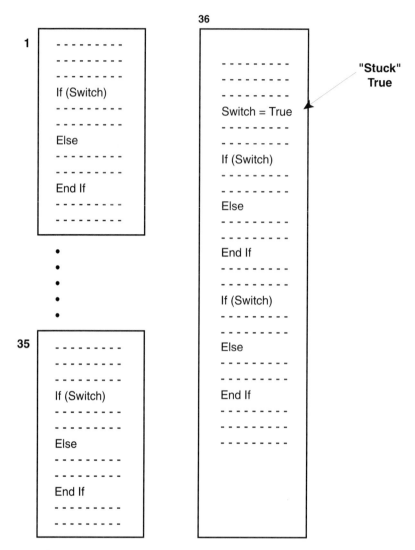

* State of the switch depends on module execution order.

Figure 2-8   The stuck switch example

is that complicated. Whether or not you eliminate the global nature of the switch, the dependencies can easily be eliminated by setting the switch in each module in the subsystem to FALSE and then programming the logic on which the switch is to be based in each module individually. If the setup code is the same, create a fan-in module. If it is similar (but not the same), use a massage module to achieve fan-in. If these solutions are not correct, use an informational strength module. This will almost always be the correct solution.

Another way of examining this would be to look at the input domain. Is there any evidence by looking at the input variables and their dependencies that you can get a clue as to whether or not the above mentioned approach is correct? In our example, the situation was too complex to quickly solve from this point of view since we needed to provide a "working" solution to the user in too short a time for such an approach to prove practical.

The "Multiple-State" Example Often a specification allows the user to implement input to the computer in an undisciplined manner. This usually leads to a multiplicity of states. An example might be allowing the user to place a set of commands in a piece of text. For example, the user may insert a tag in the text to tell the program to begin bolding the text at that point. At a later point, the user might insert another tag to tell the program to begin italicizing the text. Later on, the user can indicate when each particular "end tag" is inserted to stop either the bolding or the italicizing. While this might make the text look funny to some people, it does not cause any problems, as the system merely executes the commands.

But suppose you insert other commands such as "make the text larger" or "change the font." If the rule for these types of commands is "Whenever such a command is found, it is applied to the entire text defined by a set of delimiters," it still may run correctly. But suppose you wish to run a translation program that changes the tags in the existing text to a set of tags in a different operating environment with a different set of rules. If you attempt to write the translation program as one program, the variations of patterns will cause a set of dependencies that will be almost impossible to deal with. Normally, in this sort of situation, you are forced to deal with text or data that have already been created using this dependency-based algorithm, so you cannot go back and redefine the specification to make it more manageable.

The best solution—while not easy—is to define the set of all the states the various combinations of tags can take on. You then can place the knowledge of the various patterns in an executive module and call one of a set of subexecutive modules to manage each state. Each state will have a specific pattern and its evaluation and transformation to the new environment can usually involve a small number of "worker modules" that perform the various translation functions. These translation modules will be relatively generic and can usually be reused in each of the subexecutives. While the biggest problem is to enumerate all the possible states, once this has been done, how each pattern is processed can be accomplished through fan-in to the various translation modules from the subexecutives. (See Figure 2-9.)

Given the description above, you must enumerate all the states which can exist—even if there are a large number of them. This may seem like a lot of work, and it is usually much better to fix the software specification than to try to solving it in the software architecture. Sometimes you are dealing with a situation where all the users have been using this feature and will not change (though it is still better to force the change, if you can). If for some reason you cannot, then the solution is to make a list of all the states that can be generated from the users' input and then design the executive modules to eliminate the dependencies.

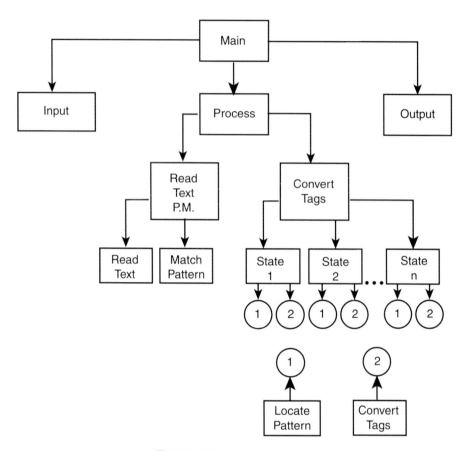

Figure 2-9   The tag example

Here is the beginning of a list of states that might need to be generated using an actual notation that was used:

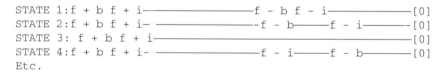

```
STATE 1:f + b f + i————————————f - b f - i————————[0]
STATE 2:f + b f + i- ——————————-f - b————f - i————-[0]
STATE 3: f + b f + i——————————————————————————————[0]
STATE 4:f + b f + i- ——————————f - i————f - b————[0]
Etc.
```

If you take all the possible states and attempt to program a parsing program to handle all of them at once, you will end up with a program that is a mass of dependencies.

There are two possible ways to program this. You can write a program that creates an intermediate program that is free of the rules of the first program. Then write a program that converts the intermediate program into a final program having the rules of the second environment. Or, you can create an executive module that "knows" the patterns of all of the states and calls an appropriate secondary executive for each state to manage that particular state. This particular approach will be used to show how executive modules can be used to "hide" the knowledge of a dependent specification so that the resultant architecture will be independent. Using the second approach, you can call reusable functions that will manage the parsing and conversion for each state.

2.3.5 Examples of the Basic Tools in Dependency Analysis at the System Level

Earlier, the basic system-level dependency analysis tools were enumerated. Each elimination tool will be described in more detail and an example will be given. The exception to this will be the use of Windows-based transaction processors. The reason for this is that many tools now exist which manage the creation of screens and create the logic for what happens when a button is selected. The menu-based transaction processor example is mainly to show that when certain criteria are used to change the state of the system, one achieves better results in terms of independence if one uses transaction processors than if one attempts to level state/transition diagrams, which are presented in most real-time methodologies.

The Use of Executive Modules to Manage Highly Independent Subsystems and to Hide Dependencies   One of the most powerful tools in software engineering is the creation of a software architecture using executive modules. They are useful in several ways because they allow us to

- create and implement independent subsystems in such a manner as to guarantee that the product is built in stages and that the subsystem is completely implemented
- package functionality in one independent subsystem
- repackage completed software in many different subsystems without changing the basic functionality of the entire system or losing traceability back to the specification
- complete a software project on time and within budget
- hide dependencies within the executive module

An example of how executive modules may be used in shown in Figure 2-10.

The Use of Fan-in to Create Highly Independent, Reusable Modules   Sometimes a person is tempted to hardcode data into modules. Some examples are dates, tax rates, business parameters, company name(s), headings, etc. While this eliminates the need to pass data to these modules, it makes them highly specialized and hard to reuse. What this leads to is recoding the same module over and over again for specialized environments. Whenever a better algorithm for implementing that module becomes available, you must implement it in a large number of places in the software (which can lead to errors), rather than just coding it once and calling it when it is needed.

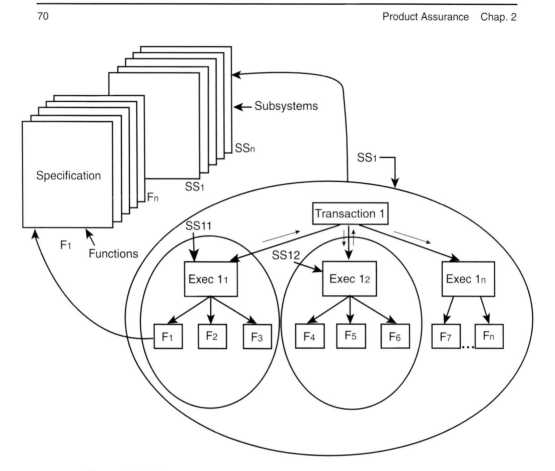

Figure 2-10 Process model—an architecture for using executive modules

The same idea of reuse applies not only to modules which are complete functions; it also applies to code segments which contain a piece of knowledge that may be highly volatile and may change across time. Figure 2-11 shows how fan-in works.

The Use of Massage Modules to Create Highly Independent, Reusable Modules   As was mentioned earlier, massage modules are used when you want to "hide" a volatile piece of knowledge so it can be accessed by all the modules that need the knowledge as a part of their execution, but where each of the calling modules perceives the module containing that knowledge differently.

Figure 2-12 shows an example of how massage modules work. In this example, we assume that there are three places in a software system where one wishes to use a SORT routine. One routine needs to use a three-dimensional sort wherein an array is sorted on row × column within level. Another needs to use a two-dimensional sort wherein an array is sorted on row within column. Still another needs to use a three-dimensional sort wherein an array is sorted on row

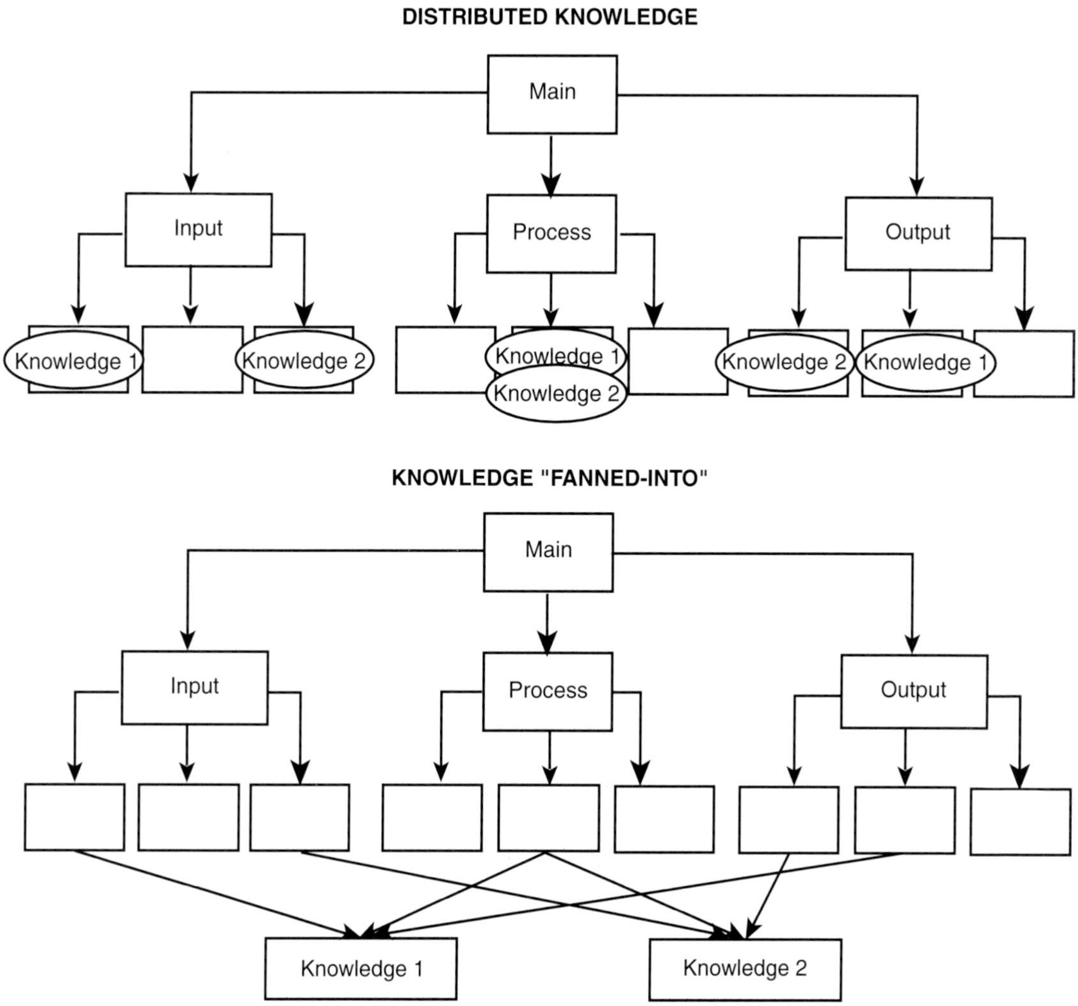
DISTRIBUTED KNOWLEDGE
Main
Input
Process
Output
Knowledge 1
Knowledge 2
Knowledge 1
Knowledge 2
Knowledge 2
Knowledge 1
KNOWLEDGE "FANNED-INTO"
Main
Input
Process
Output
Knowledge 1
Knowledge 2

Figure 2-11 Module fan-in

× level within column. Normally, you would code a separate routine for each situation, since they all perceive the sort differently.

However, the best solution is to recognize that all sorting routines can be reduced to a one-dimensional SORT. Although there are actually better ways to solve this particular sorting problem than the one we are proposing, this is an easy way to see how massage modules are implemented. You then use a massage module, called from each the modules which needs the SORT routine, to convert the desired sorting algorithm into the standard library routine. You might be tempted to code the massage module inside the calling module, rather than letting it be called directly. The reason not to do this is that it places two functions inside the module, instead of just the one the module is designed to perform. Fur-

SEPARATE FUNCTIONS

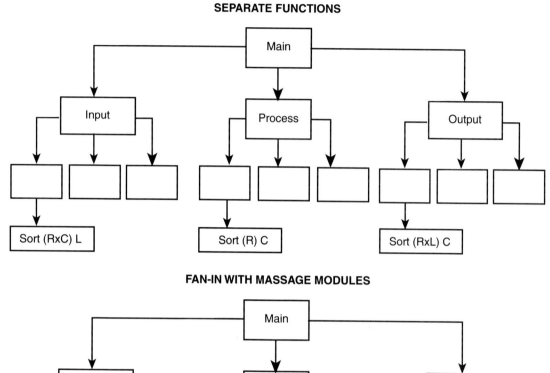

FAN-IN WITH MASSAGE MODULES

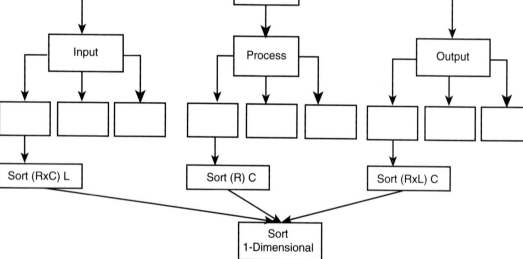

Figure 2-12 Massage modules

ther, having the massage modules on the outside of the calling module makes the structure of the system more visible, and thus easier to verify as being correct. This example was referred to earlier.

The Use of Informational Strength Modules to Create Highly Independent, Reusable Modules   Sometimes, massage modules cannot be used to convert the calling module's perception to a "fan-in-type" environment. The results of the perception are just too different. But still, the piece of knowledge must still be isolated—and all the different perceptions must be packaged in the same place. This leads to the concept of an informational strength module.

The most common use of informational strength modules is to eliminate the impact of dependencies based on data structures. An example is a situation in which a company creates a software system to process personnel records. These personnel records exist as data structures. Had these been created in the 1960s, they would have been required to not contain any information regarding sex, religion, ethnic background, age, etc. This was based on government regulations against discrimination. In the 1980s, these records were forced to be reestablished containing this information to demonstrate affirmative action. Had the same software system been in place, it would probably have needed to be rewritten due to the fact that the knowledge of the data structure was contained in every module in the system. This type of situation occurs often in systems with long lives such as those on mainframes for major corporations.

Remember that data structures may not be the only knowledge that needs to be hidden from the program. Other knowledge might be related to "cursor control," "different databases," "different hardware platforms," or anything else where the knowledge cannot be "fanned into" using simple fan-in or massage modules. Note also that one informational strength module may call one or more other informational strength modules. Figure 2-13 shows how informational strength modules might be used to "hide" the knowledge of an entire data structure from the various parts of the program, thus making the data structure independent of the system using it.

The Use of Menu-Based Transaction Processors to Create Highly Independent, Reusable Modules   The concept of transaction processors which are "menu-driven" is easy to grasp—but it is not elegant. It seems far more mathematically sound to use state/transition diagrams or other more mathematically elegant approaches. But they tend to introduce dependencies and become very complex as they are successively leveled. Transaction processors, as models, can be used any time the system is forced to change its state and provides an extremely high degree of reuse and independence to its components. Figure 2-14 shows the basic structure in a generic sense of how a transaction processor works. Myers (1978, 1979a) shows that they can be created where the transactions are defined both inside and outside the actual program. We have mainly used them with externally specified transactions.

SEPARATE MODULES

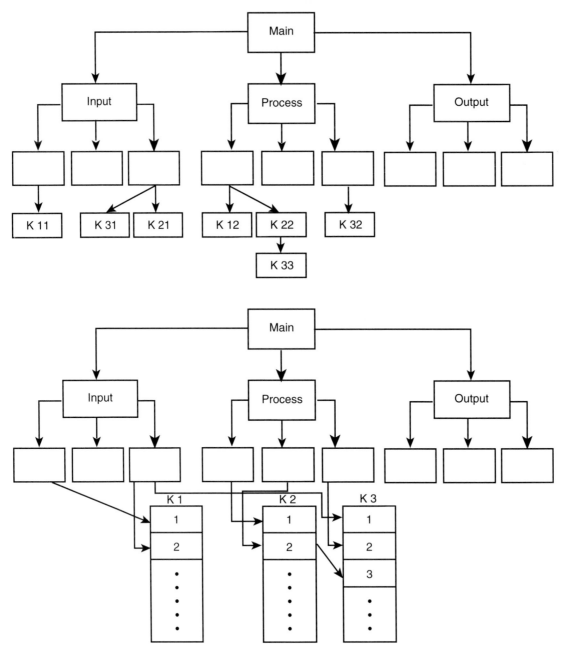

Figure 2-13 Informational strength modules

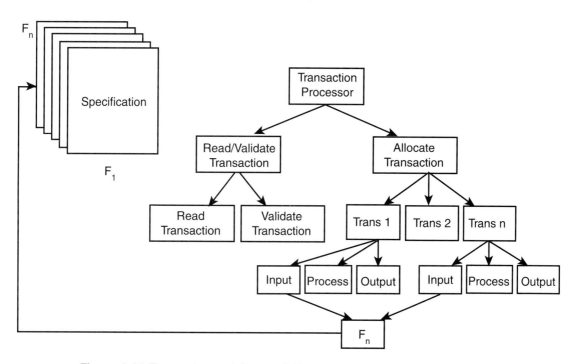

Figure 2-14 Transaction model—a model based on a menu-oriented transaction processor

2.3.6 Final Comments

Dependency analysis, once you understand it, is fairly simple conceptually. At the module level, it is fairly easy to implement. A trade-off is with efficiency; most of the constructs used in eliminating dependencies and making it possible to pattern match for correctness are often not as efficient as the "classical" violations of structured programming conventions. However most of these violations are based on views such as, "we've always done it that way, so it must be right." Because of the extremely negative impact these violations have on maintenance, each time they are proposed, the algorithm should be coded each way, run through some sort of software monitor, and proven to be necessary. Because of the 80/20 rule, there are only rare circumstances when this "efficiency" actually makes a difference in the performance. But there are times when efficiency must prevail; idealism must be tempered with reality. Various examples of these issues have been addressed at earlier points. Because of the extremely negative impact dependencies and spaghetti programming have on software maintenance, it is better to program for ease of maintenance and ability to eliminate functional testing and then go back and reprogram the few areas where such poor-quality constructs make a difference. But this should be done in the context of the performance of the entire software system, not just for small segments of code.

Dependency analysis is extremely cost-effective. The time spent eliminating dependencies—especially at the system level—pays for itself many times over in terms of both maintainability and reuse. In fact, libraries of reusable software are relatively easy to create and maintain especially when massage modules are used.

Several years ago, one of the authors was consulting with a company that was attempting to evaluate the cost-effectiveness of "higher order software (HOS)." It turned out that for systems in the neighborhood of 48,000 to 50,000 lines of code, HOS proved extremely effective, but for systems over 100,000, it was not true. This was because the nature of the methodology was to generate a large number of small functions. (Think of creating 1,000 weights of 1 oz. each, attaching them to one cord, and trying to lift them all at once. The physics involved tends to make it difficult, if not impossible. For this reason, everywhere we attempted to use HOS, the resultant system tended to fall apart and become unusable.) As larger and larger object class libraries tend to be created and marketed, this same pattern appears to be developing in the object-oriented paradigm. The use of informational strength modules, massage modules, and executive modules tends to alleviate that problem with respect to reusable libraries of functions (or subfunctions based on the conclusions of dependency analysis). Another problem in the object-oriented paradigm tends to be the incompatibility of class libraries from one organization to another. We also referred to this earlier as we discussed reuse. We referred to caveats by Carma McClure and Ken Orr regarding "too many" little functions in a class library.

These concepts can be implemented in almost all of the software methodologies currently in vogue including those in the object-oriented paradigm, since parts of almost all methodologies are based somewhat on the concepts of the Yourdon methodology. As stated earlier, dependency analysis leads to the ability to deliver high quality software—on time, maintainable, and changeable. Because you can eliminate expensive, inefficient unit testing and regression testing, it is possible to create software more cost-effectively as well.

2.4 CONCLUSION

In this chapter we have talked about methods of establishing quality standards and we have also discussed product assurance as it relates to JAD, prototyping, disaster recovery and configuration management. In doing so, we have talked about some of the issues that you need to know with respect to creating and implementing quality standards within your company. There are other product assurance strategies that you can use depending on your specific needs. In addition, we have shown you a new development methodology which allows you to eliminate testing.

Software Quality Assurance (SQA)

Now that we have looked at process assurance and product assurance, we will discuss a Software Quality Assurance (SQA) organization, what its components should be, how to justify and staff a software test organization, and how to make it effective. We have seen that when hard times come upon a software company, the quality assurance and testing organizations are among the first to be downsized. This is an unfortunate occurrence and usually comes about because management does not understand the value and leverage of such organizations. Keeping a quality assurance or test organization alive and viable is a challenging proposition. We will discuss ways in which you can cost justify quality to your upper-level management.

3.1 REQUIRED COMPONENTS OF SOFTWARE QUALITY

A quality plan should be part of a product specification and will be shown and described as a part of that deliverable in Chapter 4. Software quality assurance must be taken very seriously if an organization is to produce quality products. Later in this chapter, we will review the impact of the new paradigm on this area of software development.

The number of people involved in quality assurance, along with their political power, makes a distinct difference. In order for these individuals to be effective, they must be organized into one or several organizations which interact with the entire company. Each organization's mandate must be well defined and their authority defined and accepted at all levels of management. This is especially true if an ill-managed product is in danger of missing a marketing window and realistic management decisions must be made.

3.2 BUILDING AN EFFECTIVE SOFTWARE QUALITY ASSURANCE ORGANIZATION

In order to have an effective quality assurance organization, you should consider the following four components:

- quality assurance
- verification and validation
- simulation
- testing

Depending on your analysis—along with some experimentation and feedback— you may place all of these in one organization, or you may create one or more other organizational structures. For your particular organization, some of these components may not be necessary at all.

3.2.1 Quality Assurance

Quality assurance is an activity to make sure that quality standards are adhered to and that the quality plan is being followed. Those belonging to this group make certain that entry/exit criteria are being met at each stage and refuse to allow the software product(s) to proceed farther unless appropriate criteria have been met.

3.2.2 Verification and Validation

As was mentioned in Chapters 1 and 2, validation asks the question, "Am I building the right product?" and verification asks the question, "Am I building the product the right way?"

The first question relates to the software development life cycle model in place and whether strategies are used to make certain that the appropriate people are involved in the gathering of the requirements. These people would also make certain that the necessary changes to the specification are kept under control through the appropriate configuration control processes so that the product is build according to the requirements.

The second question relates to whether appropriate software development strategies are being employed and whether the product is being built properly.

3.2.3 Simulation

Simulation is related to the effective use of prototypes to show either a proof of concept or performance issues. It is also used to build early versions of the software system using independent modules, subsystems, and executive modules to accomplish the same goals. You can use simulation based on mathematical models to simulate and extend software behavior when little is known.

3.2.4 Testing

This is the traditional testing organization. Its cost-effectiveness will be described later on, as we discuss how to build an effective test organization as a part of a quality assurance program. We will then discuss—in the context of the new paradigm—how this organization might be completely refocused to concentrate on software behavior rather than software functional correctness.

3.3 BUILDING A SEPARATE QUALITY ASSURANCE ORGANIZATION

If the quality assurance part of the organization is to be established separately from the test organization, it will probably have more political power—especially if it reports to a Corporate Quality Committee which is responsible for overall corporate quality and adhering to corporate quality standards and goals, especially those relating to conforming to ISO-9003, SEI-CMM, and Malcolm Baldrige standards. Such a committee should report to the senior vice-president's level and be made up of qualified, interested persons from all levels of the corporate structure.

With this structure, quality assurance is a "police" organization, and it is viewed as such by the rest of the company. This can lead either to conformance to quality standards or to deliberate "stonewalling" and sabotaging of corporate quality initiatives depending on how healthy the company is in terms of employee morale and commitment. Just how many individuals and how they should be trained are determined by how large their efforts should be. You may need to experiment with such a group to see how it should be organized.

If verification and validation must be established outside of the software testing organization, then it would be good to have it assigned to the Corporate Quality Committee, as well. If for software contractual reasons it needs to be supplemented by independent verification and validation methods, then this is ideally where it should report. You will need to experiment with the best way to organize this group and how many should belong.

Having a separate organization for simulation depends on your organization's needs as well. Usually, this can be done most effectively by senior engineers on an ad hoc basis or as part of a research and development organization, which is responsible for acquiring, evaluating, and experimenting with new technology. If you find you are constantly shifting between a waterfall and a spiral life cycle, you may want to look at this as an alternative.

Because of its importance, software testing will be considered as a separate section below. One comment, relating to testing and quality assurance, is that both terms have negative connotations. For example,

- If you call your quality organization Quality Assurance, it brings to mind poorly qualified policemen who get in the way of doing a good job and must be satisfied without letting them interfere too much with software developers' major activity, with is getting the product out.

- If you call your quality organization Software Testing, it brings to mind poorly qualified data-entry people who blindly enter test cases and eat up the company's most needed resources (such as more programmers and equipment) and when the test cases don't run, waste programmers' time showing the testers what they did wrong.

Both of these concepts will get in the way of your putting in place an effective quality plan with accompanying organizations. Whichever approach you use, you must make very certain that a well-established life cycle is in place and that the points where it interacts with either Quality Assurance Teams, Test Teams, or both are "well defined" and that entry/exit criteria are well established and adhered to.

3.4 THE COST-EFFECTIVENESS OF SOFTWARE TESTING

Software testing will never find a place in a software development system unless it is cost-justified. In many companies, when downsizing needs to take place, it is the testing and quality assurance people who are laid off first (Crandall, 1993).[1]

3.4.1 Credibility and Return on Investment

In attempting to sell any particular program or idea to management, one must have credibility. Good managers tend to evaluate the value of a particular idea, program, or organization based on return on investment to the company. For this reason, a case must be built which satisfies these two conditions. This is most effectively done by basing your metrics and measurements on the costs and benefits of finding and fixing errors and the risk involved and cost of letting errors slip through on what has happened (and is happening) in your organization. This is the best way to gain credibility.

If you need credibility to even get started, it can be gained by one of two methods. First, you may begin by informally gathering information on the cost of fixing errors in certain of your own products. If this is difficult or impossible to do without management support, credibility sometimes can be gained by showing data from other companies. Often this is difficult to obtain because companies do not like to "air their dirty linen in public." Some companies, like IBM, do make this useful data available—even if it proves embarrassing.

---

1. The following material was originally published in *The Journal of the Quality Assurance Institute*, October 1993, pp. 8-20. Reprinted by permission.

3.4.2 Different Projects Require Different Approaches

Once you have made a case for software testing, you must begin in an effective manner. On some high-risk projects, you may be able to go back to the start and incrementally test each module or unit of code, successively integrating them into a working product which can be system tested. At other times, you may need to wait until you can start at the beginning of a project. We will discuss good methods for starting a successful test organization later. Usually, the best place to start implementing testing is with the unit test. Later on you can move testing principles earlier into the life cycle as you gain credibility. As will be seen later, you must continue to "sell" testing and its cost to upper-level management. Error tracking, to determine where and when in the life cycle the error should have been found; and cost allocation, to determine just how much the error costs to fix, should become a fundamental part of the testing process.

3.4.3 Begin Collecting Data

You must begin to collect data from your own organization. If you begin checking with others in your organization, you may find individuals who are aware of problems resulting in costs to your company. You may be aware of historical situations as well. In addition, you should talk to people at conferences and trade association meetings. Often they will be willing to "swap war stories" with you or share their experiences.

You can also collect "war stories" and data from publications. For example, *Information Week* (1992) told of an ambulance that "took over 30 minutes to reach a dying man because the computer dispatch system used by New York's Emergency Medical Service was not designed to recognize street addresses with more than two digits following a hyphen. A lawsuit prompted the city agency to rate the problem a 'high priority.' Seven months later, a list of all addresses not recognized by the dispatch system was made a part of the system." This was obviously a specification problem, but after seven months, it still could not be resolved within the computer system. This seems to indicate serious problems with the maintainability of the system. There was no indication as to the amount or status of the lawsuit, so it is difficult to affix a "risk." It could be in the millions of dollars just from one small error (that should have been easy to fix) (Francisco, 1992). Stories such as these can lend credence to your cause.

3.4.4 Making a Case for Finding Errors Early in the Life Cycle

For a test organization to become effective, and ultimately to pay for itself, it must gain credibility in several ways. It must

- reduce the number of errors which slip through to the customer

- measure the cost of finding and fixing errors at whatever point they are found in the life cycle

- demonstrate that the testing process is improving and becoming more cost-effective

This latter idea can best be achieved through automation, first, using off-the-shelf tools which are later enhanced by in-house tools.

The first observation of the fact that the cost of fixing errors increases asymptotically the further into the life cycle one progresses comes from a study by Barry Boehm (1976). This study was based on data from TRW, IBM, and GTE. Others have found similar results. In the 1982–85 time frame the data in Table 3-1 were collected by one of the authors, as related to the life cycle.

Table 3-1   Cost of Fixing Errors at Various Points in the Software Development Life Cycle

Company	Specific. Design	Programming	Testing	Installation and Maintenance
IBM/Raleigh	$10	$100	$1000	$25000
IBM/Rochester				$8000 ($10000)
Large LA Firm		$900	$19000	$19000
Hewlett-Packard	1 Unit	10 Units	100 Units	Infinity
IBM/Santa Teresa	1 Unit	27 Units	64 Units	127 Units

We have not been able to update these data to 1994 or 1995. Obviously the potential costs are higher now than they were then. The Raleigh data is for telecommunications software. Rochester data is for the System/38 and are the cost per "APAR," defined by IBM to be a customer reported error. The large Los Angeles firm was a mainframe customer of IBM's who built their own software in-house. They used the Yourdon methodology and felt that they had their testing "under control"—until they started logging their errors. The HP data were based on one of their desktop computer lines. The software under test was "burned into ROM" and frozen when it was shipped. HP did not report their data in dollars; only in units of effort and money. The Santa Teresa data is from 1976; they also only reported units of effort or money.

Guidelines for the Cost of Fixing Errors Across the Software Development Life Cycle   The guidelines reported in Table 3-2 are "potential" and "actual" dollar amounts observed in several companies and "averaged" for presentation here.

Building Your Own Cost Database   You will need to generate your own figures. Specification/design errors are found mainly through design reviews. If ten people participate in a one-hour design or specification review and find one error,

Table 3-2 Guidelines for the Cost of Fixing Errors Across the Software Development Life Cycle

	Specific. Design	Programming	Testing	Installation and Maintenance
Guidelines	$10 – $100	$100 – $300	$500 – $1500	$10000 – Millions

you would calculate the salaries (and overhead) for the people present, say, $30 per person present. This would give $300 per error. On the other hand, should you find multiple errors during the hour, the cost would decrease rapidly. Also, the effort to correct an error might be merely to change an interface on a prototype screen, change a bubble in a data flow diagram, or a module in a structure chart. Or, you might revise a functional description to make it more specific, accurate, or testable. This might involve only an hour of someone's time. Similar calculations can be made during the programming phase using code reviews and unit testing. In this phase, one would factor in both the review and test time and the time and effort necessary to fix the error. You might also include computer costs in some circumstances. But you must collect and maintain data routinely for each of these phases.

When the major software packages were mainframe, the IBM figures seemed appropriate, since there were only tens of thousands to hundreds of thousands of users. Errors could be fixed, and because of the small number of users, with sophisticated employees/users, the impact of the errors was not so severe. In the PC marketplace, there are millions of users. For some products like word processors, the "risk" is small. If a secretary loses a file, it might mean a few hours time wasted.

But when one of the authors was a vice-president at Novell, he found that with 4 million users and the potential of a data degradation occurring which was mandatory to fix, it might easily be fixed for $10 per user. But multiplying that times 4 million users led to a potential of $40 million to fix the error. Although such a problem did not a actually occur at Novell, the potential was always there. Fortunately, most errors affect only a small number of the possible users and can be fixed on a user-by-user basis or through publicity in newsletters or on user bulletin boards. There always remains the risk, however of an airline's or bank's network crashing. Even if it were down for only a few minutes, potentially millions of dollars worth of business could be lost.

In the early 1980s a company in Utah had a group of employees lobby for creating a test organization. Upper-level management resisted, stating, "Let the users find the errors. It will not hurt them." Within six months they had a data degradation error in the software driving a piece of their hardware. It was too disastrous to the user community not to fix, and it would have had legal ramifications if very many users had encountered the error in the product. For this reason, they had to recall the product and ship a corrected version. This cost them around $500,000, a sum that would have bought them a lot of testing time.

Risk versus Cost   The potential cost of errors in control systems which involve human lives cannot be ignored. If your business is not impacted by those types of costs, then potential risks should be identified, based on your customer base and the impact to them of lost business, lost data, late (or inappropriate) data, etc. should be assessed. Real and potential costs of errors which are realistically assessed can help you make a preliminary case to management of the need to build an effective test organization.

Employees attempting to sell upper-level management on the need for adequate software testing must be prepared to face the issue of risk realistically from upper-level management's point-of-view. For example, if a company sells around $400 million worth of product per year, and sales of the older version stop when a new version is announced, the company could be losing over $1 million per day that the new product is not shipped. If the risk is that it will cost $100,000 to fix an unknown, but potential error, it is better not to delay the shipping. The company would rather take the risk—assuming it could be sure that the risk would be less than $1 or $2 million, or even $5 or $6 million. It is easy in the test environment to be too altruistic and demand perfection, which may be unachievable, regardless of how much testing is done. Becoming a valuable test organization has as much to do with realistic assessment of risk as it does with effective testing.

3.4.5 Steps to Creating an Effective Test Organization

If you stumble in creating your first test organization, or if you oversell it, it will be that much more difficult to start over later on and obtain adequate resources. As mentioned in the introduction, there are two ways to get started. Which way to start depends on the risk your company is facing.

When Risk Is Small   If risk in current product development is small, then take a nonessential product and begin testing it with a small test team, possibly with acquired off-the-shelf test software. Keep accurate accounts of the costs involved. As software testing proves itself, expand the test organization to include more and more products, additional essential products with time. Be patient, but continue to sell upper-level management on the idea of testing. Keep accurate records on the cost of finding and fixing errors in the existing products which were not tested according to the new organization's strategy.

When Risk Is Large   If risk in current product development is large, you cannot afford to wait or to begin slowly or cautiously. You must begin testing the existing products at whatever point they are in the development cycle. What tends to make this difficult is the lack of an effective software development life cycle and well-defined process and methodology for getting products to market (or just completing and installing them, if you are building for your own company in an MIS environment).

The important consideration, which we will see in the next section, is that there must be management support at the time you formally start your test organization. If you are starting with a small product to build credibility, then this may not be critical; if you are starting in the middle of an existing high-risk product, then management support is mandatory. They must make a commitment from day one that there will be an effective, well-staffed, well-supplied test organization. Sometimes this will be difficult to get them to do, mainly because there has not been enough evidence presented to indicate the risk involved or possibly to give them the feel for the cost of building the test organization.

The Impact of Testing on the Development Organization   Another issue that must ultimately be addressed is the impact of testing on the development organization. Initially, this impact should be minimized until everyone starts to "buy on." Later, the impact of testability on the specifications and software design must be integrated into the development process. At some point a life cycle must be imposed on the development organization and test activities must be integrated with development activities. This must be agreed on by both organizations. Entry and exit criteria relating to each of the phases must be defined and agreed upon. Finally, the project plan must be created according to the order in which the various modules and components will be implemented and integrated. This is critical if incremental testing takes place and if integration testing is effective without massive numbers of stubs and drivers being needed. All of this calls for massive cooperation between the test and development organizations and commitment to a high-quality, error-free product. To reach this point, management must very early on give its blessing and commitment to the process.

3.4.6 How to Create an Effective, Stable Test Organization

We will now turn our attention to how to create an effective test organization.

Management Support   As was stated, in order to create an effective test organization, there must be management support very high up in the corporate organization, Without it, the test organization cannot be effective. Testing must have the power to stop release of a defective product—even if there is an important marketing window that will be missed—should the product prove unfixable within the appropriate time frame. Management also must commit to adequate testing resources, both in terms of personnel, equipment, and software. These resources do not come cheaply, but they are extremely cost-effective when the organization is built correctly. You cannot "soft pedal" this to management. They must be ready to make a strong commitment if this is to succeed.

The head of this organization should have enough prestige and power to withstand the political pressures associated with a test organization. He or she should report to at least one level above the managers responsible for the products being created, preferably at the vice-president's level or at least at the second- or third-level manager's level.

Organization Size   The ultimate number of test engineers in the test organization should be based on whether or not these engineers are to perform the unit and integration testing or whether these testing levels will be performed by the development engineers. When the development engineers perform unit and integration testing, the ratio should be approximately two development engineers for each test engineer. When the test engineers must perform all the testing, the ratio should be one development engineer for each test engineer. In addition, there should be technicians to set up equipment, keep tests running, log test results, and so forth. The appropriate ratio of these will depend on the specific needs of the particular test organization.

Salaries and Status   These individuals should be called test engineers and have equal pay and status with development engineers, if the organization is to become a first-class test organization. This often involves a battle with a company's Human Resources Department. A high-level manager, hopefully at the vice-president's level, may need to overrule the hiring policies of the Human Resources Department. Without this parity, the test organization will be viewed as an organization for entry-level individuals, who rapidly begin plotting how they can get into the development organization, and one will not be able to attract and train effective, career-oriented test engineers.

Defining the Organization   A map or structure showing how the test organization will relate to the various players from software development, marketing, documentation, and maintenance should be established. Once the test organization is well established and is gaining credibility, attempts should be made to move its impact to as early a point in the life cycle as possible. This will be discussed in the next section. Standards must be established against which the deliverables for a product will be measured. These relate to

- Documentation standards—inside and outside the code, in user's manuals, etc.
- Programming and systems design standards (see Crandall, 1987; 1990a; 1990b)
- Management sign-off procedures

This latter area relates to the need, at times, to allow for certain "violations" of standards, without losing control. A manager hears the reasons for the violation and then signs off that it is a valid reason to violate the standard. These standards must be agreed to by all the individuals involved from all the organizations.

Process Control Procedures and Policies   These involve design reviews of product specifications and test plans, code inspections prior to unit testing a module, and walk-throughs of either area, as appropriate.

Basic Testing Strategies and Tools   These involve formats and standards for test plans, test case generation procedures, testing strategies, and standards (based on risk analysis) for each of the testing levels with which a test organization should be concerned. These will be expanded on in the next section, but they might be classified as

- Unit test
- Integration test
- Subsystem/system test
- Beta test
- Acceptance/regression test

These classifications will have the least impact on the development organization when one is first establishing a test organization. Later they can be refined to include the early part of the life cycle, as described in the following section. A library of test tools should begin to be assembled to support each of these levels.

Project Management Policies, Strategies, and Standards These may impinge on the development area but are an important part of quality assurance, as it is the project plan which makes it possible to get a product out on schedule, within an appropriate marketing window, if used correctly.

Configuration Management Policies, Strategies, and Standards These are best handled in terms of managing versions and builds through effective use of a program library facility. A company should be able to reconstruct any previous version or build of a product, and error fixes and enhancements should be tied to a particular build or version of the product. Builds tend to relate to incompletely built portions of an entire product, while versions relate to an entire product with given characteristics and functions. More discussion of this topic will be provided in the next section.

Evaluation Policies, Strategies, and Standards Evaluation policies, strategies, and standards should be established for

- Software development
- Testing
- Project management
- Appropriate development and testing tools
- Measurements and metrics
- Employees and employee policies

There is not space to discuss all of these areas, but it is important that they be evaluated with well-defined and well-known criteria.

3.4.7 Making a Test Organization More Effective

For an overall test strategy to be effective, it must be based on a well-thought-out software engineering infrastructure. Once a test organization begins to acquire credibility, the development organization must be restructured to allow for better integration of test awareness into the software development process. Ideally, software projects should be organized in two ways (Crandall, 1990a):

- the development organization structure
- the product development life cycle

The Development Organization Structure Most software development organizations should have the following components:

- Marketing organization
- Software development organization
- Software testing organization
- Software maintenance organization
- Documentation organization
- Human factors organization

Companies might also have other component organizations such as human resources, sales, distribution, or support, but these will not be described here. The above six areas impact the software development process. [The paper (Crandall, 1990a) referenced above describes how to get software products to market. Here the interest lies in how to build "test awareness" into the process (Crandall, 1990b).]

People from each of the six areas should be organized into product development teams and made responsible for taking a product from conception to release to maintenance. The size of a product team may vary from 6 to 20+ people, depending on the product, but ultimately, large teams should be subdivided into development teams of around 5 to 6 people. Experimentation should determine the best structure, organization, and makeup of the teams. The team members should be loyal to the product and totally committed to its development, but actual personnel management, in terms of recruitment, training, salary, and advancement, should take place within the appropriate organization rather than through the team.

As was mentioned in an earlier section, experience tends to indicate that the ideal ratios of individuals in the above organizations are as follows (Crandall, 1989a). For every two development engineers, there should be

1 marketing person

1 – 2 test engineers

1 – 3 maintenance engineers (depending on the size and age of the organization, i.e., the number of products being maintained)

1.5 documentation persons (one to write the documentation and 0.5 person to test the documentation)

0.5 – 1 human factors persons

As was mentioned earlier, not only should test engineers receive the same pay as development engineers or maintenance engineers, but movement among the three groups should be encouraged. Personnel evaluations should be made on the same basis for all three groups. A good strategy is to hire new engineers into the testing group, after a year or two move them to the maintenance organization for a couple of years, then move them to support for a couple of months (to see what people think of the products and how maintainable and usable they are), and then move them into development. After they have worked on development for several years, move them back to either testing or maintenance. This provides extremely "testing aware," "maintenance aware," and "service aware" individuals to the organization. However, there are many times when you do not have the luxury of hiring this way. Much of the time, you need experts immediately in some phase of software engineering.

Test engineers, maintenance engineers, and development engineers should be trained in software testing through formal, in-house courses. They should not simply be told to test. If a company is near a university, the university might be willing to underwrite a testing course for that university's curriculum in Computer Science (see Crandall, 1989b, for more information).

The test organization oversees the entire testing process, from specification design through software design, through inspecting the code, through unit testing the code through integration testing the modules, through subsystem and system testing, through beta testing through maintenance testing. They have the final sign-off on exit criteria from each phase.

Definition of an Effective Product Life Cycle   In the development of commercial software products, the "waterfall" (Pressman, 1992; Humphrey, 1989), or "sequential" (IBM, 1978) type life cycle model will not work, as it adds too much time to the development cycle. The "spiral life" cycle has gained much favor in recent years, mainly in the area of Rapid Application Development (RAD). As mentioned elsewhere, this approach tends to cause you to lose control of the software architecture and does not seem to be any faster than the proposal which follows. Something more closely related to Metzger's model (1981) is better. The model used most effectively at Novell (Crandall, 1990a) was one in which the life cycle was broken into the phases shown in Figure 3-1.

In this life cycle model, the major part of software development takes place simultaneously among all the development teams. Code reviews and inspections are attended by all groups, as appropriate to their backgrounds and potential contribution. Incremental testing takes place as early in the development life cycle as possible—as soon as software engineers have units and subsystems ready to test. After a module's code is reviewed, unit tested (with the test plan and test cases reviewed and signed off by the test organization, though performed by development), integration testing takes place (at which time the code is "frozen" and is available on a "read-only" basis to everyone—including the programmer). On completion of integration, the subsystem is turned over to the test organization. The maintenance organization begins during this time to maintain the various versions and builds (to be discussed later on).

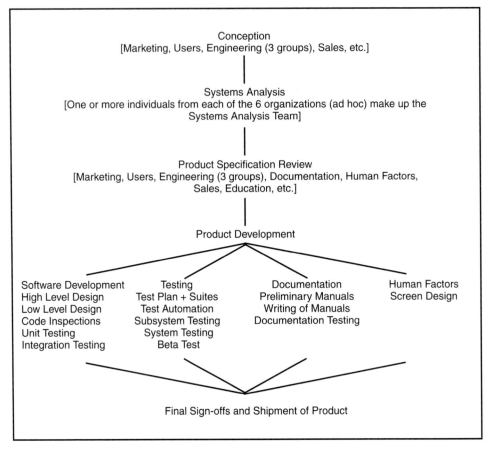

Figure 3-1   A parallel life cycle

Corporate Testing Strategy   A possible corporate testing strategy (Crandall, 1989a; Crandall 1990b) might be created as follows. Five test levels, refined
from the earlier section, are defined as a part of the testing strategy:

- requirements and specification
- unit and integration
- subsystem/system
- beta
- regression/acceptance

While different test techniques exist at each level, the basic strategy is
based on the testing relationships among the levels. The test-level activities are
tied together through Cascaded Value Added Testing (CVAT). The goal is to minimize the cascading effect. Note that while this concept is related to the idea of

filters, it is very different in its approach, though that difference may seem rather subtle. Here we are using basic testing strategies to successively remove errors. In the new paradigm, we are eliminating them through filters based on pattern matching.

Testing Relationships   Because it is demonstrably less expensive to remove errors early in the life cycle rather than later, the emphasis of cascaded value added testing is to employ strategies which will allow for removal of most of the errors early in the life cycle, with fewer and fewer errors being found the farther you progress into the life cycle.

Requirements and Specification   In the context of the infrastructure described above, a systems analysis team, usually made up of a subset of the product development team, creates the product specification. Initially, errors should be removed from the requirements and specification through a number of design reviews. These reviews should involve "typical" customers, "advanced" customers, development engineering, test engineering, documentation, marketing, sales, support, and others.

Software Design   The software development team usually creates a software product architecture, or an internal design of the software. The software design should also be reviewed, but usually only the product development team would be involved, plus invited experts.

Module and Subsystem Coding   Once the code has passed its first successful compile (as determined by the programmer), it should pass through a code review, which would include the team member from the test organization. Following this sign-off, the code is ready for the unit test. Ideally, the programmer should unit test his or her own code, with the test plan and test cases reviewed by the team member from the test organization. DeMarco (1982) recommends that the programmer never see the code after it is programmed. As a variation on the above, a testing SWAT team (or unit and integration team) from the test organization might be assigned to unit test the code, or it might be routinely tested by the test organization. You must experiment to find out what works best for a particular organization. At any rate, the test cases must be captured and retained for regression testing. Specific unit testing techniques and strategies are covered by people such as Beizer (1991, 1995) and Hetzel (1988). They will not be covered in this chapter.

When the code has passed the unit test, it is "frozen," and promoted to integration. When a number of modules are ready, subsystems are integrated and tested in preparation for promotion to the test organization. Again, the unit and integration team can play a role here.

Programmers often do not understand either the need for, nor how to perform, unit and integration testing. Often, they are unwilling to take the time. Sometimes, because of production schedules, it is unrealistic to expect them to. The unit and integration team provides a means of solving training, motivation, and scheduling problems encountered at these levels of testing. Applying a strong methodology such as object-oriented design can be beneficial—especially when used with automated tools, as explained in the next section.

Subsystem/System Testing   Rather than wait for the entire product to be built before formal testing begins, it seems best to begin incrementally testing the subsystems as they are completed. Once a subsystem has passed the exit criteria for integration testing, it is promoted to subsystem testing. A strategy for implementing this is presented later.

At the time the product specification is frozen and signed off, the product test team begins to create a formal test plan, which is evaluated and signed off. Then the team begins to acquire the equipment necessary to perform the testing. The team also begins to acquire the automated tools to test that particular product, either those available commercially or those built internally by a tools research and development group (which would be created within the test organization). Then they begin to specify and write the test suites. When the code finally becomes available, they are ready to begin testing.

The subsystem/system test strategy basically involves defining all the functions contained in a given subsystem to be tested and then making certain that all of them work in connection with the rest of the system. There are many different techniques which can be used, and it seems inappropriate to list all of them in this book. See Beizer (1984) and Hetzel (1988) for more details. As with unit and integration testing, the test cases are captured, as much as possible, and are retained for regression testing. A testing log is maintained by each tester indicating test cases run, errors found, anomalies encountered during testing, and so forth. Exit criteria from this phase are related to the stability of the product, decrease in error rates, errors corrected and retested, and so forth.

Beta Testing   A beta test group should be part of an effective test organization. For popular products, many companies desire to become beta test sites, and it is necessary to place testing standards and restrictions on them. Companies chosen as beta test sites should be required to perform testing difficult to do by the company itself and to operate in environments difficult to re-create at the software company. The beta test group coordinates and manages the beta testing. Errors found at this stage are reported back to the development organization, fixed, and regression tested. Corrected versions are sent back to the beta test sites.

It should be noted that at this stage of the development cycle, the product is close to shipping. Documentation must also have been prepared for the beta sites and must be tested and evaluated along with the code. In fact, recall that the documentation team, which makes up a part of the product development team, not only contains individuals writing the users manuals and other documentation to accompany the product, it also contains individuals who must test the documentation against the product to verify that it adequately and clearly represents what the product is to do in a given situation. These individuals also make certain that no undocumented features have been allowed to creep into the product, that there are no missing functions, and that functions operate in the way in which they were originally defined.

Regression/Acceptance Testing   Once beta testing is completed, the product passes through a final regression/acceptance test. This testing is extensive and is to make certain that all reported errors have been correctly fixed, that all documentation errors have been fixed, and that the product is ready for "first customer shipment."

Customer   Through the cascaded value-added testing process, the number of errors should be radically reduced as one moves from one level of testing to the next. Ideally, subsystem/system testing should only locate errors which were impossible to detect through unit and integration testing. Beta testing should only find errors which exist in environments impossible to create outside of a user's shop. Regression/acceptance testing should only verify that all reported errors have been properly corrected.

When the product reaches the customer, no errors should remain in the code. Obviously, this is an unreachable ideal, but it should be the stated goal of any test organization, and software should be in place to allow for error tracking to provide feedback to help reach that goal. Note that in the new paradigm, it is not.

Risk Analysis (Risk, Time, Resources)   The problem with the cascaded value-added testing process is that it is an ideal, not a solution. At the unit test level, there are a potentially infinite number of test cases which could be written and executed. Such a high level of testing is impossible. Many times, to be able to test a particular function or subsystem, more code must be written to create the test environment than exists in the actual piece of code itself. You must, therefore, also evaluate and test for the errors which may be created by the test organization itself as it writes these drivers and stubs.

Often, there are not adequate resources, nor is there adequate time for the developer to test the piece of code or subsystem to the degree it needs to be tested. One solution has been to implement the unit and integration team. This team moves from product to product, testing critical code and helping the programmers perform tricky tests which their training does not prepare them to do. This helps minimize the risk of programmers failing to incrementally test their code. It also helps the programmers avoid the temptation to simply bang away on the keyboard performing ad hoc tests which are neither planned nor documented.

But even this approach is not enough. There are still rarely enough resources to adequately test a piece of code or a subsystem. For this reason, the product test plan is built around risk analysis. During the unit test, modules and functions within modules are identified and evaluated as to high, medium, or low risk. Decisions are then made as to whether to exhaustively test, moderately test, lightly test, or ignore a particular function.

The evaluation should consider module complexity, error history, customer impact, whether it is a new or existing feature, schedule (time available to test), and programmer confidence level.

Risk Analysis Applied to Cascaded Value-Added Testing   Applying risk analysis to the cascaded value-added testing process, it can be seen that, initially, you eliminate as much potential error as possible from the product specification by having a large number of individuals from a broad set of backgrounds, goals, and expectations evaluate the product through product specification reviews. Product designs are also reviewed as to design quality. Code is reviewed prior to the unit test.

At the unit test level, a module is analyzed and evaluated to determine the amount of time to be spent testing it and which parts of the module are to be singled out. This type of evaluation is also applied to the integration testing.

At the subsystem/system test level, you may also be limited with respect to time and resources; in fact, some resources are just not available. Some environments are impossible to create or are prohibitively expensive. A reasonable assessment of the risk in this environment must be made, and effective selection of beta test sites which can test specific environments to minimize this risk must be made.

The basic goal of this entire process is minimal customer impact. As can be seen from the previous discussion, the concept of cascading is related to allowing fewer and fewer errors to pass from one level to another. Ideally, only errors impossible to find at one level should be allowed to pass to the next, where test procedures minimize the risk of their getting past the phase where they should have been caught. On the other hand, some of the risk is associated with lack of time or resources. One may not have time to test all functions, so those associated with obscure, unlikely paths, or those which will have little or no impact on the user, are not tested.

Change Control   Because products rarely remain static during their life cycles, provision must be made to handle change. Uncontrolled change leads to creeping featurism, undocumented features, poorly planned integration of the new features, and loss of traceability back to the specification.

No matter how well the original specification is researched and created (Crandall, 1990a), there will be changes to it during the development cycle. Managing this change can be accomplished by a Configuration Control Board, which ideally would exist fairly high up in the organization. At Novell, it was at the Divisional Vice-President's level. The approach taken is to have a proposed change evaluated by all individuals involved: marketing, development, testing, documentation, sales, and so forth. Each group provides an impact assessment for each proposed option (or action) which could be taken with respect to the change, and a decision is made based upon what appears best to upper-level management in terms of the overall corporate policy and direction. This allows changes to be made in a controlled manner and for adjustments to be made with a complete understanding of their impact on the current product, and possibly on other products. The ability to deal with these changes also requires a CASE tool for the specification, a code library (and librarian) for the management of the code, and a CASE/TEST tool for managing the test cases. An example of how this is being done at Digital Technology International is provided in the Appendix.

Versions of the product should be specified and maintained during the development cycle where major changes are made—especially when they occur late in the development cycle and copies of the product are in the hands of key or critical users (Crandall, 1990a). When minor changes are made or when errors have been corrected, builds should be specified and tied to particular dates. Information regarding various versions and builds should be managed by the Maintenance Organization and they should see that everyone involved knows what is going on. Feedback should be obtained periodically and the basic approach to change control should be modified and managed with respect to the specific needs of the particular organization's problems and needs to make things function in an effective manner.

3.4.8 Conclusion

Note that the new product delivery process takes all the concepts described above and makes them more efficient. With enough discipline on the part of management and developers, this new paradigm has a high probability of providing you with a strategy for reaching Six Sigma or any other quality goal you would like to achieve. As you will see, you never do away with the test organization just because you no longer need to test software in the traditional sense. You are actually shifting your emphasis to behavioral testing.

Without strong, committed management support, it is extremely difficult to build a strong, effective test organization. Good test organizations require a large amount of computer and human resources. For a test organization to be effective, it must exist in an environment with a large amount of automation. Initially, much of this automation is achieved by acquiring off-the-shelf testware. Later on this testware must be modified and customized to fit your own unique test environment.

Once you have strong management commitment and support for a test organization, you must then put the organization together in such a way that it can be effective right from the start. A major consideration is that for this organization to be effective it must impact heavily and early in the software development life cycle. Indeed, a software development life cycle should be imposed on the software development process. Further, plans to build the product should reflect the order in which components will be integrated together to allow system testing to begin as early as possible in the development process. The latter part of this section is directed to the concepts and principles which will help you achieve that goal.

3.5 THE IMPACT OF THE NEW PARADIGM

As can be seen, the life cycle model for the product delivery system of the new paradigm is very similar to the parallel life cycle of Figure 3-1. A major difference between the approach of Section 3.4. and the new paradigm is in the use of filters, with which quality measures are associated. Instead of dealing with error rates and trying to eliminate bugs, one is dealing with quality and trying to show through pattern matching and evaluation that there are no errors in the product. Similar to CVAT, we are attempting to remove all the errors that are available to the process at each given point in the life cycle. The new paradigm, however, has more points at which these errors can be filtered out, and emphasis is on quality, rather than errors. In terms of efficiency (the time and effort necessary to remove errors versus the percent of errors removed), the new paradigm is more efficient.

3.5.1 Management Aspects (Return on Investment) under the New Paradigm

The efficiency and effectiveness of the new paradigm must be demonstrated just as they are for a traditional test environment. If possible, you should start on smaller projects and then proceed to larger ones as you learn the process and gain control of it in your organization. It cannot be stressed enough that it requires enormous discipline on the part of management—from the very start of a project—for this new paradigm to work effectively.

Leverage   From a management perspective, there is another concept which is extremely important—leverage. Leverage is providing a certain return on investment for a given outlay. Many companies have been going through downsizing in an attempt to counteract a loss in sales and/or profits and flatten management to eliminate the "fat" in the organization. We feel that when these fads are followed, it is merely an indication that there is a lack of leadership among management and an admission of failure to properly manage the company. This will be discussed further in the next section.

A better approach is to use a feedback mechanism, coupled with leverage. Whenever programmers must perform rework, there is zero leverage. Testing has zero leverage. For maintenance programmers, there is zero leverage. For support people, there is zero leverage even if you charge for their help. Companies must decide on what type of business they are in. If you sell services or custom software, or if you build for internal MIS use, you probably have little leverage; on the other hand, if you build for "shrink-wrapped" markets, you can—with discipline—achieve a high degree of leverage.

3.5.2 Leverage at the Software Product Level

As we indicated earlier, leverage is providing a certain return on investment for a given outlay in building a software product. Leverage at the employee level is the return on investment to the company for that employee's salary (and overhead).

Earlier in this section, we stated that "flat management" and "downsizing" were fads and that their use indicated incompetent management. These statements are based on the following two observations:

- If a company is managed using an effective feedback mechanism based on the implementation of the corporate mission statement and strategic plan, then the need to employ fad-type management strategies is nonexistent. An effective feedback mechanism would indicate early on if there were anything wrong with the corporate management structure.

- If there is a sudden need for downsizing, this is an even more important issue. You should never manage employees on the basis of budget or cash flow. You should manage on the basis of employee leverage. This means that each employee is considered an investment and is managed in such a manner as to maximize that investment. An employee is not hired because there is a budget; an employee is hired because there is opportunity. As we mentioned earlier in the book, leveraging a software engineer to 1,000 times his or her salary is not unreasonable. This is also true for almost all employees in an organization. Therefore, if a software engineer makes $50,000 per year, he or she should be generating around $50 million in profits. In some organizations, such a goal may be totally unrealistic. On the other hand, a company's market can be adjusted to make such goals attainable.

In a recent article, Tom Peters (1995) decried the "fad management" that has been in place since the 1950s, when America was just coping with the massive productivity gains. Peters points out that at that time, Peter Drucker proposed "management by objective." While that was appropriate for that time, management has continued to use it and has then relied on other fads that have come along. Peters's current feeling is that management lacks leadership, which he illustrated by the example that even poorly funded schools can have outstanding programs under a school principal who is a strong leader.

Further, good managers are more than good leaders; they also are usually good coaches, as well, and are not unwilling to get in and get their hands dirty in an emergency or crisis. But they also employ a feedback mechanism based on their corporate mission statement and goals. By managing a system against standards of productivity, performance, quality, and leverage, they will always know what is happening to their organization (and the competition) and can adapt immediately and correctly.

Many have felt that managing by income, sales, or profit, per employee and laying off and rehiring based on these numbers is an effective management strategy. Indeed many have used this approach to justify layoffs. Such strategies are usually followed when senior management manages toward quarterly earnings to the exclusion of almost everything else. Five-year marketing plans based on corporate mission statements require a bigger picture and a more long-range solution. Statistics show that where downsizing occurs, 86 percent of the remain-

ing employees experience morale problems. Yet only 50.6 percent of the companies using downsizing to help their profit margins actually show a profit.
[Bernard Wysockl, *The Wall Street Journal* (July 5, 1995), as quoted in Gill,
1995.]

Achieving and maintaining a high degree of leverage in a company require
a high degree of management discipline. Flat management goes completely
counter to this goal. Because employee leverage is based on a highly volatile
environment, it requires an extremely effective feedback mechanism and a high
degree of management attention—from top to bottom. This tends to indicate that
at certain levels of the management chain, the employee/management ratio
must be fairly low. How does one assure such leverage? It is based on the leverage associated with the products the company is building. The next section
shows some examples of how such assurance can be guaranteed.

3.5.3 Guaranteeing Leverage

Creating an environment where leverage can be maximized requires a high
degree of planning and discipline. But there are many ways such leverage can be
guaranteed. This idea relates to making sales estimates realistic and to building
products to guarantee such estimates.

**An Example of the Power of Using Filters and Plans to Guarantee Lever-
age at the Product Level**   An example of how filters and plans can be used to
effectively define a new software product—in practical terms—might be illustrated by the relationship between the marketing analysis (and its filter) and the
preliminary sales plan (and its filter). Initially, the marketing analysis document
provides a preliminary estimate of both the cost of building the system and the
amount of sales it will generate. Neither of these figures is well known at this
point. They may be accurate, but they are not precise. You will not have a tight
figure for the cost of building the software until the software architecture with
its accompanying project plan is in place.

But suppose the preliminary estimates from the marketing analysis are
such that there is high probability that the software product can be built for
around $1 million and should sell around $100 million—provided a particular
marketing window can be opened. The sales organization then looks on a region-
by-region or salesperson-by-salesperson basis at what parameters must be met
to achieve that goal for the first year of sales.

The sales organization would then create a preliminary sales plan. It might
indicate that in Seattle, Washington, there are 25,000 potential customers. A
reasonable success rate would be around 20 percent, meaning 5,000 sales for the
year. The salesperson decides if he or she can make a sale, close it, install and
train the customer on the product in one hour provided certain criteria are met
with respect to the software system, i.e., the "usability" of its interface, accessibility of its training materials, etc.

A reality check indicates that to meet this goal, a salesperson can "realistically" make around 3 sales per day—based on 15 calls, yielding around 700 sales

for the year. If there is only one salesperson in Seattle, then six more salespeople need to be hired. If there is a cash flow problem, then the first salesperson's sales would be used to hire the other six salespeople—unless they work purely on commission. This sales plan not only contains this information, it also should include the names of the companies to be contacted, which will be contacted first, what sales tools will be needed, and what backup help will be necessary (training staff, help desks, etc.). A similar activity would be carried out for each territory or salesperson.

It should be noted that this activity leads to some constraints on the software being specified.

- It must be capable of being easily and quickly installed in the user's environment on whatever software and hardware the customer is expected to have.

- The user interface must be simple enough to be intuitively and quickly learned by the customer.

- The on-line help must be responsive and easy to use.

- Training must be available and have been validated on interactive video or CD-ROM, so that the amount of training the salesperson must provide is efficient and minimized.

When a specific sales plan is created and filtered, it has a major impact on the software specification. The value of the requirements definition document and filter becomes more apparent in this context.

In order for employee leverage to be effective, it usually requires an employee to create or build something once and then to have it reused over and over again. This is obvious in the programming environment, but it is also true for documentation and training. If the cost per sale can be made even more efficient, it merely adds to the leverage applied to the salespeople. But this must be specifically designed into the product.

Using a Gantt Chart to Improve Leverage   Using a Gantt chart to schedule employee activities provides several benefits to the organization attempting to improve employee leverage. Critical Path Method (CPM) and PERT charts tend to be "overkill"—especially since the data and probability distributions necessary for their use tend not to be available in some business contexts. Gantt charts—to whatever level of granularity is necessary—can be used to both schedule and measure an employee's time. When this approach is used properly, it is ordinarily not a simplistic activity. Depending on their responsibilities and the products they are building, employees may be moved from activity to activity to maximize the construction and delivery of a product. Care is taken to manage the critical path, while maximizing the leverage of the employees at each point in time. Advanced planning along with effective feedback make this possible. Care must be taken to factor into shifting employee assignments the negative impact of start/stop on the schedule and the possible negative impact on creativity.

Often, several products can be built simultaneously using a minimal number of people. At Novell, we called this "running lean and mean." But this can only be done in the context of an effective product delivery system.

Conclusions   In most software development environments, software is being built for a rapidly changing market. Not only do users' needs change, but new platforms also come on the market, competitors bring out products having an unexpected impact, new technology becomes available. This requires an effective configuration control process to be in place. The important concept is that of identifying and managing change. When everything has been identified and placed in a manageable environment, then it is possible to respond rapidly to changes in the market place without losing control or damaging the employee or product leverage.

Many marketing managers maintain that the software market is changing so fast that five-year plans are a thing of the past. They cite marketing disasters in the software area as reasons why this is so. Our experience is that the software field, while changing rapidly, is not discontinuous. Whether you are dealing with a five-year plan for a company's product line or the marketing plan for a single product, the facts are all there and are obtainable far enough in advance to be useful. Things may change faster or slower than you expect—but they are not discontinuous. If you plan on selling a word processor when the world "suddenly" wants an office suite of integrated tools, it is because you have not talked to enough people—customers and noncustomers—or studied the market through marketing surveys and competitive analyses. That is the major reason why the first thing we did on coming to Digital Technology International was to make certain the product delivery process was marketing driven.

3.6 TECHNIQUES AND CONTENTS OF A SQA PLAN

Now that we have discussed how to build an effective quality organization and how to implement software testing, we turn to how you develop a software quality assurance plan. You should note that the SQA plan is developed on a project-by-project basis and it is not a static plan that is created only once. The SQA plan describes the project's quality objectives and how these objectives will be met. The plan focuses on aspects of process and product assurance that are most critical to the project.

3.6.1 What to Address in Your SQA Plan

Given the objectives of the quality assurance plan, it should include activities to assure the product meets quality objectives, and activities to assure the development process follows your internal system development process.

Objective   The objective reflects the purpose and scope of the SQA plan. It will list all the functions of the system that will be addressed by the SQA plan.

Significantly Impacted Departments (SIDs)   This section will identify all the organizations that will be affected by the new software. These organizations have the ability to influence the contents of the software and they may control some of the activities related to the development.

Resources   This paragraph lists all the resources, and their respective departments that are responsible to carry out the activities that will contribute to the overall quality of the system.

Document Quality   List all the documents to be developed and identify how the quality and robustness of these documents will be maintained.

- Software Requirements: This section identifies how the requirement document will be written to ensure there are no missing or unambiguous requirements and that each requirement is testable and measurable.
- Design Document: This section identifies how the software architecture will be designed to ensure that the requirements are met.
- The Validation and Verification Plan: This section should identify verification activities, the schedule, and who would be responsible for conducting them. The following activities should be considered in a validation and verification plan:

(a) reviews

(b) walk-through

(c) sign-offs

(d) inspections

(e) audits and/or testing

Any entrance or exit requirement for each of these activities should be identified in the verification and validation plan.

Deliverable   This section identifies different phases of the system development life cycle and defines the inputs and outputs for each phase. The paragraph also lists how the outputs will be verified for the following:

- the relevant requirements of the output are met
- the output meets the acceptance criteria
- the output meets any internal or external development standards
- the outputs meet regulatory requirements

Test   This section, at a high level, identifies all the tests to be carried out. If any field testing or beta testing is to be conducted, it should be listed in this section. A test plan will indicate how these tests will be carried out. See Chapter 5 for a format for test plan.

Acceptance Criteria   List who will be developing the acceptance criteria, the time-frame of the acceptance criteria walk-through, who will be invited, and if there are any issues, how they will be resolved. The acceptance criteria should be based on specified user profile and user interfaces. Further it should state the complete set of functions and the event list through which they will be demonstrated.

Delivery   If the software is developed for outside customers, this paragraph identifies

- number of copies to be delivered
- delivery schedule
- type of media

This should be coordinated under release management (see Chapter 4).

Maintenance   This section should list all the maintenance activities that will be carried out and how they will be accomplished. It will include

- identification of maintenance activities
- scope of maintenance
- reports related to maintenance
- department responsible for maintenance

Configuration Management   This section states how various versions of the software will be identified and tracked. Consideration should be given to

- version control
- limiting updating of project documents by more than one individual at any given time
- updating of project documents with ongoing changes
- configuration management tools to be used
- the stage when a project-related item will be brought under configuration

Document Changes   This section identifies how the documentation will be updated, specifically, user manual, operations manual, system development life cycle instruction manual, etc. The following items should be addressed:

- How will the changes to the documents be approved?
- How often will be documents be updated?
- How will the old copies of the documents be retrieved?
- Will all the documents reside under document control?
- Where will the master list, with latest revisions reside?
- How often will the document be reissued?

Quality Records   This paragraph should identify the quality records and how these records will be stored and maintained. The paragraph should also specify how long the quality records will be kept and the schedule of when they are to be destroyed. Quality records include

- Development plan
- Test plan
- Verification and validation plan
- Measurement plan
- Test plan
- Test cases
- Test results
- Regression test results
- Minutes of various reviews
- Audit results

Metrics   This paragraph should identify what types of data will be collected for measurement purpose so that the development process can be continuously monitored and improved. (See Chapter 8 for details on measurement.)

Practices and Standards   Identify methodology that will be used to ensure the product is developed according to the internal/external company standards and that preestablished practices are being followed. The standards include

- coding standards
- documentation standards
- comments standards

Training   List all the training needs of the project team of the project under development. Indicate

- the type of training to be given
- how often it will be given
- how end users get their training
- how the need for training will be assessed
- how the training records will be kept

3.7 CONCLUSION

In Chapters 1 and 2, we defined process and product assurance techniques. You should have noticed that process was separated from product. Basically, quality is not a vague term but it is a very specific term and has an enormous impact on both the product and the process through which it was developed. If you try to build a product without a quality process, you will encounter serious problems. In this chapter we have discussed the type of organization that needs to be in place to address quality and testing. Some of the problems you may encounter in putting such an organization in place and the cost-effectiveness of establishing quality are also mentioned.

Software Quality Standards

The major thrust of our book has been on quality. In this chapter we will consider some quality standards that have been used by companies such as Motorola, IBM, and others to achieve quality awards. This material is mainly based on the authors' experience consulting with IBM and other companies, but parts are based on personal conversations with Connie Marchewka of Texas Instruments Software Engineering Process (STEP) and on "The Baldrige Process" by William F. Hayes (1995), Executive Vice-President of Texas Instruments. In addition, we reference "IBM's Rochester Facility Strives for 'a Perfect 10'" (1990). We will revisit our product delivery process and give some additional definitions of various components.

4.1 SOME STANDARDS FOR SOFTWARE QUALITY

In the context of the new paradigm, here are some quality standards for you to consider. The first standards will apply to some industry goals in terms of quality criteria that many companies aspire to: Six Sigma, or 3.4 defects per million opportunities, Two Times Theoretical Cycle Times, and continuous improvement. These basic concepts come from a program initiated by Motorola in the 1980s.

4.1.1 The Concept of Six Sigma

Six Sigma is one of the major concepts that has been used in an attempt to increase quality. It is basically a strategy to reduce the number of errors in a software system to less than 3.4 defects per million lines of code. It relates to being six "standard deviations" away from the mean in a "normal distribution." Malcolm Baldrige winners including IBM and Texas Instruments have followed Motorola's lead. One of Motorola's first steps was to form Motorola University, where they developed courses on quality software design, Deming's and Crosby's concepts of quality, etc. Most quality-oriented companies understand the importance of education in building quality into a corporation—and especially into a corporate culture. Most programmers are committed to attending courses on technology, but they are rarely committed to courses on quality concepts, thinking them to be a lot of "hype," with little substance. This tends to be true—regardless of whom you present the material—unless you have a quality organization and a quality process in place. Our new paradigm puts total emphasis on quality deliverables throughout the product delivery process. Whatever process you use should do the same.

Motorola also moved the decision level as far down the management hierarchy as possible, flattening out the organization through the use of self-directed teams. The corporate paradigm was changed to reflect quality and employees were encouraged to "buy on."

Motorola then employed the Six Steps to Six Sigma, which involved:

1. determining what your product is
2. determining who the customer is for that product
3. identifying the suppliers you need for your product
4. mapping out the process you must use to put it together
5. examining that process to eliminate errors and wasted steps
6. establishing measurement means to feed continuous improvement

Quality programs based on Six Sigma tend to work only when there is an executive champion high up in the organization who has a clear vision of what must happen and where the company is going. Often companies that are well on their way toward quality awards stumble and lose sight of their goals when such an executive leaves without an adequate transition (see Crandall, 1989c).

Unfortunately, while several companies have been able to use the Six Steps to Six Sigma to achieve quality, other than the idea of teams and goals and focus on the customer, little is given to help other companies to achieve similar goals. How do you achieve 3.4 defects per million in a testing environment? Suppose your intermediate goal is to achieve 1 error per 1,000 lines of code and you achieve 2 errors per 1,000 lines of code? When you look at your testing strategy, it appears that you have around 90 percent coverage with little chance of accounting for more? What do you do?

Texas Instruments (TI), another Malcolm Baldrige winner, followed almost the same procedure that one of the authors did while at Sun. They also set up their version of a six-step strategy leading to Six Sigma. The TI strategy looked like this:

- identify product
- identify customer
- identify suppliers
- design (development) process
  - make process mistake proof
  - reduce cycle time
    - everything has value
    - measure

- ensure continuous improvement
  - measure
  - analyze
  - control
  - improve process
    - Gantt chart/PERT chart
      - dependency
      - sequential
      - simultaneous

4.1.2 Reducing Cycle Times

This concept relates to our measure of life cycle efficiency. No matter what life cycle model you use, you should try to make it as efficient as possible. Some concepts that may help are related to cycle reduction. While this concept originated in quality movements on the hardware side, it has application on the software side, as well.

This is another quality issue directly related to Six Sigma. The concept of theoretical cycle time that was addressed at TI is used where the individual components of a product life cycle are studied and unnecessary, inefficient steps are removed from it or modified in the process. Its formal definition is: "Actual time required to produce one unit of work with a specified procedure through all steps of the process with no set up waste or delays of any kind" (Connie Marchewka, personal communication). Strategies for reducing cycle time at TI were based on the following activities:

- evaluate every step to shipping
- use critical path analysis (parallel)
- reuse
- minimize work in process ("just in time" manufacturing of software)

All of these activities are related to continuous process improvement, and some version of them is found at most companies who have won the Malcolm Baldrige National Award for Quality. Against the various process models proposed in the software industry, these concepts can be placed, and used to evaluate their efficiency relative to one another. In the next section, we address process efficiency in this context.

4.1.3 Continuous Process Improvement

Once a quality program is in place and goals are being met, there is a tendency for the goals to become an end in themselves. Whenever a team stretches to meet a goal, they let up afterward. It is just as important to create the idea of continuous improvement within the corporate culture. A spokesperson for Motorola stated, shortly after they won the Malcolm Baldrige award, "We have achieved Five Sigma, and we are rapidly approaching Six Sigma."

4.2 THE PRODUCT DELIVERY PROCESS

Two of the most important documents you will use will be explained next. First, we show the entire set of deliverables which can be used as part of the new paradigm. Then, the marketing requirements definition document (Figure 4-1) will be explained briefly. (In the Appendix all the "frontend" filters which relate to marketing orientation and to the product delivery process used with the new paradigm are presented and commented upon.) All the earlier filters feed into this document. Following this, we will present and explain the software specification document (Figure 4-2). Following this, we will look at coding standards and system-level standards—in a fairly general way, tying them back to the concepts of Chapter 2.

4.2.1 Deliverables Associated with a Product Delivery Process

The following list consists of a set of deliverables associated with various stages of the delivery system for which we have created filters to help us ascertain their quality. Filters exist at the following points in our product delivery process. Within some of these areas there may be several filters.

- Marketing analysis
- General product description
- Market positioning plan
- Preliminary sales plan
- Preliminary budget
- Requirements definition
- System specification
- Software architecture
- Project plan
- Product development*
- Software audit (module level)*
- Behavioral testing*
- User profile testing (work flow/task/products)*
- Documentation development*
- Final marketing plan*
- Marketing documents*
- Marketing demonstrations*
- Final sales plan*
- Sales kit*
- Sales subproducts*
- Sales demonstration versions*

- Training plan*
- Training tools*
- Delivery plan*
- Support plan*

We keep a log of all our filters and review them as necessary to keep them current. All documents are filtered by an ad hoc team to verify that the documents are high quality, accurate, and complete. Sometimes these filters are evaluated linearly via e-mail—sequentially passing from one team member to the next. But should any particular member of the ad hoc team feel the filter-based evaluation would be more effective as a full-team effort, he or she can call for a meeting. These actions by any member are always approved. If it turns out later the meeting should not have been held, the decision is evaluated later on. It should be noted that this should be very much a team effort and everyone should take it seriously and make an effort to ensure quality.

Note that in this model, the traditional feasibility study is replaced by the marketing orientation and marketing studies that are a part of the marketing analysis. Whether one should take a "risk" trying to build a product and get it to market (or within contract) is here based upon the concept of "leverage," as explained at several points in this book. If management feels that feasibility is an appropriate approach, it is easy to add to one of the filters or to create another deliverable with its accompanying filter. Our product delivery process is extremely versatile and allows for constant process improvement through its feedback mechanism.

4.2.2 A Description of the Marketing Requirements Definition

There are other ways this document can be defined, depending on which life cycle you use. We feel this one is appropriate because it covers everything from a marketing point of view. If your organization operates in a different context, you should change this document to make it more appropriate to your organization. Figure 4-1 shows this document.

The Introduction portion of this document creates a marketing context for the software product to be constructed. The marketing document/filter in I.A.1.c defines the preliminary leverage of the product. It will be refined as you progress through the various parts of the delivery system. Often management wants to produce a product without any understanding of its benefit to the company. Leverage provides a measure of this benefit.

The marketing window (I.A.2) helps place constraints on the time frame to build the product. Ideally, advanced planning should begin early enough so that if it should take around 18 months to build the product, the developers know about it—and have this document in their hands—about two years in advance.

---

*Denotes parallel activities based on or related to the project plan.

They can then work backwards to find an appropriate starting date. If, as is usually the case, management has not planned far enough ahead, then a realistic compromise must be reached in terms of what can be realistically built and still meet the marketing window. It does not pay to start programing without planning, figuring that the time saved by eliminating the planning will give more time for programming. This has never been true and it never will be true.

Another important consideration is the impact of this product on current products in your product line (I.A.3). Can people upgrade easily? Do you intend to make money from upgrades? Will there be a lot of training necessary to learn the new product—especially in terms of an upgrade? The latter part of A.4 is important for the "human factors" and "documentation" people, who must understand the user. They must create a paradigm that makes it easy for the user to simply start using the product using "intuition," rather than "training."

The need to base this document on a competitive analysis is extremely important. It can have a major impact on how the product is built—and how it will compete in the marketplace. Part 2 is very important from this point of view. Can the salespeople use the product to get in the door of companies where competitors already have their products installed? How does this help your company reach its five-year plan?

Section II provides knowledge of the hardware background and whether the system is to be built as a client/server-type application. It also indicates what types of devices are to be supported by the software product. This allows, fairly early on, developers to do "proof of concept" development against unknown—or poorly understood—environments.

Section III is an iteration through all the functions that are in the product. Note that this is the first view of the functional specification. It is given in terms of the marketability of each of the functions. As can be seen, this is not just a list of the functions; it is a fairly complete description and involves the user profiles as well as a description of their data inputs and outputs.

Section IV provides a preliminary view of the user interface. It is related to the user profiles of III.G.1 and also to the various interface standards (such as CUA^{TM}, Macintosh®, etc.) that one must interface with. Budgets and other considerations are also included in this document. Notice that this document can be viewed as a filter. It is merely an outline of what the filter could be. If some parts are considered unnecessary, you do not include them as "boiler plate"; they are only included if they are relevant.

Filter for a Marketing Requirements Definition Document

This is a preliminary view of what a marketing requirements definition document should contain. It is the final output of the Marketing/Sales part of a product delivery process. It is the definition of what the requirements are for the software specifications document.

I INTRODUCTION

A General context for the product

1. What is the justification for the product?
   (a) Why should it be created?
   (b) How does this help our customers?
   (c) What is the leverage for the product (expected costs against anticipated sales)?

2. What marketing window(s) must we reach?
   (a) What is the earliest date we should try for?
   (b) What is the latest date we can meet and still be within the window?
   (c) What is the anticipated risk/impact if we miss it?

3. What is the impact on current products?
   (a) Which products does this replace?
   (b) With which products must this product interface?
   (c) What alternatives for how this product interacts with current products are possible?
   (d) In what ways will this product impact the user profile(s)?
   (e) In what ways will this product impact the current products with which it interacts/interfaces?

4. To what level of user is this product directed?
   (a) How does this level of experience impact the interface?
   (b) With what interface standards will they be familiar (Macintosh, Windows, etc.)?
   (c) What impacts are expected on their work flows, paradigms of use, ability to master product's use without training, additional training, etc.?
   1- What patterns should we attempt to capture or reproduce?
   2- To what level should our user manuals and training manuals be pitched?

Figure 4-1 Filter for a marketing requirements definition document

3-　Will purchasers/users require additional training? How should it be provided?

B　How will this product be used?

1. Description of how it will be used.
2. Description of user problems it will solve.
3. Will it be retrofitted into existing automated products?
    (a)　Ours?
    (b)　Competitors (interoperability)?
    (c)　Ancillary products they will need to purchase to extend usability (interoperability)?
4. Must it be backward compatible with earlier products or databases?
5. Is this a part of a sequence of products described in the five-year plan?
    (a)　How and where does it fit in the five-year plan?
    (b)　How does the technology involved help us evolve toward future products?
    1-　What are the technologies involved?
    2-　What training is it anticipated we will need?
    3-　Where and how can it be obtained?

II　PLATFORMS AND DEVICE INTERFACES

A　Upon which platforms must this product be operable?

B　What type(s) of hardware configuration(s) will be required?

1. Should this run in a client/server environment?
2. What types of configurations should be supported?
3. Toward what types of parameters should this be directed (number of users, hardware requirements, network requirements, performance, etc.)?

C　With what types of devices should this product interface?

1. Competing devices
2. Vendors
3. Type of support available/needed (us, them, value-added resellers (VARs), third-party maintenance, etc.)
4. Specifications (documents, etc.) for these devices

Figure　4-1 Filter for a marketing requirements definition document (Continued)

III FUNCTIONALITY

List of functions. For each function, the following outline might be used.

A Name of function

B Description of function

C Problem solved by function (justification)

D Relative importance of function to marketability of the product (associated risk analysis)

E Data required

F Data produced

G Function is part of which:

1. User profiles

2. Tasks

3. Events

4. Screens (and menus)

H Constraints

IV PROTOTYPE SCREENS AND OTHER INTERFACES

A Interface standards

B Relation(s) to user profiles

C Examples (with protocols)

V PRELIMINARY FINANCIAL CONSIDERATIONS

A Budget

B Hardware requirements

C Manpower requirements

D Training requirements (programmers, etc.)
Needs analysis (from five-year marketing plan)

VI COMMENTS AND SIGN-OFF BY REVIEWERS

A Comments

B Signatures

Figure 4-1 Filter for a marketing requirements definition document (Continued)

VII ACTION(S) TO BE TAKEN

A   Action

B   Person assigned

C   Date results expected

D   Manager to sign off

VIII GENERAL INFORMATION

A   Author

B   Date

C   Revision number

Figure 4-1 Filter for a marketing requirements definition document (Continued)

4.3 COMPONENTS OF A SPECIFICATION

Although there are several references on the market that purport to describe what should go into a specification, most of them are oriented more to how different methodologies look in their software models than to what all the components of a good specification are. (See Davis, 1990, for an example.) Figure 4-2 presents an overview of what we believe a "good" specification should contain.

The need for stability in a specification can be addressed by making it as complete as possible. This requires either accurate identification of the ultimate users of the software and a large amount of communication with them, or if the users are internal to the company, then JAD (Joint Application Development) or some similar approach is employed, leading to a similar result (see Chapter 1). While this book will not address methods for identifying users (see Crandall, 1993), it will address methods for keeping the specification and product current with changing user needs and changing software environments.

In some environments, a process is begun using a requirements document. Usually this is created at the beginning of a project as the document to drive the systems analysis process. Regardless of whether this is a "one-pager," or is a relatively complete description of the requirements, it becomes the mandate for the project. Yet the document which has the most impact on the software development process is the product specification. This section will describe briefly the components which should go into a good product specification. It should be noted that there are many other approaches to the contents of a good specification and that this is only one example. Another description of this is given in the Front-end Filters section of the Appendix.

---

1. **Functional Specification**
- User Profiles
- External Interface Specification
- User Interfaces
- Usability (Pattern Matching, Paradigm Shift, Function Access)
- Interface Standards (Macintosh, X/Open™, Windows, Common User Access, etc.)
- Third-Party Software Interfaces (Interoperability)
- Hardware Interfaces
- Database Interfaces
2. **Information Model**
- Process-Oriented (Object-Oriented) Model
- Event List
- Entity Relationship Model
- Database Model
- Data Dictionary
3. **Constraint Document**
4. **Performance Criteria Document**
5. **Hardware Specification**
6. **Preliminary Budget**
7. **Preliminary Project Plan**
8. **Preliminary Manpower Allocation**
9. **Standards Document**
10. **Quality Plan**
11. **Master Test Plan**
12. **Documentation Plan**
13. **Product Release Plan**

Figure 4-2   The components of a product specification

4.3.1 Functional Specification

This part of the specification is most often the part which is provided to developers. The functional specification is usually a list, alphabetized or grouped by component or type, of the basic functions that make up the product. There are usually one or two pages of description, with some accompanying information on data formats and types, etc. This description may be somewhat formal in nature, using structured English, or it may be a rambling monologue. (If this is the case, deriving the functions from the monologue may require semantic analysis.

While semantic analysis is an important concept in software engineering, it is beyond the scope of this book to discuss it.) At times, a description of the interfaces to other modules or functions may be included. However they are created and represented, functional specifications are the fundamental part of a product specification.

When new technology is being implemented, it often pays to use prototypes—or to create your own prototype—to quickly create "working models" of parts of the system to assure that the technology can be implemented correctly and efficiently. There is a tendency to use all or part of the prototype as the actual product. This should always be avoided. There is a philosophy which states that to build a product correctly, you should build it once to find out how to do it and then rebuild it to take into account what was learned. This will almost always make a far, far better product. Unfortunately, rarely are there the time and resources to allow this. Using the prototype as the actual product is a misuse of this concept. Management sign-off, as a justification for using all or part of a prototype, is an effective way to limit and control the use and misuse of prototypes in software development.

User Profiles   User profiles are basically descriptions or representations of how one uses the software product. They are typically made up of tasks, which are made up of functions contained in the product. Rather than providing a user with a product containing 100 functions, a user is presented with a set of tasks which, when used appropriately, will allow the user to create the products the software was designed to do. When the set of products or activities the program makes available to the user are taken as a set, it constitutes the user profile. Usually it is connected to the implementation of an efficient, effective work flow. For example, "How does a pilot use the functionality—both old and new—of a Boeing 787 given he or she has flown a 727, 737, and/or 747?"

Graphical User Interfaces (GUIs) should be created in such a manner that there is an easily identifiable pattern available to the user for performing tasks and creating products. The user would be trained to use paradigm shifts to convert from his or her view of the problem or product to the one represented by the software. For each task or activity, additional functions appropriate to the tasks are also made available to the user. If a particular function is to be made available on several screens or menus, it is found in exactly the same place and performs in exactly the same way—in terms of the current context. This constitutes the most effective implementation of usability.

Defining the software system around user profiles and restricting the functional use to only these profiles—with variations based on additional related functions—makes the software easier to use and makes it less error-prone from the user's perspective. It is also easier to test, as, rather than having 100 functions available with little or no context (requiring 10^{157} possible tests), developers limit the use of the functions to only those tasks for which they are appropriate. Once this is done, you can finish testing as soon as all the user profiles have been tested (in the context of system testing).

External Interface Specification The external interface specification constitutes a complete description of how the software product interacts with the "outside world."

User Interfaces To be used effectively, user interfaces should be created to easily represent patterns the user is familiar with, as he or she goes about performing tasks and creating products. This is much like getting into your own automobile and unconsciously working within the familiar surroundings to perform the tasks of starting the car, turning on the lights, putting the car in gear, etc. Paradigm shift, on the other hand, is like getting into a rental car and seeing where all the familiar tools—provided to help one operate the automobile—are located and then proceeding to use them in the appropriate, familiar manner.

Usability As defined earlier, usability should be measured in terms of the accelerated learning concept (which everyone already uses) of

- pattern matching
- paradigm shift
- function access

Interface Standards Just as automobile makers attempt to build usability into automobiles by putting driving functions in the same place across the industry (with a few exceptions) and adding additional features/functions in logical places (stereo, automatic temperature controls, cruise control, etc.), so software designers should make use of similar standards:

- Macintosh
- Common User Access (CUA)
- X/Open
- Windows

Database Interfaces As many, if not most, products make use of database systems, provision should be made in the specification for database interfaces to be defined—in such a manner that many different models and products can be compatible, so long as the data structures required by the software are acquired accurately and efficiently.

Third-Party Software Interfaces (Interoperability) Very few software products exist or operate in a vacuum; they must operate and interact with other commercial products. Effective interfaces to these other products must be designed into the product being designed and built. (Apple's OPEN DOC project is an attempt to create a technology which makes interoperability extremely cost-effective and attractive to developers.)

Hardware Interfaces Many commercial products, in order to be marketable, must reside on several platforms. Further, they must make available the use of many different input/output/storage devices. Each of these must be specified and designed into the product specification and the software architecture.

Thus, it involves interfaces to the user—in the form of screens, interfaces to the database, interfaces to APIs (Application Program Interfaces)—so users/ developers can create their software packages and interface them to the operating system and other software—interfaces to support hardware devices, and interfaces to other software systems. One of the major parts of this specification to be considered is related to two things:

- the protocols by which one passes from one screen to another

- the interface standard or standards which are in use, such as Windows, OPEN LOOK®, etc.

Screen prototypes—either created within the software organization or purchased from the outside—should be used to create views of these interfaces. Whether all, or only a part, of the external interface is modeled at this time should be discussed by the development team—with input from users and upper-level management. 4GLs often prove useful in this environment, when they are used correctly.

If interfaces to other software are not considered, examined, and specified in this part of the specification, it is possible that incompatibilities will hamper the product's use in the commercial world and may later require patches and reengineered parts of the system to be created and implemented.

4.3.2 Information Model

An information model is made up of several parts. Part of this is product-oriented in the traditional software development methodology sense, but as software evolves into multicomponent, multiprocessing-oriented systems, data modeling and state modeling become more and more important. Although it will not be covered here, software models based on client/server orientation also become important to the information model. But the client/server relationship is easy to design—when dependency analysis is used. This is because the independence of the functions allows them to be moved between the client and the server and back until the proper performance, usability, and reliability have been achieved.

Process-Oriented/Data-Oriented/Object-Oriented   Software   Model
Although it is not always necessary, sometimes it is useful to create an information model to allow for traceability between the software specification and the software architecture. There are other methods, however. The use of data flow diagrams—through executive modules—will always provide traceability. Just as there are many life cycle models, there are many software development models. They all have points in their favor, depending on your company goals. From our point of view, it does not especially matter what information model you use; what is important is the software architecture that comes as its byproduct. A useful book relating to these concepts is *Behavioral Models: Specifying Users' Expectations* by Kowal (1994).

Event Lists Event lists are used to give an operational view of the functionality. From these, it is easy to tie the functions to appropriate GUI interfaces and test them. Further, each event is accompanied by a corresponding set of triggers. While there may be many triggers for one event, the system must return only one response. The basic approach is:

1. An event is defined, usually some function—or possibly even a subsystem.
2. A trigger is defined, usually some activity performed by a user, such as pushing a button on a screen or entering a piece of data and using it as a key.
3. A response is defined, usually the execution of a function or subsystem.

A software system must always provide the same response each time a trigger is employed regardless of where it is accessed in the entire software system. This is part of the strategy to minimize the number of "states" the system can take on. It ties directly to the architectural goals relating to eliminating dependencies and minimizing the number of states. An alternative view is the use of assertions. Assertions provide an active method of viewing the specifications. From our point of view, this leads more to behavior testing than to functional testing.

Entity Relationship Model   As a part of the data modeling, it is usually important to define the business rules that pertain to the software environment you are building. This modeling should be related to enterprise analysis—or strategic data modeling (at IBM, this has been called enterprisewide information modeling). Books relating to software models at this level are in the area of information engineering (see, for example, Martin, 1989, 1990a, 1990b). In extremely large projects, this tends to be where the software breaks down. One of the major approaches to data modeling is the entity/relationship modeling approach (see Yourdon, 1989, although there are other excellent books, such as Chen, 1977, and Flavin, 1981).

Database Model   Most complex systems today need to have a database model. This needs to be built around database theory and modeling, and unless the software is for commercial, off-the-shelf use, it should be tied to the enterprise modeling described above. A brief overview of these approaches—with the names of their originators—is contained in Table 4-1. Some of these models are described in *Encyclopedia of Software Engineering* (Marciniak, 1994).

In extremely large database systems an error in the database model may cause incompatibilities that you will need to live with for years. This is because sometimes the database is so large that if it is wrong, you cannot off-load it, reconfigure it, and reload it between the times it needs to be accessed—especially for large batch runs. New, modern database technologies, coupled with extremely fast processors, make it much more likely you can overcome these issues for most software systems, including fairly large ones.

Data Dictionary   This part of the specification is required as a part of structured analysis and design. Whether you use object-oriented or some other methodology, you still need some type of definition for your data. This—or something similar—is important to make sure that the data are defined appropriately

Table 4-1 Architecture of Software Development Methodology

Modeling Approach Assumes an Underlying Structure	Modeling Approach Assumes No Underlying Structure
Enterprise Level	
Nonrecursive Business Modeling Tools	**Since these approaches assume no underlying structure, they cannot be recursive.**
BIAT (Henderson et al.)	BSP (Zachman et al.)
BICS (Kerner et al.)	ISS (Michele Veys et al.)
Business Entities (Tabory)	ASYST (Atkinson)
BMT (Pentleton)	DSSD (Orr)
	Structured Analysis (DeMarco)
	SADT (Softech)
	Business Structure (Martin)
	RAD Methodology (Appleton)
	Information Engineering (Finklestein)
	Entity/Attribute/Relationship Modeling (Chen)
	RDA (Mills and Wilson)
Recursive Business Modeling Tools	
LCS (Warnier's Management Units)	
DSSD (Orr's Generic Model)	
ASYST (LeMoigne's General Systems Model)	
Application or Information System Level Tools and Methodologies	
Finite State Machine Models	**Data Structure Decomposition**
Box Method (Mills et al.)	DSSD (Orr)
	LCS (Warnier)
	JSD (Jackson)
	Arthur Anderson Method 1
	Data Flow Decomposition
	Yourdon/Constantine
	DeMarco
	McMenamin/Palmer
	Gane/Sarson
	Page-Jones
	Myers
	Stevens
	Weinberg
	The Vienna Method
	The Swedish Method

Table 4-1 Architecture of Software Development Methodology (Continued)

Modeling Approach Assumes an Underlying Structure	Modeling Approach Assumes No Underlying Structure
	Object-Based Analysis/ Decomposition
	Booch
	Rumbaugh
	Shlaer/Mellor
	Meyer
	Jacobson
	Fusion
	Coad/Yourdon
	Real Time-Oriented
	Ward/Mellor
	Hatley/Pirbhai
	Ward/Jensen
	Structure Analysis
	SADT (Softech)
	SAMM (Boeing)
	MASCOT 3 (Ken Jackson)
	DART (General Dynamics)
	SARA (Hughes Aircraft Company)
	Mathematical Proof-Oriented
	Clean Room
	High-Level Language-Based
	HOS (Higher-Order Software)
	PSL/PSA (Problem Statement Language/Problem Statement Analyzer)

and consistently throughout their use in the product. Often the same data are called by different names, causing problems within the software; at other times, a data element is defined with different characteristics at different points within the program. These and other considerations leading to potential errors must be taken into account in the specification and during the programming effort.

Data dictionaries are part of the various CASE tools currently on the market, but whether these tools are used or not, the data dictionary should be used— in one form or other—as a part of the product specification to assure data usage of high integrity and quality. Several different notations exist (see, for example, DeMarco, 1979, or Gane and Sarson, 1979).

4.3.3 Constraint Document

Sometimes constraints are well known and well established in advance; at other times, they are ill-defined, and they are not well understood until the developers have actually attempted to implement the software—or portions of the software—they have created. Wherever possible, outside knowledge should be used to help in establishing these issues in advance.

4.3.4 Performance Criteria Document

Where enough information is known, performance criteria for all or various parts of the software should be specified in advance. When the developers and test engineers have enough of the product available to perform subsystem/system testing on that part of the software, then tests designed to highlight and measure performance should be instigated. For some parts of the system, this can be done fairly early in the development cycle; for other parts, it may be necessary to await the final acceptance test. (Sometimes special drivers and harnesses must be created to manage this performance testing appropriately; other times, probes inserted in the code in order to instrument it can actually interfere with the measurement of the product's performance.)

4.3.5 Hardware Specification

When the software is to reside on new hardware, or when it must run on several platforms, then the hardware specification leads to a substantial effort to make it portable. The comment regarding structured design, given above, indicates that the developers should refine the software architecture to make it easily adaptable to the different platforms, i.e., to make it run relatively independent of its hardware environment. In addition, the test engineers must work to create harnesses and drivers which make it possible to efficiently test the product across all the specified platforms.

A major requirement at this point is to look at the preliminary schedule to see that appropriate hardware is ordered and/or scheduled to be available when development needs it (for unit and integration testing, should it prove necessary) and when testing needs it (for subsystem and system testing, especially for behavioral and user profile testing). Usually, more hardware is required for system testing by the test organization than for unit testing by the development organization—especially if extensive code auditing is used.

4.3.6 Preliminary Budget/Preliminary Schedule/ Preliminary Manpower Allocation

Part of a high quality specification should involve a preliminary budget. The word preliminary is used because at this point it may not be easy to establish the actual budget to a great degree of accuracy. Yet you should have a general feel for how much it will cost—based on other, similar, projects. This document, along with the preliminary schedule and the preliminary manpower allocation, should allow one to get a fairly accurate view of what the costs will be. Information from the hardware specification is also important input at this stage.

Ideally, you should obtain an estimate of the amount of sales, income/profit to be obtained by this product from marketing. This should be tied to windows of opportunity, as closely as possible, to allow the schedule to be fixed in terms of first customer ship. Ordinarily, this is fixed too late, and product development is tied to too short a development cycle to allow for a quality product to be built. The shortcuts taken to meet the marketing deadlines have, therefore, a detrimental effect on the product quality—in terms of all the quality measures which should be met (Crandall, 1993). Often missed deadlines cause bad reports and resentment or confusion on the part of customers, who have been planning on the announced delivery date. Marketing must do a better job of identifying marketing windows of opportunity far enough into the future to allow quality products to be built.

If it is known that a project will begin 3 to 6 months into the future and that 20 programmers (having a certain skill mix) will be required to build the product and that it will take 18 months to build, then an appropriate manpower allocation can be made. Manpower allocation involves several activities—some of which cannot be performed accurately until after the software architecture has been defined and finalized. Initially, the project leaders may know that of the 20 programmers needed, 10 will be available on the starting date, 5 "experts" will need to be hired, and 5 developers can be shifted 4 months into development from projects they will be finishing at that point in time. The 5 "new-hires" are looked upon as an investment needed to achieve the sales income specified by marketing; the same is true of the hardware. (Often companies make the most current hardware available to their customers, providing only hardware several versions old to the developers and test engineers. This is a short-sighted approach to software development.)

It should be noted that these parts of the product specification are preliminary. They cannot be firmed up until after the structured design of the software architecture, in the form of a structure chart (or something similar), has been created. At that point, these documents should be reworked, and the more finalized form included in the updated product specification. All three of these components must be monitored during the life of the project, to update them to reflect new information, changes to the software, modifications to the specification, personnel leaving/being hired/being transferred to other projects, and so forth.

No product or product specification will remain constant during a development cycle—no matter how short. Changes will be proposed by customers based on usage of current products; changes will be mandated by new technology which was not anticipated when the specification was written; changes will be proposed by developers, test engineers, and marketers based on new ideas generated by the actual building and/or testing of the product. Some of these changes are mandatory; some are extremely useful, and others are merely "nice."

In order to manage these changes, a Configuration Control Board (or similar body) must be put in place to review the changes as they are proposed. Everyone influenced by these changes—developers, test engineers, documentation personnel, and marketers—submits an impact assessment statement, which indicates what will happen to the budget, schedule, and manpower allocation, if the proposed change is made. The Control Board then makes a decision, and the appropriate changes are made to everything that is affected. (For very simple or minor changes, if the involved individuals reach consensus and there is no appreciable change to these three parts of the product specification, then the changes are made without appeal to the Configuration Control Board, but appropriate changes are made—with management sign-off—to each affected part of the specification and the software architecture.) We include in the Appendix a copy of one of our recent Configuration Control Board forms from Digital Technology International. The management signatures at the end are individuals from the CEO and the President through the Senior Programmer and the Product Manager. The author, as Vice-President of Software Development, is the last manager to sign in order to manage any conflicts or issues that need to go before the entire Configuration Control Board.

As we indicated earlier, if a change has an impact on the project schedule, there are only three things that can be changed. Of the three, the most care must be taken in adding new developers to the project. Often the time they take coming up to speed offsets the gain expected from changing arbitrarily person/months, with emphasis only placed on the numbers/calculations. Further, care needs to be taken when functionality is dropped, if that functionality is critical to outside software developers whose software depends on certain functionality being present.

4.3.7 Standards Document

Most software houses must be concerned with many standards to which their products must conform or against which they must interface. This standards document becomes a fundamental part of the product specification of most products. At most, it provides a complete specification of the standards to which this product must conform; at least, it provides a reference to these specifications in already existing documents.

These standards may relate to how the code is to be written (see Crandall, 1993), what the user interfaces are to be, and other quality standards which impact the product. Performance standards may also be included. Standards for internal and external documentation might also be included. Still other standards might relate to the screen interfaces, hardware interfaces, APIs, etc.

Standards requiring training of personnel in languages, new development technologies, project planning, and so forth, are also specified. This document relates closely to the quality plan described next. The standards document describes the what; the quality plan describes the how.

4.3.8 Quality Plan

The quality plan is basically a description of how quality will be built into both the product and the process. It relates to how training in quality standards, metrics, and technology will be provided (if any courses need to be developed and/or modified, or if they are already in the curriculum) and how it will be enforced (i.e., through management sign-off). It relates to how the schedule will be maintained (i.e., through biweekly deliverables schedules—with demonstrations of the parts of the product contained in the deliverables), what levels of test coverage (for both unit and integration and for subsystem and system tests) will be required, and how risk analysis will be managed throughout the software development life cycle—especially as it applies to the test process (see Crandall, 1993). (Most of the actual risk analysis standards and other considerations will be general; they do not become specific until the product is actually under development. This latter part is also related to the master test plan, to be covered next.)

4.3.9 Master Test Plan

This describes the strategy for how the product will be tested. It involves nine areas:

1. Who will perform unit and integration testing or the code audits?
2. Who will perform subsystem and system testing?
3. What will constitute the final acceptance test?
4. What test strategies will be used at each phase?
5. What automated tools are available?
6. What automated tools will need to be built or purchased?
7. What will the criteria be for risk analysis?
8. What entry/exit criteria will be used for all phases of the project?
9. Who has sign-off authority for the various components of the project?

These questions are covered in more detail in Chapter 6. Note that when asking who will perform unit and integration testing or the code audits, you should decide which approach—or combination of approaches—to use for testing the product. If you are going to use dependency analysis with the accompanying code audits to establish code correctness, you should estimate how much time it will take to achieve the desired level of quality using this approach versus traditional testing. In either case, an accurate estimate of time and resources must be made. In addition, asking who will perform subsystem and system testing especially applies to the behavioral testing strategy at the system level. Spending enough time and resources on the behavior of the system is highly cost-effective—more so than spending time and expending resources on functional testing, when that can be done more effectively—and with better results—using dependency analysis and pattern matching.

As with several of the other components of the product specification, certain parts of this specification will need to be modified/updated/enhanced as product development goes forward. A major part of this enhancement takes place after the software architecture is in place. Moving from the product specification to the creation of the software architecture is a major step in the software development life cycle. Indeed, the formal starting date for the project is normally tied to the formal acceptance of the software architecture, the project plan, and the test plan. The development of the product specification and the software architecture are preliminary steps—a "research project"—before the actual individuals/equipment/resources are actually assigned to the software project itself.

4.3.10 Documentation Plan

This part of the specification is related to the development and specification of the documentation. It involves whether it will be delivered on CD-ROM, diskettes, or hard copy. It estimates the total number of pages, potential number of illustrations (based on the external interface), potential number of examples, what types and number of manuals will be provided, the level at which each part will be written, and how these will be related to help files, etc. Also addressed will be the need for national language design in both the product (internal messages in the code), external (screens), external (help files) and in the manuals themselves. (Most of Digital Technology International's products are marketed throughout Europe, the Middle East, and Asia, so national language considerations are very important to us. If things are managed correctly, and far enough in advance, both the internal and external documentation can be adequately planned for. Internal documentation for the code is important if, as DTI has, your company has resellers and licensees who have access to your code and the right to modify it for their markets.)

The estimated number of documentation personnel and approximate length of time the documentation will take should also be specified. A preliminary schedule for the documentation should also be included. The parts of this document which impact the structure and makeup of the software product should also be reflected in the appropriate documents.

4.3.11 Product Release Plan

This is the preliminary plan, on the part of the release organization, as to how the product will be released. This can also be updated as the project proceeds. Work on earlier projects may indicate packaging considerations, i.e., the number of diskettes (or CD-ROM), etc., that will be needed (so they can be ordered/manufactured in plenty of time, as well as their labels and packaging materials). This will need to be revised and refined the closer the project gets to FCS (First Customer Ship).

4.3.12 A Test Plan for System Testing

When performing system testing, it is just as necessary to prepare a test plan as it is when performing code audits and any accompanying "unit and integration testing" deemed necessary. In code audits and/or unit and integration testing, the bug fixes and regression testing are performed by the programmers involved—with sign-off for the test plan and regression test completion performed by someone from the test organization. This person is also responsible to fix the filters that may have been broken, causing the errors to occur at a point later than they should have been caught (see Chapter 6 for more detail).

Most system testing is related to the behavior of the system rather than its functionality. This means that instead of testing the functionality at the system level, you test the behavior of the functionality.

At Digital Technology International, we test against various user profiles. Before doing so, we actually run automated test scripts against our entire set of functions to assure that they all run correctly. While this is done at the system level, we consider it to be functional testing, and it is done in addition to our code audits and "little bang" integration strategies. Following this, one of our release criteria is that each release has been run against at least three user profiles: once by development and twice by the release organization. In each case, an entire product must be constructed. In much of our software, this involves putting out an entire newspaper. Under some conditions, we run a product at one or more customer sites before formally releasing it.

4.4 RELEASE MANAGEMENT

Another part of putting together and delivering a complete product is related to release management. As you recall, this was mentioned as a fundamental part of the specification presented earlier. But often, how a product is released is ignored—or worse, marketing simply announces the product to satisfy either a whim or the desire to be "first," bringing disaster to all concerned. We will outline the components of a release process and then comment on some of the caveats which we feel exist in releasing a product.

Until the project plan has been put in place, product development has not yet started. After the marketing documents have initiated the process, sales, support, and others can validate various user profiles, screens, and functions against particular users and/or potential users. This information is a fundamental part of creating the specification. But these individuals sign nondisclosure agreements, as these potential products are part of your corporate strategy and mission.

The project plan is the first indication of how long it will reasonably take to get a particular product to market. A product should never be announced until it is clear that the project plan is realistic and on schedule. The marketing strategy can be used to help development decide in what order the product should be built. Often, a preliminary version can be implemented to create credibility in the marketplace; intermediate products can also be created and sold—if they are built using the paradigm we have presented here—using executive modules to create and maintain independence. Documentation, training materials, courses for support and installation people, and courses for salespeople can also be created and implemented at an early point.

Most products, especially those which require custom installations, must have filters during the release process. This is just as important as having filters at the beginning of the product delivery process. Often this is a major source of customer feedback. Further, for complex products, checklists relating to hardware setup, software setup, database setup, network configuration verification, and whatever else is appropriate to your environment are important feedback mechanisms. As is typical of the product development process, these checklists are deliverables and must be filtered for quality, completeness, and accuracy, just like any other deliverable in the process. Failure to install a system correctly is as much an "error" as a bug in the software.

If a product is to be marketed "off the shelf," then a sales forecast needs to be made well in advance. This must be based on the rate at which it will be sold and how it will be distributed and through what distribution channels. Once this is determined, you need to figure out how large the program—and its documentation—will be. Will the program be issued on CD-ROMs or diskettes? Or both? Which versions of OS and hardware will be supported? Will the documentation be hard copy, soft copy, or both? Will the software contain on-line help files? Will these be context-based?

Once these decisions have been made, you must order the materials far enough in advance for them not only to be available, but also to allow time for your product(s) to be copied to the media. Once copies have been made, how do you intend to distribute them? Is it realistic? Can you cover the channels adequately? Off-the-shelf software products usually contain information regarding marketing feedback issues, i.e., questionnaires, etc. Feedback should actually start early in the process to guarantee quality is not lost at any point. Filters should be established for this purpose and should be updated, as necessary, to assure that the deliverables at each point of the release process are maintained at a high level of quality, completeness, and accuracy. Some method of identifying the purchasers of your product should be created, either through free software or some other approach. Questionnaires and telephone surveys, measured against filters, should be part of the release process.

The product delivery process, must include "hand-off" processes. Development must have performed "adequate" behavioral testing (functional testing should have been handled in the other paradigm). The support/release organization should run additional user profiles to make certain that the behavior of the system is "robust," and that there are no fundamental weaknesses in the product. This should include making sure that response times and other performance issues are resolved well in advance of first customer shipment.

4.5 SOFTWARE QUALITY STANDARDS IN THE PRODUCT DELIVERY PROCESS

When Humphrey (1989) and others define software quality, they tend to talk about it in terms of error rates. In the first part of this chapter, we discuss quality goals based on Six Sigma. The measurement, 3.4 errors per million lines of code, deals with the number of errors allowed to get through to the customer. This number is based on six standard deviations away from the mean in a normal distribution, but the above goal is all that need concern us.

There are some other problems, however.

- Are errors that cause a misspelling on a screen or report as important as an error that causes corruption in a database record? Where do you draw the line between their severity in terms of reporting or not reporting? How are errors in the documentation within the code used in calculating error rates?

- Does this deal with only errors that are reported back from the field (APARs, using IBM's term), or should we include those from inspections or functional testing? What about true behavioral testing? What about errors based on the debugging a programmer does with his/her compiler before first public release to the testing organization by the development team?

Do these errors we have described have equal importance? It depends.

1. Errors that get to the customer should always be counted higher than those caught before they leave the software house.

2. Errors that are found late in the life cycle, cause a lot of rework, and negatively impact the schedule should be counted higher than other types of errors.

But just as with using lines of code as a metric, you must find away of being consistent across all your products. In our definition, we have used the term to apply to bugs that reach the customer, but we have made no attempt to separate high-severity from low-severity bugs.

4.5.1 What Is Software Quality?

Just as it is naive and damaging for educators to attempt to use a letter grade to classify students as to their quality, the same is true in software quality assessment. Educators try to justify this grading practice by saying, "We know it is not the best, but what can we do?" Then—worse—they start talking about "grade inflation," which is a way of saying: "We cannot turn out too many quality products." Sadly, this is what we try to do in our typical software development paradigm. We try to increase the grades (contrary to education) by reducing the errors, but because we are measuring the wrong things, we do not usually increase quality. There are many things you can do, but whatever you do, you should be consistent. (For more discussion of measurement, see Chapter 8.) When Humphrey (1989) discusses selecting quality measures, he observes that when "no quantitative measures are available such things as functionality, performance, and human factors, other steps must be taken to ensure that these important topics are given adequate attention." This is very much our position, but we would go further.

At a recent Software Testing Conference, 70 or more speakers discussed quality code, but all their testing proposals related to functional testing. The quote above by Humphrey shows that others are thinking further ahead. Yet Humphrey also presents figures (e.g., Figure 16-1, p. 347) to show how to compare and measure effectively by normalizing defects per thousand lines of code and use it for tracking "quality" across three product releases.

To us, quality is not related at all to the number of bugs—especially those that are allowed to reach the customer. Rather these numbers are only an indication that you did not have a strategy for designing out your bugs so you would not need to test for them. That is what Deming was saying in our quote in the Preface. To us, defects or bugs of a functional type, which reach the customer, are process failures! They should have nothing to do with quality. When you base statistical charts and graphs—or worse—statistical inferences on error, defect, failure, or bug rates, you are attempting to define and fix the wrong problem. They have nothing to do with quality; only with process failure.

As an interesting sidelight, one of the authors was arguing, at a conference, against trying to use statistical inference in software activities. One of the individuals involved made the comment: "At the xyz company, they have been able to predict error rates to within 1%." When the author asked how you could achieve such accuracy in large, unrelated projects, the speaker conceded that perhaps it was related to highly similar, follow-on code and functions. Our perception of this is: "If you can predict errors from one module to another so accurately, why are you testing for them? Someone obviously has a highly repeatable process for designing errors into code! Why not *solve* the problem instead of attempting to *predict it*?" (Statistical "predictability" is based on the "persistence" of the traits you are attempting to predict—in this case, error rates.) We will discuss misuse of statistics in more detail in Chapter 8.

You will see this same concept in Chapter 11 relating to total quality management (TQM). Ideally, designing out errors is more effective than designing them in, yet we allow software designers and engineers to design them into the software and its architecture rather than out. Practically every testing strategy in Beizer's (1991, 1995) and Kaner et al.'s (1993) books relates to bugs that can be designed out through careful, filtered design. This is true for all the other testing books, as well. They are a quality approach that is in violation of Deming's approach and TQM. This is also true for inspections and walk-throughs, which we discuss in Chapter 7. Not only can the spirit of Deming's goals be met through the effective use of filters in the new paradigm, based on the product delivery process, they also provide an effective method for continuous process improvement where the measurements are fairly precise and dynamic.

4.5.2 An Alternative Approach to Quality Measurement

Suppose you use a measurement for quality based on availability (see Humphrey, 1989, p. 343). This measure is related to mean time to failure and to mean time to repair. A high value of availability is potentially an excellent measure of code quality, especially for interactive systems, as it relates to the access time an airline or other customer will have, with their system up and running.

"Availability" under the Old Paradigm   But what is availability really related to and how can we "design out" the inverse of this: lack of availability?

One measure (see Section 1.4.5) that can help is based, depending how you want to define it, on

- cycle efficiency, i.e., how rapidly we can get an entire product through the software development life cycle (in the old paradigm) and out to the customer. You should note that if you simply ship a fix without going through a quality-based release mechanism, you will "shoot yourself in the foot" and possibly destroy your credibility with the customer.

- average debugging and rework rate, i.e., do your module and system architecture make it possible for quick fixes without the need to do extensive regression testing.

As a quality measure, this should be aggregated across the entire product's life.

"Availability" under the New Paradigm (The Product Delivery Process) In our new paradigm, we take a serious look at the whole concept of "mean time to failure." The word *mean* implies that it is an average of some kind. Is it across several products or several iterations of the same product? If, more realistically, it is across iterations of the same product, what makes each iteration different from the others? If we are dealing with a mechanical device, we are dealing with the fact that for each iteration, it either experiences wear and tear or moves slightly out of alignment. For mean time to failure to have any meaning in software development, it must be related to the basic, allowable "operational profiles" (see Musa, Iannino, and Okumoto, 1987) or, as we have defined them, user profiles. Whichever definition you employ, these user profiles are

- sets of user profiles that are "countably infinite," i.e., they can be identified and numbered 1, 2, 3, 4, 5, and so on forever. You should note that this is an entirely possible outcome, depending on how you have designed your software system.

- sets of user profiles that are "large, but finite," i.e., they can be identified and enumerated completely, but it will be a big job.

- sets of user profiles that are "small and finite," i.e., the input domain is easy to define and test.

Musa et al. suggest defining these profiles through use of equivalence partitioning, which might lead to classes based on marketing studies of the uses of a system.

With the latter two characteristics, it is easy to make use of mean time to failure. The other concept we need to look at, as in the old paradigm we discussed first, is how long does it take to fix, test, and release the code in which the bug has been fixed? With code design being so highly restricted as to pattern and independence, with an accompanying design for independence at the subsystem/system level, the time the software is unavailable, i.e., the system is down and the error has not been fixed, tested, and released back to the customer, is minimized for each failure.

Stochastic Software versus Deterministic Software   But there is an even more important concept relating to mean time to failure and similar concepts. If you run a single-user profile against a software system several times, you should always get the same, predictable results. This is because all software systems should be defined, architected, and built so they are deterministic, i.e., every input should produce the same output. This is the basis for the industry definition of a test case. This should be true whether you are in the new paradigm or the old paradigm. If you cannot achieve this—even for one user profile—your code is too unstable to use, and you might just as well start over.

What happens when a complete set of user profiles are run? In either paradigm, you should be able to repair it to the point it has all the errors related to that set eliminated from the software. At that point, mean time to failure should be *infinite*. This is much easier and realistic to achieve in the product delivery process than in the old life cycle process. A consequence is that your process has produced zero defect software (see Schulmeyer, 1990).

When you face a countably infinite number of user profiles—or finite number of profiles you have not counted (or cannot)—you find yourself needing to deal with your software system stochastically, rather than deterministically. In this context, mean time to failure has great meaning. To use it effectively, you need to determine if there is an underlying frequency distribution your customers' environments impose on the profile. But to do so, you must have identified completely and correctly the profile(s) as they occur.

Another way to encounter stochastic processes in software is when you have two independent systems competing for the same resource. One has (say) 90 states and for certain ones of them, needs to use the printer; the other has 2,000 states and uses the printer 99.9 percent of the time. Since the two are independent, either could be in any state when the two collide. Depending on the number of usage configurations of the first system, you could possibly end up with 90^{2000}, possible states with transitions you need to stop, back out of, and restart. (Of course, this is "worst case.") The problem comes from the fact that usually the two systems are made to "know" each other, or at least the "controlling" system "knows" the states of the other. The excessive number of states and the randomness with which they occur leads to software which performs in a stochastic manner. Again, if you could determine empirically the frequency distribution for either the states or for the user profiles generating these states, you could calculate mean time to failure.

A better solution is to insert an executive module above the two subsystems in the architecture and allow it to know the states of both, but not make that knowledge available to the two independent subsystems. The executive module is the only one in the entire software system which knows the relative states of the two. But in addition, it needs to know and manage 2,090 states. But that is a far cry from 90^{2000}. With good design, this could be reduced further, but usually at a performance cost.

Failure Modes   At the beginning of Chapter 5 (Section 5.1.6), we will provide you with another concept of testing which usually does not find its way into the typical testing book. That is the concept of "failure modes." Even if your user profiles work for typical environments, they will "break" if users attempt to do things they should not do. They may contaminate a database, lose a major document, overwrite an unrecreatable document, or worse, contaminate their neighbor's computer software. Still even worse than this is the possibility of bringing the entire company, with all its international locations to its knees, due to how widely spread the failure is.

Arthur, in his TQM book (1993), cites several software disasters, from the real world, to sell you on the need for software quality, or total quality management. Another, less costly example is one in which one of the authors participated several years ago at IBM/Toronto. A new IBMer decided he wanted to send an electronic Christmas card to his friends at IBM. When he sent it, he mistakenly included their aliases. As the card was received by each friend, it was immediately forwarded to everyone on the friend's alias, and those people's aliases,..., until everyone at IBM received the card, not once, but every time they were on someone else's alias. The reason for mentioning this is not to isolate a poor, naive, new IBMer; it is to point out that that particular profile could just as well have happened under natural operating conditions by someone hitting one key wrong or having the wrong setting on his or her computer. As you build mission-critical software using special marketing/requirements analysis/design teams, you must take into account all the possible failure modes in the user profiles and in all the states the software system can take on.

There is some argument as to whether a massive software failure is a *virus* or a *failure mode*. The IBM example was widely known as a virus. But to us, the issue is: If someone deliberately sabotages a software system through the special creation of a user profile which causes a failure mode, it is related to a virus; if it is inadvertent or accidental, it is simply a *failure mode*. A new programmer at Novell, experimenting with some code, succeeded in bringing down Novell's entire worldwide network. He found a "previously undetected failure mode"; he did *not* create a *virus*.

We feel that this is an extremely important measure of quality. To us, software quality should be defined in terms of behavior, not functional error. As we have stated elsewhere, it does not help to give a user 100 functions as he or she can use them in 100! (factorial) or10^{156} ways. No one, with any amount of training, can understand how to use that many combinations of functions. That is why we suggest you constrain the interface to a number of user profiles that will protect the user (or customer) from failure modes while providing for easy use through pattern matching against familiar patterns and common-sense access to needed functions. To us, this is the basis of usability. In our new paradigm, it is very easy to achieve, but difficult to measure at more than an ordinal scale (see Chapter 8).

The Elimination of Functional Testing As we explained in Chapter 2, the product delivery process is a true Deming TQM process that can be installed in any organization relatively easily and efficiently. Using filters, rather than inspections and test cases, you can show the system is correct from the very start.

When the process "breaks," as it often will when you are first implementing it and your personnel are not "mature" in its use, you immediately fix the filters that were broken. In this case, most of these "software quality metrics" have little or no meaning, mainly because their use comes much too late in the software development process. If you define true "errors" as only those that have reached the customer, in the product delivery process you are dealing with far more than whether a programming or design error has "slipped through." You are dealing with whether the marketing and sales filters are broken, whether the marketing requirements, software specifications, software architecture, and project plan filters, and software audits are broken, and whether the software hand-off to support filters, final in-house customer profile testing, user profile testing at specific customer sites, support training on the profiles, trainer certification for performing customer training, and installation training and performance checklists and audits have all been performed and verified. In the new paradigm, for this to happen, usually over 18–25 filters must have broken simultaneously.

From Deming's perspective, in the new paradigm we are attempting to design quality into each of the deliverables in the product delivery process and then use filters to guarantee the correctness (accuracy), completeness, and quality of the deliverable defined by or relating to the filter. Thus, at whatever point in the product delivery process an error has been encountered, the filters and audits help us instantly fix and improve the process and the product it creates. This is our concept of quality.

4.5.3 What We Mean by Software Quality

As you will see, our view of software quality runs far counter to the software industry's view. But we believe that Deming would be pleased with our approach. First, we believe that all successful testing is behavioral testing and should be marketing-driven, i.e., the product should do what the users/potential customers want in a way that is cost-effective for them (leverage), easy for them to use, and have little or minimal risk to them as they produce their products.

We will approach quality in terms of an automobile/customer relationship. When a potential customer seeks to buy a car, it is in terms of "comfort level." This comfort level may have little to do with actuality.

A friend of one of the authors was leaving on his honeymoon with his new bride. As they were ready to pull away in their car, the author said, "Boy, wait until you see what's going to happen." While this was foolishly intended to be a message of support, both the bride and groom figured that we had done something to their car. As they drove the back roads of Kansas, they worried each time they left a town if the car would make it to the next town. They also worried if they would be stranded because the small town might not have a mechanic. Periodically, they would stop and look at everything they understood about the car (which was not very much), find nothing wrong, and nervously drive on. There was nothing wrong, but that did not matter; their perception that something might be wrong made them miserable.

So how does this relate to software? A negative review of a package in a computer journal or newspaper or "word of mouth" in a company may lead to a large number of potential users either not purchasing or not using a software package. It does not matter whether the comments are true or false.

If, in the history of brides and grooms, nobody had ever done anything to them on their wedding nights, the comment would have meant nothing. But there was a broad body of experience behind their interpretation of that comment. Second, experience had taught them that most automobile breakdowns will occur at the most inconvenient spot.

In software, consumer experience is that it is not bug free. Indeed, many novices will not buy the first release of a product because they feel it will be "too buggy." Yet they do not feel that way when they buy a small appliance or a car. In the software environment, students feel that their word processor will go down the night before an English paper is due and they are composing it on the computer, and they will be late through no fault of their own.

What about the impact of software quality initiatives on potential customers? What you find is that mean time to failure is defined to be: "The wheels on your Mercedes-Benz will probably not fall off for at least 10,000 miles." If you are driving your Mercedes 180 kph on the autobahn and you notice on the odometer that it show 9,999.9 miles, you probably will feel a bit uneasy—in spite of the fact that you paid a lot of money for the car, and it "drives like a dream."

"Drives like a dream" and "looks like a dream" (for the money) are usually the reasons we purchase a car. If we read magazines like *Consumers Reports*, we may find that the magazines rates many components of "quality."

- How does it corner?
- How does it ride on bumpy roads?
- What is its turning radius?
- Is it easy to turn?
- Does its shape look nice?
- Will it still be stylish in five years?
- Does it come in colors I like?

You should be able to see that these issues relate to both how a car (software) might look and feel, and possibly perform. Is this all there is to the analogy? No. Some other issues are:

- What is the car's "frequency of repair" record? (This is an important quality issue for software. In the analogy, this might mean: "Does it crash often and is it easy to bring it back up?" But it also might mean" "How often does the vendor need to send me a fix when it breaks or does not work the way it is supposed to?" "Does that fix always work?" "Does the fix break another part of the system that was working before?")
- Does the car go as fast as I want it to? (Performance)
- Can I put everything in it I want to—without (say) renting a trailer or truck for most of what I want to do? (Efficiency)

As you proceed with this analogy on your own, look at the behavioral testing strategies we mention in System Testing in Chapter 5. To us, this is where "customer satisfaction" is to be found. And to us, "quality" means "customer satisfaction."

4.5.4 Software Quality Standards

In other sections of the book, we have provided you with strategies for obtaining high-quality software. We have also reviewed some of the issues involved. We have shown you how to create software modules—in any language—that can be filtered (audited through pattern matching) with the elimination of dependencies to increase the quality. We have also shown you that in terms of strategy, one can create high-quality software systems that can be easily built on time and within budget, providing a high degree of customer satisfaction—without conforming to any of the traditional software quality assurance approaches but conforming closely to Deming's philosophy. These software system strategies are based on dependency analysis and also on the early work of Stevens, Constantine, and Myers (1974). Our own definitions of modularity (cohesion) and coupling are provided in Chapter 11, but with great disappointment, we realized that we could not—in this book—provide you with the entire methodology and thought process. With what we show you in Chapter 2, you have enough knowledge to do it right if you follow assiduously all our rules. But at the system level, there are many trade-offs. When you adhere to one standard, it often means that you must violate another. But these represent intelligent violations of the standards. Some of the "other measures," directly out of Myers (1978, 1979a), aid in making intelligent evaluations regarding these trade-offs. Reluctantly, we must hold a more complete discussion of these concepts for another book.

Code Quality Standards   We have found no standards in any of the programming textbooks for coding standards or measures of code quality. They do not even tell you how to build good software! Nor do they define testability. The first major article addressing this is Bertolino and Strigini (1996). They do not even address the structure theorem, though they do address using the canonical forms. Only Linger, Mills, and Witt (1979) address it correctly, plus Dijkstra (1968) and the early papers by Mills inside IBM.

There are some quality standards to which good programmers should adhere. The spirit of them is in the constraints provided in Chapter 2, from which we showed you that you only needed to use the three canonical forms, restricting loops to WHILE loops and NESTED IF THEN ELSEs to SELECT/ CASE structures, while taking care to eliminate the dependencies. Here are some guidelines to accompany these ideas.

- Readability of the code. "Readability" of the code is the most important consideration, even if you must violate other programming conventions.

This is what allows you to "pattern match" effectively in code audits. Normally, you do not need to violate other conventions to achieve this.

- Use of proper programs and proper program segments.
- Use of top-down, structured programming strategies.
- Emphasis on maintainability (and testability) of the code (use of a small numbers of patterns and structures).
- Use of the three basic structures of structured programming (i.e., canonical forms).

1. Simple sequence of statements.
2. Iteration (correct use of loops). DO WHILE structure should be used unless REPEAT UNTIL structure is justified—and we, in our entire careers have *never* seen a place where it is.
3. Selection (single and multiway branching). The CASE or SELECT/CASE structure should always be used unless use of other structures is justified (IF THEN or IF THEN ELSE). In several of the new 4GLs, they do not allow for CASE structures. Until their designers understand quality issues, you probably need to just work with them, attempting to minimize the risk they cause.

- Use "correct" structures. Under some logic conditions, it is possible to use a "zero/one-time-through DO WHILE" in place of an IF THEN structure. Their logic is the same, but their environments are different and their basic logic structure is different. Often programmers, attempting to be "cute" or "clever," make these kinds of substitutions. Good programmers *never* do it. (We have heard teachers of "C" attempt to justify clever uses of FOR-loops in "C" on the basis of their being "clever" or "creative." Such people should be fired, or retrained, or worse, forced to be maintenance programmers in industry.)
- Do not branch out of loops. All exit conditions should be specified in the boolean expression of the WHILE statement. Nested IF THEN ELSEs can be used (sequentially) to create the exit conditions. Sometimes it is better to use the CASE statement if it removes more dependencies.
- Do things the "same way" as much as possible. Use "variations" only when justified by some criteria.
- Complexity. If there are several ways to design something, use the design that is the least complex, especially in terms of dependencies.
- Do not nest IF THEN ELSEs more than two levels deep. They should not be permitted for alternative processing but are allowed for sequential error processing (or other type) processing. But you should realize that any time the order is important, it means that there is a dependency involved. Further, our position is that it is better—almost always—to use CASE structures even in this situation.
- Use the CASE structure (with documented boolean expressions) in place of nested IF THEN ELSEs for alternative processing. Use calls to external

subroutines to process duplicate code from within the alternative parts of IF THEN ELSEs.

- Affirmative programming. Test and define all default conditions. Use the CASE structure in place of the IF THEN ELSE structure. Be sure to examine the entire *set of conditions* for each type of default.
- Robustness. Always attempt to recognize and design out "failure modes."
- Code should always run to completion. System error messages should always be avoided. (What do they mean to the uninitiated user?) If the code does not run to completion, it should be intercepted and replaced with an error message (and/or a diagnostic to enhance serviceability). If possible, you should attempt to capture the state and/or the transaction to allow for easy recovery.
- Avoid the use of the REPEAT UNTIL structure.
- It is often easier to test than a DO WHILE, but it is not as stable during maintenance. As we indicated before, it always involves a dependency.
- Validate all input data to a module. This means that if this is the first time externally produced data are used by the software system, they should be validated. If the data are provided from elsewhere in the program (and they have been validated there and calculations made—and you have eliminated any dependencies)—they should be "examined" to see if they are correct. The purpose is to make sure the data values are "in range" and that "division by zero" or similar problems cannot occur in the module under observation. If you carry this concept too far, you may actually cause dependencies rather than eliminating them. Duplicate editing criteria indicate that there is a dependency between the two places it takes place. "Examining" the data is part of interface testing, through pattern matching, not placing additional, duplicate tests "in-line." If there is a "division by zero" condition in a module, it is in that module where it should be tested for and corrected. (If you do it earlier, you usually create a dependency.) If values might be "out of range" for a certain function, they should be "out of range" everywhere in the program, or you are dealing with different software "states" at different points and with the same data being both valid and invalid, depending on where they are used. *This* is the condition that should be checked for in the module wherein the data is entered into the software system.
- Avoid, correct, or document programmer assumptions.
- Avoid, minimize, or document intramodule dependencies.
- Avoid, minimize, or document intermodule dependencies.

4.6 CONCLUSION

This chapter has involved software quality standards. As you can see, we have taken a very nontraditional approach. We feel that once you have accepted the spirit of Deming and TQM, there are much better ways to approach software development and quality than the old-fashioned "testing at the end of the life cycle" and "noncustomer-based" software specifications. While some of this may appear controversial, we feel our new product delivery process conforms to good software practices and will produce positive results for all who use it.

We hope you see the possibilities of new ways to achieve quality standards. Further, your specification documents will be much more complete than being merely a list of functions. The concept of a user profile, while difficult for many people to understand and grasp, can greatly simplify the usability of your software if enough time has been taken to develop it adequately.

CHAPTER 5

Overview of Test Cycles

One of the unfortunate facts about testing is, as Kaner et al. (1993) state in their book, that most university students with a computer science degree have never heard of Beizer, Kaner, Perry, McCabe, Miller, Howden, or any of the other testing experts active in the software testing field. The majority cannot even name the major testing strategies. Neither can most professional programmers. We consider testing to be an extremely important, although neglected, activity in the software quality initiative.

In this chapter, we intend to cover the basic concepts of testing. We will begin by defining the various parts of the testing process, although we will concentrate on unit and system testing strategies. We cannot do more than give you some definitions and some basic strategies for testing. We will give you a complete view of behavior testing and some of the issues surrounding it.

5.1 OBJECTIVES OF TESTING

It should be noted that there is a difference between the four basic concepts related to software testing. These are:

- error detection
- error removal
- error tracking
- regression testing

5.1.1 Error Detection

Error detection involves identifying errors. This not only involves classical testing methods; it also involves inspections and walk-throughs or any other type of approach to error detection. It also involves the approach we use in the product delivery process model, based on pattern matching and filters. We will concentrate in this chapter on the classical approaches to software testing. At the unit level, these involve test strategies based on functional testing. At the system level, these may involve either functional testing or behavioral testing. Note that many people consider black box testing, functional testing, and behavioral testing to be the same thing. If you choose to call behavioral testing by another name and use the "traditional" terms, then simply choose a different term.

When errors are reported from a customer, they are found because a customer runs a specific user profile that was not adequately tested before the product was released. This is one of the most serious types of error detection, as it involves a customer. The error may have impacted the customer's ability to do his or her job and produce a product on time, according to a contract or government-imposed deadline. Sometimes, the user profiles involve unexpected combinations of functionality that you might never think of testing in-house. Highly independent software tends to lessen the impact of these types of errors.

In our context, behavioral testing is much more difficult to define than traditional testing. It is also difficult to locate an error related to behavioral testing. Usually you are fine-tuning the system and whether or not you have achieved your goal is somewhat arbitrary. With behavioral testing, even if you can define a behavior and test for it, what is the error you are testing for? Once you have located one, it is also difficult to remove the error, assuming you can define and find it. For example: "The system should respond 'quickly' to all database searches." Error: "The database searches are not fast enough." Which ones? All of them? Only those based on indices? How much faster do they need to be? What can be done to improve performance? What if everything you know how to do to create rapid access to the database has already been done, but you cannot market or use the product unless it is faster? This is but one example.

We will approach the concepts of software testing in this chapter mainly in the context of functional testing, beginning with unit testing and then proceeding to integration testing and system testing.

5.1.2 Error Removal

Error removal involves debugging and other strategies for identifying where the error occurs in the code, the process necessary to identify what in the code causes the error, and removing it. To us, debugging software is basically still an art rather than a science, and there are very few strategies that are precise and well defined. Performing traces; setting traps; identifying "error states"; identifying the algorithm, function, or module in which the error occurred; and other strategies require much insight into the software and are not easy to define or carry out even though the error has already been identified. Discussion of such debugging techniques will not be covered in this book.

5.1.3 Error Tracking

Error tracking is also important. Whenever an error has occurred anywhere in the software, it means that someone or something has failed. It is as important to find and correct the cause of the error as it is to fix the error itself.

Many companies fail to realize how important this is. As you have seen, this is one of the most important parts of the new product delivery paradigm.

5.1.4 Regression Testing

Regression testing is testing to see if the fix or rework to the code actually fixes the error, fixes it in one place and breaks it in another, or breaks the code in other places without actually fixing it at the point in the software where the fix was attempted. There are a lot of questions as to what constitutes true regression testing. Does it involve the fix? Does the test for the fix run in a regression test suite, or does it run as a separate test before regression testing takes place? Does it involve only the code right around the fix? Does it involve only the test case which uncovers the error? Or does it involve a complete rerun of the entire suite of test cases? What if all the code has not yet been written? Or all the potentially pertinent test suites? Can you depend on their catching a newly caused error later? See Section 5.5.7 for more details on regression testing.

5.1.5 Goals of Software Testing

Myers (1979b) states that the purpose of testing is to uncover errors. Others have said that the purpose is to show that the program runs for typical test cases. On one hand, the idea is that if a Boeing 777 crashes, it represents a successful test case; from the other point of view, if it takes off successfully, it represents another valid example that the aircraft is airworthy.

One of the major problems with all the approaches to testing is that they assume that the state of the code is given. This means that most testing strategies are based on trying to find out what happened and go from there. This indicates that one must determine the input equivalence classes and see if they are independent. With domain testing, one assumes that they are all dependent, with the restriction that the boundaries are all linear. Bugs exist in the code and it is your job as a tester to find them.

From our point of view, you can design out both the errors and the dependencies. Remember that Deming believed you could cease dependence on inspection to achieve quality. The focus is on avoiding quality problems, in place of inspecting out defects after they have occurred. This may seem trivial at first glance, but it is a major shift from the way software is built and tested.

The product delivery process should be directly in line with the goals of the quality movement—in terms of Deming's 14 points, TQM, Six Sigma, theoretical cycle reduction, and the Software Engineering Institute's Capability Maturity Model (CMM). The reason the new view of process control, software development, and testing is so controversial is that it goes so much against the traditional approaches to each of these areas.

From a traditional perspective some may say, "Testing all inputs is a straw man." However, the question is: "If you do not test all the inputs, which ones do you leave out? On what basis?" Our view is that inputs should be included or excluded from tests based on risk and usage. But a better approach is to design the inputs so that there is a reasonable number to test and the method of testing them is efficient enough so that total input domain coverage is trivial.

One testing problem is that simply finding errors or ad hoc testing tends to be the most effective method of finding errors. However, following this method, you have no way of knowing what you have tested and what you have not. On the other hand, test coverage allows you to show that for the code—or paths—covered, the program runs correctly. Sometimes capture/replay tools can help you identify and measure the results of ad hoc testing.

If you have only limited testing resources, the question is, is it better to use them to find errors or to show that the program runs correctly? Another even more troublesome question is whether or not it is possible to prove the program runs correctly, even if that is your goal. Many people attempt to show a program is correct by running previous production runs (modified to reflect the new environment) against the new program. This tends only to work for batch software, though if a capture/replay software testing tool has captured an interactive environment, it may be possible to do a reproduction of part or all of the new software environment. Using production runs tends to be extremely wasteful of testing resources, as production runs tend to follow the 80/20 rule and only test about 20 percent of the code, over and over again.

By isolating subsystems and using domain testing, equivalence class partitioning, boundary value analysis, or user profiles, you can make a test suite "zero in" on a particular part of the code. This is much like shooting with a rifle rather than a shotgun at a target (the bugs). If the interfaces tend to be independent, then this method is extremely efficient; if they are not, then approaches to building the test suites using cause-and-effect graphing, truth tables, and test coverage matrices are necessary and a lot of effort is required to obtain a reasonable level of coverage. But it still tends to be more efficient than running production runs, as one can focus on critical parts of the code. Note that there is discussion of "dated" testing strategies versus "newer" strategies. Domain testing is considered by some testing experts to replace equivalence class partitioning, boundary value analysis, and cause-and-effect graphing. This is especially true in the latter case, as a cause-and-effect graph can be extremely complex. With domain testing, as was mentioned earlier, you assume all the input classes are dependent. According to Beizer (personal conversation, April 1996), domain testing is one of the most promising and effective of the new testing strategies.

Of all these concepts, equivalence class partitioning may be the least understood. Normally equivalence classes involve sets, intervals, specific numerical values, or boolean expressions, which are independent of one another. One lists all the sets (say), or classes, and then takes each one in some sequence and tests correct values and then incorrect values for each set. This is done one at a time. Since the classes, by definition, are independent of each other, the order does not make any difference, but you do not allow multiple error conditions. If you do, you cannot tell which error condition caused a problem or whether it was handled correctly.

There is an article on domain testing from a mathematical point of view in the February 1996 issue of *IEEE Transactions on Software Engineering* (Chen and Yu, 1996) on failure rate estimation. This article, in addition to either of Beizer's books (1991, 1995), may give you additional insight into this new area of traditional testing.

5.1.6 Error-Prone Code and Failure Modes

Some authors of testing books state that experience shows that no one type of error is more prominent than another. We do not believe this is true. When one of the authors was consulting with IBM (in the division that was nominated for the Malcolm Baldrige Award), they were working on a risk-based concept called "design analysis." It was basically oriented toward measuring error rates and tracing them back against the modules in which they occurred. They would then classify these modules and keep statistics on the design, the type of module, and the type of error and use this information to focus on areas of the code which seemed most likely to contain errors. This was an early precursor of error tracing. We found definite patterns. The biggest problem was gathering accurate information and maintaining it.

Kaner et al. (1993), in the preface to their book *Testing Computer Software*, Second Edition, state: "This book is about doing testing when your co-workers don't, won't and don't have to follow the rules." How does error-prone code come into being? Because people don't follow the rules. Errors must be designed into a product; they do not occur by chance, though they may occur due to carelessness. This means we can design them out—or better—not design them in in the first place. This is the basis of Deming's quality concepts. In the product delivery process, the whole emphasis is on designing software with a thought process that minimizes the probability of errors being introduced.

Now, in the days of quality initiatives, shareholders and customers are starting to understand that they can bring lawsuits against incompetent managers and executives. If an employee (programmer, software engineer, etc.) deliberately refuses to follow quality standards—especially when they are called to his or her attention—that person is of no value to the company and should be fired for insubordination. Upper-level management knows that poor quality deliberately designed into a product (in violation of known quality standards and in the name of "creativity" or "efficiency" or whatever) is an act of sabotage and can cost the company millions of dollars.

When one of the authors was teaching a university testing course, students would ask: "Where should we look to find the most errors?" The answer was: "Look in the exception-handling routines." This still tends to be true. Most of the 80 percent of the untested code (related to batch processing) tends to be for extremely rare user profiles or for exception handling routines. Indeed, most commercial software, such as word processors, tends to be easy to break when you try to do rare or unexpected operations. Sometimes this is referred to as failure modes, or in other words, user profiles the software is not intended to execute. Whether these are referred to as undocumented features, documented limitations, or errors is very much a function of how they *are* documented. Ideally, failure modes should be documented in the code with error messages, warnings, and alternative suggestions.

Several years ago, one of the major operating systems used the C drive as the default drive. While one of the authors was visiting an insurance agent, the secretary came into the office and stated: "Something's funny. Usually it only takes a few minutes to format a disk. This is taking over 45 minutes." The author asked the agent, "Have you backed up your hard drive?" "What is a 'backup'?" was the reply. Of course, the agent lost all the insurance agency's records.

Later, at a conference, the author was commenting on the situation and explained: "The computer should have replied: 'Are you sure you want to do this?' 'You will delete all your records.' 'These are the records you will delete. Are you sure you want to?' 'Check each file you are willing to delete.' Etc." One of the attendees stated, "That is a stupid thing to do. You should just let the computer do the delete without all those comments." How much you should protect the user from such "failure modes" is obviously open to debate.

Usually, if an adequate job has been done interacting with potential users and others to ascertain appropriate user profiles, you might sometimes restrict the number of functions or profiles available to simplify the software or make it easier to use or train. These restrictions are documented to make it so users are aware of what the software will and will not do. While violation of these "restrictions" might lead to failure modes, ideally, the user should be protected from them by error messages.

Another concept related to this is that, with appropriate study of potential users of your system, you may be able to define work flows and user profiles which optimize the creation of the user's desired products (to be created using your software product). If initial use of the product is "intuitive," due to readily identifiable patterns, you have created the "usability" quality in your product.

If you provide an airline pilot—even an experienced one—with a set of 1,000 new features on an airplane, his or her chances of getting the plane off the ground successfully are probably about nil. The same features the pilot has used in the past should work the same as before, but an efficient extension of the new features which are intuitive and natural in helping the pilot do the job but constrained by whatever is necessary to prohibit the pilot from allowing the plane to crash—though allowing enough versatility to enable him or her to recover from "untoward" actions—is obviously what should be required. There are no right or wrong answers; this is based on experience with the user profiles, many "dry runs," and a lot of "fine-tuning." This is not functional testing; it is behavioral testing.

Sometimes these "features" or "software behaviors" simply end up in the code and are due either to

- programmer assumptions
- ill-defined or incompletely defined features
- missing features

In this case, we would consider these features to be errors which should either be removed or documented as software limitations.

Programmer assumptions tend to be assumptions a programmer either consciously or unconsciously makes concerning how the code will operate. Some examples we have seen are:

- One file being processed (say, year-to-date) will end before another file (say, the update file).

- A machine operator will never mount and execute the same update file twice.

- There will always be at least one record (i.e., using a REPEAT UNTIL structure rather than a DO WHILE).

- In a variable-size array, there will always be at least four columns.

The major idea is that these are difficult—if not impossible—to identify, because they are neither visible nor obvious. Further, they are not a part of any specification or constraints.

Often errors occur when there are so many potential states in the software—especially in the concurrent parts of a software system—that it can only be considered stochastic, or random. When these concurrent systems are interacting, without any executive software maintaining their states, then race conditions, deadlocking, and other similar conditions occur. With good design, these should not occur, and the system should be deterministic. If enforcing deterministicity causes performance hits, at least they can be restricted to small amounts of code or a small number of subsystems.

There are strategies which sometimes can be employed when the number of software states proliferate. Most of these strategies are related to conditions the tester can impose to achieve a high degree of coverage with a minimal number of test cases. As one of the reviewers suggested, the tester could employ "orthogonal array testing," which would allow him or her to pick the set of tests which would provide the most efficient coverage. This concept is related to the creation of "multiply independent tests," as opposed to our strategy of imposing independence on the code and the states it takes on itself.

Error-prone code, on the other hand, is a concept related to statistical quality control. Instead of trying to make software quality assurance (QA) techniques meet hardware definitions, a better solution is simply to define error-prone modules according to a preestablished set of criteria. For example, you might choose criteria based on

- error rate within the module
- conformity of the module to coding standards
- readability or "understandability"
- relative complexity, based on "typical modules" from that application type
- "environmental" stability of the module
- "environmental" independence of the module

In your company, you might find other issues to also be important. Whenever a module has exceeded one of these measures, based upon whatever threshold you have set, then the module should be rejected, redesigned, and reprogrammed from scratch.

5.1.7 Effective Test Team Validation Strategies

One of the most difficult things software development management must do is gain confidence in the testing effort. As we discuss later in this chapter, it is easy to see code being written, but it is hard to tell if effective testing is taking place. As you implement the product delivery system, especially in terms of the "nontesting, pattern-matching paradigm," sceptics will often criticize the approach as being too radical and too risky. Any time a person or test team begins testing for the first time, it is a good idea to validate their efforts. What this means is that you assign two independent teams the same code or subsystem to test at the same time. You then compare the errors found and the responses of the two teams as to what they discovered and how they approached the testing effort.

Whether both teams find the same errors, the same number of errors, or the same severity of errors, you gain insight into the effectiveness of the testing effort. This is true whether you use traditional testing techniques or the new paradigm in the product delivery process. In the new paradigm, both teams would pattern match the code independently and compare results. Or you can use the results of pattern matching against the results of traditional testing. You should note, however, that the code audit, based on pattern matching is a filter, not a test or inspection. For this reason, it tends to enforce and affirm quality as well as functional completeness and correctness.

If you cannot afford the luxury of having two teams test the same software twice, another approach is to perform what is sometimes called "morphological testing." This is where you deliberately insert errors into the code and see if your test cases uncover them. Attempts to automate this process have led to fairly expensive testing for the results obtained, so it is usually not a good idea to try to use this approach for operational testing. This is true for two reasons. First, you must have some sort of interpretive compiler so you can insert the mutation operators without expensive, time-consuming compiles of the code. Second, most of the mutation operators (i.e., deliberate errors such as + instead of −, * instead of ", 2.5 instead of A, and so forth) cause the software to crash without running to completion, making the offending operator ineffective. But if you plan carefully, often you can get a good feel for how effective your testing is. Usually, only a small portion of the code can be verified against the testing effectiveness using this approach, but it may be enough to tell whether your test team is effective.

Once you have validated your teams to your satisfaction, you can proceed to the testing approach you have decided to use. This is probably one of the best ways you can gain confidence in the new paradigm.

5.2 BLACK BOX TESTING VERSUS WHITE BOX TESTING

While black box testing and white box testing are called by several different names, they basically involve looking at the structure of the code (white box) or looking at the functionality of the code (black box). There is some question as to which approach is the most effective or efficient. There is also an argument as to how much is—or should be—involved in white box testing. White box testing tends to involve coverage, while black box testing tends to involve functionality. An inherent weakness of white box testing is that you tend to find errors when the function is partly wrong, but if it is the wrong function programmed correctly, it is almost impossible to detect with white box testing. On the other hand, black box testing tends to uncover it immediately. But a weakness of black box testing is that it tends to be insensitive to missing functions (how do you test it if it isn't there?).

An effective user profile will tend to find missing functions within a work flow or set of tasks related to one or more events. A problem with user profiles is that they are difficult for programmers and users to define. If a user profile can be defined in terms of basic work flows, which can be combined in various ways to perform more complex tasks—or to complete various desired products—then user profiles tend to be very stable. The idea is: "What are the user profiles necessary to combine the basic functions of a Boeing 787 to allow a plane to take off? To fly through the air? To land at another airport?" Users typically want to define the user profile as: "How to fly the plane from San Francisco to New York." And they make the profile too complex and not generic enough. They then want the software customized for the flight to each city from the other city, thus creating many "off-by-one" versions and customized software. (This is impossible to train and support, regardless of whether it is in one MIS environment or at many sites. In a shrink-wrapped environment, the impossibility of support is obvious.)

Many companies feel that if they achieve fairly adequate statement coverage, they are doing well. But a large number of companies fail to achieve even this to a reasonable level. We are aware of several major companies who ship code where, while it all has compiled, over 40 percent has never executed, with the idea that, "if the software compiles, it must be all right." We tend to look with horror at the fact that many companies ship software where they cannot show that 100 percent of the statements have even executed, let alone have been tested, yet they do not see this as even being a problem (or a risk). To us, 100 percent statement coverage is not anywhere near minimum coverage. What about covering all the branches or nodes within the code? A more difficult question is, do you do them one at a time or in all possible combinations? Or do you do something "in between"? As you might suspect, there is no right answer to this, especially when dependencies are taken into account.

As you can see, there is a major gap between the state of the art in software testing and the state of the industry. We will attempt to straddle the fence on this issue, leaning toward the strategies that seem easiest to use or the most efficient. Later on, we will show you the efficient approach of our new paradigm.

We will start by addressing white box testing, and then proceed to black box testing. Realize that there are entire books on both these subjects, so the most we can do is give you a general idea of how to perform various types of testing and refer you to other books which specialize on these topics. You may be surprised to see us defending and criticizing some of the techniques in current testing references. If the testing industry were stable, each testing book should be a "rehash" of the others. This is not true. There is a lot of controversy about how to test and which techniques are the best. Since we are limited to one chapter on the topic, we can merely point out some points of disagreement and where we stand on some of them. In the early years of testing, one of the least-understood concepts was not "what test techniques do you use?" It was "what testing strategies do you use to employ the available test techniques?"

5.3 Unit Testing

In the classical approach to unit testing, you perform a set of basic tests at the module level. None of them are related to the behavior of the system; each is related to whether the functions work—especially when they have been executed in each of their potential states. Software testing at the unit or module level is basically of three types:

- ad hoc or ad lib testing

- white box testing

- black box testing

Each of these will be covered in a separate section.

5.3.1 Ad Hoc Testing

Ad hoc or ad lib testing means you simply play with the program, trying whatever comes to mind, in an attempt to break the program or make it fail. The problem is that while you usually find many errors, you can never be sure what was or was not tested. You have no idea just how much of the code or its functionality was covered. The reason it is so effective is that the tester tends to begin to "identify psychologically" with the programmer. Once when one of the authors was ad hoc testing a program written by some programmers from Italy, he identified which programmers had written which parts merely by the different ways they performed. This was true even though a different programming culture was involved. This psychological interaction tends to lead the tester to parts of the software where the software tends to perform in a "flaky" or "weird but undefinable" manner. While this may lead to a lot of errors being detected, unless there is some sort of capture/replay tool to trace where the tester has been, the functional, subsystem, interface, or statement coverage is almost impossible to evaluate.

5.3.2 White Box Testing

When using white box testing, you are involved directly with the structure of the code within a module or code segment. You draw a directed graph (similar to a flowchart without the logic, as we described in Chapter 2) and use it to plan tests which adequately cover all the code in a given module. While these definitions and descriptions sound simple, they are not always easy to accomplish. Code coverage is defined in terms of six types. Loop coverage is also part of white box testing.

Segment Coverage   Each segment of code between control structures is executed at least once.

Branch Coverage or Node Testing   Each branch in the code is taken in each possible direction at least once. One of Boris Beizer's favorite comments is: "If you see a graph, cover it." (Beizer, 1991, 1995)

Compound Condition Coverage   When there are multiple conditions such as

```
(0 < X < 100) OR (150< X < 200) AND (Y > 0)
```

you must test not only each direction, but also each possible combination of conditions, which is usually done by using a "truth table."

Basis Path Testing   Each independent path through the code is taken in a predetermined order. This is considered by some testing engineers to be the minimum condition for path testing. When there are dependencies in the code—especially among the paths—basis path testing is not adequate. You must, in addition, test each of the paths for which a dependency exists. This "basis path" testing technique is also known as structured testing and is "marketed" by Tom McCabe (1982) as part of his complexity measure, cyclomatic complexity, and his automated tools. Many people, Beizer included, do not feel that this is an adequate level of coverage.

Data Flow Testing   This approach is an attempt to find an analyzable, repeatable strategy that lies between basis path testing and full path testing. In this approach, you track specific variables through each possible calculation, thus defining a set of intermediate paths through the code, i.e., those based on each piece of data chosen to be tracked. For more on this, see Beizer (1990, 1995). We feel the intuitive feelings and experiences of Beizer and others are justified, when basis path testing is evaluated in terms of dependencies. Even though the paths are considered independent, dependencies across multiple paths are not really tested for by this approach. This is also true for full path testing, as well. Most test cases do not uncover dependencies, even though they cover the paths or code segments in which the dependencies occur. Dependencies do not make the code incorrect; they only make it so that it is difficult to fix and test. Our new paradigm takes this into account.

Data flow testing does tend to reflect dependencies, but it is mainly through sequences of data manipulations. This approach tends to uncover anomalies such as variables that are "used, but not initialized," "declared, but not used," and so on. It is not used to show how to package data usages to minimize dependencies among them, just as path testing is not used to package control structures with code segments to minimize dependencies. This dependency analysis strategy seems to be wholly absent from both software development concepts and software testing concepts. At present, data flow testing is not effectively supported by commercial test tools, so it must be performed manually.

Path Testing   Path testing is where all possible paths through the code are defined and covered. While basis path testing and data flow testing seem simple to define, to actually test them is extremely laborious and time-consuming. While basis paths constitute a relatively small set of tests, full path testing can number into the billions of tests. Though many testing experts deny that the numbers of paths can go this high, in other writings we have given examples of how this happens. Some testing experts feel that the need to achieve full path coverage is a "straw man." Our position is that if you do not achieve full coverage, you must have some criteria to decide what to test and what not to test. While this may be done by defining certain equivalence classes and using them to minimize the number of paths, it is better to recognize and constrain the tests in terms of dependencies, which also affect the equivalence classes.

Loop Testing   In addition to these coverage measures, there are testing strategies based on loop testing. These strategies relate to testing single loops (WHILE loops, REPEAT-UNTIL loops, and FOR loops), concatenated loops (sequences of loops), and nested loops (one or more loops inside another loop). Loops are fairly simple to test unless dependencies exist among the loops or between a loop and the code it contains. In that case, the number of permutations of tests approaches infinity.

There are many published strategies for testing loops, mainly in books on unit testing, but they do not tend to take into account dependencies and their impact. Some of the verification strategies relating to loops (see Humphrey, 1995) provide examples in the "clean room" environment. But they tend to be complex and contain poorly written, unreadable code. This simply makes it harder to locate the dependencies that might be there or to pattern match to show that the algorithm is correct. Beizer (1990, 1995) provides comments on loop testing as does Pressman (1992).

If loops are written correctly and without dependencies, they should be fairly easy to test. To us, the major concept should be "loop invariance." This means more than what is usually part of the mathematical definition. If you run a WHILE loop that processes an array by advancing the subscript number, say, from 1 to 100, this should not constitute 100 "states" of the loop; it should constitute one "state" processed 100 times for different subscripts. If states of loops are evaluated in this manner, it is fairly easy to identify dependencies. Further, loops were originally used to keep from having to write all 100 processing structures for the array (or whatever else could be repetitively processed) as separate pieces of code. Loops should involve doing the same thing over and over. When nesting occurs, either with additional loops, or more obscurely, through subroutine calls, it is possible to create large numbers of states. This is especially true when the states the subroutines take on contain dependencies on other input data than whatever is caused by the loop variable. This is one of the major areas where the number of states can be radically reduced. Normally the problem is still based on dependencies.

Beizer does make a distinction between deterministic (FOR) loops and non-deterministic (WHILE) loops. We feel, on the other hand, that all loops can be placed in the WHILE-loop structure. As we mentioned in Chapter 2, FOR loops tend to be hard to read. In C they tend to be so "versatile" as to be "undecipherable."

The proper idea is that deterministic is related to any logic structure in which the number of times through the loop is predetermined, and the structure of the logic will be the same regardless of whether the loop is deterministic or not. As we mentioned earlier, this is not a complete enough description; indeed, nondeterministic is misleading. Software systems deal with three types of conditions. These are all related to states of the system. Each time a loop increases in value or changes state according to some characteristic, the entire system is considered to have changed state. If the various subsystems are independent of each other, they may or may not have changed state. Basically, we define them to be

- deterministic
- stochastic (nondeterministic)

The question is, if a count from 1 to 10 is deterministic, what about one where a user enters a value for n to be used in a count? It is still deterministic. What if a loop processes until two values get close to an arbitrarily small value but the values never converge to within that value? It is still deterministic; you simply have an additional state that must be managed—that of nonconvergence. A software system that is stochastic or random in its behavior, is when you have two concurrent systems, completely independent of each other—except that they compete for some common resource. "Compete" can be interpreted in many ways. When one system reaches a certain state, it has some sort of effect on the other, which cannot be predicted in advance. Reaching a particular state of the other system is completely independent of state of the first and also cannot be predicted in advance. Almost always, this can be designed out.

Many testing experts and software design experts see no difference between the logic structure for WHILE loops and REPEAT-UNTIL loops, except for the fact that one passes through the latter before testing for the loop condition. They do not recognize that this always causes a dependency between the logic and loop variable of the loop structure and the loop condition. This can always be avoided by setting up the loop condition to be initialized before entering the loop. This lack of distinction is an example of thinking in terms of an old paradigm.

The example in Chapter 2 of a dependency between a WHILE-loop structure and a CASE statement leads to an explosion of tests. This explosion cannot be removed by defining an equivalence class; the relationship between the logic structure of the loop's boolean expression and the logic and logic structure of the branches must be separated and repackaged so as to eliminate the dependency across logic structures. When someone says that branching out of a loop structure when a condition occurs is an example of a nondeterministic loop, you should say that it is an example of a violation of good programming standards and be rejected. The "horrible loops" that Beizer (1990, 1995) discusses are similar. Reject them and have them redesigned and reprogrammed. Do not even try to test them.

5.3.3 Black Box Testing

In addition to white box testing there is also black box testing. Mainly, this consists of assuming that the logic structure of the code is unknown—that it is a "black box." This is the point at which the function of a module is tested. There are several tests one can make at this point.

Error Guessing   In this approach you merely write test cases which test functions or parts of functions which, experience has shown, tend to be error-prone. This can be highly effective and is somewhat related to ad hoc testing, though it is ordinarily better planned and control of coverage is more adequate. Some feel that this is an "archaic" concept left over from Myers (1979b) and, to a degree, it is. But when design analysis and other techniques based on error tracking and root cause analysis are used to guide testing efforts, it becomes a very "modern" approach. Our new paradigm, with its filters, also makes use of this concept. When a bug slips through a filter, it is tracked back against all the filters and each one is corrected to capture the class of errors it allowed to pass through. You also fix the deliverable in which the error occurred.

Equivalence Class Partitioning   As has been previously stated, many programmers run production runs against software systems to find bugs, hoping that they will have enough different use patterns to find any bugs that might exist. This approach is extremely inefficient, and 80 to 90 percent of the transactions merely execute the same test case with different data. This can happen at the unit level, as well. If you test a sort routine with five numbers and then rerun it with five different numbers, this is not two tests; it is one test with two different sets of data. It accomplishes absolutely nothing after the first test has been run.

Traditional equivalence class partitioning takes this inefficiency into account. You only run one test for each class of input (to the module). But in addition, you run additional tests using invalid data for that class to make sure the error routines are working correctly. The number of invalid tests depends on whether the class is a set, interval, data element, or boolean variable. Since there are usually several different equivalence classes (input data elements or structures) on the module interface, all but the one being tested must run with correct data, changing to incorrect data one equivalence class at a time.

One of the problems we are concerned with is the fact that while there often seem to be only a small number of equivalence classes, there are often hundreds of thousands of states which exist later in the program. This indicates that some of the equivalence classes contain subsets related to other classes based on dependencies that are not visible when one is setting up domain testing strategies. More study needs to be devoted to this situation.

Boundary Value Analysis Many errors tend to occur on the boundaries of equivalence classes, so another approach is to test the boundaries. Usually, you test just inside, on the boundary, and just outside—wherever the variable type allows this to be done.

Cause-and-Effect Graphing When dependencies exist among variables on the module interface, they cannot be handled effectively with equivalence class partitioning. Instead, a technique known as cause-and-effect graphing is employed to create tests which reflect the dependencies present. In our new approach, these dependencies would be eliminated from the interface variables. Although there are some software packages available in the PC environment to deal with cause-and-effect graphing, the most appropriate one is used to define specifications upfront and create a minimum set of tests, rather than testing them at the end.

Domain Testing Domain testing is a more "modern" equivalent of boundary value analysis and cause-and-effect graphing (due to dependencies among the equivalence classes). It also takes into account methods of testing on the boundaries of the classes. The entire approach is clearly explained in Beizer (1995) and is a bit too complex to explain here. The major thing to consider is that the approach is generic and assumes that all equivalence classes are dependent. It then uses linear transformations to create sets where the linear boundaries can be tested. The idea that interclass boundaries can be reduced to linear ones is asserted to be "adequate" by Beizer. This is true as well, but a problem is that there are no commercial test tools yet available to provide effective support for this approach.

Module Interface Testing In module interface testing, you attempt to test whether the values along the interface are correct as they relate to modules which call them. This means that the specific calls in the calling modules must be tested to see that they are in the right sequence and of the right type. As you move more toward the system level, this might also involve "calling chains" or sequences.

Command-Line Testing When the interface is external to the software system, i.e., a user interface, for which the operation of the program is caused by a command line, then you must test each of the "setups" to show that the software system operates correctly and that appropriate error messages are given whenever the command line is set up improperly. Normally, there is a type of grammar or pattern associated with the command line that must be taken into account. When there are dependencies, these dependencies must often be tested using cause-and-effect graphs. In the Windows and Macintosh interface environments, these types of interfaces no longer exist. But where they do (UNIX® operating system, for example), they are not user friendly and are difficult for uninitiated users to implement correctly. It is probably most effective to approach them in terms of the generic approach of domain testing.

Of course, you are not prohibited from using any of these traditional unit testing strategies as part of your software verification efforts as you move to the new paradigm. Initially, until everyone in your organization matures in the new paradigm, you should do a certain amount of dual testing. But once you have proven the paradigm to your own satisfaction, you can move directly to the approach described in the earlier chapters. You will see that it is extremely efficient for high-quality code, with a minimal number of patterns.

5.4 INTEGRATION TESTING

One of the most frustrating parts of software development and testing is software integration. We have seen projects where the entire code base was written in less than six months but it was still unintegrated over a year later. This comes when the system is neither designed correctly nor built correctly. Normally, the purpose of software integration is to adequately test whether or not the software actually runs as one program. The question is how to achieve this. If interface testing shows that the calling/called structure is compatible and that the called module works with a driver and the calling module works with a stub, then interface testing should show that this relationship is true when the two modules are actually put together and further linked to other modules that were similarly tested.

Testing performed at this level is usually black box testing, although it is possible to link processing or logic paths between two modules. Herrold (1989) describes how to do this using data flow testing. We suggest that this only be done—whether with data flow testing or path testing—if there is reason to believe that there is some sort of anomoly which is hard to define. A better approach is to redesign the software so that this can be pattern matched using the new paradigm.

Typically, software integration is viewed from the following nine perspectives:

- incremental versus nonincremental
- big bang
- top down
- bottom up
- risk based
- threaded
- outside-in (Essential Systems Analysis)
- inside-out [Orr Data Structured Systems Development (DSSD)]
- little bang

Actually, all of these, except perhaps the latter three, are based on the wrong concept. We will discuss this view at the end of this section.

5.4.1 Incremental versus Nonincremental

Usually, the reason you might use nonincremental integration is because you have no design or development plan and all the programmers on the project are "doing their thing" and hoping things will come together in the end. When the time comes to ship the product (with less than a couple of days for system testing), everyone brings his or her code and an attempt is made to integrate it.

This is an incredibly naive way to build software. It is far better to "build a little, test a little." Typically, if software development is somewhat organized, you build the software using a Gantt chart with the software built in the order of the dependencies present. The idea might be that you need to build the database software first; then you can build the software that accesses the database, test it against the database software, and then proceed to the next set of dependencies.

With the new paradigm, all these dependencies are designed out, and it makes no difference when the modules are programmed in the sequence defined by the project plan. You can build them in such a manner that an executive module manages whatever subsystem is important at each milestone of the software development process. Usually, in software development, the most important issue is building the software to maintain credibility with upper-level management and with the customers. This can best be done if you can demonstrate working code early on, and continue to demonstrate that more and more of the system is working at key points in the development process—and that these deliverables are on schedule. In commercial environments, very often the ability to demonstrate and possibly ship early versions of your product can provide a distinct competitive advantage.

5.4.2 Big-Bang Integration

Of all the types of software integration, big-bang integration is the most common. It follows directly from the reasons mentioned in an earlier section. The major problem with this is that you tend to uncover a large number of bugs "all at once," without any indication as to what the environment was that generated them. If there are a lot of dependencies, which is usually the case in this type of situation since the code probably has no distinct or recognizable architecture, it is almost impossible to isolate causes of one bug from another. In addition, making it so two modules work together and then adding a third can often break the other two. When this is proliferated, it is in an impossible situation. There is never any justification for big-bang integration. It is always the result of incompetence and naivity.

5.4.3 Top-Down Integration

For these remaining implementation strategies, there is a lot of discussion about the pro's and con's of each. Top down implies that you start with the highest-level main program and gradually add stubs until you reach the bottom. Stubs tend to be less complex than drivers, which must be used if you program "bottom up." One of the problems is that many systems do not have a top or they may have several tops. Another problem is that often the way the program must function is not known until you get close to the bottom. Specifications usually deal with the lower-level, more detailed part of the software product. Still another problem is that, with the stubs, the program often can be made to appear as though it has been completely programmed, since the stubs appear to be doing the work. This leads management to be overly optimistic and sometimes unrealistic in terms of the actual state of the software.

Originally the DeMarco (1979) approach to software development was based on the concept of starting with a context diagram and successively decomposing it functionally until you reached the bottom. The constraints were that no module should call more than 10 other modules and the calling sequence should never be more than nine deep. This allowed for some excellent guidelines as to how to design systems that were "not too flat" or "not too steep." As you gained experience with this approach, such a feel was very useful. The problem was that as you decomposed the system from the top to the bottom, often, at the lowest level, the functionality—while completely accurate and well defined—was not grouped appropriately for the user to access. In the Orr DSSD methodology, this was the starting point, i.e., defining the concurrent users and the users' data needs and then moving outward to the system boundaries. McMenamin and Palmer (1984) later developed essential systems analysis as a way of resolving this. We will talk about this in Section 5.4.7. They started with a definition of the concurrent "processors" and the data interactions or transactions among them. But of course, this is talking about software design, not implementation.

5.4.4 Bottom-Up Integration

An alternative to top down is bottom up. As was mentioned earlier, you start with the lowest-level modules and build up from there, integrating them using drivers, rather than stubs. One problem here is that drivers tend to be more complex and error-prone than stubs. In some cases, the size of the drivers necessary to create an adequate testing environment may constitute more code than the rest of the entire program. Often, this approach requires a substantial amount of rewriting or reprogramming as you move up the calling chain. In addition, the bottom is not always the same distance from the top for the various calling chains and sometimes the functionality of the subsystems becomes unplanned or unstable, or the architecture disintegrates.

5.4.5 Risk-Based Integration Testing

Risk-based integration testing is based on the concept of building parts of the system associated with risk early on. This risk can be defined in many ways. It may relate to schedule and missing marketing windows, or it may be related to creating "credibility" in the minds of management and customers, or it may be related to the fact that certain parts of the code must run for long periods of time as part of extensive behavior-oriented testing. Traditionally, creating an architecture that contains this risk-oriented type of integration is effective, but it is difficult to achieve. Yet within our new paradigm, with its accompanying executive module-based architecture, it is a fairly trivial exercise.

5.4.6 Threaded Integration Testing

With this approach to integrating software, an attempt is made to take pieces of code from each of a critical subset of modules and use them to build a function that crosses the entire product. Often this approach is used to build credibility or proof of concept regarding a new product. The problem is that often, management gets the idea that the product is farther along than it actually is. This can also be done easier using the new paradigm.

5.4.7 Outside-In Integration Testing (Essential Systems Analysis)

There is a temptation to try to explain this in detail, based on McMenamin and Palmer's extensions (1984) to DeMarco's work (1979). But the concept we want to get across is that a software development methodology—even one dating from the early 1980s—can help in building a component-oriented system which can be integrated using the basic structure of the architecture leading to the product from the specification. With this approach, you start with concurrent processors and use them to create the files and databases on which they are based; then you move to the functions and processes relating the processors to each other. You then decompose downward or recompose upward.

5.4.8 Inside-Out Integration Testing
(Orr DSSD—Data Structured Systems Development)

This approach is similar in some ways to that explained in Section 5.4.7. Rather than being based on process structure—as defined by data flow diagrams—it is based on data structure and the transformation from input data structures to output data structures. This approach begins by defining the concurrent users and then the data they make use of. From this, the approach works "inside-out" to create the information model. This approach could also be used to create an implementation strategy. It should be noted that both data flow and data structured methodologies are both based on "process."

5.4.9 Little-Bang Integration Testing

When software is built using *executive modules* to manage independent functions traceable back to the original specifications, you are essentially dealing with a large number of small, independent subsystems. These can be put together using a "little-bang" approach, rather than stubs and drivers. This is an extremely efficient way to integrate systems. Each of these "little, independent systems" can be further integrated into larger systems. Their very independence is why this is efficient and relatively "error free."

5.4.10 The New Paradigm (The Product Delivery Process)

The new paradigm is built around any particular methodology which provides for

- traceability back to the specification
- executive modules
- a high degree of independence

Thus it is possible to rearrange the modules into subsets which will allow them to be integrated however you prefer without changing traceability to the specification. With this approach, any variation of the above approaches is viable, but the best is to build and rebuild with the concepts of risk, management and customer credibility, and ease of proof of concept. This is fundamentally the process used in "little-bang" integration.

5.5 SYSTEM TESTING

In a traditional software development environment, you must move rework from the developers to the maintenance engineers in order for rework not to have a negative impact on the software development schedule. In the product delivery process, these types of errors should not exist; they have been filtered out as a part of the development process. Ideally, the only kind of errors that should be found at this point are those which relate to the behavior of the system, not its functionality. If functionally related errors are found at this point, it means that one—or more—of the earlier filters is broken. The error should be tracked back into the life cycle and compared against each filter to see if it could have been caught at an earlier point.

There is such a thing as system-level functionality, but this should be captured in the subsystems created as a part of the project plan. Overall system-level functionality does not really exist, as software systems consist of many functions. These are best captured through user profiles, designed to use the software system to produce products. Sometimes it is hard to determine if one is testing the behavior of a function or the functionality of a function when one deals with it at the system level. Actually, it is semantics, as what is really important is that it be verified in some manner.

A system test is a series of different tests designed to fully exercise the system to uncover its limitations and measure its capabilities. The objective is to test an integrated system and verify that it meets specified requirements. You should note that system is where most of the testing effort should be placed. Below, you will see that there are many different behavioral tests of how the software system performs. This is where the quality of the system should be defined. For your particular environment, you may find other measures or tests of quality that you may want to consider. Remember that these will not be absolutes; many performance issues are merely judgment calls. Further, you may not feel that all the tests we propose are necessary for your environment. Our position is that if you choose to leave out a test or test classification you know about, you need to justify it in terms of risk and usage. Depending on your system and its implementation environment, there may be other behavior-oriented tests you may wish to perform.

5.5.1 System Test Considerations

Because system testing takes place at a higher level, the testing focuses on behavior rather than function or functional structure, and this cannot be tested through code audits based on pattern matching. As a part of our release process at Digital Technology International, we run automated test scripts that exercise all the functionality of our system, but not in all combinations.

In system testing, not only does the behavior of the individual functions need to be tested; further functional tests must also involve:

1. **The Event List:** All the possible triggers must be exercised and the expected results compared with the actual results. This often requires an "oracle" to generate expected results to be compared with the actual results. Sometimes this can be built as a table—such as a "truth" table. Every function should be tested by one or more events in the event list. Note that this is dynamic functional testing; it is testing the function as a part of the software system and as part of the user interface.

2. **Specific Scenarios:** The entire set of possible scenarios, or user profiles, should be specified for a given application. If it is finite, you can perform tests of all of them; if the set is extremely large, a risk analysis must be performed for those scenarios not covered. An effective method for doing this is to define the meaningful user profiles and restrict the testing to them or at least use them to help evaluate the risk.

3. **Transaction Tracking:** A list of possible transactions, either extracted from the scenarios or from the event list, are tracked through the software system (or subsystem) to ascertain that they function correctly (in sequence) from "input" to "output." You can also model the states of the system to see if they all can be reached. If they cannot, then the system contains "dead code." Note that this is also a good place to identify dependencies.

4. **Screen Mapping:** A map through all the screens through all conditions (pull-down menus and submenus) which can lead to other menus is created. Each time a screen or a pull-down menu is reached which requires input or generates input, the appropriate functions are processed to see that the functions operate correctly. When they lead to a subsystem or the main system for processing, their input is captured and passed to the subsystem as input—or is retrieved from it as output. You should ask the following questions: Can you terminate properly from each screen or navigate to other screens should you desire? To navigate between two screens, can you get there efficiently? Do you need to go through several others? Is all the functionality necessary to perform a task (part of a user profile) easy to access from the screen where it is needed?

5. **Error Message Testing:** Every error message which can be generated by the system must be extracted from the code and placed in a table, where it can be generated and tested for appropriateness and understandability from the user's perspective, with the proper response being prompted for. Error messages should also be checked from a "national language" point of view to see that they have enough room to be translated both in the table and on the screen where they are displayed. This is also true for all messages or tests displayed on the screen. Usually, they are listed in some sort of appendix to a user's manual or an installation manual. At other times, they may appear in a technical manual.

6. **Documentation Testing:** All examples used in the user's manual must be tested for correctness and for whether or not the manual gives the exact answers users will obtain when they run the examples. Further, all the functionality should be available through both parts of the manual and through an effective, accurate index. Care should be taken to see that all the accessible terminology in the manual can be understood by the user and related to his or her application or task.

7. **Help System Testing:** See that all help files are "context-based" and generate the appropriate messages when the "help" is sought from all possible approaches or contexts available. This is one of the most difficult types of testing. Often the question the user wants answered may not be easily identified by the developers nor explained adequately from the user's point of view.

8. **Performing a Complete Sequence of Functional Tasks:** A complete user profile must be performed for various applications or sets of applications (e.g., at Digital Technology, this would consist of putting out an

entire newspaper or other similar operation). A user profile involves the work flow and basic set of functions the user needs to follow to produce a product. It involves more than just performing some functions. It involves the actual steps one goes through. This may involve how several major parts of your own product work together or it may involve how your product interacts with other commercial products and is related to interoperability. Part of the problem with this is training users to identify and use "generic" user profiles rather than "specific" ones. We tried to identify and show examples of this earlier, i.e., driving a rental car in general versus driving a rental car around San Francisco.

5.5.2 Fundamental Tests (Product Verification Testing)

In addition to the functional tests based on functional behavior, as defined above, there are other tests fundamental to all software. Certain of these are difficult, if not impossible, to measure accurately. Five of these fundamental tests are described next.

Usability How easy is it for the user to figure out what to do without recourse to a training course or to a user's manual? This usability should be based on building user interfaces that have patterns already familiar to the typical user. The user then learns to use the software through pattern matching and paradigm shifts, exactly as they do in mastering any new product.

Installability How easy is it for a novice to install the software correctly and easily without recourse to an expert? Have you provided automated tools?

Reliability Given the same inputs (and/or files), does the system perform in exactly the same way each time? Do reasonable changes in various parameters still provide the same (expected) outputs? Ultimately, this is based on the user profiles we have been describing. Reliability tests are conducted, according to mathematical models of software reliability, to ensure that the system can be used/operated for periods of time before a fault is detected. Reliability is the probability of some function of the system failing within a specified time (Musa, Ionnino, Okumuto, 1987). Reliability testing is monitoring the mean time between failures. Reliability and consistency testing go hand in hand where the system behavior (inputs, outputs, response time) is measured for consistency. We have discussed various concepts related to this with respect to our new paradigm and the impact of well-tested user profiles on mean time to failure.

Performance Performance tests are conducted to ensure that the system response time meets user expectations and does not exceed the specified performance criteria under heavy stress or volume. During these tests, response time and the transaction rate are measured. The purpose of performance tests is to test-run the performance of various functions of the software within a specified hardware configuration. The performance tests can couple this test with stress testing. Questions to ask when doing performance tests are: Do standard files, structures, and activities perform exactly as warranted? When the software system loads approach the upper limits guaranteed by your company, does the performance remain at reasonable levels, or does it degrade? In what ways is it possible—during system testing—to force the program(s) to degrade in their performance?

Serviceability   When the user's software system crashes, is it possible for a support person manning the phone line to acquire enough information to enable the maintenance organization to assess the error and fix it without additional information or the need to send a programmer on site?

5.5.3 Other Tests (Measures)

These tests are more or less important—depending on the nature of the software being built and tested.

Efficiency   Does the system require a minimum amount of disk and/or memory space for the amount of and/or type of functions it is to perform? Is it reasonable as compared to other products, especially those of competitors?

Integrity   Does the software system always provide the same answers when it is provided with the same data from whatever source and in whatever format?

Dependency   Does the software system run independent of its environment, or is it dependent on either certain types and/or speeds of software, disk size, memory sizes, etc. Does it require special versions of other software systems to run effectively? To what degree has the software been made independent of such hardware/software environments? This also ties into our marketing-oriented filters found in the Appendix and in Chapter 2.

Consistency   Does the software system always behave in the same way regardless of its operating environment?

State/Transition Testing (Finite State Machines)   When concurrence requirements cause the software system either to change its state, or suspend its state, restarting when the competing system finishes, does it restart at the correct point with the correct data? A software development methodology called the "box" method makes use of the leveling of finite state machines (FSMs) into machines which perform any of the three canonical forms of structured programming. Within each of the control structures another FSM is created and the process repeated until the appropriate "lowest" level has been reached. This approach has been propounded by Harlan Mills and his associates (see Mills, 1986). (Note that for transaction processing, state/transition modeling is both needlessly complex and has a negative impact on the software. A simple "transaction processor" works better—especially for menus and pull-down menus found in DOS, Mac, and Windows environments.) Behind many of these is software which automatically implements this functionality, or at least makes it easy to interface with it.

Interrupt Handler Testing   Often interrupt handlers can be modeled using state/transition models. Under some conditions, it is appropriate to merely place them above the rest of the software systems where concurrence exists and allow the interrupt handlers to simply "interrupt" the appropriate concurrent system and sequentially (or using some other model) allow each to have its turn. Often, these can be defined in terms of, or as a part of, executive modules.

Memory Leak Testing   As systems become complex, more and more of the functions of an operating system need to be incorporated into application software. Often this means that, in order to gain efficiency—and keep control over the operations of the software system—it is necessary to perform some of the functions of the operating system such as memory allocation. This often leads to "memory leaks," where the system does not release all of the memory it has acquired. Whenever the memory allocation function of the operating system has been circumvented, it must be tested under as many conditions as possible to see that under all conditions, the entire memory space has been released. The controversy here is whether it is easy to find memory leaks because of the limited interfaces and functions involved with the memory allocation based on deterministic conditions, or whether it is difficult, in some instances because of an exceedingly large number of concurrent or interdependent conditions giving rise to rare instances of memory leaks which appear to be stochastic in nature. Automated tools exist to make memory leak testing relatively easy and effective.

Race Condition Testing   Race conditions can occur at many places in a software system. Most of them can be avoided just through effective programming practices. Global variables are a pernicious violation of good programming practice; variables should be passed explicitly among the modules that absolutely need them. If they are passed as a part of a data structure to modules where they are not needed, informational strength modules should be used to eliminate their presence and their effect. When race conditions come about from two concurrent processes needing a global or "explicitly passed" variable at the same instant, one should probably design the system so that such a problem will not occur. The same problem can occur, however, when two or more concurrent programs are accessing the same database record. Database technology now exists to make it easier to solve these problems.

When only a single variable is involved, such problems should be easy to avoid by simply making each variable available as a single variable to the module requiring it. When it is part of a larger data structure—and the entire data structure is not needed—it should be accessed through an informational strength module.

Such problems are unavoidable when the variables are part of a large data file where a transaction—or series of transactions—are necessary and multiple access becomes necessary. Usually eliminating the race condition either degrades performance for the other system—or it creates "deadlocking." Its impact can be minimized but not always easily solved.

Another occurrence of a race condition can be when two event-driven systems operate concurrently and reach a state where they need the same device or resource. The ideal solution is a design issue. You merely insert an executive module above the two independent systems and let it monitor their states. It then knows which system to interrupt under what conditions or what the protocol is for allowing access to the resource. Thus, the two independent systems are truly independent.

Maintainability   Maintainability is impossible to test using any traditional testing methods. The only way to do this is through use of a filter. The main method of creating maintainability is through the process of designing out of the system both intermodule and intramodule dependencies. These are not always easy to spot, but as more and more experience is gained—especially in recognizing them and their impact—while fixing errors in existing software, you become more proficient. Once you are accustomed to looking for them, it is possible to eliminate almost all of them through effective design—at the module level and at the system level. As we have said, effective design in this area eliminates the need for regression testing.

Testability   Testability is related to two concepts. The first is whether the specification is written in a form for which it is possible to create a test case. This will be discussed in detail in Chapter 11. The other approach is related to the ability to pattern match the software as part of a code or system audit. If you need to actually run test cases, the design that makes the software maintainable also makes the software testable. For example, inside the code of a module, it is possible to eliminate—or at least minimize—the effects of software dependencies. When this is done, a combination of segment and branch coverage is equivalent to "path" coverage. This means a minimum amount of testing can provide the same coverage as complete coverage provided you have effectively eliminated the dependencies. At the system level, a great many dependencies can be eliminated simply by effective design along with the ability to identify and "design out" other dependencies wherever they occur. When it is impossible to completely eliminate them, it is possible to minimize their impact to only a few modules or subsystems.

Interoperability   As with other "abilities" to be tested, interoperability can be designed into a software system. It involves defining the points at which an external product is to interface with the existing system and then simulate the interface. You effectively put a stub at that point and then write the program around it. This is done at each point a module or product coming from another company is to interface with the existing system. If one module is to interface at many points, one simply creates an informational strength module to capture the code from the outside module at each point it is needed in the existing software. When the code finally becomes available, it only needs to be changed in that one module. Some interfaces are very difficult to achieve, mainly because they are in major products where the authors had no intention of their ever running with anything else. Many times, in these cases, they are the "big guys" and you are the "little guys," and they are unlikely to make major changes in their product interface even if it means more sales. Almost always, if you work to make both products' interfaces independent of each other, a solution is possible—either through use of one or more massage modules or informational strength modules.

As the software industry moves into the OLE and OpenDoc environments, interoperability takes on new meaning. As with Application Program Interfaces (APIs) a standard interface is provided to software developers. In the OpenDoc environment, a "container app" is provided to which can be attached multiple software systems or packages provided by other vendors.

Stress (or Load) Testing   Stress tests subject the program to high input conditions or loads that exceed expected volume during the peak time of the operation of the system. The objective of the test is to determine the system behavior during these peak times. Heavy stress occurs when a program receives a large amount of data over a short period of time. Stress testing executes a system in a manner that demands an abnormally large quantity of resources and it is applicable to programs that operate under varying loads. When one of the authors was at Novell, we needed to "certify" that our new software would run 1,000 clients from one server without degrading. When we tested, we needed to make sure that there was a "margin for safety" in the product, i.e., that it would run more than the required number without degrading.

Migration   This is the ability to move easily from an earlier version of your product to the current version—or from a competitor's product to the current version of your product. This is important to maintain "marketability" as you move from version to subsequent version. This is an important part of our marketing requirements document and filter at Digital Technology International.

Volume Tests   These tests subject the program to a high volume of data. The purpose of these tests is to determine how many transactions can be supported by the system. The functions are executed at a high volume and slowly additional functions are put through to exhaust the system, thereby determining the break point. The volume and stress tests check the behavior of the system at the peak hours or high loads. Examples of volume tests are feeding a computer an absurdly large source program to compile or fill an operating system's job queue to full capacity and inputting thousands of customer names and addresses in an accounts payable system. It can also involve adding more and more users to an interactive system until it finally degrades or crashes.

Functional Tests   Functional tests are conducted to ensure the system behaves according to the functional requirements and that the acceptance criteria of the users will be met. Analyze the business requirements document to derive a set of test cases. The key is to compare the system functions to their original objectives, ensuring that all functions outlined in the requirements document are present in the system and work as intended. This includes

- designing a test that generates ten interruptions per second, when the normal rate is one or two seconds
- increasing input data rate by a large rate to determine how input functions will respond
- executing test cases requiring maximum memory or maximum space

Security Tests   Security tests are performed to ensure the robustness of the system. Security tests cases are designed to determine how easy it would be for an unauthorized user to access confidential data from a system. They are conducted to break the program's security checks. One way to test the robustness of the security is to hire a computer "hacker" to subvert the security checks of the system. Security tests attempt to verify that protection mechanisms built into the system will protect it from improper penetration.

Usually, it is impossible to prove that a system is completely secure. No matter what you do to make it secure, intruders can usually find their way around it; you just do not know how they are going to do it. That is the major problem with security testing. If *you* can break into it, that proves you were very naive in how you built it; if you cannot, someone else probably still can.

Conduct security tests by

- playing the role of an individual who wants to enter the system by acquiring the password(s) by external means.
- attacking the system with custom software designed to break down any constructed defenses.
- purposely causing system errors, hoping to penetrate during recovery.
- introducing a "virus" to clobber all the data/programs.

Recovery Test   It is important to ensure the system recovers from programming errors, hardware failures, abnormal conditions, or simply loss of electricity. Recovery testing forces the software to fail in a variety of ways and verifies that recovery is properly performed. One way to determine a recovery test is to inject programming errors into the system to determine if the system can recover when these errors occur. The attempt is made to diagnose the extent of damage the error may have caused. If there is a partial shutdown of the system due to failure of the electricity, for example, the system should technically be returned to the prior state. Depending on the risk of a failure, in some cases a system failure must be correctable within a specified period of time or severe financial damage can occur.

Documentation Test   These tests are conducted to test the accuracy of the document, to ensure the contents of the system are listed in the document in a manner the user can understand, and no features are missing. For example, if there are six features in the system, all these should be described in the documentation. The test cases are designed to test the reliability of the document contents and to improve the clarity so there is no confusion when the user reads it.

5.5.4 Testing/Maintenance Problems

Testing and maintenance problems tend most often to be based on three conditions.

Programmer Assumptions   These occur when a specification is incomplete and programmers do not notice it. They simply proceed as though the solution were completely straightforward and obvious (and least to them). This can be as simple as which file ends first in a file maintenance operation, whether all transactions processed on a same day are considered the same transaction or different ones, etc. Each of these is made without documentation and therefore is not tested because no one is aware such a decision (assumption) has been made. The authors know of many notable examples of this with major service companies, but we will not go beyond what we have said above.

Segment and Data Dependencies (Intramodule Dependencies)   These dependencies are not as serious as intermodule dependencies (mentioned next) since they impact less code. But when a change is made to a module, they can require thousands of test cases, rather than hundreds. Indeed, if segment/data dependencies are limited to only one leg of an IF THEN ELSE, or a CASE statement, only two or three test cases may be necessary. When maintenance programmers are looking at 100,000 lines of code to find an error, being able to look only at one small piece of a module/program makes their job much easier. Many of those who teach programming classes are not aware of these issues and therefore do not see why FOR loops and other constructs should be eliminated, especially in "C." They tend to think in terms of only 100 to 200 lines of code. Maintenance programmers rarely have that luxury.

Intermodule Dependencies   Intermodule dependencies, by their very nature, are very insidious to maintenance programmers—let alone test engineers. There are many ways such dependencies show up. Global data structures/ elements are among the worst. No matter how they are restricted, their effects ripple through every module that accesses them. They create dependencies that are often impossible to unravel.

Other types of dependencies depend on entire data structures being passed among modules, when only one or two variables contained in the data structure are actually needed. When any of the unnecessary variables (such as zip code, date, field size for some variable) change, even though their change should affect only two or three modules, *all* the modules need to be changed.

Still another sort of change is not where data change, but rather where the state of the system changes because of something that occurs in one part of the system and it affects something in another seemingly "unrelated" part of the system. It usually affects two or three modules many modules' distance apart and is, therefore, hard to document, let alone to fix. The best solution is to package the dependency at one place. And when one part of the system changes state, the others—packaged in the same place—also know about it and can change. But all these dependencies require a lot of effort to seek and identify them during the design review filter at the software design level.

5.5.5 The Credibility of Software Testing

Since it is impossible to look at "lines of code" or other similar measures of productivity in relation to testing activities, the credibility of software testing tends to rest on the following measures. Did someone not find errors because there were none there? Or were they lazy or ineffective? At least these measures give some semblance of credibility:

- Number of test cases
- Number of errors detected
- Severity of errors found
- Amount of time spent
- Amount of time spent per test case
- Testing framework and strategies
- War stories
- Drops in error rates
- Amount—and type—of coverage

With our new paradigm, these do not have much meaning at the unit level, but they do at the system level. You must show that you used this testing activity, which if done right is a nontrivial activity requiring a lot of corporate resources (including time), but that it is an effective activity providing enormous return on investment to your company.

5.5.6 A Comment on Beta Testing

Beta testing is normally used as an ad hoc approach where the software is given to key users, who then use the product in a "production environment" and report any errors they find to the software company. In our mind, this is extremely nonproductive. The best approach to beta testing is to define it in terms of tests that cannot be performed in the developer's environment due to lack of equipment, lack of software, or lack of personnel. For example, when one of the authors was at Novell, we needed to test how our LAN software ran across a gateway to a mainframe. It was not practical for us to purchase one just to test our software, but it was easy for us to have one of our users provide us with the

test environment. The same thing was true with the 1,000 clients that needed to run off one server. In a beta testing environment, the software company should provide automated test cases and testing criteria to the user performing the beta testing and require that those tests be performed as a part of the beta testing agreement.

5.5.7 A Comment on Regression Testing

Regression testing has now become a buzzword in the industry—just as beta test has become a buzzword. Often, people say they are doing it when they do not even understand what it is. Many people feel that if they have "automated" their test suites, they are doing an adequate job of regression testing. One of the phenomena one of the authors observed when working with maintenance programmers in IBM was that some tests in the regression test suite were extremely sensitive to errors while others would not find any, even when they executed the code in which an error occurred. We did some studies, under contract with IBM at Brigham Young University, in an attempt to find ways of identifying and labeling effective regression test cases. It was almost impossible to accomplish, though we did find that the regression test cases needed to be kept and referenced in a database by the part of the code executed.

Many times, a regression test is merely a production run against the changed code, using last month's data. When you apply the 80/20 rule, you see that the majority of test cases are merely testing the same code over and over again with different data. This is a naive, ineffective approach to regression testing.

What becomes obvious now is that effective regression tests are those which uncover dependencies. As such, the test cases can be designed and implemented provided you can recognize the dependency. But if you can identify it, why not simply design it out of the system and save later maintenance programmers the problems of attempting to fix the dependency-related problem—after analyzing its ripple effect.

Regression tests are used to retest the system after functional improvements or fixes are made to the product. The regression test confirms that the fix to resolve the original problem has not created any new problems. You perform regression tests by reexecuting some subset of the program's test cases. It is important to test the function directly affected by the change or fix, and also other functions that may have been indirectly affected. Document all tests you perform. Fixes to the code can often break existing test cases and test suites, especially automated test suites.

Changes and error corrections tend to be more error-prone than the original code in the program; therefore special attention should be given to them before entering the regression test phase. In terms of our new paradigm, if the software architecture is high quality, it is possible to design in these changes through a re-architecting of the system or subsystem. This can actually make the system better than it was originally. In the traditional paradigm, this is rarely the case.

Regression tests can be accomplished by adhering to the following steps:

1. Plan the general approach, obtain resources, estimate schedule, identify the test cases needed to retest the system, and add more cases as required.
2. Determine the completeness of the fix by retesting the system's functions where the original problem was encountered.
3. After successful completion, run additional test cases to ensure that no new problems arises. Document all results.
4. If any new problems are encountered, complete a problem report and send it to the development team members for the fix.
5. If no new problems are encountered, consider the test successful.

5.5.8 Acceptance Tests

The purpose of acceptance tests is to confirm that the system is developed according to the user requirements and it is ready for operational use. Normally, it is part of a formal handoff or release process. During an acceptance test, end-users or customers of the system compare the system to its requirements. Remember user involvement plays a major role in the success of the acceptance testing. The best way to devise an acceptance test is to show that the program meets the initial requirements. If the product delivery process is used, the marketing requirements document and the product specification can be tied to the handoff or acceptance test and it is fairly straightforward. This is true whether the marketing requirements document is generated from a marketing analysis, a contract based on a request for proposal, or simply an internal "contract" for an MIS product or other such product.

This test exists as a final stage of confidence building for the users and as a protection against overly risky implementation. There may be a few surprises but there should be no major discrepancies discovered during acceptance testing. Acceptance testing ends when the customer/end users feel confident that the system is ready to be used. The procedures for effective acceptance tests are:

1. Plan the acceptance test:
   (a) Plan the general approach; obtain resources, and estimate schedule. Identify the procedures to report any discrepancies discovered during testing.
   (b) Develop test cases based on the features of the system so each major function and performance requirement can be tested.
   (c) Test how the system handles invalid input; verify the system's error messages.
2. Measure the acceptance test:
   (a) Execute the test procedures.
   (b) Evaluate test results.
   (c) Check for discrepancies.
   (d) Accept or reject the system based on the acceptance test criteria established in the beginning of the project.

5.6 CONCLUSIONS

One constant question we have faced in our classes, seminars, and conferences is: What are the criteria for deciding that "testing is complete"? In our less-than-ideal world, we would like to say that testing is complete when you have developed and executed test cases for every function of the system you are testing and when all the problems that had been identified are fixed. However, in today's competitive world, such a strategy would increase the time to market the product, thus affecting the financial bottom line and would be ruled as being impractical. We suggest you conduct thorough risk analysis of what to test and what not to test. Based on the analysis, make a determination of when you will consider the testing complete. Usually, you consider it "complete" when the risk of missing the marketing window is greater than the risk of shipping with so many bugs that the customers will lose confidence in the product. This is a particularly awful corner to paint yourself into. Often, the facts that the software was never adequately specified, architected from a quality standpoint, or managed correctly, you are stuck with a late schedule, which can only make things worse. (We are aware of very few software projects that actually finish ahead of schedule and allow enough time for testing.) And you are only talking about errors, not quality. In other environments such as building internal products, your criteria may be different, but they will still be built around some evaluation of risk. Refer to Section 11.3, Risk Issues in Software Quality Assurance.

Many statisticians have attempted to provide mathematical models and statistical estimates for determining when you are finished testing. One of the authors repeatedly told his students: "You never finish testing; you quit testing." With the new paradigm, this is no longer true. If you follow our product delivery process, when all the code has passed through the appropriate filters or code audits, then that part is through; when the system has passed all the automated test scripts, then that part is through; when all the behavior criteria specified in the product description/positioning document have been met and measured, then that part is through; when all the appropriate user profiles have been run, then that part is through. When all these criteria have been met, then the product is ready to enter the release process. The reason this works is because everything has passed through filters, 18 or more. If you relate this to the "picture" of our delivery process in Chapter 1 or with the list of frontend filters in the Appendix, the value of this approach should be obvious. Further, the risk is based on "schedule," which is fairly easy to manage, rather than "errors getting through," which is almost impossible to manage, from the traditional software development/testing point-of-view.

Remember the analogy of pouring coffee through a filter rather than picking out the grounds. When you pick out the grounds, you can never be sure you are through; when you filter the coffee, you are through as soon as all the coffee has passed through the filter. That is what we are trying to say in this conclusion and throughout the book. When you do not use filters but rely on traditional testing, as explained in this chapter, then the first paragraph of this conclusion indicates what you are stuck with having to do. Everything is based on risk assessment, which is almost impossible to accomplish effectively and with confidence.

As we said at the beginning of this chapter, we do not have the space to include a complete discussion of software testing. On the other hand, we tried to provide you with a unique view of some parts of software testing which might not appear in a typical test and reference book. Most testing references tend to focus on test strategies related to the functionality of the software. We hope that now you will see that there are major issues related to software behavior as well.

Test Planning

*I*n earlier chapters, we have tried to straddle the fence between traditional software testing and the new product development process. In this chapter, we are concentrating on the traditional approach, knowing that is the most likely place for you to begin your test planning.

6.1 BENEFITS OF A TEST PLAN

It is difficult to manage the testing of a large system, considering the numerous test cases, problem reporting, and problem fixes. Just as you must plan and manage a project by estimating resources, schedule, cost, and so forth, you must plan the testing of a software product. The planning activities let you do strategic thinking on what types of tests should be executed within the constraints of time and budget. During the preparation of the test plan, as each test scenario is planned, you must estimate the time it would take to test the system. In many companies, the data of previous completed projects are not kept and there is no record of "lessons learned," thus making estimation difficult.

The mistake most testers make is not planning the test schedule upfront. They fail to allocate adequate time to test the product and conduct regression testing. Often, even if the entire project schedule slips, the end date still remains the same. Since the test phase is the last step before the product goes out, the allocated test time is usually reduced; thereby the quality of the software is sacrificed. If one of the test dependencies identified upfront in the planning stage is receiving the code on time for testing, the management personnel as well as the project team members will realize immediately that if the code does not arrive in testing at the required time frame, the entire project schedule will slip.

The test plan acts as a service level agreement between the test department and other significantly impacted departments. The testing efficiency can be monitored and improved by developing a thorough test plan. This plan also identifies the test deliverables, functions to be tested, and risks. One of the most important advantages of a test plan is that it communicates to the audience

- the methodology which will be used to test the product
- the resources:
  - hardware
  - software
  - manpower
- the schedule during which tests will be accomplished
- the process used to manage the testing project

This information helps create a common understanding regarding the testing of the product. The test plan serves as a quality control document for test activities, thus letting the project team monitor costs, time delays and requirement changes.

6.1.1 Techniques

Before writing the test plan, you should obtain the names of all test analysts, select the automated test tools you will use for the project, and decide on the environment required to conduct the testing. In addition, you should obtain sign-offs on service-level agreements with other departments that may be involved with your testing activities. When developing a test plan, ensure that it is kept simple and complete, current, and accessible. The test plan should be frequently routed to the appropriate people for feedback and sign-offs. Depending on the organizational structure of your company, the test plan can be either written by the test leader, test coordinator, or test manager.

6.1.2 Steps to Perform

Except for minor enhancements to an existing system, ensure that all major releases have a test plan. The following steps will give you guidance in developing a test plan.

1. Depending on the features of the system, from the tests listed in Section 5.5 for system testing, determine which tests you need to perform.
2. Once you have identified the types of tests needed to test the system, plan how each of these tests will be performed. Develop test cases.
3. Use the Test Plan template in the Appendix to guide you into developing your test plan. You may also want to refer to the test plan sample.
4. When the contents of the test plan are finalized, conduct a review for completeness of the test plan.
5. Incorporate the feedback from the review in the test plan.
6. Get approvals on the contents of the test plan from managers of all the departments that will be impacted by this new product, for example, managers of Development, Customer Support, Marketing, Operations, Integrated Technology, Product Assurance, Quality, and User Management.

7. Follow the test plan to ensure that everyone on the test team uses the process outlined in the test plan and if there are any exceptions to this, the deviations are logged as "addenda" to the test plan. For consistency, these addenda should be approved by the same group of individuals who approved the original test plan.

6.2 DEVELOPING THE SUCCESSFUL TEST PLAN

As mentioned before, the test plan is crucial for the management of the test process. The contents of a test plan are important since the test plan is a technical document and requires technical discipline. In addition to being a road map for testing, the plan is a contract among participants to perform said activities within a specified time frame. A well thought-out plan will save hours of frustration at the end of the test cycle, reduce risks, and provide a tool for management reporting.

Ideally, all the participants for the project should contribute to the test plan document through reviews and discussion. All participants will feel committed to the plan since they helped to create it and this fosters a high degree of dedication among participants to follow what is being said in the test plan. If participants accept responsibilities and later do not fulfill them, the test plan provides evidence of the initial agreement. It provides criteria for measurement, deadlines for test deliverables, and describes procedures for documenting and resolving problems.

A test plan table of contents lists the main topics and should be updated as new techniques and tools are introduced or functions of the application are changed. Depending on the size of the system, a separate test plan for unit testing, system testing and acceptance testing should be developed. The following are the typical contents of a test plan.

Introduction   The introduction gives a brief description of the system being tested so anyone reading the test plan would get an overview of the features.

Scope   The scope describes at a high level what will be tested and what will not be tested in order to avoid ambiguity and identifies what is going to be addressed by the testers.

Test Plan Strategy   The test plan strategy outlines the objectives for developing the test plan and establishes the procedures for conducting the tests. For example, "The objective of this test plan is to ensure there is a uniform understanding among anyone who reads the test plan, regarding the test methodology as well as the number of resources, schedules, etc." The strategy should also identify all the tests that will be performed to check the robustness of the product. A brief description of each test should be given so there is common understanding of the test itself and how a specific test will be conducted.

Test Environment   The test environment section lists the hardware and software configurations required to perform tests. It determines the type of help required from other departments to support the environment tests.

Schedule   The overall test schedule is identified in the project plan indicating the start date and end date of test activities. However, the detailed schedule of testing should be developed during test planning process, identifying the start and end dates for

- development of the test plan
- designing test cases
- executing test cases
- problem reporting
- developing the test summary report

Control Procedures   Since the test plan is the primary document and means of giving control to the project, it should serve as a vehicle for raising participants' consciousness regarding the project by raising issues early and documenting them. This section should have detailed instructions for problem reporting. You must establish and publish a procedure for communicating defects to the development group in which you indicate

- whether an automated on-line system will be used to record and report problems
- whether the problem fixes will be accepted daily or once a week
- how the problems should be prioritized, for example 1, 2, or 3. The number circled identifies the severity level of the incident as determined by the testing analyst. Priority 1, being the highest severity level, may be classified as a missing function, a function not working, or a defect which may impact implementation. Priority 2 may be a function not working but a work-around exists and Priority 3 may be minor cosmetic errors or spelling mistakes.

Control Activities   The control activities section indicates when walkthroughs or reviews will be conducted and list the individuals who would participate in these activities.

Functions to Be Tested   This section lists all the functions to be tested.

Functions Not to Be Tested   This section lists all functions not to be tested, along with the reason for not testing, for example, "low risk," "code reused and previously tested with 100% satisfaction."

Risks and Assumptions   This section lists assumptions taken into consideration when developing the test schedule, such as

- Unit testing will be done prior to receiving code for system testing.
- All testing personnel will have the knowledge of the product and will be experienced testers.
- The computers will be available during all work hours.

Deliverable The deliverable section lists what will be delivered at the end of test phase, such as,

- Test plan
- Test cases
- Test incident report
- Test summary report

Test Tools This section identifies all test tools you plan to use during testing, whether they are in-house or need to be purchased. For example, test coverage analyzers might be used to provide information on the thoroughness of one or more test runs of the program. At the end of the analysis process, the analyzer produces a visual listing of program with all unexecuted code flagged.

Approvals This section ensures that the plan is reviewed and approved by the individuals who will either be affected by it, or on whom you are dependent to either receive code or other support in order to conduct testing.

Exit Criteria This section identifies the exit criteria for the test phase. Some of the examples of the exit criteria:

No priority-one open problems.

All functions identified in the requirement document are present and working.

No more than three priority-two problems open.

6.3 TEST PLAN SAMPLE

This section presents a sample test plan document.

TEST PLAN FOR THE KENYA LIMITED COMPANY PAYROLL SYSTEM

TABLE OF CONTENTS

NOTE: None of the addenda mentioned in the test plan are attached with this sample test plan. In reality, all addenda should be attached.

1.0 INTRODUCTION

The Kenya Limited Company is the client for this project. They currently process their payroll on a Sperry 9200 mainframe. They plan to downsize the application to run on their PC/LAN. The current payroll system is quite complex. It does the following:

- handles the update/addition/deletion of employee information
- allows payroll clerks to enter employee timekeeping information for each two-week pay circle
- allows for corrections and adjustments of past payroll processing
- provides various payroll reports and handles the issuance of the payroll checks

Kenya Limited Company plans to migrate the application to a PC/LAN-based system in stages. Our company has contracted to develop the first stage. Kenya Limited Company will decide whether to continue with downsizing this application after receiving and evaluating our system.

1.1 Test Plan Objectives

The Master Plan for Payroll System supports the following objectives:

- Define the activities required to prepare for and conduct both manual and automated System Integration, Batch and Regression testing.
- Communicate to all responsible parties the tasks which they are responsible for.
- Define various deliverable and responsible parties.
- To catch problems early in the development cycle. If corrections are made early in the development cycle, project costs will be kept down and the customer will receive a timely product of quality.
- Provide a structure for testing within the system development life cycle. This will keep the effort focused and on schedule.
- Define responsibilities within the testing framework. This plan holds participants accountable for agreed-upon responsibilities.
- Coordinate test efforts and provide overall direction for all testing activity. This will prevent duplication of efforts and provide sharing of test data throughout phases of testing.

2.0 SCOPE

2.1 Payroll Data Entry

We are to develop a system to allow payroll clerks to enter the time-keeping information for each pay cycle. The system should allow the payroll clerks to enter data from IBM/PC compatible workstations that are modes of Kenya Limited Company's PC/LAN.

2.2 Reports

The system is to provide a few reports. However, the large majority of reports and check issuance will continue to be processed on the Sperry mainframe.

2.3 Sperry Interface

Our application is dependent on an interface between the Sperry mainframe and the PC/LAN. We will need to use information on the Sperry and provide payroll data to it. The Company already has an interface in place. Kenya Limited will take care of downloading information needed by our application. The application must provide a user-friendly means of creating the pay period payroll file and uploading it to the Sperry System.

3.0 TESTING STRATEGY

The testing strategy will include the Unit, System, Integration, Performance and Stress, Batch, User Acceptance, Batch and Automated tests. A fundamental guideline of this strategy is to ensure that the developers conduct only the Unit Testing. While conducting testing, it is vital to have a full test coverage where each function is tested to ensure that it works according to the original specifications and also to ensure that all the functions indicated in the requirement document of the Payroll system. The goal is to produce a high quality, user-friendly product.

Detailed step-by-step test cases with expected results will be developed. The purpose of the test cases is to identify all the functions of the system that will be tested and the process that will be followed. The test cases will be developed from the Requirements Document and a Requirements Validation Matrix will be prepared. The test cases for the Acceptance Tests will be developed by the users/customers.

3.1 Unit Testing

Definition: Unit Test consists of testing individual programs or subroutines as they are written instead of testing the entire system after it has been written. The testing of smaller building blocks is done first and then these blocks are combined and tested. Unit Test means testing each function independently to verify correct processing in a stand-alone environment.

Participants: Developers, Test Team, Marketing personnel.

Methodology:

(a) Initial Unit Test will be conducted by the developers.

(b) As the completed modules are received from the Development Department, the Test Team will start the Unit Test on these modules. The members of the Test Team will be responsible for creating tests and executing the tests.

(c) Testing Tools Services will be responsible for setting up the "testing tool" [*insert name of the tool here*] and assist in capturing test cases. [*Insert the name of the tool here*] will be used in a "Capture-Play" mode to provide a trail to reproduce defects.

(d) Testing Tool Services will supply examples of the Unit Test matrix to ensure that developers conduct positive and negative tests for all code modules and associated functionality.

3.2 System and Integration Testing

System Test: A System Test is a series of different tests whose primary purpose is to fully exercise the system to uncover its limitations and measure its full capabilities. The objective of the System Test is to test the integrated system to verify that it meets specified requirements.

Integration Test: An Integration Test is an orderly progression of testing in which software and/or hardware elements are combined and tested until the entire system has been integrated. The purpose is to measure the correctness of each program unit's behavior once the program has been combined with other programs.

Participants: Test Team, Testing Tool Services

Methodology:

(a) Team Leaders will be responsible for developing test cases. The test cases created by the Team Leaders will serve only as a foundation for testing. Members from the Payroll Department are expected to lend their expertise (specially in the FICA and state taxes areas) by locating and identifying problems that may not necessarily be documented in the form of a test case.

(b) The Test Team and Payroll Department will be responsible for identifying data requirements, functions, and accounts to be included in the testing region. They will also be responsible for preparing the testing region.

(c) The Test Team will be responsible for executing test cases and assigning one person to maintain the automated testing environment, become familiar with automated test tool and automated testing techniques, and run the Regression Test for the entire testing team.

(d) Test Tool Services will be responsible for setting up the test lab and building the infrastructure to support Payroll testing.

3.3   Performance and Stress Testing

Performance Testing: To test the system to determine if the performance meets the requirements as stated in the User Requirements Document dated xx/xx/xx.

Stress Testing: Stress testing involves subjecting the program to heavy loads or stresses. A heavy stress is a peak volume of data encountered over a short span of time. Stress testing executes a system in a manner that demands resources in abnormal quantity. Stress testing is applicable to programs that operate under varying loads.

Participants: Test Team, Payroll Department members, and Test Tool Services

Methodology:

(a) Test Tool Services will be responsible for using the automated test tool to run the test cases and get the performance/stress information. They will record and evaluate the results and present it to the Team Leader and Test Team.

(b) The Test Team will be responsible for testing the network.

(c) Testing Coordinator will review the results, get assistance from developers to resolve issues, and the Team Leaders will create additional test cases needed to test any changes.

3.4 User Acceptance Testing

Definition: The purpose of the Acceptance Test is to confirm the system is ready for operational use. During the Acceptance Test, end users (customers) of the system compare the system to its requirements.

Participants: Test Team, Payroll Department members, Test Tool Services

Methodology:

(a) Test Team will be responsible for changing previously developed test cases slightly to conduct the user acceptance testing.

(b) The developers will be responsible to assist the Test Team in resolving any outstanding problems or issues.

(c) Test Tool Services will assist in the use of the automated test tool to execute the user acceptance test cases.

(d) Payroll Team members will assist with the development of any new test cases.

(e) Criteria for completion of the Acceptance Test include general concurrence between users and developers that the minimum level of testing has been accomplished; adequate resolution of outstanding problem reports is achieved; and assurance that the product meets the original business objectives.

3.5 Automated Regression Testing

Definition: Regression testing is the selective retesting of a system or a component to verify the modifications have not caused unintended effects and that the system or component still works as specified.

Participants: Test Team

Methodology:

(a) Test Tool Services will be responsible for setting up a workstation-based testing lab to support automated regression testing.

(b) Product Manager/Testing Coordinator will be responsible for assigning one member of the test team to become their automated testing specialist and maintain Regression Test environment.

(c) Team Leaders will be responsible for providing complete testing conditions and test cases.

4.0 ENVIRONMENT REQUIREMENTS

4.1 Mainframe

- Block of sign-on IDs for all testers via Security Administration
- Complete special request for registered reps
- Databases
- CICS regions
- Etc....

4.2 Workstation

- Configurations
- Software
- LAN requirements
- Etc....

5.0 TEST SCHEDULE

Requirements Testing	Begin	End
Unit Testing	10•07•YY	10•11•YY
System and Integration Testing	11•25•YY	11•29•YY
Acceptance Testing	12•09•YY	12•20•YY
User Sign-off	01•20•YY	01•23•YY

6.0 CONTROL PROCEDURES

6.1 Reviews

Reviews will be conducted at the end of each phase for sign-off, i.e., Requirements Review, Design Review, Code Review, Test Plan Review and Final Test Review. The project team and user participants will be informed of the review session two weeks prior to the meeting. Any related document will be given to the participants at this time so they will be prepared to give their feedback during the review session. A few days prior to the session, the project team will be requested to submit their expectations, concerns, and criteria for the success of the review. The project leader is responsible for preparing written reports of the reviews.

6.2 "Kickoff" Meeting

To ensure that all testers and Team Leaders have a thorough understanding of the problem reporting process, the Testing Coordinator and Project Managers will conduct a Testing "kickoff" meeting. This meeting will officially begin the system testing effort for the Payroll Project. At that time, we will provide an overview of the new software, detailed procedures for "bug" reporting, roles, and responsibilities, etc. All the members of the entire Test Team are encouraged to attend the "kickoff" meeting.

6.3 Daily/Regular Payroll "Bug" meetings

Due to the complexity of the Payroll Project, regular testing meetings will be held in order to ensure ongoing communication and coordination. Tentatively, the software developer will provide weekly updates noting all fixes, based on "bugs" reported during the previous week(s), as well as an updated diskette reflecting new screens and functionality.

6.4 Change Requests

Once user testing begins, changes to the Payroll System are not encouraged; however functional changes are sometimes required, usually as a result of testing. Testers should discuss all proposed changes with Change Control Board (CCB). The CCB will determine the impact of the change and when it should be implemented.

6.5 Problem Reporting

1. When problems occur (i.e., actual result does not match expected result), all testers will be required to complete a problem report. Supporting documentation in the form of print screens, design specs, etc., must also be attached in order to resolve the problem

2. Each time a problem is discovered, the Tester will complete and submit problem report to the QA Manager who will determine if in fact the problem should be forwarded to the Test Coordinator ("features" of the system are sometimes mistaken for a problem).

QA Manager will also eliminate any duplicate problem reports before forwarding to the Test Coordinator.

3. The Test Coordinator will be responsible for loading all new and resubmitted "bugs" into the On-line Problem Reporting (OPR) system. The Test Coordinator will forward all reports to the software developer on a regular basis, and in turn update the OPR system based on feedback from the developer.

4. Unless a fix is of an emergency nature, all fixes will be sent once a week. Every Friday, the developer will send the fixes to the Test Coordinator who will ensure the installation and retesting of the fixes.

5. The Test Coordinator will officially close all reports when the retesting is completed satisfactorily.

6. At the end of the testing phase, a summary report will be prepared and routed to appropriate individuals. The summary report will contain the number of problems discovered, magnitude of the problems, and explanation of any existing, known cosmetic problems.

7.0   FUNCTIONS TO BE TESTED

The following is a list of all the functions that will be tested:

- Online Help
- Error Messages
- FICA Calculations
- State Tax Calculations
- Hardware
- Print
- Check Setup
- Gross Earning Report
- Net Earning Report
- Bonus Deductions
- Year-To-Date Earnings
- Net Calculations
- State Disability Insurance Calculation
- Health Insurance Deductions
- Vision Plan Deduction
- Dental Plan Deduction

- Tax Calculations (based on number of dependents)

- Sick Leave Accrual

- 401K Deductions

- Direct Deposit Message

8.0 RESOURCES AND RESPONSIBILITIES

The Test Team consists of Technical Leader, Project Manager, Testers, Test Coordinator, QA Manager, and Configuration Manager. The Technical Leader and the Project Manager are responsible for deciding when system tests will start and end. The Testers will be responsible for developing Test Cases and executing tests. Test Coordinator will be in charge of the progress of testing and will coordinate problem reports and related fixes between the Test Team and the developers. The coordinator will also be responsible for coordinating facilities, schedules, materials and tools for the testers. The QA Manager will be responsible for keeping the Test Plan current and obtaining appropriate sign-offs whenever any changes are made to the Test Plan.

Resources:

Business Sponsor:	Kamau Ormani	VP, Human Resources (H.R.)
Payroll Project Manager:	Pito Abdulla	Dir., H.R.
Product Manager:	Wygazo Petrs	Human Testing
Test Coordinator:	Julie Andrews	Human Resources
Team Leaders:	Hsali Jamo	Tech. Support
	Michale Lee	Tech. Support
	Frank Samuel	Cust. Service
Team Leaders:	Karen Brown	Cust. Service
	Michelle Yen	H.R.
	Danny Martinez	Cust. Service

Responsibilities:

Payroll Project Manager	Responsible for the overall success of the project; primary contact to Senior Management
Product Manager	Serves as primary contact/liaison with the software developer
Test Coordinator	Ensures the overall success of the alpha test effort; communicates all updates from the vendor and coordinates weekly testing
Team Leaders	Ensures that base-case test cases are developed for each module to be tested within his/her group; ensures that testing is adequately and accurately performed; attend regular "bug" meetings
Project Team	Subcommittee comprised of H.R. and Customer Support; team meets once a week to review project status and to resolve any issues impacting the progress of the project
Testing Team	All individuals who are participating in the testing effort

9.0   MAJOR DELIVERABLES

There is a major deliverable associated with each task related to a Test Plan. The person responsible for creating the deliverable is defined further in this section. A preliminary deliverable should be written by each of these individuals for his/her task and this should be reviewed and signed off by the other project team members. If a similar document exists for other projects, you can use it as a prototype.

Task	Responsibility	Dates
A. Pre/Testing		
1. Develop test cases	Team Leaders	9/21/XX– 1/28/XX
2. Identify data requirements, functions, and accounts to be included in the testing region; prepare testing region	Project Team	By 2/1/XX

Task	Responsibility	Dates
3. Obtain a block of sign-on IDs for all testers via Security Administration; complete special request for registered reps	Testing Coordinator	By 2/1/XX
4. Confirm/verify testers (specific individuals) from all impacted areas	Testing Coordinator	2/15/XX
B. Testing (both informal and formal testing)		
1. Execute tests and document all actual results	All Testing Teams	2/1/XX– 8/23/XX
2. Complete problem reports	All Testing Teams	2/1/93– 8/23/XX
3. Conduct regression tests	All Testing Teams	2/1/93– 8/23/XX
4. Conduct and attend daily/scheduled "bug" meeting	Testing Coordinator Team Leaders	As Scheduled
C. Post /Testing		
1. Participate in beta test, as needed	Team Leaders, etc.	5/28/XX– 7/26/XX
2. Prepare for product rollout	Project Team	8/15/XX– 9/19/XX

10.0 SUSPENSION/EXIT CRITERIA

At any time, bugs in the software may prohibit or seriously impact the test progress. Under these circumstances, QA Manager may choose to suspend testing. This prerogative will be exercised if any of the following conditions exist:

- source code contains one or more major category bugs that prevent or limit testing
- assigned test personnel are unavailable at times when needed by the Test Team
- hardware or software is not available at the times indicated in the schedule

11.0 Dependencies

11.1 Personnel Dependencies

The Test Team requires skills that must be available to analyze, develop, perform, validate, witness, and direct tests. Personnel with these skills must be made available to the Test Team.

11.2 Software Dependencies

- Source code and supporting documentation must be unit tested and provided within the schedule outlined in the overall project plan. Delay of the transfer of the code to the Test Team will affect the test schedule.
- Code has to be installed on all the test hardware.
- All appropriate tables with current employee data should be set up by the developer.

11.3 Hardware Dependencies

The Sperry 9200 mainframe as well as the PC/LAN environments will be available during normal work hours to conduct testing. Any downtime will affect the test schedule.

11.4 Personnel Dependencies

Application developers, project leader, testing services, and support technicians.

12.0 Risks

12.1 Schedule

The schedules for design and code phases are generally aggressive and could indirectly affect testing. A slip in the these phases may result in a subsequent slip in the testing phase and may push testing beyond the forecasted completion time.

12.2 Technical

The technical risk for the overall project is considered low. The existing payroll system performs nearly all the required functions requested in the new system. Since we are going to run parallel tests with the current payroll system, in the event of the new system failure, we can switch to the existing system.

12.3 Financial

Due to the financial risk, the new system will be run parallel for a number of weeks with the current system and the disbursement reports of the new system will be compared with the disbursement reports of the current system to ensure that there is no discrepancy. This parallel runs will be continued even after transition to the new system for as long as is deemed necessary.

12.4 Management

Management support is required so when the project falls behind, the previously allocated test time is not automatically reduced to make up the delay. The Test Team is staffed by members from organizations whose help is needed to bring together the mix of talent and expertise required of a good Test Team. Supporting organizations have other priorities and objectives that may compete with the goals of the Test Team in the area of talent and resources at this critical time. This success of this plan depends on the effort and talents of individuals who are called upon to assist in testing. Management can reduce this risk of delays by supporting the Test Team throughout the testing phase and assigning people to this project with the required skills to ensure success.

13.0 TOOLS

The following tools are needed:

- A Sperry mainframe comparator tool to compare files generated by running the parallel systems

- Automated test tool to conduct Regression Testing

14.0 DOCUMENTATION

The following documentation will be available at the end of the test phase:

Test Plan
Test Cases
Incident Report
Test Summary Report

15.0 APPROVALS

Name (In Capital Letters)	Signature	Date
1.		
2.		
3.		
4.		

6.4 CREATING TEST CASES

It is extremely difficult to test a large system without proper test planning and test cases. The test case describes how each test is to be conducted and input/output details. Development of test cases assist in keeping track of what is tested, when it was tested, and the outcome of the test. If a defect is found while testing, a documented test case makes it easy for the developer to re-create the problem so that proper analysis can be done to fix it.

6.4.1 Techniques and Characteristics

Although there are no standards or simple rules for designing test cases, test cases should be designed for testing each function, with expected results. In order to determine what will break the system, the tester has to be creative and want to break the system. In order to accomplish this, the most important consideration is the development of effective test cases and test design. The test cases should be repeatable, i.e., when a test case is rerun, it should give the same results each time, except in a real-time environment. Organize and develop test cases around system requirements and for key functions of the system.

The three steps for test cases are creating, executing, and ensuring the end results are correct. While creating test cases, reference back to the requirements document to ensure proper test coverage of the requirements. The test design emphasizes

- the type of test needed to test the requirements
- how a test will run
- how all requirements will be addressed by the tests

Good test cases catch the errors and demonstrate that the system works according to the requirements and expose anything that is abnormal. Develop test cases in such a way that each test case covers as many related functions as possible. This will minimize the total number of test cases. Figure 6-1 outlines main characteristics of a test case.

The test case should consist of at least the following:

- test case identifier
- the name of the person responsible for executing the test
- the date the test was executed and the version of the system tested
- description of the functions to be tested and a list of actions to be carried out
- input values
- output values (expected results). In most cases, the success of a test depends on obtaining the predefined expected results.
- actual results (outputs received when the test case was executed). Indicate whether or not errors were detected, and if so, complete a "problem report."

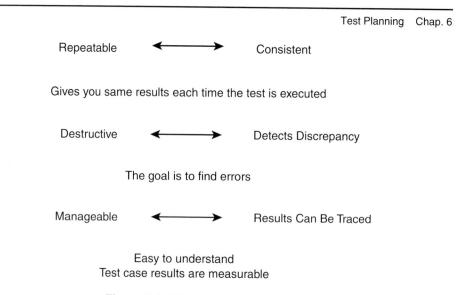

Figure 6-1   Test case characteristics

Other pertinent information may be included in a test case, such as, description of the test environment, entrance criteria for the test, exit criteria for the test, testing objectives (what does the test accomplish and what would indicate that the test was successful), and special instructions or additional information regarding the test case. This additional information may include any related test cases which should be executed prior to this one; which files, if any, are to be purged prior to or after test; and any processing options or other table settings to be changed as a part of the test. Depending on the nature of your system, in addition to function testing you may want to develop test cases for abnormal system end, stress test, volume test, computation and boundary analysis, cause-and-effect logic, and security test.

Functional Test Cases   The requirements validation matrix, discussed in Chapter 1, will assist in ensuring every requirement has a related test case. Functional test cases should produce clear, measurable results that can be verified easily. The test cases are developed by referencing the requirements document and ensuring that various functions of the system work as noted in the requirements document. At a later time, if the requirements are changed, the test cases and expected results should also be altered to incorporate the change. Function testing seems straightforward; however, in order to be successful, you must know the system functionality well and how the functions interact with each other.

It is important to make sure the system can recover from an abnormal end. These test cases will ensure no data is lost or corrupted when the system crashes suddenly. Stress test and volume test cases also fall under function testing, revealing how the system behaves under certain conditions.

Computation and Boundary Analysis Test Cases These tests verify the mathematical calculations and accuracy. They are for normal processing, with no error conditions purposely created. The boundary analysis test cases are designed by inputting the maximum and minimum allowed values. When creating boundary analysis classes, include boundary values of ±1 to check the system behavior. If the valid numbers of the boundary are from 0 to 50, then any number between 0 through 50 should be handled in the same way by the software. In other words, if the software works for number 2, it will also work correctly for other numbers such as 35, 42, 19, 8, and so forth. Any value less than 0 would be considered invalid.

Cause-Effect and Logic Cases The input to software can be divided into valid and invalid data. Test cases should be developed for both of these categories to verify how the system behaves when invalid data is entered. Ideally, when the invalid data is encountered, the system should give an error message. Ensure the error message is easy to understand and is accurate. The cause-effect cases should demonstrate that the program logic operates within established constraints. The critical decisions of the program should be checked for completeness.

Security Test Cases In the current environment of "hackers," security is of prime concern. The test cases are developed to validate the security features by penetrating the security and "breaking" the system by inputting data in the protected fields or protected transactions. The purpose is to prevent unauthorized users from accessing the system. The data security test cases test errors in data transmission between program components to ensure the program does not stray into areas where it does not belong.

Test Case Development Considerations You should consider the following when developing test cases.

- All valid system input must be accepted.

- All invalid system input must be rejected with clear error messages.

- All functions—including generation of reports—should be tested.

- Any reports generated by the system should be tested and verified.

- Any interfacing systems must be invoked and verified that the data is passed to and from the interfacing system.

The following checklist will help you create test cases to validate "transaction screens" of a new system:

- Is the field in the proper row and column?

- Does each field display proper attributes?
- Is the field length correct?
- Did you enter alpha data in numeric fields and vice versa?
- Did you attempt to input data in display-only fields?
- Are "help" features working and is the explanation clear and unambiguous?
- Are the screen field names consistent with other screens?
- Are required and optional fields properly processed?
- Are defaults processed as documented?
- Are date fields properly validated?
- Are error messages correct and clear?

To test the internal logic of a program, develop test cases that

- guarantee all independent paths within a module are exercised at least once
- exercise all logical decisions on their true and false sides
- execute all loops at their boundaries and within their operational bounds
- exercise internal data structures to assure their validity

6.5 AUTOMATED TEST TOOLS

For the test phase of the development life cycle, the most important type of tool provides automated execution from a black box perspective. These tools either capture a test as it is performed manually or as it is described in a script language, then replay it, and compare the actual results to the original or expected responses. This enables repeatability and consistency of test execution as well as productivity, enabling large volumes of tests to be performed unattended. Some tool suites also provide the ability to distribute or simulate the execution of tests over multiple processors, thus providing performance and stress tests to measure the system's ability to handle high volumes of transactions and users.

This section will cover the evaluation of automated execution tools and selection of an appropriate vendor, as well as suggest an approach for validating both.

6.5.1 Evaluation Criteria

There are four primary criteria for evaluating an automated test execution tool. Briefly, they are:

1. Compatibility—Does the tool support the platform(s) and environment(s) of the system under test?

2. Usability—Does it provide the necessary functionality, and are the testers able to make effective use of it without a prohibitive learning curve?

3. Maintainability—Can changes to the system under test be accommodated in the automated tests without undue effort?

4. Manageability—Does the tool provide sufficient and meaningful information to enable management of the test library and measurement of the test results?

Each of these criteria is discussed in more detail below.

Compatibility In today's complex client/server environment, the system being tested may involve multiple platforms: The client portion may execute on a workstation which is attached via a network or other communications link to a host, which could be a mainframe or mid-tier server that provides data access and other services. It is important that the automated test tool be compatible with each and all of these components at some level.

Client-Level Compatibility At the client level, fundamental compatibility requires that the test tool be able to co-exist with the system under test or at least the portion of it that executes on the client. This means the two must not compete for the same memory or other resources, or that one or the other may be configured to accommodate the other. This type of compatibility can be established by installing and executing the test tool through the basic steps of loading, operating, and exiting the system under test. If these steps can be automated and executed without errors, the probability is that the two are compatible at the resource level. For graphical interfaces, the issue is more complex. The majority of Windows-based applications are comprised of windows and controls or objects that support a given set of behaviors. For a particular operating environment, such as Windows, there is a set of so-called standard controls that are common to the environment and addressable through the window manager. These include such control types as edit controls, list boxes, push buttons, check boxes, radio buttons, and so forth. Not all standard controls that are standard to a single operating environment are common to all; for example, notebook controls are available in OS/2 but not in Windows. This raises the portability issue of compatibility, which is addressed in more detail below.

The reason that compatibility is important at the control level is that the quality of the test script is affected. A recognized control can be addressed by the tool by name or class instead of by its screen location, thus providing readability to the script as well as long-term flexibility and maintainability. For example, a script which says "Select list box item USA" is more readable than one that says "Click left mouse button at 245, 841." Further, if the list box is moved within the window or the position of the option "USA" is moved within the list, the former script would still operate correctly while the latter would not. This is also an example of maintainability, which is reviewed in depth in a later section.

Problems with control compatibility arise when the system under test either makes use of custom or nonstandard controls, or avoids using the window manager at all in favor of rendering bitmap images of controls. In the former case, the system may require a unique presentation of information, such as a data grid or spreadsheet-like layout, that is not native to the operating system.

In this case, the test tool must provide the ability to register the custom control so that it can be recognized, or provide a driver that already contains the custom control class or an API (Application Program Interface) that allows the tool to address it. These types of drivers or API calls may already be available for popular development tools, or the vendor may be persuaded to develop one.

In the second case, using bitmap images of controls, the tool might not be able to address the controls at all through the window manager, and so must either revert to using window pixel coordinates or rely on an API that permits the tool to obtain the required information directly from the application. The bit-mapped rendering approach is more common among development tools that strive for cross-platform compatibility and/or performance; using bitmap images does not rely on the window manager, and thus can be more easily ported between them and also operate faster.

To ascertain the level of compatibility, capture a script that covers a representative sample of the screens, windows, or controls that comprise the application; then review the results. Ideally, coordinates will not be necessary.

Communications-Level Compatibility   The second layer of compatibility for client/server systems is the communications layer. This may consist of a network, a terminal emulator, remote communications or some combination of all of these. There must of course be resource compatibility: The test tool must be able to peacefully coexist with the communications layer while it is operating. There is also a another layer that is important in this context, and that is synchronization.

Synchronization is the ability of the test tool and the system being tested to remain in step with each other. For example, if the system being tested must make a data request to a remote host, the timing of the response may vary from one session to the next depending on the traffic on the system or the state of the database. If the test tool is not able to detect the actual response time and instead executes at the original recorded speed or some other standard rate, then the test tool may get ahead of the system being tested and attempt to execute steps which the system is not ready to receive. This will cause the test to fail.

There are several ways to deal with synchronization, some more elegant than others. The most elegant requires that the system being tested or its communication layer provide a visual clue or other indicator of a busy state or readiness. A common indicator of a busy state is an hourglass cursor or status line containing (X). There may also be lower-level functions, such as a call that can be made to the terminal emulator or another communications facility that will return the busy or readiness state. However provided, this indicator must be available to the test tool and it must take advantage of it in a transparent manner. Some test tools allow a driver to be invoked that maintains synchronization automatically, while others may require that it be explicitly called within the script. If an indicator is not available or is not reliable, the next best solution is for the test tool to provide the ability to wait until the system is ready by, for example, checking that a particular window or control has focus.

This wait period should not be a fixed amount of time, although an upper limit should be defined for purposes of detecting a system failure through a timeout. This approach is not as global as an indicator, but it can nevertheless accommodate varying execution speeds. The last and least acceptable means of maintaining synchronization is to simply slow the script down to the point that it will never outpace the system under test. This naturally leads to a degradation of performance and may significantly reduce the productivity gains from using an automated tool and still leave open the opportunity for instability in the case where the system speeds vary widely. The system under test may itself timeout if too much time passes before the next input is performed, or it may exceed the expected wait delay and the tool gets out of step anyway. Review the tool documentation to see how synchronization is addressed; then verify its effectiveness in your environment by creating a script that performs data requests to the host, and execute it at different times of the day when traffic on the system affects the performance. Observe whether the script stays in step with the system under test: Does it execute as quickly as possible without getting ahead? Although it may be necessary to fine-tune the tool for your environment, assure yourself that the tool provides the means to do so.

Host-Level Compatibility   If the test tool or any part of it operates on the host, then the resource compatibility issue is somewhat more complex than on the client because the installation and execution of software on a shared resource such as a host are often more tightly controlled than on the client. Thus, it may be necessary for the tester to schedule the use of the tool with systems administration and provide ample resource planning to assure that the tool does not consume excessive system resources. If the test tool resides on the client, then host-level compatibility requires that the tool be able to co-reside with—and stay in synchronization with—the layers of the platform that communicate with the host, and also that the tool be able to detect and respond to host-generated messages. In some cases an error on the host is broadcast to the client via a high-priority message that suspends execution on the client. In these cases, the priority of the message may be so high that the tool itself is suspended from operation and is thus unable to detect and respond to the message. This type of circumstance should be evaluated to see whether a lower-level priority message can be used, or, if not, whether the client can be monitored so that human intervention can be taken when such a message is issued.

Portability   The last aspect of compatibility involves systems that are designed and intended to execute in multiple operating environments. For example, some development tools permit the application to be generated for more than one window manager, such as OS/2 or Windows or X Windows. If the system under test is itself intended to be portable, then the test tool (or versions of it) must support all target platforms, and the test scripts must have some level of portability. Portability in this context means that a test script which is created for one environment is able to execute within another with minimal or no modification. Without this capability, the test effort will be multiplied across platforms even though the development effort may be transparent. This will cause testing to become a bottleneck to the delivery of the system. Because compatibility determines whether the test tool will function in harmony with the system under test and within the platform and environment in which it must execute, the more diverse the platforms and the more complex the environment, the more important this issue becomes.

Usability   The usability of a test tool has three aspects: the functionality which is available, its extensibility, and the learning curve required to take advantage of it.

Functionality   Functionality of the tool determines whether it is capable of performing the types of tests needed to exercise the system under test. For example, an application that provides graphical output whose content is distinguished by color and font attributes would require a test tool that is able to distinguish one color or font from another; conversely, a tool which allows the end user to freely customize colors and fonts may require a tool that makes these attributes transparent. Therefore, the critical characteristics of the system under test should be identified and compared against the feature set of the test tool.

Extensibility   The extensibility of a test tool refers to its ability to take advantage of external functions such as other utilities or sources of data. For example, can scripts be created and edited in a word processor or text editor that is already familiar to the user, or must the tool's editor be learned and employed? Also, can the tool introduce test data from outside sources, such as production databases, spreadsheets, or other sources? The capability of extending the native functions of the test tool through the use of external applications and data can introduce substantial economies for leveraging the test effort and reducing the learning curve.

Learning Curve   The learning curve requirement means that the functionality of the tool is available or can be implemented in a manner which makes it usable by the skill level of the intended user. Because many testers are recruited for their business or application expertise and not for their technical prowess, a test tool which presumes programming skills may not be usable by the tester without a steep learning curve. Since time and resources are always scarce during the test phase, imposing a substantial training burden may not be feasible. Thus, the tool should be usable with a reasonable investment in training or take advantage of utilities that the tester is already familiar with.

Maintainability   It is essential to realize that automated test scripts possess all of the attributes of software: They are comprised of computer-based instructions that will, over time, require modification as the behavior of the system under test changes. In fact, a single change to the system being tested may result in multiple changes to the test scripts; a modified window, for example, might appear in dozens or even hundreds of test scripts. Because of this, maintainability is crucial to the long-term viability of an automated test library. The maintainability question can be divided into three key areas: the necessity of making changes, the ability to identify necessary changes, and the level of effort required.

The necessity of making a change is affected by the compatibility level of the tool with the user interface. As discussed above, a tool which relies on pixel coordinates instead of control names will be much more sensitive to changes, even cosmetic ones. If an item in a list changes position, the pixel coordinates must be changed; if the item is referred to by name, no change is needed. Ideally, windows and controls or fields should be able to be repositioned without affecting the test script. If changes are necessary, however, being able to find them is obviously a prerequisite to making them. If, for example, windows or screens are identified in the test scripts by their name or title, then it would be fairly straightforward to locate the scripts in which they are referenced should a change be needed. On the other hand, if components of the system are identified only by their pixel coordinates or other obscure convention, then it may be a virtual impossibility to find affected scripts. Therefore, review the means by which components of the system under test are referenced in the associated test scripts and determine whether they can be identified with a reasonable effort.

Once the changes can be identified, the next question is the level of effort required to actually make the changes. Does the tool provide for a search and replace capability? Can the scripts be edited in an external editor or word processor, or must they be accessed through a proprietary interface? Is there a central database or repository of test scripts or components that permit centralized maintenance? These types of capabilities can dramatically affect the maintainability, and thus the useful life, of your automated test scripts.

Manageability A comprehensive automated test library will most likely consist of large volumes of tests and their results. Since test scripts have the attributes of software, they require change management and version control just as the system under test. Also, since test results provide the metrics to inform management of the status and quality of the system, the data analysis and reporting capabilities must also be robust.

Test Library Management In terms of change management and version control, the test tool should be evaluated for how scripts are named and stored, and whether there are either intrinsic functions to manage them or for support for external utilities which provide this capability. The amount of effort required to manage changes and new versions to test scripts is also a function of the complexity inherent in the process of creating them: How many different files comprise a test? Are there naming conventions or other techniques for associating all related files? Without a practical means of managing the tests as changes are made or as new versions are introduced, the test library can lose integrity.

6.5.2 Test Results

Test results, which basically represent the final product of an automated test effort, should be meaningful enough to inform management of the status of the system under test and its quality relative to expectations. This means, for example, that a simple count of errors may not be sufficient to be meaningful: Are the errors serious or cosmetic? A single high-priority requirement which fails may be enough to halt release, while a hundred low-priority problems may be acceptable. Review the test tool reporting capabilities to assure that tests can be tied to or identified by priority or requirements that can be used as an indicator of readiness.

Also, there will almost certainly be multiple iterations of test execution during a single cycle: As errors are discovered and corrected, the same tests will be repeated. Without an ability to plot or track the error discovery and correction rate across test cycles, it will not be possible to determine whether quality is improving or regressing. Similarly, measuring the arrival rate of errors—the number of errors uncovered over a period of time—can provide a basis for projecting schedules and estimate remaining errors to be discovered.

Test tools should be reviewed to determine the amount and quality of test result information; analysis and reporting capabilities are either included or can be made available.

6.5.3 Test Case Generation

The generation of test cases refers to the programmatic creation of test case data or instances, as opposed to sampling or other techniques. The advantage of this method is that high volumes of test conditions can be created; the disadvantage is that volume alone is not a guarantor of coverage or efficacy.

There are two techniques that can be used. The first utilizes equivalence classes to generate the total possible number of combinations. Although this approach will in fact yield a large number of test cases, it may not take into account the impact of interdependencies, for example, if the value or state of one data element controls the validity of others. This means that there may be more than one test case that exercises the same path, or too few to cover all the paths.

The second technique, known as cause-effect node graphing, adopts the approach used to test hardware. In this case, the requirements are stated as mathematical formulas yielding the optimum, as opposed to maximum, number of test conditions. For example, if two test conditions both cause the same path or gateway to be chosen, then only one is necessary. This relationship of conditions can be summarized in a "truth table." The key here is that the interdependencies are incorporated so as to generate the precise test conditions necessary to test all pathways once. Although more efficient in terms of coverage, the primary disadvantage of this technique is that few requirements are defined rigorously enough.

6.5.4 Vendor Selection

Equally important to evaluating the tool is selecting the appropriate vendor. Some tools are available from only one source, while others may be available from a number of different channels such as resellers and consultants. The crucial considerations in vendor selection are summarized as

- Experience—What level of experience does the vendor offer in the implementation of automated test tools?

- Services—What services does the vendor offer for training as well as implementation to assure that the tool is properly deployed?

- Support—How readily available and responsive is the vendor to technical questions and issues?

- Commitment—Is the vendor committed to the automated test tools market or is this only one of several offerings?

Experience An automated test tool is only as good as the vendor behind it and their level of experience in test automation. Many issues that arise in the effective use of automated tools are not technical; they are related to organizational, planning, and implementation considerations. Therefore, verify the amount of time the vendor has been in the automated test industry and how many customers have successfully implemented their tool.

The best way to evaluate the vendor's experience, of course, is to talk to other customers. Although most vendors will provide a list of references, take certain precautions. For example, find out how long each reference has been using the tool; if they are new users, there won't be enough time to have uncovered long-term issues such as maintainability and manageability. Also, try to talk to more than one person; in some instances the management may have one view of the tool and the end users another. Try to get as broad a perspective as possible.

Another way to evaluate a vendor's experience is to post inquiries on newsgroups, bulletin boards, and other resources such as the Internet. This will help you locate customers who may not have been mentioned by the vendor but who nevertheless have valuable information. As with the vendor's reference list, be careful in evaluating volunteers as well. In some cases a tool may succeed or fail for reasons that are unique to the customer instead of the tool.

Services The most common type of service is a training class, which may be offered at the vendor's location or at the customer's site. In either case, determine whether the class is "canned" or whether it is tailored to your specific requirements. Although standardized training in the operation of the product is important, this may be more effective in the form of a self-paced tutorial. Classroom training should, whenever possible, be customized to the application and task at hand.

In addition to training or tutorials, implementation services are highly advisable. Unless your organization has successfully implemented test tools before, you will most likely require some assistance to make the most effective use of the tool. Implementation issues cover such topics as how to staff your test team with the proper skills, how to organize the test effort and plan both schedules and resources, how to distribute the workload, and useful approaches for naming conventions and design standards that will simplify long-term management and maintenance.

In some cases, your organization might be resource constrained; find out whether the vendor can provide on-site assistance to actually use the tool, or whether they train or certify independent consultants who can provide assistance. Naturally, local expertise is more accessible and less expensive, as a rule, and is therefore preferable.

Support   Product support usually involves either answering questions or resolving technical problems. In either case, both the quality and timeliness of the response are critical. The quality of the response is determined by the skill level of the person: Are they experienced with the product, or must they consult the documentation or another person? Although in some instances it may be proper to direct you to the relevant area of the documentation, the support personnel should offer broader insight and assistance.

The timeliness of the response is also important. Depending on the severity of the problem, the response may make the difference between being able to use the tool or not. Although for some problems an immediate solution may not be available, at least a prompt acknowledgment of the problem and a plan for resolution should be forthcoming. Ironically, a "fix" that is made available too quickly may actually be a liability, as it may indicate that the change was not sufficiently tested.

Commitment   The commitment level of the vendor to their product and customers can be evaluated by the frequency of maintenance, enhancement, and new product releases. How often are new releases made available for corrections? What is the process for submitting enhancement requests, and how often are they evaluated and incorporated? Does the vendor have plans or active projects to support new platforms or versions of operating systems?

Commitment is important because, as a customer, you are making a significant commitment to purchasing and implementing a tool. If the vendor does not invest in continuous efforts to keep the tool current and continue to expand its functionality, it may eventually become obsolete, thus risking the investment you have made in the test cases and scripts developed with it.

6.5.5 The Pilot Project Approach

The ideal means of performing a thorough evaluation and validating your vendor selection is to implement the tool on a pilot project. A pilot project is one which addresses a small, well-defined subset of the application and its functionality from beginning to end, with a small core team. Preferably, the scope of the effort should require no more than one to three months to complete and involve no more than three to five persons.

During the pilot, detailed records should be maintained as to the amount of time required for each task and for each member of the test team. This information will help you validate your planning assumptions, project resources, and schedules more accurately. Expected and actual benefits versus costs should also be documented and evaluated.

The tool should be evaluated according to the four areas previously discussed, and any unexpected issues should be carefully documented and resolved.

The vendor should also be evaluated. Were the training courses effective? Were the services useful? What level of support was required? Were the quality and timeliness of the response satisfactory? Assure yourself that the vendor is able and willing to meet it commitments and provide prompt, quality service.

Aside from validating the tool, the vendor, your approach, and team, a pilot project will invariably uncover issues that, on a larger scale, would be much more problematic. Discovering flaws in the test library design, or determining that the skill levels of the team members aren't appropriate are much easier to correct during a pilot than in the middle of a large-scale, mission-critical implementation.

The final outcome of the project should be an analysis of the expected and actual results and a set of recommendations on how—or even whether—to proceed with the rest of the application. It should not necessarily be a usable set of tests. The pilot team should be free to decide to throw away the tests developed during the pilot and start anew with the information learned. This prototype approach will free the team to experiment freely and objectively evaluate assumptions before they are cast in concrete.

But perhaps most important, the pilot project will often raise issues that are completely outside the tool or the vendor's experience—the process and organizational constraints that exist in every company—and must be resolved before the test effort —whether manual or automated—can be a success. After all, if tools were the answer, word processors would write letters.

6.6 OUTSOURCING

Outsourcing is basically when a company decides to have another company build their software systems for them. It can also involve a maintenance agreement whereby the outsourcing company agrees to maintain the software system for an annual or monthly fee. Sometimes it involves one-time testing of a company's software system or systems. Outsourcing differs from building a custom system for someone in the sense that there tends to be a one-to-one relationship between the two companies, rather than a software company building a software system and then selling and installing it at sites across several companies, perhaps customizing it to each company's needs.

6.6.1 Background

Outsourcing is becoming a way of life for many companies who either cannot afford the equipment or trained personnel to create or test their software. Sometimes this outsourcing goes to Third World countries; other times it goes to American companies. As with most other software activities, there are successes and notable failures. As you will see later, it is important to make sure that your contract negotiations protect both you and the company to which you are outsourcing your software development or testing.

6.6.2 Potential Problems

The authors have had several experiences with outsourcing, some positive and some negative. To give you some insight into potential problems, we will characterize several of these experiences for you.

One experience related to outsourcing a commercial product to a company that had expertise with a certain mainframe product. It seemed practical to have them develop that mainframe version of the company's product. Unfortunately, they not only violated the contract in terms of confidentiality and noncompetition, they also held our company hostage and blatantly marketed the product in direct competition to us. We decided that it would have given us more leverage to have simply trained our own personnel, taken a bit longer to build the product, and kept it in-house.

Another experience related to our sending the specifications for several products to a Third World country. While it took us around six months to establish proper communication, the programmers worked to our specifications, stayed within our quality guidelines, and delivered the product on time and within budget. It was extremely cost-effective.

In a third situation, we decided we did not have the expertise to build a particular product. We held several interviews with the outsourcing company, checked out their references, talked to them about quality and methodologies, and tried to be extremely cautious in our contract negotiations. while they were considered experts with rapid application development and 4GLs, they also indicated their commitment to quality and staying within specifications. As it turned out, they—on a cost plus basis—were 2 1/2 times over budget, 2 times over schedule, and did not even bother to test their product or guarantee it would compile or run when they delivered it. They wanted to charge us to fix their bugs. They ignored our specification and tried to use a RAD approach to what they provided us. When we reread the contract, we found we were totally naive and unprotected.

As you define the deliverables for the project, you should also define software quality. As we have said, it is not error rates; it is related to behavior and to coding and architectural quality standards. The latter two standards are relatively easy to adhere to, except that sometimes architectural quality standards conflict with performance standards. Behavioral standards often must be negotiated between your company and the outsourcing company.

6.6.3 Contract Negotiations

The single most important document when outsourcing is a contract between the purchaser and the supplier. The contract is an agreement which outlines obligations, services to be performed, and in some cases, identifies methods for resolving contractual issues that may arise between the supplier and the purchaser. The management personnel of both the entities need to understand the scope of the contract, each organization's responsibilities, and risks associated with the contract.

The purpose of developing a detailed contract upfront is to eliminate any misunderstanding and having a clear knowledge of what will be the final deliverable. The contract may also specify how each activity is to be performed and when these activities are to be performed. In the event the purchaser insists upon seeing the supplier's test plan, test cases, and test results, these items should be made part of the contract. If periodic joint reviews are to be held between the supplier and the purchaser, the contract should identify when and where the review will take place, what material will be reviewed, and how the action items arising from the review will be handled.

As we have observed many different outsourcing experiences, there are several things we would make explicit in a contract. First of all, as we have mentioned elsewhere, we consider there to be a major difference between error rates and code quality. Error-free code can still be of poor quality because of excessive dependencies or behavioral problems. These criteria should be explicitly stated in the specification and in the contract. The outsourcing company should be required to follow a prescribed product delivery process, or at least a software development life cycle. The project plan should allow for frequent deliverables which you can review and evaluate for quality and conformity to the specification. This should protect you if the company gets too far out of control or their quality deteriorates below standards. Provision should be made for how the product will be handed off, who will do the sign-off, who will evaluate code quality and programming standards, how acceptance testing will be done, what happens if the outsourcing company is over budget or outside the schedule, etc.

Contract Review The contract should be reviewed between the supplier and purchaser to ensure there is consistent understanding of what will be expected from both of them. The minutes of the review should be signed and acknowledged by both the parties. Possible risks regarding the schedule or technology should be identified and documented in the contract and the development costs and schedules must be agreed to by both and should also be included in the contract. The supplier should never commit to developing a system that exactly matches the purchaser requirements. According to Richard Raysman (1992), "A vendor should not agree to a provision which promises that the software delivered conforms exactly to the general business functional description. Software evolves during a development project and is rarely delivered in exactly the form the parties envisioned at the outset. The parties should agree that if the software substantially performs the agreed business functions it will be accepted by the user. Variations from the functional specifications which are not substantive may be used by a user as an excuse for failure to pay for custom software."

Dictionary of Technical Terms A dictionary of technical terms used in the contract in regard to the development of the system should be kept and a walkthrough of the terminology should be conducted to ensure both the supplier and the purchaser are aware of terms and conditions.

Quality Records   The contract should also identify the quality record-keeping. For example, the contract might read, "Minutes of all the reviews must be kept and shared with the purchaser; or results of all the tests must be shared with the purchaser." The quality records may include

- test plan
- test cases
- problem reports
- minutes of all reviews and inspections

The time frame during which the purchaser will be allowed to inspect these quality records should be indicated in the contract. For example, the contract might read, "The test plan will be available for purchaser inspection by (date)."

Deliverables   The names of documents that will be provided to the purchaser should be listed in the deliverables section. The deliverables may include

- instructions for using the automated test script tool
- executable code (object files)
- specific recommendations for using the test script tool for maximum effectiveness in testing
- weekly progress reports (project status summary)

Product Ownership   Identify who will own all the items listed in the deliverables section. For example, the contract might read, "All items referred to as deliverables will be the property of the purchaser and are hereby assigned to the Purchaser, unless indicated otherwise. All deliverables generated by ABC & Company (supplier) during the performance of this contract will become the property of the purchaser, but may not be disclosed or otherwise distributed by the purchaser without the express written consent of ABC Company (supplier)."

Acceptance Criteria/Acceptance Testing   The acceptance criteria of the system must be developed by the purchaser upfront, and they should be reviewed and agreed to by the supplier. This should be attached to the contract as an addendum so there is no mistake as to what would be acceptable by the purchaser. If the supplier wishes to review the acceptance test cases, this should be made part of the contract. This will bind the purchaser to review the acceptance test cases with the supplier so there are no surprises at the end. The schedule for acceptance testing, with start and end dates, should be identified in the contract.

Procedures and Standards   If the purchaser requires special standards that need to be adhered to while developing the software, these standards should be described in the contract. Similarly any special procedure requirements should also be mentioned in the contract.

Roles and Responsibilities   The contract should clearly indicate the roles and responsibilities for both the purchaser and supplier during various phases of development. Key individuals should be identified, from both the purchaser and supplier organizations, to ensure the product is specified, developed, tested, and installed as stated. If a technical contact is to be made available at the purchaser's site for the duration of the project to answer questions and provide technical information, this should be made part of the contract. Individuals who will act as the key contacts for both the supplier as well as the purchaser, should be identified and mentioned in the contract.

Staffing   The supplier should indicate the qualifications of the staff to be used in the development of the product. For example, the contract might read, "ABC Company (Supplier) will use senior test engineers, with seven or more years of testing experience on this project. The role of the senior test engineers will be to write test plan, develop test cases, and execute the cases."

Cost Summary and Schedule   All the expenses associated with the project should be identified and listed in the contract and each individual activity of the project should also be listed separately with costs. An entire project schedule should be developed and listed, along with the start and end date of each system development phase and related activity.

Compensation   A clause compensating the purchaser, for any delays caused by the supplier, should be present in the contract. At the same time, statement should be made to compensate the supplier for time and effort caused by the purchaser's failure to provide the requirements document on time or for purchaser's failure to perform other contractual activities which may result in delay of the final product.

Facilities and Tools   The contract should clearly state the purchaser's obligation in providing facilities for development and test or special tools required for either development or tests.

Confidential Information   Both the supplier and the purchaser should identify what material is confidential. They should agree to hold all confidential and/or trade secret information in strict confidence, not to disclose it to others or use it in any way, commercially or otherwise, and not to allow any unauthorized person access to it either before or after termination of the contract. The supplier should further agree to take all actions reasonably necessary and satisfactory to the purchaser to protect the confidentiality of the information, including implementing and enforcing operating procedures to minimize the possibility of unauthorized use or copying of confidential information.

Contingencies   Any known contingencies should be identified and included in the contract. For example, the contract might read, "The parties expect that testing will be done with Version 5.1 of the Brand X Test Tool. If Version 5.1 is not available for us by November 19, 19XX, or if it is unreliable, then supplier will be allowed a reasonable time to find and gain experience in the use of a replacement tool." If you can agree on how long a "reasonable time" would be, you should record it in the contract. But if you are not sure, and if you think it would take a lot of discussion time to settle a minor issue, you may agree to leave this term open.

Agreement Modifications   The contract should include the procedures for modifying the services and deliverables described in the contract. For example, the contract might read, "Any changes will be implemented only after both parties agree to do so. A written change order procedure will be used by the supplier to inform the purchaser of project cost and schedule implications for all requested changes."

Other Related Topics   In addition to the above topics, special attention should also be given to

- indemnity

- advertising procedures

- the termination clauses for the contract

- description of prepayments for the services

- when and how invoicing will begin

- how arbitration will be conducted in the event of controversy or claim arising out of or related to the contract or the breach

Readers may consider using a form of abbreviated arbitration. In the contract, you list a group of qualified arbitrators. When there is a dispute, you call one of them (use the first one on the list; if unavailable, use the second one on the list, etc.). This arbitrator should be technically knowledgeable as well as a good negotiator with high integrity.

The arbitrator meets with the two parties for not longer than one day. Both sides present their arguments and describe the problem. The arbitrator makes a decision. For example, he or she may order the supplier to complete programming and the purchaser to pay an additional $10,000 to defray the expenses. The idea here is a fast decision that specifies an achievable result and is cheap. Rather than arguing in courts for months who is right and who is wrong, arbitration resolves the issues quickly. In summary, we suggest a detailed contract between the purchaser and the supplier should be written by a legal counsel.

CHAPTER 7

Software Quality Assurance Reviews

*I*n this chapter we define software quality assurance reviews. To illustrate this, we will show reviews in the context of an MIS application which might be reviewed in a company.

A formal product assurance is a set of activities carried out during the system development that ensures quality of deliverables and overall system. It focuses on activities that are conducted to assure deliverables meet customer requirements. According to the *IEEE Standard Glossary of Software Engineering Terminology* (IEEE, Std. 610.12-1990), a review is: "A process or meeting during which a work product, or set of work products, is presented to project personnel, managers, users, customers, or other interested parties for comment or approval. Types include code reviews, design review, formal qualification review, requirements review, test readiness reviews." In short, a review consists of activities conducted by a team of people to identify problems. The purpose of software quality assurance reviews is to assure the quality of a deliverable before the development process is allowed to continue. Once a deliverable has been reviewed, revised as necessary, and approved, it can safely be used as the basis for further development.

7.1 OBJECTIVE

The objectives of the quality assurance review can be broken down into the following:

- identify required improvements in a product
- assure that the deliverable is complete (i.e., all the pieces are present)
- assure that the deliverable is technically correct (e.g., all the data flow diagrams are correct)
- measure the progress of the project
- identify any defects early, thus resulting in cost and time savings

7.1.1 Business Review

The business review ensures that the MIS software supports the business functionality specified in the requirements document. This can be further broken down into the following objectives:

- The deliverable is complete.
- The deliverable provides the information required for the next phase (i.e., can the system design be developed from the requirements document?).
- The deliverable is correct (i.e., does the code conform to predefined standards?).
- There is adherence to the procedures and policies.

7.1.2 Technical Review

The technical review ensures that the software conforms to your company's standards of development. These standards may include, but are not limited to, any standards for GUI, windows, screens, user interface, naming conventions, repository completeness, and so forth. The technical review process also ensures that any changes to the software are implemented according to pre-defined procedures and standards.

7.1.3 Management Review

The intent of the management review is to

- validate from a management perspective that the project is making progress according to the project plan
- ensure a deliverable is ready for management approval
- resolve issues that require management's attention
- identify if the project needs a change of direction
- control the project through adequate allocation of resources

Generally, these reviews are not planned and they may occur on an "as needed" basis. The management review team consists of the representatives of all the areas affected by the development effort.

The project manager is responsible for formally reporting the status of the project, ensuring that all supporting documents of the review are available for distribution to the appropriate managers and distributing the minutes. Each member of the management review team is responsible for reviewing the documents and making notes for issues before attending the review meeting. During the review, the team

- examines the project status
- determines if the project fulfills user requirements and performance criteria
- ensures that properly trained resources are allocated to the project

- generates a list of issues, associated risks, recommendations, and course of actions to be taken to resolve the issues

- examines the project cost

- reviews the initial project plan; notes variations to the cost and identifies the possible occurrences causing the variations; identifies strategic activities and time frame to address the variations

- recommends authorization for additional management reviews if necessary

The output from the management review process is the management review report which lists action items, ownership and status; issues and recommendations identified by the management review team that must be addressed for the project to meet its milestone; and process improvement recommendations to avoid the same defects from occurring in the future.

7.1.4 Roles and Responsibilities

Whenever a group problem-solving session is held, there is a classic set of roles that are played by the participants. This is true whether you are talking about a review, inspection, or any other type of problem solving. One way in which these roles can be defined is as follows.

Facilitator The facilitator is the individual who thoroughly understands the subject matter under review and can present the background information and assign roles to other members. The facilitator also encourages participation for all the attendees and ensures all problems are adequately reviewed. The facilitator understands the issues and keeps the meeting focused and moving. In addition, he or she gains consensus on problems and makes sure that everyone has a chance to express views or receive clarification on any misunderstanding. The facilitator is required to perform the duties of a reviewer and records issues if the recorder is not present.

Author (Producer) The author ensures that the subject material is ready for the review and distributes it. During the meeting, the author paraphrases the document a section at a time. The author is responsible for scheduling the review; selecting the review participants; determining if entry criteria for the review are met; providing information about the product during all stages; clarifying any unclear issues; correcting any problems identified; and providing dates for reworks and resolution.

Recorder The recorder collects and records each defect uncovered during the review meeting. Then, the recorder develops an issues list and identifies whose responsibility it is to resolve each issue. In addition, he or she records meeting decisions on the issues, prepares the minutes, and publishes the minutes while continually tracking the action items.

Reviewer   Each member of the review team spends time prior to the meeting reviewing the information, makes notes of defects and becomes familiar with the product to be reviewed; identifies strengths of the product; verifies that the rework is done; and insists upon clarifying any issues that are not clear.

Observer   The observer is a new member to the project team who learns the product and observes the review techniques.

7.2 GENERAL GUIDELINES

Guidelines for reviews must be established in advance, agreed upon, and adhered to. A review that is uncontrolled can bring unpredictable results and ultimately be worse than no review at all. The following principles will assist in the success of your review.

Preparation   Materials to be reviewed should be distributed to the participants in advance, with expectations, guidelines, and deadlines clearly established at the time of distribution. In addition, adequate preparation time should be provided to review the document.

Discussions   Limit the debate and discussions during the review. Issues should be recorded and investigated at a later time. The review meeting is not the right place to discuss any specific issues.

Respect   The reviews, when conducted properly, should leave all the attendees with the feeling of accomplishment. Mutual respect is a key factor for the success of the review. Avoid discussions of style. Criticizing the author or being overly aggressive in expressing a viewpoint can evoke hostility, thus resulting in reviewing the attendees and not the product. Avoid direct accusations and debates.

Agenda   Follow the agenda strictly. If the discussions tend to sway from the agenda, gently remind the attendees of the purpose of the review and the agenda and reiterate the time frame. Stick to the technical issues.

Review Records   Take notes of all the issues raised during the review. If possible, use a flip-chart for recording so everyone can see what is being recorded, and if there is any discrepancy, it is identified and cleared immediately. Document who the issues are assigned to and the resolution date.

Resources   Allocate adequate, qualified resources for the review. The participants should have received formal training in how to conduct reviews and there should be written corporate standards or guidelines on the review methodology.

Attendees   Limit the number of attendees. This will allow the meetings to be focused. Ensure that each attendee has received the review package and that he/she is prepared for the review.

7.2.1 Review Frequency

The reviews can occur at various phases of the life cycle. Some of the major review checkpoints are as listed below.

- at the beginning/end of the requirements phase
- at the beginning/end of the design phase
- at the beginning/end of the code phase
- at the beginning/end of the test phase
- approval of the test plan

Select a series of formal review checkpoints during the development cycle. Conducting the review at the beginning and at the end of each phase will ensure the phase is completed according to predefined standards. Focus on a small part of the overall software; for example, rather than attempting to review an entire design, review the design a few modules at a time. By narrowing the focus, the review tends to uncover a larger number of defects.

7.2.2 Review Planning

Since most reviews tend to be time-consuming and exhausting, do not schedule more than two review sessions per team. Once the review meeting is scheduled, distribute the review package one week in advance. The review package should consist of

- document to be reviewed
- review agenda
- identification of the individual who will manage the agenda and schedule
- exit and entrance criteria for the review
- objective of the review
- names of attendees, their roles and responsibilities
- review location
- date and time of the review
- list of classifications that will be used for defects discovered during the review. Defects may be classified into three categories:
  - (1) Defect type such as incorrect, missing, extra features not originally requested, unambiguous, produces incorrect results, includes features not requested by the customer, or functions inconsistent;

(2) Origin which lists the phase where the defect was originated, such as requirements, design, code, or test; and

(3) Severity which might be high, medium, or low

- procedures for handling issues raised during the review and escalation process

7.2.3 Review Meeting

The facilitator begins the review meeting with an introduction of the agenda, people, and a description of their roles.   The author of the document proceeds to explain the materials, while reviewers raise issues based on advance preparation. When valid problems, issues, or defects are discovered, they are classified according to their origin or severity and then recorded. These are accompanied with the names of individuals who are responsible for resolution and the time frame during which the item will be resolved. Any related recommendations made during the review are recorded.

At the end of the review, all attendees must decide whether to

- accept the product without further modification
- reject the product due to severe errors (once corrected, another review must be conducted)
- accept the product provisionally (minor errors must be corrected within preestablished time frame)
- hold a follow-up review session

Once the decision is made, all the attendees of the review should sign off, indicating their participation and concurrence with the results of the review. The recorder documents all details of the review meeting and publishes the report within one week. The report consists of

- elements reviewed
- names of the individuals who participated in the review
- specific inputs to the review
- list of unresolved items
- list of issues that need to be escalated to management
- action items/ownership/status
- suggested recommendations

7.2.4 Rework

It is important to establish a follow-up procedure to assure that issues raised during the review have been properly addressed and resolved. Unless this is done, it is possible that issues raised may "fall through the cracks." The project manager ensures that all major defects identified in the review are fixed and retested.

7.2.5 Follow-Up

During the follow-up, it is important to ensure that all the discrepancies identified are resolved and the exit criteria for the review have been met. You should also develop recommendations for the future reviews based on the "lessons learned" and distribute the final report consisting of the review findings and resolutions to appropriate staff members.

7.3 WALK-THROUGHS AND INSPECTIONS

Walk-throughs and inspections are other product assurance activities conducted to improve the quality of deliverables. According to the *IEEE Standard Glossary of Software Engineering Terminology* (1990), a walk-through is a review process in which the designer leads one or more others through a segment design or code and the participants ask questions and make comments about possible errors, violation of development standards, and other problems (Std. 610.12-1990). Edward Yourdon (1985) is credited for documenting a detailed walk-through process. The walk-through is conducted for each activity of the project, and the objective of the walk-through is to

- detect errors early
- ensure preestablished standards are followed
- train and exchange technical information among the project team who participate in the walk-through
- improve morale due to increased communication regarding the quality of the project via participating in the walk-through

The inspections are peer reviews of software which were developed by Michael Fagan in 1976 (1976, 1986). The inspection process, as defined by Fagan, involves the following steps:

1. Planning: To identify participants, get materials together, and schedule the overview
2. Overview: To educate the participants
3. Preparation: Individual preparation for the inspections
4. Inspection: Actual inspection to identify defects
5. Rework: Rework to correct any defects
6. Follow-up: Follow-up to ensure all defects are corrected

The inspection team consists of four participants: author or designer who ensures the reader understands the work being inspected and performs any rework required; the reader who paraphrases each design statement or line of code being inspected; the tester who keeps track of all aspects of data compilation and file handling; and the moderator who facilitates the process. There are a number of books on inspections and walk-throughs which we have suggested in the References at the end of this book.

CHAPTER 8

Basic Concepts of Measurements

Measurements and metrics are very troublesome concepts, regardless of what it is you are trying to measure. Everyone tries to reduce very complex systems, processes, organisms, and activities to simple numbers. The study of measurements, especially outside the physical sciences, has led to many disasters whether in the field of health, government, or computer science.

In this chapter we will survey many types of measurements, some tips on how to gather and use them, and some major caveats with respect to their use and misuse. We will also discuss how filters can be used in place of tests, metrics, and measurements to provide more effective feedback mechanisms than the alternatives typically provide.

8.1 DEFINITIONS

There are many popular sayings related to measurements. Almost all of them point to the fact that without measurement, there is no room for improvement. For example, James Clark said, "To measure is to know." Tom DeMarco said, "You cannot control what you cannot measure." Tom Gilb said, "Invisible targets are usually hard to hit," and Deming said, "Plan, do, check, act." These sayings have become so commonplace that we feel like adding, "If you don't know where you are going, how do you know if you have arrived?" We are sure someone else probably made this comment before as well.

At this time, we do not know of any research that indicates what users mean when they request an application with quality. However, Gerald E. Murine (1988) listed the aspects commonly sought in an application by the users. According to Murine, they are

- correctness—the extent to which a program satisfies specifications and fulfills user's mission
- reliability—the extent to which a program can be expected to perform the intended function with accuracy (acceptable level of downtime)

- efficiency—the extent to which a computer uses minimum resources to perform a function

- integrity—the extent to which access to software by unauthorized persons can be controlled

- usability—the effort required to use or learn the application

- maintainability—how difficult it is to find and fix the problem

- testability— the effort required to test the system in order to ensure it functions according to the requirement

- flexibility—the ease of updating or modifying a program

- portability—the efforts required to transfer a program from one hardware configuration to another, or from one software system to another.

- reusability—the extent to which a code could be reused for another application

We have referred to most of these as our measures of quality and indicated that they are related to behavioral tests which can be performed. We indicated that they first appear in relationship to our marketing/document filter: product description/positioning. These then become the basis of how we develop our products.

There are several useful reports on the subject of software metrics which have proven to be practical and result-oriented. For more information, see Gilb (1977); Boehm (1976, 1981); Jones (1986); DeMarco (1982); McCabe (1976); and Halstead (1977). In addition, in the *IEEE Transactions on Software Engineering*, Basili (see Briand et al., 1996) presented a mathematical framework for metrics, with excellent mathematical-based definitions. While the math is basically set theory, those of you with good math backgrounds may wish to explore this paper.

8.2 UNDERSTANDING THE NEED FOR COLLECTING METRICS

Industrial competition is forcing software companies to investigate approaches to producing reliable software. Software reliability and consistency are becoming two of the most competitive areas today. Defects in software are causing various problems in business and are also causing numerous lawsuits. Without reliable data, it is difficult to estimate schedules, work efforts, and costs of software projects. It is evident software quality and reliability measures are required to determine the quality of software and whether it will meet end-user expectations. The *IEEE Standard Glossary of Software Engineering Terminology* (1990) defines "measure" as an activity that ascertains or appraises by comparing to a standard. The most effective method to increase the efficiency of software is to implement a defect prevention methodology by measuring the past defects, identifying the causes, and eliminating them.

There are several reasons for establishing measurement systems in a workplace including

- Conduct performance appraisals to evaluate individual productivity.
- Justify existence, particularly in the era of company downsizing, justification may be needed for the existence of a separate test group. For example, if the test group is constantly able to detect major defects in black box testing, this may be sufficient to justify the existence of the group.
- Compare the quality of one system with another. This becomes difficult if the systems differ dramatically in the size and complexity.
- Monitor if the quality level is affected when any changes are introduced to the software.
- Estimate time and cost required to develop a system.
- Evaluate the quality of service and support provided to the customer.

8.3 BENEFITS OF METRICS

The interpretation of software metrics can improve the overall quality of the product. Without a predictable and reproducible measurement of software quality, you are caught in a never-ending loop of failed estimates and unhappy customers. The information derived from these measures can assist you in implementing processes that would allow you to

- increase customer satisfaction
- improve productivity and quality by quantifying development and maintenance processes
- develop, identify, and analyze trends
- provide useful information for the planning cycle
- provide a baseline against which future efforts can be measured
- determine the skill level and the number of resources required to support a given application
- identify programs that require special attention or additional maintenance time
- identify complex programs that may cause unpredictable results
- provide constructive means of making decisions about product quality

8.4 COST OF METRICS

While *quality is free*, there is initial cost associated with setting up a measurement system. Note that long-term gains derived by measuring and implementing process improvement programs certainly outweigh the cost. The most well known cost estimation models are Boehm's (1981) Cocomo model and L.H. Putnam's (1978) model. Areas that require cost consideration when implementing a measurement program are:

- **Training:** Required for the quality assurance group or other administrative group for collecting, analyzing, and reporting the data. This team of individuals will require skills to identify the root causes of problems and suggest process improvement to eliminate the root cause.

- **System Development Methodology:** Based on the metrics evaluation, there may be changes required in the suggested procedures for developing the application. This may result in rewriting the development methodology, training the staff in the new procedures, updating the current documentation, and replacing the old copies with the new ones.
- **Tools:** New equipment may be required for data collection and counting (function points, errors, etc.). Training on how to use these new tools may be required.
- **Organization change**: Based on metrics, some organizational changes may be desired.

8.5 COMMON MEASUREMENTS AND TIPS

Useful measurements are those that help the software practitioners or managers conduct analysis.

8.5.1 Requirements

Some of the common measures relating to requirements documents include

- Size of the document which includes number of words, number of pages, number of functions.
- Number of changes to the original requirements, which were developed later in the life cycle but not specified in the original requirements document. This measure indicates how complete the original requirements document was.
- Consistency measures to ensure that the requirements are consistent with interfaces from other systems.
- Testability measures to evaluate if the requirements are written in such a way that the test cases can be developed and traced to the requirements.

Often problems detected in the requirements are related to unclear requirements which are difficult to measure and test, such as

- The system must be user friendly. (What does user friendly mean?)
- The system must give speedy response time (What is speedy response time?...10 seconds, 13 seconds?)
- The system must have state-of-the-art technology (What is considered state of the art?)
- The system must have clear management reports (What should these reports look like? What is the definition of clear?)

When stating functional requirements, you must emphasize what the system must do, how well it should do it, and what is expected from it in terms of

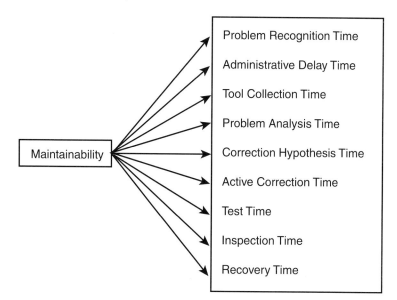

Figure 8-1 A decomposition of maintainability

quality. In addition, when the requirements state that the system should be maintainable, the author of the requirements document should explain what is meant by maintainability. The following explanation of maintainability, based on ideas originated by Tom Gilb (1988), clarifies what the author should address when the word maintainability is used. Figure 8-1 displays our view of Gilb's point.

8.5.2 Code/Design

Measures related to design and programming modules include

- number of external data items from which a module reads
- number of external data items to which a module writes
- number of modules specified at a later phase of the product and not specified in the original design
- number of modules which the given module calls
- number of lines of code (noncommented source statements)
- data usage, measured in terms of the number of primitive data items accessed
- entries/exits per module which predict the completion time of the system

8.5.3 Testing

Measures connected to the testing include

- number of planned test cases in the test plan that ran successfully

- success/effectiveness of test cases against the original test plan
- number of new, unplanned test cases which were developed at a later time

8.6 SEVEN COMMONLY TRACKED MEASURES

Though there are several items in an organization that can be tracked, measured, and improved, there are seven measures that are commonly tracked.

8.6.1 Number of Defects

Defects are the number of reported instances when the software did not meet requirements or performance criteria. Defects are counted throughout the life cycle. The defect count can be kept at three different stages:

1. during white box testing to evaluate the quality of original code
2. during black box testing to evaluate the number of errors that escaped white box or unit test
3. after the product is released to the customer to evaluate the number of errors not found during both the unit and black box tests

Along with the defect, the origin of the defect should be evaluated. For example the requirements phase, design phase, code, and also the severity of the defect should be noted. Identifying the origin of the defect gives you the information for process improvement. For example, if there are too many defects whose origin is traced to the requirements document, you may want to review how the requirements are collected, documented, and inspected since it appears that the current procedure for developing the requirements document is not working. Therefore, the process must be changed to ensure that future requirements documents have quality in them.

The metrics on the defect severity identify the software quality and reliability. Too many show-stopper defects would indicate a weakness in test planning and testing. This information will allow you to either train the staff in thorough test methods or to put procedures such as test plan inspection in place to identify any weakness in testing upfront. For defect severity, refer to defect classification in Section 7.2.2.

8.6.2 Work Effort

Work effort constitutes the number of hours spent on development of a new system, system enhancement, or the support and maintenance of an existing system. The hours are collected throughout the project life cycle, across all the development phases to track commitments, expectations made to the clients, and to provide historical data to improve estimating for future work efforts. Effort is normally tracked for the purpose of planning for the resources and for estimating future project needs. It warns the management of changes and deviations from the original plan that could impact the overall budget of the project.   The data for effort may be collected via timecards or an on-line time tracking system where any time spent on activities related to the project is documented and tracked. Tracking efforts can give early warnings regarding budget overruns and schedule delays. Wolfhart Goethert (1992) has given a framework for counting and reporting staff hours in his book *Software Effort Measurement: An Architecture for Counting Staff-hour and Reporting Schedule Information*.

8.6.3 Schedule

Software development projects often suffer from tight schedules and related problems such as poor quality of the system due to lack of time to test and employee fatigue. The schedule metrics are the variations between planned versus actual. The schedules cannot be met by adding more people to the project since this often causes confusion and chaos. The purpose of schedule measurements is to track the performance of the project team toward meeting the committed schedule. The data from this measure helps management to predict if the original planned delivery dates can be met. In the event that meeting the delivery date seems to be in jeopardy, management can take timely and appropriate steps to control the schedule.

The Cocomo model described by Boehm (1981) in *Software Engineering Economics* may be used to provide feasible elapsed times for projects. For schedule measurement, each major activity of the development cycle is tracked for

- planned start date versus actual date
- planned completion date versus actual completion date

The original planned schedule represents the baseline. Each new estimate is then documented as a revised schedule so that the comparisons can be made between various new estimates and changes to the original dates. The schedule data is typically used in determining the effectiveness of planning and managing. There are a number of project management tools on the market that would verify the data for the actual planned start dates against the actual start date and give variance reports.

8.6.4 Number of Changes to the Requirements

The number of additions, changes, and deletions to requirements should be measured as soon as the requirements document is checked into the formal configuration management. This measure reflects the quality of requirements and the need to change the process of either collecting the requirements or documenting them. The measure is also used to determine system stability, since evidence of constantly changing requirements may affect the overall quality of the product.

The changes to the requirements are counted as they occur. Also the determination of the mean time from the requirement completion to when the first change was introduced is considered. This data tells you how thorough the original requirement-gathering phase was. Once the software system goes into production or is released to the general public, enhancement requests resulting from customer calls or updates due to problem fixes are also counted as changes are made.

8.6.5 Size

The size measures are important because the amount of effort required to perform most tasks is directly related to the size of the program involved. When the size grows larger than expected, the cost of the project as well as the estimated time for completion also grow. The size of the software is also used for estimating the number of resources required. The measure used to estimate program size should be easy to use early in the project life cycle. Subsequent comparisons of the early estimates of the actual measured product size provide input for improved estimates for future projects.

Lines of Code   The size measure is usually accomplished by either using the lines of code or function points. There are no standard counting methods for lines of source code. It is difficult to estimate the lines of code early in the life cycle. The count should be baselined after the first unit test and recounted for each subsequent test version, prior to and including installation of the system. When using the lines of code measure, the following items are usually tracked:

- empty lines
- comments/statements
- source lines
- reused lines
- lines used from other programs

Counting the source lines of code is not a trivial activity and sometimes it is difficult getting consistency, i.e., if an assignment statement takes up multiple lines or if a C programmer places brackets next to a reserve word or in the line below. The safest approach is to use a compiler or other automated tool which counts according to the same algorithm each time. In the authors' experience in testing, very often more errors are found in the comments than in the executable lines of code. How should these be counted—or should they?

Function Points   Allan J. Albrecht from IBM introduced function points in 1979. Function points start from the characteristics and functionality of the system. It is a method of quantifying the size and complexity of a software system based on a weighted user view of the number of external inputs to the application; number of outputs from the application; inquiries end users can make; interface files; and internal logical files updated by an application. In order to measure the program, the developer counts these five items and multiplies the total by weight factors that adjust for complexity. These adjusted function points becomes the unit of measure for the application.

There are several benefits to using function points. They are independent of languages, can be used to measure productivity and number of defects, are available early during functional design, and the entire product can be counted in a short time. Function points can be easy to understand and a nontechnical user can calculate them. They are used for a number of productivity and quality metrics, including defects, schedules, and resource utilization

8.6.6 Documentation Defects

The documentation errors are counted throughout the project life cycle. These defects are collected when they are encountered in any project-related documents, such as requirements, detail designs, test plans, user manuals, and operations manuals. Defects of the following nature are tracked:

- missing functionality
- unclear explanation
- spelling
- not user friendly

8.6.7 Complexity

This metric gives data on the complexity of the software code. As the complexity of software increases, the required development effort increases and the probability of defects increases. Complexity can be measured at as many successive levels as possible beginning at the individual software module level. The purpose is to evaluate the number of resources and time that would be required to develop the application, since complex programs require more time for the programmer to code, test, and become familiar with the program. The complexity of a module can be evaluated by

- number of files
- program size (noncommented source statements)
- number of verbs
- number of IF statements
- number of paragraphs
- total line of code
- number of loops (GO TO-based loops)
- architecture metrics such as
  (a) GO TOs
  (b) entry points
  (c) termination verbs
- diagnostic metrics which are the measure of programming language violations which may not cause compile errors or warnings but which are confusing, such as
  (a) dead code
  (b) unresolved procedure exits

- design complexity which is measured by
  - (a) modularity (how well a design is decomposed into small, manageable modules)
  - (b) coupling (the interfaces between units)

McCabe's (1976) cyclomatic complexity is a measure derived from a flow graph model of a program's control flow. The McCabe metric is a number that represents the complexity of a module and is a measure of the complexity of the program's control structure. It is based on the number of decision statements in the module. If the complexity measure of a module exceeds 10, the chances of the module being error-prone also increases. The McCabe metric is expressed as a unitless number. However, industry experience states that a complexity measure in the rank of 1 to 10 per code module is optimal for producing quality code (William T. Ward, 1989). The cyclomatic complexity can be used to identify which modules should be subjected to vigorous testing. Halstead's software science metrics for complexity are derived from a source code listing for volume, effort, vocabulary, and the like (Halstead, 1977).

8.7 ESTABLISHING A MEASUREMENT PROGRAM AND PROTOTYPING

Within the concept of leverage defined as the part of the new paradigm based on the product delivery process, measurements play an enormous role in being able to manage effectively. Cost accounting as a means of capturing and managing employee activities is absolutely necessary. In this context employees understand that true professionals such as doctors and lawyers attain maximum use of their time often by measuring their activities to within 10 or 15 minutes. When software professionals understand the professionalism and discipline associated with time measurements, they become more enthusiastic about participating. But measurement data is involved in other aspects of software development besides accounting for and maximizing employee effectiveness. As you will see in Section 8.8, we feel that very often filters provide more effective feedback than the more classical measurements defined in this chapter.

Establishing a process to capture and publish measurement data plays a vital role in the success of a measurement program. The selection of the actual metrics is not the only vital factor. The collection and publication of accurate, reliable data are important to gain confidence from the software engineers and managers. If there is no trust in the data collection, the results will not be taken seriously by the recipients. Thus, any suggested process improvements will also not be taken seriously.

Upper-management involvement and support in a metrics program are crucial factors. In companies where middle managers feel threatened if they publish their department's data for either quality or productivity, executive management must guarantee introduction of a fair metrics program. Then these concepts will be received more openly. The idea is to implement a program that makes the employees feel comfortable so they are not afraid that the data may be used against them.

The real issue here is that you should measure things in order to improve them. Thus, in the Deming paradigm, you measure things in order to improve the process and the quality of the deliverables. If measurements are used to place blame for failure, or if layoffs are related to measurements, then you will find people covering up. The whole purpose of measurement is continuous process improvement. We found that when we used filters and leverage, rather than other, more popular, metrics and measurements, the emphasis was on the quality produced by the use of filters against deliverables and the discipline of managers in seeing that their employees were placed in the most favorable productivity environment.

This management approach is in direct alignment with Deming's philosophy, as represented in Figure 11-1. It is also a fundamental part of total quality management. To us, meeting the schedule within budget with a highly leveraged product is far more important than the lines of code or function points involved. The purpose of a schedule, managed in terms of a Gantt chart or other tool, is to allow for an employee's improved productivity, not to force excessive programmer code production at the expense of quality. Ideally, the productivity in terms of product development should come through a more efficient process and an architecture which provides for extensive reuse.

To us, the most important measures are defined in terms of customer satisfaction and increased profits. Our product delivery process begins and ends with the customer, through the initial marketing and sales filters to those associated with the release management process.

Robert B. Grady from Hewlett-Packard has written two books on software measurement that focus on how to establish a metrics program (1987, 1992). We recommend both of these books to anyone trying to establish a software measurement program in software metrics. Grady focuses on how Hewlett-Packard dealt with cultural and technical issues and why the company established the Software Metrics Council to address software engineering problems.

When establishing a measurement program, you should phase in each measure in the organization, resulting in an ultimate integrated measurement program. The general approach to establishing a successful measurement program is to

- identify the reason for establishing a measurement program
- identify the needs of your audience and stakeholders
- determine the level of organizational resistance and how you would address it
- involve as many staff members as you can to overcome resistance
- determine how much time you have
- investigate if there are any measures already in place that you can use
- decide which metrics to start collecting first
- ensure there is compatibility of measurement goals with the goals of the organization
- establish a phased implementation plan

- establish quantifiable targets such as cost, personnel, and schedule targets for the activities and outputs of each phase of the development process
- review the measurement plan with appropriate managers and executive management
- obtain commitment from upper management to provide you with additional resources or tools, if the need arises
- measure the actual values against the targets
- determine the variances and the reasons for the variances
- establish a plan to address the variance and standardize the plan to prevent these variances from occurring in the future
- establish history with which to compare future data
- integrate metrics into the development process as a part of the way you do business
- focus on success

Most measurement programs fail for one of several reasons. They may fail because they did not have executive management support. Or, the measurement plan focused on only one measure and when the data was collected and evaluated, no one knew what to do next. Another reason measurement programs may fail is that the data was not utilized as intended. For example, a process was not put in place to eliminate similar defects in the future or far too many metrics were collected and no one had time to do anything with the data. Beware of all of these symptoms before you start.

When establishing a measurement requirement, use a direct metric value—a numerical target for a factor to be met in the final product. You might have results like the following:

- system response time—4.2 sec.
- system availability—99%
- user satisfaction—95%
- network availability—98%
- predictive metric value—a numerical target related to a factor to be met during system development. This is an intermediate requirement that is an early indicator of final system performance. For instance, design or code errors may be early predictors of final system error rate.

8.7.1 Prototyping

Changing the culture of an organization is an extremely difficult task. When establishing a measurement plan, you may have to face a hostile environment where individual department managers may not want you to collect metrics of their work area due to the fear that these metrics may be used against them. After you go through a rough and hard sell, you want to ensure the measurement plan is successful right from the start. Consider prototyping the plan before actually publishing the data. The idea is to address any unforeseen glitches that you may face and to test the entire process of data collection and dissemination.

Once the results of the prototyping are reliable, implement the measurement plan on a small scale. Keep all the stakeholders informed of the data and validate the data you collect on a continuous basis. For example, ask yourself: Are these the right data? Are there areas that need improvement? Based on the results of the validation activity, adjust the measurement plan. Apply the measurement activities in other projects and finally expand the scope of your metrics program to include management commitment and support

8.7.2 Measurement Cycle

After the data for a particular measure is collected, you should do the following:

1. analyze the data
2. identify the problem area
3. develop procedures to address the problem area
4. get buy-in from appropriate staff
5. train staff in the new procedures
6. implement new procedures
7. continue the measurement activity
8. change the process if need be

Any measure when implemented and applied correctly can prove beneficial to your organization. But we feel that there is an effective alternative. The next section discusses the use of filters as an alternative to measurement and other feedback mechanisms.

8.8 THE IMPACT OF FILTERS AS FEEDBACK MECHANISMS

Filters versus tests, metrics, and measurements constitute a powerful change of paradigm. The concept is that it is possible to filter out errors in marketing documents, sales documents, software specifications, software architecture, and software products without traditional testing and inspections. The management strategy using our product delivery process allows continuous process improvement through immediate feedback. In traditional software development organizations, the emphasis is on metrics and measurements which are used to evaluate changes to the software development process and to prove to management that investing in software development methodologies and tools provides good payback or return on investment, but they are evaluated over a long period of time. Project postmortems are used to evaluate just-completed projects so future projects can be improved upon. This means a development team fixes or improves future projects rather than current ones. You should note that the concept of a filter exists in many different forms within the software development

community. From one point of view, any sort of testing or review process is a filter. There is nothing wrong with this.

Our approach uses filters to provide immediate feedback. These filters and
the errors they uncover can be evaluated, and the filters fixed many times during
the current project, should it prove necessary. Filters relating to such deliverables as marketing documents, sales documents, training plans, delivery plans,
and so forth, tend to be very stable, and once they are established, they rarely
are changed. On the other hand, filters relating to the area of software development tend to be very technology dependent and may change several times per
month or even per project per week.

When an error is uncovered, especially late in the software development life
cycle, we pass the error through each of the earlier filters to see why they did not
catch it. For those filters that should have caught it, a change is made to make it
more sensitive—not to the error, but to that class of error. We also fix the deliverable in which the error occurred. When an error gets through to the customer,
especially after the organization and the filters have matured, the error means
that 18+ filters have broken simultaneously. An example of a filter is the market-
oriented requirements definition filter (see Figure 4-1). This deliverable creates
the context in which the software product is to be built. It is the foundation on
which the product specification is built. A discussion of the frontend filters at
Digital Technology International is provided in the Appendix.

8.9 THE MISUSE OF STATISTICS IN SOFTWARE DEVELOPMENT

There have been many metrics that have been used in software development as
software experts have attempted to discover which techniques are best for providing effective software development. A major problem with the use of statistics
is the failure to recognize the basic concepts on which they are based. We will
comment on a few of the major misuses.

8.9.1 Statistical Measurements

First of all, just what should we be measuring? If we measure error rates,
we reduce error rates; if we measure lines of code produced, we get a lot of lines
of code; if we measure functions produced, we get a lot of functions produced. But
what happens when we attempt to tie programmer productivity to familiar versus unfamiliar specifications or environments? Then productivity is related to
the ability of a programmer to pattern match.

There are some things that are difficult to measure objectively (or accurately). What about effectiveness of a technology? What about the effectiveness
of "design before implementation"? Looking at that, how do you measure the
effectiveness of using pseudocode versus "just programming directly, without
design"? Is it measured in terms of errors? Lines of code produced? Functions
produced? Adherence to quality standards? Amount of time to code and compile?
Or what?

None of these questions, nor their solutions, is very satisfying. One of the authors required university students to submit a pseudocode version and a preliminary code version of each problem to the programming lab before they would be admitted. Semester after semester, those students tended to average 20 minutes in the lab to complete an assignment, while students from other comparable classes took over three hours. What do you conclude? Would you apply this result or observation to all students? To all programmers? What happened to these observations when most students began having personal computers where they could program without this enforced discipline? What actually was being measured by these conditions?

You should be very careful how you use metrics—whatever they are. Yet it is true: "If you can't measure it, you can't manage it." A parallel comment is: "You get what you measure." A good feedback mechanism will allow you to adapt measurements as you attempt to find those that help you.

The strategy proposed in the new paradigm allows for effective metrics, as it is based on five-year plans, mission statements, marketing strategies, strategic competitive advantage, etc. If you build products to achieve these goals, the measurements and metrics you use will naturally adapt to give you an efficient way of achieving them.

8.9.2 Sampling versus Case Studies

There have been several studies which have attempted to use university students to prove that "pseudocode is unnecessary" or "productivity is better if you teach them to..." The problem with these studies is that they are based on presentation samples; that is, they are not selected at random from the entire population of professional and nonprofessional programmers but are selected from students who have chosen to attend a particular university and take a particular class at a particular time. Further, they may be beginning students who are learning their first programming language. Even though they are divided at random into two (or more) groups, inferences drawn from the sample can only be applied to other students who attend that university at that particular time. The sample is self-selecting. To be statistically valid, you must select your sample from the entire population about which you wish to make the inference. Studies based on small programs do not necessarily carry over to large programs, especially not exceedingly large programs. It is difficult to find even one company that will agree to divide its programmers or projects into two groups to program with two methodologies—or to build the same project two ways.

The best solution is to use case studies. These are used in medicine and other fields all the time. In case studies, you do not really make inferences; you observe what happens and use that experience to make intelligent judgments—tempered with common sense—regarding what the implications are. The careful use of experience and feedback is extremely helpful in establishing strategies that are experientially based. This is the approach we have recommended in using our new paradigm. It does not need statistical validation. It needs effective use with feedback.

You should also note that statistical methods applied to the hard sciences are fairly easy to measure and control. It is also easy to make inferences that are fairly accurate. However, computer science—especially software development—is a soft science, like psychology or social science. As such, it is difficult to define measurements and experimental conditions and to control them adequately. Thus, the basic problems of statistics, as applied to software engineering, are related to measurement, defining populations, sampling, and inference (such as estimation and tests of hypothesis) and the fact that effective, controlled experimental conditions are extremely difficult to achieve.

8.9.3 Errors of the Estimate in Statistical Inference

Not only do we measure things (in a sample) incorrectly and attempt to use the results of the statistics to make inferences about programmers or methodologies to the wrong populations; we also often draw the wrong conclusions. A test of a hypothesis is merely an estimate that has a value 1 or 0 (true or false). Suppose someone performed a test of hypothesis involving a number of companies where each company tested its software using two techniques, like structured testing (by McCabe's definition) and simple statement coverage, assigned at random across, say, 100,000 lines of C code, broken into modules by some methodology. If they reach the conclusion that "there is no significant difference in the number of errors found" and use that conclusion to show that you need only perform statement coverage, they have grossly misinformed the testing community. The proper conclusion is that "given the sample size and makeup, it was not possible to show any significant difference, assuming there was one." Perhaps with a different, larger, or more sensitive sample, it would have been possible to detect a significant difference.

On the other hand, if a researcher sent out a million questionnaires to ask how much time programmers spent at lunch and found that senior programmers spent an average of 63.25 minutes and junior programmers spent an average of 63.20, he or she would probably find the difference to be statistically significant because in large samples, statistical tests converge to significance. Yet it is obvious that the actual average difference is negligible.

Another caveat in using statistics is when statistics are used to make estimates such as "time to complete an application or task," "programming knowledge," or "projected number of errors remaining in the code." Many people treat these numbers as exact. They are not. They are statistical approximations against which there is an error involved if they are to be used as estimates. For example, if some sort of statistical regression were used in creating an estimate, there are three types of errors:

1. The error associated with a prediction for the average number of errors per thousand lines of code for everyone who got the average measurement on whatever was being used to make the prediction (such as base salary), would be the smallest possible error of the estimate. The larger the sample, the smaller the error of the estimate.

2. The error associated with a prediction based on the average of everyone who had a given base salary, which would be larger than the estimate of the average by a factor related to the distance from the overall mean of the variable being used to make the prediction.

3. The error associated with a prediction for a particular individual who scored a certain distance from the overall mean is the largest possible error, as it involves an individual, rather than an average.

To illustrate this more explicitly, assume that someone uses a set of pairs of scores from a sample of programmers to see if the score on a programming test can be used to predict the speed of programming a given function. If the average score of 60% on the programming test predicts that the average time to program the function would be 10 hours, with an error of $\pm$ 1.5 hours, you could say that the average of all programmers from the population from which the sample was taken would be estimated to be between 8.5 and 11.5 hours, with a confidence level of 95%. On the other hand, for the average of all the programmers who scored 80% on the test, the estimate might be 6 hours. With an error of $\pm$ 2 hours, you would expect the average for the population of all programmers who would have scored 80% had they taken the test to be between 4 and 8 hours, with a confidence level of 95%.

But what if you have a programmer who has taken the test and scored 60% but has not yet programmed the function? What would be the error of the estimate? Our best guess is 10 hours, but the error of the estimate is no longer between 8.5 and 11.5; it could be somewhere around 3 and 17, with that 95% confidence level. Thus, this individual could be the worst programmer in terms of time—or the best. That is what is wrong with most statistical predictions. You must be very careful to take into account the error of the estimate, even when the predictions are based on a fairly large sample. You might fail to hire an outstanding programmer (in terms of programming efficiency) simply because he or she could not score well on a test.

Think about the implications of these ideas when you are estimating time to project completion based on linear or multiple regression results. Your estimates are better than nothing; in fact, they may be quite good. But you must be aware that there are errors involved. See Humphrey (1995) or any good statistics text for examples of how to calculate these errors. We also indicated in an earlier chapter that you often can get a fairly good estimate simply by using information from an earlier, similar project as an experiential basis for the time it might take you on a current project. Later on, you can make these "empirical estimates" more precise with mathematical calculations.

We commented earlier on using statistical studies to predict error rates. While there are people who claim to achieve around 1% accuracy of prediction, we remain skeptical. The only way common sense tells you these measurements could possibly be that accurate is if they are measuring and predicting using code that is extremely similar. If this is true, as we stated earlier, programmers must be making the same predictable errors in the second version as in the first. Regression estimates are based on the persistence of the traits being measured from one project to another. This means the programmers are persisting in making the same errors. If they are, you are looking at the wrong problem. You do not want to test these errors out; you want to find out why the programmers keep designing the same errors in!

8.9.4 Statistics as Applied to Quality Control

We mentioned the problems related to measuring quality in Chapter 4. In fact, we are inclined to measure quality in terms of software behavior, rather than error rates. We consider failure to conform to the specification to be a set of error conditions. If the specification-conforming software does not do what the customer wants it to do, then the marketing filters (or JAD filters) are broken—and you are still dealing with an error condition or set of conditions. When quality control and sampling concepts are carried directly over from hardware, things tend to fall apart.

Lot acceptance sampling, where someone selects random samples of a particular size from a lot (or set of products) and rejects the lot when the number of defects is above a particular number, does not fit software. Errors are rarely uniformly distributed along a logic path, control flow, or code sequence. Typically, they spike—or group together—when a programmer is tired, does not understand a function, or for some other reason is not at peak efficiency. These spikes are not predictable and do not follow a pattern. Further, even if you select a program statement at random using some sampling strategy, you cannot know whether or not it is correct, as it must be taken in the context of, or as a part of, the environment in which it exists. This might be a control structure, a small code sequence, or an entire module—or it might even involve an entire subsystem.

Statistical process control, where you attempt to plot the error rates as a continuous process takes place and stop the process when the consecutive errors exceed a certain range, also does not work for software—for the same reason as that described above. The basic concept in hardware is that a device is getting farther and farther "out of alignment" and needs to be replaced or readjusted. That is not what happens with software. The concept of a process control strategy going "out of range" is perfectly valid in software development, but it cannot be measured using the traditional hardware-oriented process control techniques. This is because software development is not a linear process and is based on several to many programmers, rather than on a single device. Rarely do you find all the programmers going out of control at once.

But the entire software quality assurance process can go "out of control." The new software paradigm tends to catch this type of situation better than the traditional approaches based on traditional life cycles. Sometimes plotting error rates and other metrics will help you catch things like this, but usually it is during a project postmortem and is more useful in applying your results to follow-on or future projects, as is the case with most metrics used in the traditional manner. Using the product delivery process paradigm, you are checking the process almost continuously, far more often than with traditional metrics and measurements. Since the process is self-correcting, it not only follows Deming's quality framework, it also provides a better, more valid solution than that obtained by attempting to measure it "statistically."

Myers (1979b) suggests that code that contains a large number of errors should be focused on as error-prone code and tested even more completely—or re-designed and reprogrammed. This is the concept we need to use in software, rather than process control. You will need to experiment to find out what this rate should be. In the new paradigm, we propose zero percent. There are other quality measures and strategies also proposed which involve the concept of "zero defects" (see Schulmeyer, 1990). As can be seen, this is not a metric that is only visible in follow-on or future projects; it is seen and corrected for immediately.

IBM found that leaving error-prone modules in some of their large systems, rather than reprogramming them (at great cost, in some cases), ended up being even more expensive to maintain and upgrade over the years of the products' lives. This will almost always be true, and the larger the product, the more impact leaving such modules in the software will have on its overall mainte-nance. Often these modules will be extremely sensitive to their environments, and even though they do not actually contain errors, the fact that they are error-prone tends to make them break when changes are made in other related mod-ules.

In small programs, or off-the-shelf programs in the Mac or PC environment, product life is much shorter. Trying to maintain these short-lived products allows more room for these error-prone modules to fail and not have much impact. In the large mainframe software, the life cycle is much longer. Now, how-ever, there is the potential of these error-prone modules ending up in libraries where they can be reused. While it is not as likely that they will get into such libraries due to the amount of testing that *should* take place before admitting them, exactly what constitutes an error-prone module should be taken into account and tested for.

Statistical sampling may be useful in auditing and/or validating a data-base, but it is rarely effective in testing code. Using a concept like design analy-sis is much more effective, as it is based on descriptive statistics and observed relationships and experience, rather than on statistical inference and error.

We talked about mean time to failure earlier and explained why it did not seem like a good concept. This is mainly because it is based on sets of user pro-files or scenarios. If there are no dependencies among modules and subsystems, then the system is deterministic and should run forever. If, on the other hand, there are massive dependencies and the sets of user profiles are infinite, then mean time to failure is a random concept and it is based upon which particular profile it is running which causes the failure. Since there is an infinite number, you cannot really predict which ones will cause failures or when they will occur. It is possible that user profiles based on the frequency distribution of use pat-terns may give a reasonable prediction of mean time to failure, but it still shows that the input domain is out of control. If you enforce a finite number of user pro-files through constraints, you should be able to design or test out all the errors. If you cannot design or test them out, it is because the dependencies cause too many states for the input variables, and under those conditions, mean time to failure definitely has meaning. But the problem is with your dependencies.

8.10 CONCLUSION

As you have seen in this chapter there is a wide variety of metrics and measurements available for use. For practically any one you choose, there is a controversy regarding another which competes with it. Yet the truism of the first paragraph in the chapter remains true. While installing a measurement program can be extremely frustrating and difficult, if it is approached correctly, it can be extremely beneficial and cost-effective

You may note that we cast a rather jaundiced eye on a large number of measurements and metrics because of their misuse. However, we enthusiastically recommend measurement programs such as Grady has created and validated at Hewlett-Packard.

The purpose of the previous section has been to show you why you should be very cautious in your use of statistics in your work. You should not rely too heavily on any published statistical results that you have not verified in your own company. Use your own experience on small projects to validate whatever measurements or metrics you use. Notice that we made similar comments in Chapter 3 as to how you should justify the development of a formal test organization and how it should be installed in your organization.

Whenever you use a new methodology such as the new product delivery process paradigm we are proposing, you must validate it within your own software development environment. This is also true of any technology that impacts your environment. You should especially be cautious of using estimators associated with software size, time to completion, etc. Some very excellent companies claim they can come within 10 percent of any estimate they make; we believe that it is true, and it is achievable by any company that takes the time to do things right—and measure them meaningfully.

CHAPTER 9

Process Improvement Road Map

America's quality guru, W. Edwards Deming, won the respect of American management by preaching a philosophy of commitment to quality and continuously improving the companywide processes. His recognition that "quality cannot be inspected in, it must be built in" raised an awareness in American businesses regarding quality. Many U.S. companies have recognized the fact that the way to survive through the tough economic times is to understand the needs of the customers and satisfy these needs. The companies that are industry leaders and retain their customer base are the ones that continuously evaluate their processes, services, and delivery mechanisms and improve them.

When thinking about the word "quality," the phrase "process improvement" immediately comes to mind. There is a strong relationship between the process and the outcome of that process. When no attention is paid to the process, it results in unhappy customers, poor quality products, cost overruns, and lost market share.

Before any process improvements can be implemented, consideration should be given to the organizational culture and how the change will be received. Among other things, a change in corporate culture means that working adults must learn new methods to do their jobs. Learning new methods may be an uncomfortable thought for many individuals who are used to doing things in a certain way. To help manage the change, it is important to identify the scope of such things as who will be affected and to what extent they will be affected. The change process should be gradual in order to have successful results. We recommend you hold a meeting and invite all the individuals who will be affected by the change. The following are some steps you can adhere to.

1. Explain the problem, discuss why the change is necessary, and spell out the reasons in terms that are meaningful. Outline the strategy to address the problem. This will allow the attendees to learn about what is it that you plan to address and what you intend to do.
2. Create a comfortable atmosphere where people will feel free to openly voice their concerns and their opinions. Address every concern voiced.

241

3. Explain the details of the change, elaborate on the return on investment, how it will affect the staff, and when the change will take place. People are resistant to change due to fear of the unknown. When a change is introduced, the first questions that come to mind of those who will be affected by it are "What's in it for me? Why should I accept the change?" Generally, individuals would like to become change agents because of some of the following reasons:

   (a) gives opportunities to take active part in decisions affecting them and their job

   (b) gives greater satisfaction in knowing problems they identify will be addressed and eliminated

   (c) gives opportunity to expose problems that make it difficult for them to do their job

   (d) helps them to do better job by teaching techniques of identifying problems and solving them

   (e) helps them get the recognition deserved for ideas and efforts

   (f) helps them to come to a realization that teamwork can be very effective and satisfying

   (g) assists in understanding how to effectively measure progress

4. Explain how the change will be implemented and measured.

5. Identify the individuals who are open-minded to accept the change more easily. These individuals will support the implementation of the change.

6. Train employees to help them acquire needed skills. Remember that every employee should receive some training in problem-solving skills. Not knowing how to implement whatever is recommended via this change causes uneasiness. This will help ease the transition.

7. Encourage teamwork at all times and all levels.

8. Address each concern with care so there is no fear left and value each opinion.

9. Make decisions based on factual data rather than opinions or gut feelings.

10. Enforce decisions to reinforce the change.

9.1 SEVEN STEPS OF THE PROCESS IMPROVEMENT ROAD MAP

In order to implement a change, it is necessary to have a standardized method that will be adhered to each time. In addition, it has been proven frequently that resolving process-related issues in teams results in better solutions that are likely to be implemented and to be successful. For this reason, we have developed a seven-phase, easy-to-follow process which we call the "Process Improvement Road Map (PIR)." This team approach to resolve issues and eliminate roadblocks can be implemented on departmental level as well as overall organization level. There are several benefits of using PIR.

- establishes a common way to identify the problem and address it
- avoids re-inventing the process
- creates consistent problem solving from one project to another
- makes training and related materials easily accessible since everyone in the company is required to use it

Each phase identified in the PIR is accompanied with the activities to be performed. Since most process output conditions require combinations of quality tools to monitor and/or control process effectively, we have listed and explained a number of quality tools. Depending on your needs, you may select the tool that is appropriate for you.

Each problem-solving opportunity should be addressed by a team consisting of individuals from each functional area of the organization. The individuals selected should have the credibility necessary to influence the management and staff to accept the process change recommendations and provide support. The team members should be given training on the use of the seven basic problem-solving tools: cause-and-effect, multivoting, Pareto chart, scatter diagrams, histograms, brainstorming, and line graphs. Figure 9-1 describes this process.

Step 1: Plan

The purpose of this step is to obtain consensus on the goal, charter, and direction. It is important to pay special attention to certain activities in the planing stage. These activities will ensure the overall success of the implementation of methods for process improvement:

Obtain a Sponsor The sponsor will assist in obtaining the budget and properly qualified resources for the project. The sponsor is the spokesperson for the project. We recommend the sponsor be from the upper-management team who has the power and authority to change the course of the process improvement team if need be.

Select Team Members The selection process should be based on experience, team spirit, and the enthusiasm for implementing processes that contribute towards overall quality and productivity. The team members should be from cross-functional areas, so that there is representation from all the departments. Each member should be fully aware of the business processes and areas of improvement within his or her department.

Decide and Obtain Consensus on the Team Charter Identify the scope and the goal of the team. This sets expectations and communicates the purpose of the team to the team members as well as the rest of the organization. Each member should have a say in building the charter. This will encourage ownership of the team results.

Identify and Select Area for Improvement Let each member discuss his or her department and related issues that need improvement. List all the improvement needs on a flip-chart where they can be viewed by everyone. Ask the group to define areas of improvement and issues. With the help of the team members, prioritize the list based on business impact, cost, and schedule. At this

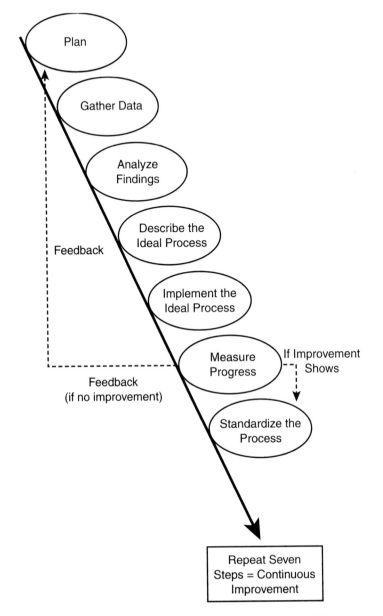

Figure 9-1 Seven steps of the process improvement roadway. These are used to identify and address areas that need analysis and improvement.

early stage, the primary focus is on involving all the team members so they can learn about the entire process improvement through team participation. It is best to pick just one or two areas to improve. This allows full concentration and speeds up the process of implementation of necessary procedures.

Prepare Project Plan, Identify Activities, Schedule, and Resources Once the area of improvement is selected, identify individual activities that need to take place and the number of resources needed to accomplish the activities. Develop a project schedule, outlining major milestones and activities.

Identify How Data Will Be Collected, Distributed and Used Decide on how the progress of the project will be measured and how the results will be distributed, who will get the results, and how often these results will be announced.

Tools of Quality to Be Used Today's software quality managers increasingly recognize nontechnical skills as the foundation of process improvement. In the past, the training for frequently used quality tools such as cause-and-effect and Pareto analysis was given only to the technical individuals. But now, quality managers have integrated the problem-solving tools for all employees. The use of nontechnical tools and skills such as interpersonal communication, teamwork, and group problem solving are playing a major role in identifying issues and initiating quality processes. The following quality tools are valuable in problem-solving activities and improvement opportunities for the "plan" step.

Meeting Agenda Develop an agenda to set the direction. An agenda should include the following:

- introduction of each team member
- purpose of the meeting and discussion of the goal
- scope of the project
- identification of action items
- time, date, and place of the next meeting

Roles and Responsibilities/Schedule Indicate what will be done, when, and who will do it. For example: "Identification of handling customer complaints, June 15, Shruti Gandhi." See Figure 9-2.

Multivoting Multivoting is used to obtain quick decisions on which areas to work on first; out of two or three suggestions, which one should be selected. You use multivoting to decrease the number of items identified during a brainstorm session so that you can reduce a large list to a manageable few (refer to step 4 for details). It is an ideal technique to obtain consensus from a group of people as to which problem you should work on first. Each member of the team votes several times on the list of problems. The multivoting narrows down to three or five high-impact problems that you should start addressing. If you answer "yes" to the following questions, use the multivote technique:

- Is the list from your brainstorming session large and unmanageable?
- Are you having difficulties in obtaining consensus on which areas to work on first?
- Due to time constraints, do you want a method to focus on selecting improvement opportunities?

The steps for the multivote technique are simple.

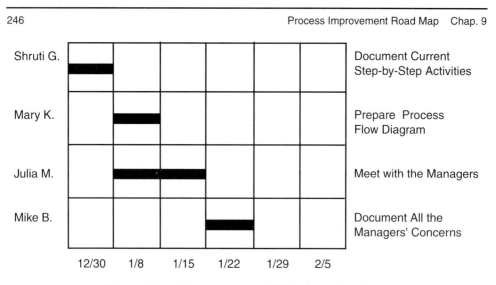

Figure 9-2   Roles and responsibilities/schedule chart

1. Count the number of problems to be addressed on the list.
2. Divide the number in half and add "1" (If you have six ideas, you will come up with four.)
3. Each person then votes on the number of times determined in the above step (i.e., four times)
4. If you have six ideas on the list, keep the top two vote-getters.
5. Keep on voting until you reduce the number of ideas to two.

Checklist   A checklist ensures all necessary issues have been identified and addressed. Some of the questions you may want to include in the checklist are:

1. Has the charter of the team been identified?
2. Has consensus on the charter been obtained from other affected departments and staff members?
3. Are the team members selected?
4. Has the project sponsor been defined?
5. Is the project plan identified and defined?
6. Are all the individual activities defined?
7. Is each member's role defined?
8. Has a meeting time been agreed upon?
9. Has the methodology to identify and select problems agreed upon?
10. Is it decided how the data will be collected and distributed?
11. Is it decided how the data will be used?
12. What will be the format of the data reporting?
13. Is it identified how often the team will meet?

Step 2: Gather Data

In this step you collect metrics on the results of current process with the intention to understand what is currently being done and also to understand the relationship between processes. In order to do this,

1. Review current process and difficulties; study the area of improvement and identify all the current processes. Meet with individuals who are the owners of the process. Discuss and document the difficulties.

2. Prepare flowcharts of the current process; "A picture is worth a thousand words." Develop data flow diagrams of current practices and procedures that are causing difficulties.

3. Describe each process in detail; identify and document each activity and write clear explanation on what the problems are.

4. Prioritize the improvement opportunities; if there is more than one process that needs improvement, prioritize which one needs to be addressed first by evaluating the impact on the business.

5. Obtain consensus from the team members; discuss your findings with other team members and obtain their "buy-in" as to which area should be worked on first and also the approach.

6. Perform cause-and-effect analysis on the problem.

Tools of Quality to Be Used   The following quality tools can be helpful in gathering the data.

Cause-and-Effect Graph   The late Kaoru Ishikawa developed the cause-and-effect diagram in 1943 at the University of Tokyo to explain to the engineers from Kawasaki Steel Works how various factors could be evaluated. The cause-and-effect diagram is a method for analyzing causes and their related effects. Since the completed diagram resembles a skeleton of a fish, it is also known as a fishbone diagram or Ishikawa diagram. This tool is one of the most popular tools in the industry as there is very little training involved to use it and it is easily understood by everyone. Figure 9-3 indicates the main causes for a large number of software defects. For example, the main cause "Management" has a direct relationship to the effect of "Too Many Software Defects." Each subcause mentioned in Figure 9-4 has influence over the main cause. Continue analysis to the level of actionable root causes. Select the root causes that have the greatest impact and obtain the data to verify the selection.

Process Flow Diagram   This technique is a good way to identify and graphically describe all the steps that are undertaken to accomplish a certain business activity within an organization. The process flow diagram is used to evaluate any duplicate efforts or redundant activity that should be eliminated. For accurate results, be sure to get feedback from the individuals who are actually involved in the process and title the flowchart. Figure 9-5 shows a simple process flow from the point a customer walks into a bank to open an account to the point when the customer leaves the bank. The diamond symbol is used for a

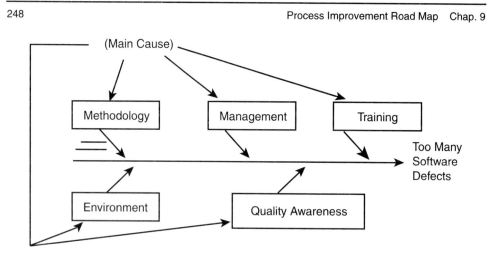

Figure 9-3   Main causes for software defects

decision point, a box is used for activities in the process, and an arrow is used for the flow of direction from one activity to the next.

Assessment   An assessment is an activity to evaluate how well an organization is doing. It is also a review of an organization to let management know how well the organization is performing. It makes the management aware of any areas of the organization that need improvement. The reason for an assessment

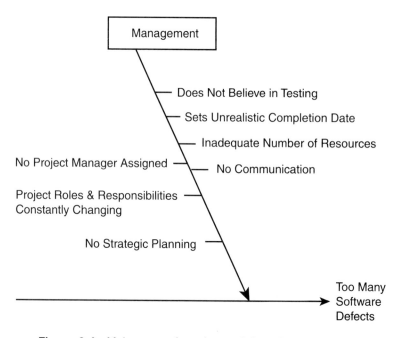

Figure 9-4   Main causes for software defects (management)

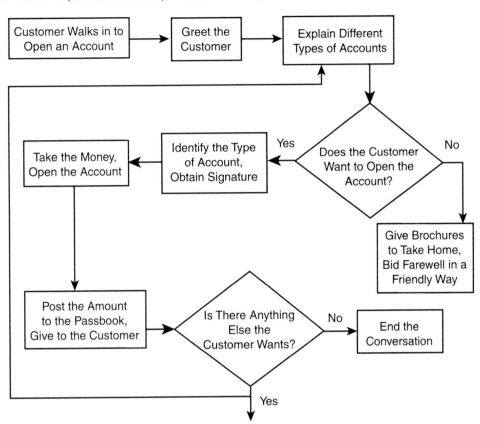

Figure 9-5   Process flow diagram: handling a walk-in customer

is to identify if processes are working well or if they are contributing to poor quality or service. Each department's processes are flowcharted and areas of improvement are identified. These areas are then prioritized based on the impact to business. The high-impact areas are addressed first. All the findings during an assessment, along with the root causes, are discussed with the appropriate managers and personnel.

Checklist   A checklist ensures all necessary issues have been identified and addressed. Some of the questions you may want to include in the checklist are:

1. Have all the staff of the identified area been interviewed?

2. Is the current process understood and reviewed by the team?

3. Are the flowcharts of all the current process prepared?

4. Is each process described in detail?

5. Does everyone on the team understand flowcharts?

6. Is there a consensus on the improvement opportunities and what determines whether the process is working?

7. Are there any quality records kept for the current process and who reviews them and how are they used?

8. Have all the improvement opportunities been prioritized based on the business impact?

9. Do all the team members agree on the priority rating?

Step 3: Analyze Findings

Once the data is collected on the process flow, use them to analyze and understand the process difficulties. The next step is to analyze the "root cause" of the difficulty by evaluating what is causing the problem and where things are going wrong. Decide how this problem can be addressed. Investigate the interrelationships and dependencies between processes. This will enable you to understand other areas that may be affected by the problem. Also identify the departments and staff that are being affected.

Tools of Quality to Be Used   The following quality tools can be used to analyze findings.

Cause & Effect Diagram   Refer to step 2.

Process Flow Diagram   Refer to step 2.

Scatter Diagram   A scatter diagram is used for identifying if there is a relationship between two factors (variables) and any possible cause-and-effect relationships. Understanding the relationship between two factors is important whether the root cause is responsible for a problem or not. Figure 9-6 shows the varying amount of fuel used in relationship to automobile speed. The data points on the chart are the amount of fuel utilized at the speed of 100 mph, 90 mph, etc. After plotting the points, you need to look for patterns. Do the dots form a distinctive line or curve? Understanding the relationship between two factors is important whether the root cause is responsible for a problem or not.

Scatter diagrams are used when trying to evaluate the performance of a current process, to show the data distribution, or to show if there is a cause-and-effect relationship between two variables. Here are simple steps that you can perform to create a scatter diagram.

1. Identify two variables suspected of having a causal relationship.

2. Collect and plot samples of "paired" data that may be related.

3. Plot the data from the summary data sheet (see Figure 9-7). For each week, the data should be captured daily and then summarized.

4. Review patterns formed by the data and analyze trends. The probability of a possible cause-and-effect relationship is higher if the data points resemble a straight line, as every time one variable changes, the other changes by the same amount.

If there is no line, that means there is no cause-and-effect relationship.

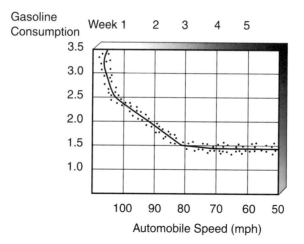

Figure 9-6 Scatter diagram: relationship between gasoline consumption and speed. A line is superimposed along the path suggested by the data points. The pattern indicates that the variables have a definite effect on one another. The more speed, the higher utilization of the fuel; however, after reducing the speed to 50 mph, additional reduction in the speed seems to have no effect on the utilization of the fuel. If there were no relationship between fuel and speed, the pattern of dots would be randomly scattered.

Sometimes the data in a scatter diagram can be supplemented in a summary data sheet. This may help in understanding the data. The data can also be used as input dots for the scatter diagram.

As you look at scatter diagrams, you need to be very cautious, in the light of what we stated in Chapter 8. There are three dangers in putting too much faith in scatter diagrams.

- There is a relationship, but what you have called the "independent variable," i.e., the one that "causes" the "dependent variable" to change, may actually be the "effect" of the other. In other words, there is a "correlation" or relationship, but you do not really know the causes and effects.

- There is a relationship, but it is "spurious." Both the variables you are measuring are actually related to each other by the fact that both are related to a third, unknown, unmeasured independent variable.

- While you see a pattern or relationship in the scattergram, it is not statistically significant, i.e., it occurred simply due to chance.

Sometimes the problem is that you fail to look at the complete environment. An example is that if in your company's strategic planning you plot sales against months, you might see a staggering increase, but if you plot market share

Weeks

	1	2	3	4	5	6	7
8	2.2	1.6	1.3	1.2	1.2	1.1	1.0
7	2.3	1.9	1.4	1.3	1.3	1.2	1.3
6	2.6	2.2	1.4	1.4	1.4	1.3	1.1
5	2.7	2.1	1.5	1.7	1.6	1.4	1.1
4	2.9	2.1	1.6	1.8	1.7	1.5	1.2
3	3.1	2.2	1.7	1.7	1.8	1.6	1.3
2	3.3	2.3	1.8	1.8	1.9	1.6	1.4
1	3.4	2.4	1.9	1.6	1.9	1.7	1.4

8 Automobiles

100 90 80 70 60 50 40

Miles Per Automobile

Figure 9-7 Summary data sheet for scatter diagram: amount of gasoline per week per automobile with varying speed

against months, you see it going down drastically. So while your sales are increasing, you are losing out to the competition—because of a growing market.

Pareto Chart The Pareto chart allows you to decide which improvement opportunity or problem you need to work on first. The Pareto analysis is the study and results of related subjects to decide if one is more important than the other. You should use the Pareto chart to

- identify major causes or costs
- decide which one of the problems your team should work on first
- identify the most critical area which causes the majority of the problems
- convince others why the area you have selected needs to be worked on first
- plan a strategy when there are too many problem areas and you do not know where to start your improvement efforts

To develop the Pareto chart, follow these simple steps:

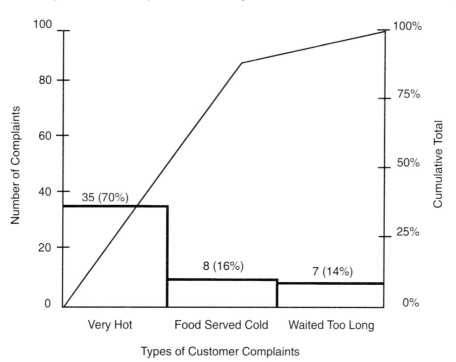

Figure 9-8 Pareto graph showing customer complaints per month

1. Decide on the data which need to be analyzed (e.g., types of customer complaints).
2. Collect the data by preparing a simple "data sheet" (i.e., all the customer complaints are recorded according to the type of complaint, for example very hot food; waited too long; food served cold, etc.).
3. When the complaints are collected for a month, total individual types of complaints and develop a chart with the largest number of complaints on the left. The Pareto graph in Figure 9-8 indicates the largest number of complaints received was for food that was too hot. This indication now gives you direction as to what complaint warrants your attention and what should be addressed first (i.e., controlling the temperature of the food).

Checklist A checklist ensures all necessary issues have been identified and addressed. Some of the questions you may want to include in the checklist are:

1. Are the process difficulties clearly understood?
2. Is the "root cause" of the difficulty clear?
3. Do all the team members understand the root cause?
4. Have the appropriate data been collected?

   5. Have the data been verified for accuracy?

   6. Is there a common understanding of where things are going wrong?

   7. Are the interrelationships between the processes clearly understood?

   8. Are the dependencies between the processes clearly understood?

   9. Has the affected department been clearly identified?

   10. Has the impacted staff been clearly identified?

Step 4: Describe the Ideal Process

The purpose of this step is to obtain a consensus on what the ideal process should be and to communicate the dependencies as well as the critical factors for the success of the ideal process. With your team members, generate a number of ideas and suggestions as to what the perfect process should look like and the dependencies of this perfect process. Document the process in detail and evaluate the critical factors which may hinder the implementation of the ideal process. Generate and document ideas from the team members on how to address these critical factors. Describe the input/output and the relationships between processes. Lastly, develop a dataflow diagram of the ideal process and conduct a "walkthrough" so that the entire staff understands the new process. Discuss the training with the staff, when it will be scheduled, and who will conduct it.

Present the proposed ideal process to the management. Make sure you are prepared to answer management questions, such as: What would be the benefits of implementing the process you are suggesting? How long would it take? How will the success of this ideal plan be measured? Obtain management buy-in, update the ideal process with the input from the management, and finalize it.

Tools of Quality to Be Used   The following quality tools can be used for this step.

Brainstorm   Brainstorming is a method of using a group of people to quickly generate as many ideas as possible. It is a useful tool to generate and collect new ideas when those involved on a project are running out of ideas. The technique is used to generate lists of information about any subject known to those involved in a short period of time and to get involvement from all the participants regarding their ideas on the subject and make them feel their opinion counts. These are the steps to be performed for brainstorming.

   1. Before starting the session, clearly identify what is being brainstormed. It can be problems, solutions, findings, names, etc.

   2. Select a person who will capture all the brainstorming ideas. Use a whiteboard to do this so that everyone can review what is being captured and if there is any discrepancy on what is being discussed and what is being captured, it can be immediately cleared.

   3. Allow five minutes for each person for free thinking with no critiquing so each individual can write their ideas.

   4. Give each person the opportunity to state the idea.

5. Collect each idea by writing it on the whiteboard.

6. Once everyone in the room has given one idea, see if anyone in the room has another idea.

7. Since brainstorming is a way of freeing the thought process and breaking old paradigms, often more ideas will come from what others have said. You should allow for this by not imposing too much structure on the brainstorming process. Allow people to "speak out" at random after the initial process has been completed.

8. Consolidate the list by combining duplicate ideas and eliminating the ones that do not have any impact on what you have set out to do.

Checklist A checklist ensures all necessary issues have been identified and addressed. Some of the questions you may want to include in the checklist are:

1. Has the ideal process been identified?

2. Does everyone agree on the ideal process?

3. Have the measurement criteria for the success of ideal process been defined?

4. Has the ideal process been described and documented in detail?

5. Have the dependencies of the ideal process been identified?

6. Have the critical factors of success been identified and addressed?

7. Have the input and output of the ideal process been identified?

8. Is the relationship between the processes identified?

9. Has a data flow diagram of the ideal process been developed?

10. Does everyone understand the data flow diagram and the proposed ideal process?

11. Is it clear what part of the process will be improved due to the change and what part of the service or product will improve because of this change?

12. Are all training issues identified and addressed?

13. Does management understand how the ideal process will function and have they agreed to support it?

Step 5: Implement the Ideal Process

The purpose of this step is to implement the corrective action that will address the root cause and increase quality of the products/services, customer satisfaction, and employee productivity. Some of the key activities are to

1. Develop an "implementation plan."

2. Obtain necessary approvals on the implementation plan.

3. Obtain required hardware/software, i.e., client server, UNIX, LANs, etc.

4. Arrange joint staff meetings where the senior management lets the entire staff know about the new process improvement implementation plan by

announcing the reasons for change and training employees on total quality management principles.

5. Identify resources required to implement the ideal process.
6. Obtain additional resources, if necessary.
7. Train the resources as required.
8. Develop the following standards and procedures:
   (a) indicate how adherence of the standards and procedures will be assured
   (b) show how the affected employees will be trained
   (c) show how the changes to the standards and procedures will be made and what the frequency of the changes will be.
9. Notify all concerned staff members on the new standards.
10. Start the process that you have identified as the *ideal process*.

Tools of Quality to Be Used   The following quality tools can be used for this step:

- employee training (for the new process)
- presentations for the management

Checklist   A checklist ensures all necessary issues have been identified and addressed. Some of the questions you may want to include in the checklist are:

1. Has the presentation of the "ideal process" has been presented to management?
2. Have the issues raised by the management resolved?
3. Have the strategies to change the culture been defined?
4. Have the resources been identified and defined?
5. Has the need for additional resources been identified?
6. Has the approval for additional resources been obtained?
7. Has training been scheduled for all affected personnel?
8. Is the "ideal process" documented and accessible?
9. Is the schedule for the implementation of the ideal process identified and understood?

Step 6: Measure Progress

The purpose of this step is to ensure the problems and the root causes have been addressed, eliminated, or decreased. Some of the key activities for this step are:

1. Develop a measurement plan.
2. Identify what will be measured and how the data will be evaluated. Identify what tools will be used for measurement.

3. Identify who will receive the data.

4. Identify how data integrity will be monitored.

5. Obtain consensus on the measurement plan.

6. Start collecting data and confirm the effects of the implementation of the ideal process by checking to see if the root causes have been eliminated or reduced. Using the same indicator, compare the problem before and after the implementation of the ideal process.

7. Go back to steps 4 and 5 if desired results are not obtained.

Tools of Quality to Be Used The following quality tools are useful for this step:

Survey The survey is a method for collecting information using questions. The survey is used to understand and measure whether the implementation of the ideal process is beneficial. The survey is also successful at getting feedback from the employees regarding their feelings on how well the changed processes are working and finding out if any additional improvements need to be implemented. You need to determine what type of information you want from the individuals who will complete the survey. Based on this, develop your questions. Plan to include some "open-ended" questions which give the person responding an opportunity to add more information than just a yes or no answer; for example, What would you do differently? What is your opinion of the current process?

One-on-One Meetings These meetings are ideal to get opinions from the people who are directly involved and affected by the process change. Usually individuals are open in expressing when they are not subjected to discussing their feelings among a group of people. One-on-one meetings are effective to get personal opinion on an issue.

Checklist A checklist ensures all necessary issues have been identified and addressed. Some of the questions you may want to include in the checklist are:

1. Is there a measurement plan?

2. Has it been decided what will be measured and how these measurements correspond to customer requirements for quality service and better products?

3. Has the data evaluation process been identified?

4. Have the measurement tools been identified?

5. Has it been decided who will receive the measurement data?

6. Has the process been defined for data integrity?

7. Have all the affected parties signed off on the measurement plan?

8. Is the measurement system understood by everyone?

9. Is the measurement system repeatable and reproducible?

10. Have measurement results been shared with affected individuals?

Step 7: Standardize the Process

The purpose of this step is to ensure that everyone understands the new process and performs it in a consistent manner. Standardization ensures that the employees have made the new process part of their daily work. The steps for standardizing the process are:

1. Develop tools and methodologies to standardize the process.
2. Develop documentation outlining the process.
3. Conduct frequent training of the process.
4. Ensure that everyone has received adequate training on the new process.
5. Review lessons learned and document what went well, what could have been improved and how it could have been improved.
6. Periodically conduct internal audits to monitor adherence to the new process.
7. Start addressing remaining problems.

Tools of Quality to Be Used   The following quality tools can be used for this step.

Histogram   Histograms are used to identify the variability within a process and to improve either services or products by identifying patterns in their occurrence. To develop histogram from the data you have collected,

1. Establish the range of your data by subtracting the smallest value from the largest.
2. Calculate the number of bars you need in the histogram. To do this, take the square root of the number of data points (In Figure 9-9, four bars were chosen, each bar representing a 30-minute interval).
3. Determine the frequency of events for each interval (In Figure 9-9, the bar is drawn up to the 1500 level as 1,500 students arrived between 8:30 A.M. and 8:59 A.M.).
4. Determine the center point on the histogram by taking the total of all the data collected and divide by 2 (In Figure 9-9, starting from the left, 2,730 students came to school. When you divide 2,730 by 2, you get 1,365. Starting from the left of the graph, count the number of students arriving at school until you reach 1,365. In the example, you reach this number when you get to the bar for 8:30 to 8:59 A.M.).
5. Include clear titles on the graph.

You should understand that when using data to create a histogram, they must be at least ordinal. This means that the values defining the bounds of the rectangles of the histogram must possess the relationship greater than or less than. If you construct a histogram based on red hair color, blonde hair color, brunette hair color, and so forth, the order in which you put them might be misleading—unless you can relate it to the color spectrum in some way. On the other hand, interval data are fine. Figure 9-9 shows interval data.

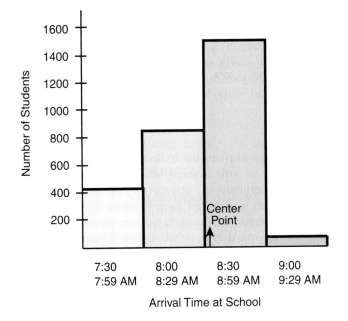

Figure 9-9   Histogram. This histogram displays the arrival time of students at the school. The school start time is 9:00 A.M. As you move away from 9:00 A.M., you will notice less frequent arrivals of students. After constructing the bars, if you draw a line over the frequency bars, you will get the "distribution" curve. Several interesting factors can be observed in the histogram: (a) Few students arrived between 7:30 and 7:59 A.M. (b) Considerable students arrived between 8:00 and 8:29 A.M. (c) Majority of the students arrived between 8:30 and 8:59 A.M. (d) Very few students arrived after 9:00 A.M.

Line Graphs   Line graphs are used to display variation in data over time and to indicate progress toward a goal. They are useful for showing improvement, identifying problems, and communicating trends. To construct a line graph:

1. Identify the item (measure) that you want to collect data on (in Figure 9-10, the item is the number of complaint letters received).

2. Develop a measurement plan and address the following in the plan:

   (a) How often will you take measurements: weekly, monthly, or yearly? (In Figure 9-10, the measurements have been taken on an annual basis.)

   (b) When will you start the measurements?

   (c) When will you end collecting data?

3. On the horizontal line (*x*-axis) track each measurement obtained. All line graphs are constructed to show time on the *x*-axis.

4. Develop a vertical line (*y*-axis) to show the frequency being measured (in Figure 9-10, it is the number of complaints).

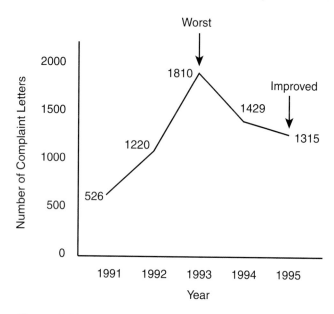

Figure 9-10 Annual number of customer complaint letters

5. Take the data point on the *y*-axis and put a dot in the corresponding date of measurement on the *x*-axis (in Figure 9-10, the first dot is placed in the data point 526 with corresponding date of 1991).

6. When all the data points have dots, connect the dots with a solid line.

7. To make the line graph easy to read, note where the data point worsened and where it improved (in Figure 9-10, the worst case was when 1,810 complaints were received and the improved case was when the number of complaints dropped to 1,315).

A line graph, because it shows connectivity due to the lines (which actually connect the midpoints of a histogram), implies interval values. While the years, 1991 through 1995 appear to be ordinal, they can be broken down into months, days, hours, minutes, seconds, and so forth—so they are interval in nature. But you need to be careful that your charts and graphs are not misleading.

Checklist A checklist ensures all necessary issues have been identified and addressed. Some of the questions you may want to include in the checklist are:

1. Have the appropriate tools been identified and selected?

2. Have the appropriate methodologies been identified and selected?

3. Have all the concerns regarding the new process been addressed?

4. Is the documentation of the new process ready?

5. Can the documentation be easily understood?

6. Have the training needs been identified?

7. Are the training materials prepared?

8. Are employees encouraged to attend the training?

9. Have you developed a plan for training future employees?

10. Are the employees given a chance to implement the new process?

11. What is the data telling you regarding the improved process?

12. Has the waste been reduced or problem been fixed? If yes, how did you measure it and by what percent has it been resolved?

13. Have process stability and capability been determined?

14. Is the measurement system working?

15. What does the customer say regarding the service or products? From the customer's viewpoint, what has improved or deteriorated?

16. Who is responsible for ongoing monitoring and updating of standards?

17. How often will monitoring and updating of standards be done?

18. Have the responsible individuals for monitoring and updating the standards been notified?

19. Have you developed a new plan to address some of the other existing issues?

9.2 CONCLUSIONS

These seven steps will assist you and your organization to start a never-ending journey toward continuous process improvement. By consistently following the steps, measuring the results, and standardizing the process which yields the highest payback in terms of quality and cost, you will experience a change in the behavior of the employees and also of management. Also by carefully following and implementing each one of these steps, your staff will experience the momentum to carry the organization through the corporate and competitive challenges.

One thing to remember is that unless management supports the idea of improving processes and is totally behind the movement, it will certainly fail regardless of how well defined your process improvement road map is. The process improvement must start with the highest-ranking executive of the company and filter down through all levels of management and then to individual staff members.

Unless the staff is empowered with a formal atmosphere to make decisions in the interest of the business, nothing will happen. Good quality-related intentions and standards are easily overwhelmed by the demands of daily work pressures. Many quality managers have discussed with us their intentions to support quality improvement efforts by holding regular root-cause evaluation meetings to address the issues of the department. However, these intentions never took effect because top management did not show interest and commitment. It is important to prepare a systematic plan to describe how the quality improvement effort will be implemented and what benefits will be derived.

Once this plan is finalized, obtain top management's support so that the process change is accepted throughout the company and there is no resistance to further change efforts. Once the plan is clearly understood by management, they must communicate to the relevant staff what is required from them to address the problem and ensure the staff introduces changes in a manner that increases the quality of the product or service. Top management must also direct and show the staff how all the elements of the change support each other to create progress.

If implemented properly, the process improvement works. However, it always fails if management misuses it, does not participate in it, or does not allow individuals to participate in developing the process. In this situation, the employee does not feel that he or she owns the process and does not commit to it. Also if there is no accountability for the success of each implemented process, no-one takes the initiative to measure the benefits derived by the change, thus allowing the employees to lose interest.

A well-trained staff will be able to face any challenges related to the process improvements and your company will become a winner in this highly competitive market if each employee brings a sense of individual responsibility, cooperation, and teamwork to the problem-solving process. The important thing to remember is to involve everyone who will be affected by the change and ensure the reason for change is well understood.

CHAPTER 10

Standards and Evaluation of Process

At many conferences when we have mentioned the word "standards," we seem to generate a lot of hot discussion. People who consider themselves creative and innovative often turn away in distaste at this word since they feel that standards will curtail their creativity and stop them from inventing new ideas! In a practitioner's view, standards are too confining and a hindrance in the progress of his or her work. On the contrary, standards reduce the activity of re-inventing the same procedures. The standards indicate what needs to be done and how it will be done.

There are several different process evaluation guidelines available in the software industry. In this chapter, we are focusing on ISO 9000-3 and for organization maturity evaluation, the Software Engineering Institute's Capability Maturity Model (CMM). We request the reader to refer to the reference section for other available standards. Note that there is no consensus as to which standards and methods will give the best results; therefore, it is in your best interest to evaluate each standard and select the one that is best for your organization.

Earlier we talked about Six Sigma and cycle time reduction. ISO 9000 and SEI CMM are both related to process evaluation, but the first two are related to quality achievement goals. As we stated then, companies like IBM, Motorola, and Texas Intruments actually used process improvement programs based on these two goals to win the prestigious Malcolm Baldrige National Award for Quality. Usually, in order to achieve such high quality standards, the company trivially qualifies for ISO 9000 registration and is well on the way to the coveted level 5 of the Capability Maturity Model. What this means is that while each of the two standards and methods we will be discussing in this chapter differ, goals based on all four have a great deal in common. We feel that a software organization that has installed our product delivery process, which has matured within the organization, will find it much easier to achieve whatever quality goals are desired than with traditional quality assurance approaches. We have also observed that organizations do not "mature"; individual projects do. Typically, the installation of an effective process may allow an organization to quickly establish a "capability" of level 5, but the maturity may vary from project to project—even under the same manager. By analogy, it is similar to learning to play tennis under an expert coach. The capability might be there, but ability is based on maturity through much practice.

10.1 ISO 9000

The International Organization for Standardization (ISO) in Geneva, Switzerland, developed the ISO 9000 standard, and it is one of the most rapidly adopted international standards at the present. Founded in 1946, ISO is a specialized world agency that develops, promotes, and publishes international standards in the area of quality assurance and quality management. The organization covers over 90 countries with chapters throughout the world, such as BSI (U.K.), AFNOR (France), CEN (Europe), ANSI (U.S.), and DIN (Germany). ISO is composed of 180 technical committees, each responsible for specialized areas ranging from asbestos to zinc. The results of the ISO technical committees' work are published as internal standards. The ISO 9000 certification signifies that a company's processes and services meet a prescribed set of quality standards.

There are several registrars that have received accreditation either by ANSI/RAB in the United States or a European accreditation body, but no registrar can guarantee that its quality systems certification will be accepted worldwide. What this means is that ISO certification in Britain may not be accepted in Germany and U.S. certification may not be recognized in Europe. Currently there are efforts between various accreditation chapters to discuss common accreditation so that the registrars would not have to seek accreditation from different bodies.

The ISO series consists of five basic related international standards on quality management and quality assurance: ISO 9000, ISO 9001, ISO 9002, ISO 9003, and ISO 9004. ISO 9000 and ISO 9004 are descriptive documents, not prescriptive requirements, and companies do not register to these; instead, companies register to ISO 9001, ISO 9002, or ISO 9003, which are conformance standards.

Table 10-1 describes the components of ISO 9000.

Table 10-1

ISO 9000	Quality management and quality assurance standards Guidelines for selection and use
ISO 9001	Quality systems model for quality assurance in design, development, production, installation, and servicing
ISO 9002	Quality systems model for quality assurance in production and installation
ISO 9003	Quality systems model for quality assurance in final inspection and test
ISO 9004	Quality management and quality system elements Guidelines

These standards are aimed at documenting an organization's quality system and related processes. The United States adopted the standards in 1987 as the ANSI/ASQC Q 90 series. Since ISO emphasizes process documentation and adherence, many companies throughout the world are pressuring their vendors and suppliers to register to the standards as a part of their contracts. Many purchasing organizations refuse to do business with suppliers who do not adhere to ISO 9000 standards.

10.1.1 ISO 9000-3

Since software development is somewhat different than manufacturing, there is a need for a standard that is specific to software development. ISO 9000-3 was prepared by Technical Committee ISO/TC 176. ISO 9000-3 is the guideline for the application of ISO 9001 to the development, supply, and maintenance of software. Implementation of ISO 9000-3 guidelines assist in

- developing improved software
- improving traceability
- improving software development processes

Organizations that have procedures in place for ISO 9001 will require only a few other elements specific to software development to comply with ISO 9000-3. There is a direct co-relationship between the ISO 9000-3 and ISO 9001 clauses. The ISO 9000-3 emphasizes the software development practices of the supplier as well as the responsibilities of the purchaser (Kehoe and Jarvis, 1995). Table 10-2, from BS EN ISO 9001:1994, gives you the cross-references between ISO 9000-3 and ISO 9001.

Table 10-2

ISO 9000-3		ISO 9001
4.1	Management responsibility	4.1
4.2	Quality system	4.2
4.3	Internal quality system audits	4.17
4.4	Corrective action	4.14
5.2	Contract review	4.3
5.3	Purchaser's requirements specification	4.3, 4.4
5.4	Development planning	4.4
5.5	Quality planning	4.2, 4.4
5.6	Design and implementation	4.4, 4.9, 4.13
5.7	Testing and validation	4.4, 4.10, 4.11, 4.13
5.8	Acceptance	4.10, 4.15

Table 10-2 (Continued)

ISO 9000-3		ISO 9001
5.9	Replication, delivery, and installation	4.10, 4.13, 4.15
5.10	Maintenance	4.13, 4.19
6.1	Configuration management	4.4, 4.5, 4.8, 4.12, 4.13
6.2	Document control	4.5
6.3	Quality records	4.16
6.4	Measurement	4.20
6.5	Rules, practices, and conventions	4.9, 4.11
6.6	Tools and techniques	4.9, 4.11
6.7	Purchasing	4.6
6.8	Included in software product	4.7
6.9	Training	4.18

Extracts from BS EN ISO 9001:1994 are reproduced with the permission of BSI. Complete editions of the standards can be obtained by mail from BSI Customer Services, 389 Chiswick High Road, London W4 4AL.

ISO 9000-3 Preparation   When you decide to apply for ISO 9000-3 registration, the first thing you want to do is to obtain top management's support which involves the budget, time, and a thorough understanding of what is required for ISO certification. Once you have the support, here are other steps to follow.

1. Form ISO implementation team.
2. Obtain a copy of the ISO standards.
3. Implement a training program for ISO overview and requirements for the rest of the staff in the organization.
4. Train the team members on the details of the standards and what needs to be accomplished. The training program should not just cover procedural and job-related issues, but also the need for change; include tools for problem solving, developing measurement criteria, and presenting data.
5. Start developing and documenting the quality policy, plan, and procedures. If you already have a manual in place, review and update it so that it is current. The quality plan should support the quality policy and the procedures must cover all of the ISO defined elements such as document control, training, internal audits, corrective action, and quality records.
6. Train staff on any new procedures and ensure the staff is following these new procedures.
7. Form an internal audit team and train the members on how to conduct the audits based on ISO standards and your internal documented procedures.
8. Schedule audits by the internal audit team members.

9. Review any nonconformance discovered by the audit members; address the nonconformance and if necessary, update the quality manual and procedures accordingly.

10. Interview and select external auditors for preregistration audit to identify any nonconformity that may have missed the internal audit process.

11. Address nonconformities found by external auditors.

12. Contact, select, and apply to a registrar.

13. Undergo formal audit by the registrar.

ISO 9000-3 Audit   Prior to the audit, the registrar sends the audit plan to the organization. The plan outlines the audit schedule, agenda and the areas to be audited. When the audit team arrives at the organization, there is an opening meeting with management during which following topics are covered:

- introduction of team members

- description of audit, scope, purpose, and procedures

- review of agenda and confirmation of the schedule

- clarification of any points not understood

After the opening meeting, the audit begins. The auditors assess predetermined aspects of the operation to the standards. They look for objective evidence that the organization is conforming to its own preestablished standards and that these standards meet the intent of the ISO standards. When the team completes the audit, they meet with the organization management to review all the findings. This meeting provides opportunity to the auditee for questioning audit teams findings. Copies of noncompliance are given to the organization and the corrective action dates are obtained by the registrar. The organization provides a documented plan on how the corrective actions will be made and implemented. Upon confirmation of the implementation of this plan, if the registrar is satisfied, it grants registration and issues a registration document to the organization. The registration is an ongoing process in which the registrar will perform periodic surveillance audits to ensure the quality system is being maintained. In the event of the failure of the quality system, the registration is canceled or suspended.

10.2 SEI MATURITY MODEL

The Software Engineering Institute (SEI) is the leading organization in the United States that addresses quality issues related to the software industry. Since software is critical in the U.S. defense system, the importance for high-quality software becomes acute. To address these needs, the Department of Defense awarded the Software Engineering Institute to Carnegie-Mellon University in 1984. The assessment methodology was developed by SEI at Carnegie-Mellon University at the request of the U.S. Department of Defense to provide leadership in establishing advanced software engineering processes. The methodology is based on assessment to determine the maturity and robustness of the organization's software development process.

Watts Humphrey joined SEI shortly after its formation. He led the initial development and introduction of the Software Capability Maturity Model (CMM) which is based on the concepts of software processes. These processes are either software tools or software engineering practices used to develop software. The model assists organizations in developing software disciplines for planning, developing, implementing, and maintaining software. The CMM model provides a baseline for software development process evaluation and it is flexible. It does not require any specific life cycle model or software engineering practices. As the organization masters the initial level and the processes mature, the organization moves to a new level to face new activities that needs to be implemented before moving to the next level. In his book *Managing the Software Process*, Humphrey (1987) describes the characteristics of a compatibility process and metrics that should be collected at each of the five process maturity levels and outlines activities that should be carried out to improve the current level in order to advance to the next level. There is a close relationship between the process maturity level of an organization and its ability to produce quality software based on the level. There are five levels in this model.

Level 1: Initial   In this level, the development organization is in a chaotic mode, leading to unpredictable cost, quality, and schedule. The overall plan is to get the job done and quality depends on the competence of the people who are put in charge of the project. Under crisis, any planned procedures are not adhered to. Since the processes are changing on a constant basis, any estimation is impossible. In order to achieve predictability of schedules and cost, the process has to be brought under control.

Level 2: Repeatable   At level two, the development organization has reasonable control over schedules and there are informal ad hoc procedures. Processes may differ from project to project. This level can be characterized as intuitive, where the department can be characterized as having achieved a stable process with repeatable, preplanned standards and verification activities such as walk-throughs and inspections in place.

Level 3: Defined   At level three, the organization has reliable costs and schedules. The development department has defined the process as a basis for consistent implementation and better understanding of the system. There are tangible deliverables and the roles and responsibilities have been established and understood.

Level 4: Managed   At level four, there are reasonable statistical controls over product quality, where the development organization is involved in measurements and improvements based upon root-cause analysis.

Level 5: Optimizing At this level, there are established procedures for continuously measuring and improving the development processes, adopting new technologies by investing in process automation, and improvement. The organization now has a basis for optimization of the process.

Levels 2 through 5 have key processes identified that should be followed by an organization to improve its development cycle. These processes identify the key activities that must take place to achieve a maturity level. Figure 10-1, based on SEI, CMU/SEI-93-TR-24, defines these activities.

Organizations can use the CMM model to identify the areas of deficiencies. When implemented with problem identification and resolution, it provides a road map for improvements.

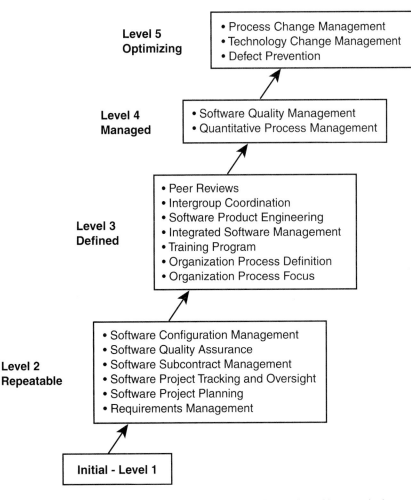

Figure 10-1 Key processes by maturity level. Reproduced by permission of SEI.

10.3 RELATIONSHIP AND DIFFERENCES BETWEEN SEI, ISO 9001, AND ISO 9001-3

The following tables, created by Apte and Iyer (1995), reflect quality systems' element relationship and differences between SEI, ISO 9001, and ISO 9001-3. These tables are reproduced by permission of the Quality Assurance Institute (QAI).

1. Organization and Resource Management

1.1 Organizational Structure

No.	SEI Question	Typical Guideline/ Document Name	ISO 9001 Clause	ISO 9001-3 Clause	Level
1.1.1	For each project involving software development, is there a designated software manager?	Organization Chart/ Project Management	Organization - Responsibility and Authority 4.1.2.1	Development Plan - Management 5.3.2.2.c	2
1.1.2	Does the project software manager report directly to the project (or project development) manager?	Organization Chart/ Project Management	Organizational and Technical Interfaces 4.4.2.2	Development Plan - Management 5.3.2.2.d	2
1.1.3	Does the software quality assurance (SQA) function have a management reporting channel separate from the software development project management?	Organization Chart	Organization - Verification Resources and Personnel 4.1.2.2	Organization - Verification Resources and Personnel 4.1.1.2.2	2
1.1.4	Is there a designated individual or team responsible for the control of software interfaces?	Project Management/ Project Plan/Quality Plan	Design Control - Design Changes 4.4.6	Quality Plan Content 5.4.2.e	3
1.1.5	Is software system engineering represented on the system design team?	Project Management/ Project Plan	Design and Development Planning - Activity Assignment 4.4.2.1	Development Plan - Management 5.3.2.2.c	3
1.1.6	Is there a software configuration control function for each project that involves software development?	Quality Plan/ Configuration Management	Design and Development Planning - Activity Assignment 4.4.2.1	Quality Plan Content 5.4.2.e	2
1.1.7	Is there a software engineering process group function?	Organization Chart/ Management Review	Quality System 4.2	Quality System 4.2.1	3

1.2 Resources, Personnel, and Training

No.	SEI Question	Typical Guideline/ Document Name	ISO 9001 Clause	ISO 9001-3 Clause	Level
1.2.1	Does each software developer have a private computer-supported workstation/terminal?	Project Management/ Project Plan	Design and Development Planning - Activity Assignment 4.4.2.1	Development Plan - Management 5.3.2.2.c	3
1.2.2	Is there a required training program for all newly appointed development managers designed to familiarize them with software project management?	Training Policy	Training 4.18	Training 6.9	2
1.2.3	Is there a required software engineering training program for software developers?	Training Policy	Training 4.18	Training 6.9	3
1.2.4	Is there a required software engineering training program for first-line supervisors of software development?	Training Policy	Training 4.18	Training 6.9	3
1.2.5	Is a formal training program required for design and code review leaders?	Training Policy	Training 4.18	Training 6.9	3

1.3 Technology Management

No.	SEI Question	Typical Guideline/ Document Name	ISO 9001 Clause	ISO 9001-3 Clause	Level
1.3.1	Is a mechanism used for maintaining awareness of the state of the art in software engineering technology?	Training Policy	Training 4.18	Training 6.9	2
1.3.2	Is a mechanism used for evaluating technologies used by the organization versus those externally available?	Technology Acquisition Plan/ Annual Budget/ Work Plan	Design and Development Planning - Activity Assignment 4.4.2.1	—	3

1.3 Technology Management (Continued)

No.	SEI Question	Typical Guideline/ Document Name	ISO 9001 Clause	ISO 9001-3 Clause	Level
1.3.3	Is a mechanism used for deciding when to insert new technology into the development process?	Technology Acquisition Plan/ Annual Budget/ Work Plan	—	—	4
1.3.4	Is a mechanism used for managing and supporting the introduction of new technologies?	Technology Acquisition Plan/ Annual Budget/ Work Plan	—	—	4
1.3.5	Is a mechanism used for identifying and replacing obsolete technologies?	Technology Acquisition Plan/ Annual Budget/ Work Plan	—	—	5

2. Software Engineering Process and Its Management

2.1 Documented Standards and Procedures

No.	SEI Question	Typical Guideline/ Document Name	ISO 9001 Clause	ISO 9001-3 Clause	Level
2.1.1	Does the software organization use a standardized and documented software development process on each project?	SDLC	Process Control 4.9.1	Development Plan - Phases 5.3.2.1	3
2.1.2	Does the standard software development process documentation describe the use of tools and techniques?	SDLC	Process Control 4.9.1	Rules, Practices, and Conventions/ Tools and Techniques 6.5/6.6	3
2.1.3	Is a formal procedure used in the management review of each software development prior to making contractual commitments?	Contract Review	Contract Review 4.3	Contract Review 5.1	2
2.1.4	Is a formal procedure used to assure periodic management review of the status of each software development project?	Progress Reports/ Time Sheets/ Weekly Reports	Design Control 4.4	Development Planning - Progress Control 5.3.3	2

2.1 Documented Standards and Procedures (Continued)

No.	SEI Question	Typical Guideline/ Document Name	ISO 9001 Clause	ISO 9001-3 Clause	Level
2.1.5	Is there a mechanism for assuring that software subcontractors, if any, follow a disciplined software development process?	Vendor Selection	Purchasing - Assessment of Subcontractors 4.6.2	Purchasing - Assessment of Subcontractors 6.7.2	2
2.1.6	Are standards used for the content of software development files/folders?	SDLC	Process Control 4.9	Design and Implementation- Implementation 5.5.3	3
2.1.7	For each project, are independent audits conducted for each step of the software development process?	Internal Audit	Internal Quality Audits 4.17	Internal Quality Systems Audits 4.3	2
2.1.8	Is a mechanism used for assessing existing designs and code for reuse in new applications?	Reuse/Design	Design Control 4.4	Development Methods and Tools 5.3.2.3	3
2.1.9	Are coding standards applied to each software development project?	Coding Standard	Process Control 4.9.1	Rules, Practices, and Conventions 6.5	2
2.1.10	Are standards applied to the preparation of unit test cases?	Unit Testing	Process Control 4.9.1	Rules, Practices, and Conventions 6.5	3
2.1.11	Are code maintainability standards applied?	Unit Testing/ Maintainability	Process Control 4.9.1	Rules, Practices, and Conventions 6.5	3
2.1.12	Are internal design review standards applied?	Design Review	Design Verification 4.4.5	Rules, Practices, and Conventions 6.5	4
2.1.13	Are code review standards applied?	Code Review	Process Control 4.9.1	Rules, Practices, and Conventions 6.5	4
2.1.14	Is a formal procedure used to make estimates of software size?	Estimation Procedure	Process Control 4.9.1	Rules, Practices, and Conventions 6.5	2

2.1 Documented Standards and Procedures (Continued)

No.	SEI Question	Typical Guideline/ Document Name	ISO 9001 Clause	ISO 9001-3 Clause	Level
2.1.15	Is a formal procedure used to produce software development schedules?	Project/Planning/ Estimation Procedure	Process Control 4.9.1	Rules, Practices, and Conventions 6.5	2
2.1.16	Are formal procedures applied to estimating software development cost?	Contract Review/ Estimation Procedure	Contract Review 4.3	Contract Reviews - General 5.1.1	2
2.1.17	Is a mechanism used for ensuring that the software design teams understand each software requirement?	Requirements Review/SDLC	Organizational and Technical Interfaces 4.4.2.2	Purchaser's Requirements Specification 5.2	2
2.1.18	Are man-machine interface standards applied to each appropriate software development project?	User Interface Guideline	Process Control 4.9.1	Rules, Practices, and Conventions 6.5	3

2.2 Process Metrics

No.	SEI Question	Typical Guideline/ Document Name	ISO 9001 Clause	ISO 9001-3 Clause	Level
2.2.1	Are software staffing profiles maintained of actual staffing versus planned staffing?	Software Metrics	Statistical Techniques 4.20	Process Measurement 6.4.2	2
2.2.2	Are profiles of software size maintained for each software configuration item over time?	Software Metrics	Statistical Techniques 4.20	Process Measurement 6.4.2	2
2.2.3	Are statistics on software design errors gathered?	Software Metrics	Statistical Techniques 4.20	Process Measurement 6.4.2	3
2.2.4	Are statistics on software code and test errors gathered?	Software Metrics	Statistical Techniques 4.20	Process Measurement 6.4.2	2
2.2.5	Are design errors projected and compared to actuals?	Software Metrics	Statistical Techniques 4.20	Process Measurement 6.4.2	4
2.2.6	Are code and test errors projected and compared to actuals?	Software Metrics	Statistical Techniques 4.20	Process Measurement 6.4.2	4

2.2 Process Metrics (Continued)

No.	SEI Question	Typical Guideline/ Document Name	ISO 9001 Clause	ISO 9001-3 Clause	Level
2.2.7	Are profiles maintained of actual versus planned software units designed over time?	Software Metrics	Statistical Techniques 4.20	Process Measurement 6.4.2	2
2.2.8	Are profiles maintained of actual versus planned software units completing unit testing over time?	Software Metrics	Statistical Techniques 4.20	Process Measurement 6.4.2	2
2.2.9	Are profiles maintained of actual versus planned software units integrated over time?	Software Metrics	Statistical Techniques 4.20	Process Measurement 6.4.2	2
2.2.10	Are target computer memory utilization estimates and actuals tracked?	Software Metrics	Statistical Techniques 4.20	Product Measurement 6.4.1	2
2.2.11	Are target computer throughput utilization estimates and actuals tracked?	Software Metrics	Statistical Techniques 4.20	Product Measurement 6.4.1	2
2.2.12	Is target computer I/O channel utilization tracked?	Software Metrics	Statistical Techniques 4.20	Product Measurement 6.4.1	2
2.2.13	Are design and code review coverages measured and recorded?	Software Metrics	Statistical Techniques 4.20	Process Measurement 6.4.2	4
2.2.14	Is test coverage measured and recorded for each phase of functional testing?	Software Metrics	Statistical Techniques 4.20	Process Measurement 6.4.2	4
2.2.15	Are the action items resulting from design reviews tracked to closure?	Defect Tracking	Corrective Action 4.14	Design and Implementation - Reviews 5.5.4	3
2.2.16	Are software trouble reports resulting from testing tracked to closure?	Defect Tracking	Corrective Action 4.14	Testing 5.6.3.b	2
2.2.17	Are the action items resulting from code reviews tracked to closure?	Defect Tracking	Corrective Action 4.14	Design and Implementation - Reviews 5.5.4	3

2.2 Process Metrics (Continued)

No.	SEI Question	Typical Guideline/ Document Name	ISO 9001 Clause	ISO 9001-3 Clause	Level
2.2.18	Is test progress tracked by deliverable software component and compared to the plan?	Test Planning	Corrective Action 4.14	Quality Plan Content 5.4.2	2
2.2.19	Are profiles maintained of software build/release content versus time?	Test Planning	Statistical Techniques 4.20	Process Measurement 6.4.2	2

2.3 Data Management and Analysis

No.	SEI Question	Typical Guideline/ Document Name	ISO 9001 Clause	ISO 9001-3 Clause	Level
2.3.1	Has a managed and controlled process data base been established for process metrics data across all projects?	Software Metrics	Statistical Techniques 4.20	Process Measurement 6.4.2	4
2.3.2	Is the review data gathered during design reviews analyzed?	Software Metrics	Corrective Action 4.14	Corrective Action 4.4	4
2.3.3	Is the error data from code reviews and tests analyzed to determine the likely distribution and characteristics of the errors remaining in the product?	Software Metrics	Statistical Techniques 4.20	Measurement 6.4	4
2.3.4	Are analyses of errors conducted to determine their process-related causes?	Error Analysis	Corrective Action 4.14	Corrective Action 4.4	4
2.3.5	Is a mechanism used for error cause analysis?	Error Analysis	Corrective Action 4.14	Corrective Action 4.4	5
2.3.6	Are the error causes reviewed to determine the process changes required to prevent them?	Error Analysis	Corrective Action 4.14	Corrective Action 4.4	5
2.3.7	Is a mechanism used for initiating error-prevention actions?	Error Prevention	Corrective Action 4.14	Corrective Action 4.4	5
2.3.8	Is review efficiency analyzed for each project?	Review Efficiency	Statistical Techniques 4.20	Process Measurement 6.4.2	4

2.3 Data Management and Analysis (Continued)

No.	SEI Question	Typical Guideline/ Document Name	ISO 9001 Clause	ISO 9001-3 Clause	Level
2.3.9	Is software productivity analyzed for major process steps?	Software Productivity	Statistical Techniques 4.20	Process Measurement 6.4.2	4

2.4 Process Control

No.	SEI Question	Typical Guideline/ Document Name	ISO 9001 Clause	ISO 9001-3 Clause	Level
2.4.1	Does senior management have a mechanism for the regular review of the status of software development projects?	Quarterly/Monthly Management Review	Design Control 4.4	Development Planning - Progress Control 5.3.3	2
2.4.2	Is a mechanism used for periodically assessing the software engineering process and implementing indicated improvements?	Quality Assurance/ Internal Audit	Quality System 4.2	Quality System 4.2	4
2.4.3	Is a mechanism used for identifying and resolving system engineering issues that affect software?	Requirements/ Design Review/ System Engineering Coordination Group	Organizational and Technical Interfaces 4.4.2.2	Development Plan - Management 5.3.2.2.d	3
2.4.4	Is a mechanism used for independently calling integration and test issues to the attention of the project manager?	Test Planning/ Integration and Test Review	Organization - Responsibility and Authority 4.1.2.1	Testing 5.6.3.b	3
2.4.5	Is a mechanism used for regular technical interchanges with the customer?	Customer Interaction Group/User Group	—	Joint Reviews 4.1.3	2
2.4.6	Is a mechanism used for ensuring compliance with the software engineering standards?	Final Inspection/ Technical Reviews	Internal Quality Audits 4.17	Internal Quality System Audits 4.3	3
2.4.7	Do software development first-line managers sign off on their schedules and cost estimates?	Project Planning	Design and Development Planning - Activity Assignment 4.4.2.1	Development Plan - Management 5.3.2.2	2

2.4 Process Control (Continued)

No.	SEI Question	Typical Guideline/ Document Name	ISO 9001 Clause	ISO 9001-3 Clause	Level
2.4.8	Is a mechanism used for ensuring traceability between the software requirements and top-level design?	Configuration Management	Product Identification and Traceability 4.8	Configuration Identification and Traceability 6.1.3.1	3
2.4.9	Is a mechanism used for controlling changes to the software requirements?	Change Control/ Configuration Management	Document Control 4.5	Mutual Cooperation 5.2.2	2
2.4.10	Is there a formal management process for determining if the prototyping of software functions is an appropriate part of the design process?	Project Plan/ Design Standards	Design Verification 4.4.5	Development Plan 5.3.2	4
2.4.11	Is a mechanism used for ensuring traceability between the software top-level and detailed designs?	Configuration Management	Product Identification and Traceability 4.8	Configuration Identification and Traceability 6.1.3.1	3
2.4.12	Are internal software design reviews conducted?	Design Review	Design Control 4.4	Design and Implementation - Reviews 5.5.4	3
2.4.13	Is a mechanism used for controlling changes to the software design?	Change Control/ Design Control	Design Changes 4.4.6	Change Control 6.1.3.2	3
2.4.14	Is a mechanism used for ensuring traceability between the software detailed design and the code?	Coding Standard	Product Identification and Traceability 4.8	Configuration Identification and Traceability 6.1.3.1	3
2.4.15	Are formal records maintained of unit (module) development progress?	Unit Development Folders	Process Control 4.9	Rules, Practices, and Conventions 6.5	3
2.4.16	Are software code reviews conducted?	Project Plan	In-process Inspection and Testing 4.10.2	Design and Implementation - Reviews 5.5.4	3
2.4.17	Is a mechanism used for controlling changes to the code?	Configuration Management/ Change Control	Corrective Action 4.14	Change Control 6.1.3.2	2
2.4.18	Is a mechanism used for configuration management of software tools?	Configuration Management/ Environment Management	Process Control 4.9.1.c	Configuration Identification and Traceability 6.1.3.1	3

2.4 Process Control (Continued)

No.	SEI Question	Typical Guideline/ Document Name	ISO 9001 Clause	ISO 9001-3 Clause	Level
2.4.19	Is a mechanism used for verifying that the samples examined by software quality assurance are truly representative of the work performed?	Quality Assurance/ Internal Audit	Internal Quality Audits 4.17	Internal Quality System Audits 4.3	3
2.4.20	Is there a mechanism for assuring that regression testing is routinely performed?	Test Planning	Final Inspection and Testing 4.10.3	Rules, Practices, and Conventions 6.5	2
2.4.21	Is there a mechanism for assuring the adequacy of regression testing?	Test Planning/ Regression Testing	Final Inspection and Testing 4.10.3	Rules, Practices, and Conventions 6.5	3
2.4.22	Are formal test case reviews conducted?	Test Planning	Inspection, Measurement, and Test Equipment 4.11	Test Planning 5.6.2	3

10.4 CONCLUSION

In order to develop your own internal quality system, you should become familiar with ISO 9000-3 standards, the CMM model, and the established Malcolm Baldrige Award criteria. For a history of the Malcolm Baldrige Quality Award we recommend the article written by Neil J. DeCarlo and W. Kent Sterett (1990) which appeared in *Quality Progress*. Also available are standards published by the Institute of Electrical and Electronics Engineers (IEEE) and the U.S. Department of Defense (DOD).

Select the standards which encompass your organization's environment and develop a quality system. You may want certain individuals to get training on ISO 9000-3 or IEEE regarding the implementation of standards or guidelines. All affected staff members should be able to understand the standards and be able to implement them. Assess your current practices against these standards and document all the nonconformance. Take actions to address the nonconformance. Periodically review the revised process to ensure that it brings desired results.

CHAPTER 11

Software Development, Total Quality Management, and Risk Management

One of the quality initiatives—crossing multiple disciplines and businesses—is total quality management (TQM). In this chapter, we will put our material in the context of total quality management; then we will provide insight into the new paradigm and its role in TQM. Following this, we will present material on how to minimize risk as you attempt implement a quality program and get software products ready for release. No matter how high the software quality is, there is always a potential risk, and it should always be recognized and managed.

11.1 THE UMBRELLA OF TOTAL QUALITY MANAGEMENT

Arthur, in his book *Improving Quality: An Insider's Guide to TQM* (1993), observes that the problem with software is not quality. Quality is the solution to the problem. With respect to problem-solving processes, he makes several observations with which we agree.

- Problem-solving processes evolve to make it possible to solve problems that were outside the reach of our problem-solving processes. He cites the move from process-oriented to data-oriented to process-oriented and data-oriented (i.e., the object-oriented paradigm). He feels that Quality Improvement (QI) is the next problem-solving process we will need to embrace.

- A new paradigm should be based on the fact that we will be moving from defect detection to defect prevention. Arthur observes that software engineering is stuck between the "search for magic solutions and CASE (Computer-aided Software Engineering) and massive inspection/testing which consumes 50 percent of the software life cycle." It is interesting to observe that at this point, Arthur is citing Brooks's 1976 text for these observations. Where have we been for 20 years?

- You cannot improve the software without improving the process.
- Quality is everyone's job, but it is management's responsibility (an observation of Deming's).

Arthur also stresses customer-oriented software development, leadership over measurement, and continuous process improvement. Looking back over our book, you will see that this is very much in the spirit of what we have presented. Indeed, the product delivery process is as close as we can come to an implementation of Deming's philosophy and TQM in the software development field. You should also notice that our emphasis is on the product delivery process, not the software development life cycle—although we have referred you to the major life cycle models. Although there are several good books in the area of TQM, Arthur's book is the only one we are currently aware of in the software area. As you compared Six Sigma, cycle reduction time, Malcolm Baldrige National Quality awards, ISO 9000, total quality management, and software quality assurance, you should have noticed that there are many similarities. A lot of the tools and emphases overlap among the various quality approaches.

Three of the major concepts of TQM are expressed in the following three figures taken from Arthur (© 1993 by John Wiley & Sons, Inc.; reproduced by permission of John Wiley & Sons, Inc.). For a more complete explanation of TQM, we encourage you to read Arthur's book. Figure 11-1 is a view of the Deming chain with the emphasis on using quality to capture market share, grow the business, and provide more jobs. This is done through continuous improvement of both quality products and processes, with a goal toward increasing productivity. (In the interest of accuracy, you should note that Deming never called this the Deming chain; others have called it that.)

Figure 11-2 shows a schema for the components of total quality management, an iterative process involving seven quality management tools, and seven quality improvement tools. We will not provide a discussion of these tools here but will refer you to Arthur's book instead. Our purpose is to provide you with a view of what TQM is all about.

Figure 11-3 is a TQM flowchart. It shows a process of moving from customer-oriented requirements through quality plans to the production and delivery of a high-quality product. While this flowchart shows similarities to the product delivery process we have presented in our new paradigm, our paradigm also adds many filters and feedback processes to help keep the product and its quality under control and on track.

11.2 TQM AND THE NEW PARADIGM

Our new paradigm begins with a marketing orientation. Obviously, effective marketing cannot exist if one ignores the customer. That is why marketing is the trigger to the entire product delivery process. This also involves an extensive competitive analysis. As one of our reviewers stated: "This approach really puts a lot of pressure on the marketing organization." That is exactly where it should be. But we feel that sales plays an equally vital role. Specific customers under the direction of appropriate sales or site managers should have an enormous

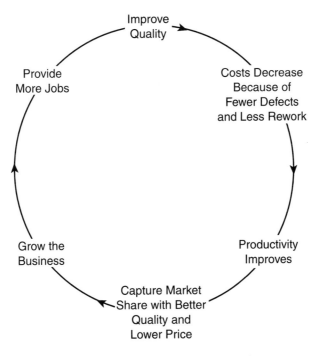

Figure 11-1 View of the Deming chain

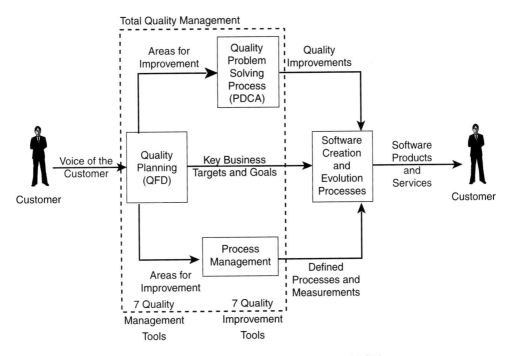

Figure 11-2 Schema of the components of TQM

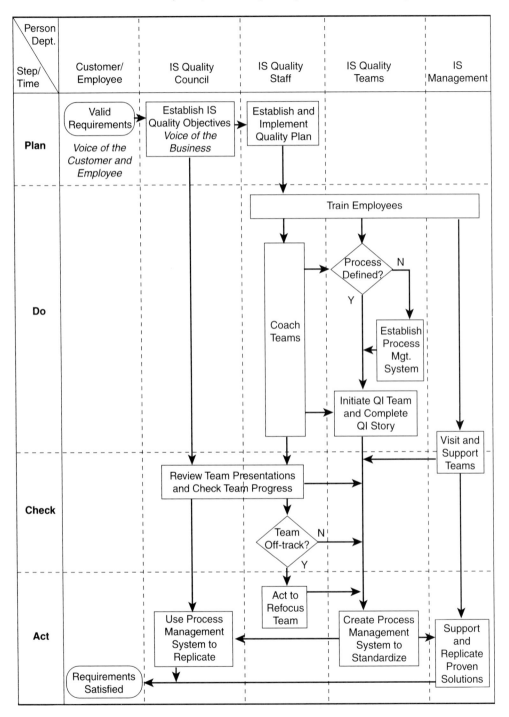

Figure 11-3 TQM flowchart

input on how and when you build your product. In our filters, a major component is the preliminary sales plan wherein actual salespeople take prototypes to customers and potential customers for their input. This is the "certification" of the marketing plan. Their input should also greatly reflect how the customers intend to use the user profiles you make available. For commercial products, identifying the right customers is one of the most important things you can do. We will discuss this later in relation to risk. Almost everything else in that section relates to solutions proposed by our new paradigm.

In the new paradigm, the concept of errors (defects), how they occur, and how they can be removed is addressed in a completely different manner from the traditional approach. As we have repeatedly stated, you can always go back to traditional testing methods if you do not feel secure, but usually, the pattern-matching approach combined with dependency analysis will enable you to assure that the errors are not there. One of the first things you will notice when you start to make it work is how efficient it is. Often seeing that there are, or are not, errors present in 100 lines of code only takes a matter of seconds. But whether this works or not is a function of whether the minimal number of patterns is used and whether only WHILE loops and CASE statements are present (with no nesting). The pattern-matching approach does not replace behavioral testing. It is never replaced by either code audits or system audits which only assure that the functionality is correct.

In terms of quality standards at the code level, the coding standards we have presented are always correct. Note that this does not relate to functional correctness. At the system level, executive modules, fan-in, massage modules, and informational strength modules almost always involve some trade-off with reality—usually involving performance or efficiency. At this level, there are no right answers, only intelligent trade-offs. If care is taken, only a few differing patterns will solve the problem—even if they involve some dependencies. But just as at the code level, there are a potentially infinite number of patterns involving undisciplined implementation of dependencies and structures.

11.3 RISK ISSUES IN SOFTWARE QUALITY ASSURANCE

There is a tendency for SQA experts to concentrate on how TQM and other quality initiatives will help provide for quality software. In our view, this is not so straightforward. Everyone wants to have a quality product—to have awards and to have reached standards. But the way to achieve these standards is unclear. The product delivery paradigm provides an approach to attaining these quality standards. It offers tools and insights to help achieve quality regardless of how you choose to define it. In addition, we also recognize that a large component to successfully ensuring quality is to manage the risk involved in any quality assurance process. In this section, we will describe several kinds of risk and ways to minimize the risks. This information will help you anticipate possible problems and have solutions for them before they hinder your quality processes. (This material originally appeared in *The Journal of the QAI* in January and April 1994. See Crandall, 1994a and 1994b. Permission to republish has been granted by QAI.)

11.3.1 Areas of Risk

Risks relating to software can be characterized in several ways. We will examine several types of risk and discuss what can be done to overcome—or at least minimize—the risks or their impact.

The Risk of Missing Deadlines   One major risk is not getting a product to market in time to exploit the marketing window. The end of the marketing window is fixed; how much of a product a company sells depends on how early their product reaches the marketplace within that marketing window. A similar risk is related to MIS-type software. Rather than missing the marketing window, a company instead loses its competitive advantage.

The Risk of Poorly Defined Users   When there is a potential of millions of users, it is often very difficult to characterize the user environment. If a software product is perceived as being too difficult to use, going down too often for too extended a period of time, or not doing exactly what users want or what their business needs, users tend to look toward the competition. In today's PC/workstation or Mac environment, there is little brand loyalty. If users do not "trust" a company's product, they will look elsewhere.

The Risk of Creeping Featurism   In an attempt to meet the needs of the "elusive user," programmers and marketers tend to keep "fiddling" with a product, adding and modifying features as they think of them. This often causes thousands of test cases to become invalid, and documentation to be rewritten. Code that was tested before becomes broken and needs to be tested over and over again, adding to the software development life cycle, and allowing error-prone code to get past the test organization. This leads to a substantial increase in time to market. Test engineers and documentation personnel give up trying to keep everything current and wait for development to finish before beginning their testing and documentation activities. This can add 100 percent to 125 percent to the time to market for the product.

The Risk of New Technology   Often a software development house must adapt or create their software in the presence of new technology such as moving from a 386 to a 486 chip, moving from a command line to a windows environment, or interfacing with a new type of device. Typically, such changes mean that those who program to this interface or platform must "come up to speed" on it. Whenever new technology is involved there is always the potential risk that it will take longer than anticipated to create the desired software. There is also a potential for creating highly error-prone code or architectures.

The Risk of Nontestability Of all the risks, nontestability should be the easiest to solve, yet it is the hardest to implement in an ongoing organization. Computer science students are rarely taught to make their code "testable." Experienced programmers are rewarded for getting their code running on time and with a desired performance; rarely does quality mean more than "low error rates." Even if there is a "testing life cycle" in place, the test engineers find themselves up against a brick wall. Systems testing is done by the test organization in the absence of effective unit testing. The product—as defined in the specification and as the code actually exists—is almost impossible to test, as the two components are rarely compatible. Thousands of test cases are required where hundreds should have done the job. Cries for higher quality code fall on deaf ears or on programmers who are up against unrealistic deadlines and have little or no time for code design or unit testing. Testability is also affected by such things as complexity, nested loops versus module calls, nested IF THEN ELSE structures versus CASE structures and module calls, dependencies, programmer assumptions, inconsistent patterns, poor modularity, and environmental dependencies.

Complexity The difficulty of testing and error rates are often tied to code complexity. Surprisingly, code complexity occurs with "structured code" as much as with "spaghetti code." This can be measured using McCabe's measure of cyclomatic complexity or by Halstead's measures, or you can simply observe it as you attempt to figure out how to test the code with a certain degree of coverage. A better solution is to program it to quality coding standards.

Nested Loops versus Module Calls If care is taken to eliminate dependencies between nested loops, they are fairly easy to test. However, if dependencies exist between the loop variables or between the loop variables and the internal code, an exceedingly large number of test cases must be written to adequately test the code. We showed you examples of this in Chapter 2. Sometimes attempts are made to minimize the problem by replacing the innermost loops with calls to subordinate subroutines. This usually creates intermodule dependencies instead of really helping solve the problem. With dependencies, the standard nested loop testing techniques in various testing texts are not adequate.

Nested IF THEN ELSE Structures versus CASE Structures and Module Calls A similar nontestability problem exists with IF THEN ELSE structures which are nested—a natural consequence of "top-down" programming. Not only does it have a negative impact on testing, it also makes the code difficult to maintain. Usually, the problem can be minimized by converting the nested IF THEN ELSEs to a large CASE structure. The CASE structure will have compound boolean expressions, but if these are documented, they are easier to test and to maintain. When the development language does not support boolean expressions, you can resort to a SELECT structure. Duplicate code, resulting from changing a set of IF THEN ELSES into a CASE statement, can be placed in external modules which are called from appropriate points in the CASE statement. In this situation, it is also sometimes helpful to place nested structures in subordinate modules to help minimize the problem. This was also discussed in Chapter 2.

Dependencies   The most error-prone condition which can exist in a program is when there are segment (intramodule) dependencies. They are rarely documented and often are not recognized. Their biggest impact is during maintenance when a minor change at one point in the program "breaks" something somewhere else. This is called the "push-and-pop syndrome" by some maintenance programmers. Unfortunately, since no one recognizes the problem, it is not tested. The program often breaks when the user environment changes. These dependencies are bad enough when they are within a module; they are even worse when the dependency crosses module boundaries. Intermodule dependencies and intramodule dependencies are explained in Chapter 2.

Programmer Assumptions   Programmer assumptions are rarely recognized by the person making them. They are caused by a "hole" in the specification which is "unconsciously filled" by the programmer. These programmer assumptions are rarely observed and tested; they only show up when something changes during maintenance. Programmers and test engineers need to be trained to look for them.

When we were reverse-engineering major programs for a large computer vendor, we discovered large numbers of programmer assumptions. Perhaps the most flagrant was an assumption that a year-to-date file would always end after an update file had finished. This worked fine until the key was changed and the update file finished last. When it did, it broke the system.

An example which provides insight into the problem is a program which was given at Brigham Young University in a large FORTRAN class to over 1,000 students over a five-year period. The problem read: "Write a program which, for each row of a matrix, will find the average of the first 4 elements in the row and place it in the location of the largest value." A 5×8 matrix was given with one largest value per row and the students ran this problem year after year, never recognizing that there was no solution because without fail, they assumed there would always be more than 3 columns. (What do you do if there are only 3, 2, or 1?) They also assumed only one largest value per row. (What do you do if there are 2, 3, or more largest values?) You don't know whether to print an error message, calculate the mean for however many values there are, or what. If there is more than one largest value, do you put it in place of the first? The last? All of them? Or do you write an error message? There is nothing in the specification to tell you, so there is no right answer. This example has also been given as a "structured programming problem" during in-house courses with only about 10 percent of the students recognizing the programmer assumptions.

Inconsistent Patterns   Another problem relating to nontestability is that some programmers try to be "creative" by never doing the same thing in the same way twice. This is an error-prone habit. Once something has been found to be efficient and correct, it should be used each time it is appropriate. Thus, often a test suite from one place in the program can be used at many other locations where that same pattern occurs. These consistent patterns are easier to maintain and are more likely to be evaluated quickly during a code inspection or a code audit. One of the major effects of the new paradigm is to enforce standard and correct patterns which can be easily audited.

Poor Modularity Poor modularity occurs when the knowledge of a data element (such as zip code) is passed among a large number of modules (as part of the name and address). It is only needed in one or two modules in the software system, but if it changes from five to nine places, every module that references it must be modified and recompiled—giving a large chance of introducing an error. These are both hard to recognize and test. Another example is that in the year 2000, a great many computer systems will "break" because of the knowledge of "19xx" being carried across a large number of modules. The same thing happened when Social Security went from $999.99 to more than a thousand dollars several years ago. Someone estimated that it cost several million dollars to make the appropriate correction in the country's payroll programs.

Environmental Dependencies Nontestability is also an issue when there are environmental dependencies. A software system should be designed so that it runs relatively independent of its environment. It ought to be fairly simple to convert from a menu-driven system to a windows-oriented system by simply reprogramming the interface. The knowledge of what kind of system is providing the data should be irrelevant to the software system—only the interface should "know." This is especially true now that there are many interface design languages available, such as FaceSpan™. If every time you change environments you need to modify the code and retest it, you enter a very error-prone environment.

The Risk of Low Reusability If a program is designed so that large portions are written so they can be reused at other points, preferably through "fan-in" where a large number of modules call that "one module" or "subsystem," then it only needs to be tested once and the interface checked for each of the calling modules. If, on the other hand, a programmer decides that the code is just a little bit different and recodes it for each place it is used, it must be tested in all those places. If a component of the module or subsystem needs to be changed during maintenance, the maintenance programmer must look in each place, make the change, and retest all the places the "somewhat" similar code was used, a highly error-prone process.

A better strategy for the programmer who sees that the code is "almost the same" is to create a massage module which converts the part of the function which is similar into one which is the same. The use of massage modules was also explained in Chapter 2. The massage module contains code which makes it possible to use the reusable module without modifying it. This is also discussed in Chapter 2.

The Risk of Personnel Shortages This risk is based on the fact that corporate planning extended over several years does not always take into account what software is going to be built, how many people will be needed to build it, or who will be available to test it (and on what equipment). This happens when upper-level management manages the personnel based on current income per employee, rather than income to be generated by the proposed software. While this is a very conservative, laudable approach, it tends to put projects just starting up "at risk" both in terms of having the programmers and test engineers available to start the project, and even more important, having them trained and up to speed so they are productive from the start. We discussed a better approach to personnel in the context of leverage.

The Risk of Poor Training   Some companies refuse to send their employees to conferences or take commercial courses—either in-house or at some outside location. Over the years, these employees get out of the main stream and have a difficult time keeping up with the technology. This means that they either make a lot of mistakes or do not design and build software which is "state of the art." In healthy companies, subscriptions to scholarly journals and to commercial trade-oriented journals and newspapers are freely provided and most employees feel an informal obligation to read them.

11.3.2 Decision Making Based on Risk

When a company begins to manage its risks, it identifies all the places in its organization where it is or has the potential of being "at risk." We have tried to illustrate which types of risk are most likely to have a negative impact on the software organization. Many of the quality design strategies of our new paradigm will minimize or eliminate certain of the above risks, but it should be obvious to you that management-oriented and training-oriented risks will remain no matter what quality has been designed in. The risk will be different for each software system created, but deciding where to put testing resources is a good indicator. You should realize, however, that there are multiple parts of the software system competing for a limited number of testing resources. All potential risks should be taken into account and a knowledge-driven trade-off should be taken.

In the new paradigm, testing emphasis is not on the functionality of the system, which is usually the case in standard testing strategies; it is in testing the behavior of the system, as we have said many times. Managing risk and the limited testing resources you have should not be forced to relate to module or system functionality, though that is where the risk usually is greatest when the software is poorly designed. Rather, they should be freed to test things that are more important to the user such as usability, installability, performance, etc. This works best when it is related to user profiles. These were explained in Chapter 5. When deciding where to put testing resources, given you are forced to do functional testing, the following factors should be considered.

Customer Impact   This is usually the most serious risk one can take. A company should look at the characteristics of the software system which is being created and recognize that if you cannot test everything exhaustively—which is usually the case—you should concentrate on parts of the system which will have the most customer impact if errors are undetected until the software reaches the user.

On a word processor, it may be fairly simple to reconstruct a day's work should that be the impact of an error. On the other hand, should the local area network handling an airline reservation system goes down, the airline might stand to loose $20,000 per minute. That is a major impact. Attempting to define, measure, or estimate mean time to failure in this environment is a risky enterprise. We have mentioned earlier that it is better to test (behaviorally) all the user profiles which are appropriate and enforce their use through effective programming and interface definition. As we said elsewhere, if the software is programmed so it is deterministic, systems should not go down because of a software failure. But from a behavioral point of view, you should make it easy to reestablish the system if there should be a hardware failure through appropriate diagnostics and system backups. A similar negative impact might occur if certain activities using a software system tended to contaminate a company's database, with the effects not showing up for several days or weeks.

New Technology   The best way to minimize the impact of new technology is to begin early to send people to training courses in the new technology. Before the rest of the software development process begins, advanced teams should begin building prototypes to create a "proof of concept" before too much time and effort are committed to the entire software product. The impact of the new technology on the rest of the product should be assessed and the part of the system which is based on the new technology should be built first using as much of the prototype as is appropriate. This would include acquiring the necessary new hardware very early so it is available from the outset of the project.

The idea here is that software development strategies should often begin up to two years before the actual specification is written and the new project actually begun. This is almost always involved with the most risk of missing the production schedule deadline. Any product development for which the approximate time to completion is not known should be started first.

Error History   As various software products are built and evaluated, people find that errors tend to group around certain modules, functions, and technology. High-risk areas should be identified early on and both development and testing should focus on these areas. If design analysis, related to the software architecture, allows for identification of error-prone code, first an attempt should be made to reduce complexity and increase the testability of the software; then for the areas difficult to improve, a testing strategy which focuses on these areas will help reduce the risk. With appropriate design strategies, based on the new paradigm, often, complex interaction and intricate relationships in the system can be identified, simplified, and audited, rather than needing to go through exhaustive traditional functional testing. Again, we stress that this does not preclude well thought-out behavioral testing.

New or Existing Feature   If the software being built is a follow-on to an existing product and the earlier product was designed correctly, a large part of the earlier product should be directly transportable into the new product. The automated test cases used to test the earlier product should accompany the code, and little additional testing may be necessary, allowing one to concentrate efforts on the new features. Mainly, the interfaces from the existing features to the new features would be where testing efforts should be concentrated.

Complexity   Complex code tends to be more error-prone than simple code. The same is true of complex interfaces. First, an attempt should be made (through design analysis) to reduce the complexity. Then that which remains should be the focus of additional testing efforts. Typically, simple code tends also to be more efficient than complex code. This is why a sequence of structured code, even though it often tends to be 25 percent to 100 percent longer than spaghetti code, tends to be the same or better than equivalent spaghetti code in performance. Where such considerations are questioned by programmers, it is worth a little extra effort to code a module both ways and examine its performance.

System Complexity   Some system complexity can be identified with McCabe's Battlemap and other similar tools. In addition, care should be taken to locate and eliminate intermodule dependencies. Usually this can be done by packaging the dependencies together in the same module, directly adjacent to each other. Where this is not possible, you can sometimes remove the dependency from both modules, making them independent of each other, and document the dependency in the new module to which it has been moved. This was discussed in Chapter 2.

System complexity can also be related to improper allocation of dissimilar functions to the same module. Or, parts of a function may be spread across multiple modules. Proper "packaging" of modules into highly functional subsystems helps reduce this complexity. This also adds to the "reuse" discussed earlier. Modules should not access any data which is not directly processed by the code within that module, or subsystem of modules. The use of global data structures should be discouraged regardless of the reason people give for their use. Where the global data structures cannot be eliminated, testing should focus on such areas. Audits in the new paradigm are effective in assessing their impact, but often software states that impact modules which are caused to be dependent by the global data structures can only be evaluated through behavioral testing. Defining user profiles which force the dependent states is terribly difficult and the results are hard to verify.

Module Complexity   Module complexity can usually be easier to identify than system complexity, but, as with system complexity, initially, an attempt should be made through design analysis to locate and minimize or eliminate as much of the complexity as possible. Where segment dependencies are recognized, an attempt should be made to package them as close together as possible. Usually, if a module appears to be unusually complex, having a different programmer reprogram the module from its specification can sometimes lead to a better solution. Modules which cannot be reduced in complexity become the target for increased testing emphasis.

Interface Complexity   Passing complex data structures among modules, or allowing modules to reference complex global data structures should be questioned and attempts should be made to reduce the complexity. Where such conditions continue to exist, testing efforts should focus on them.

Programmer Confidence Level Programmers are all different in their coding rates and error rates. While programmers should not be isolated and ridiculed (or punished) for errors, peers should use this knowledge to better assess the testing effort. Their experience levels differ as well.

Programmer Experience with Environment Programmers who have had little or no experience with a particular environment tend to make more mistakes than programmers who are more experienced. Sometimes it is not years of experience, but rather amount of time involved in a particular environment or technology that is most important. Whenever the environment is new to a given programmer, more testing effort should be focused on that particular area.

Programmer Error History We have observed two programmers working on a project. One programmer produced around 100 lines of code per week; the other 1,000 lines of code per week. The first had an error rate of around 2 to 3 errors, while the other had around 50 errors. Who is the better programmer? The answer is that both are valuable—for different reasons! That is why one cannot look at error rate alone. A high-quality code inspection may be all that is necessary to eliminate the 50 errors, thus providing the project with an extremely efficient programming effort. Note, however, that under the new paradigm, behavior of this sort tends to disappear. When programmers all conform to the same standards, there tends to be less chance for error—and the filtering process, based on code audits, tends to be more effective and efficient than traditional inspection and testing techniques.

Time Available to Test Unfortunately, many projects suffer from unrealistic time constraints. While upper-level management insists on quality, they do not allow enough time for adequate testing to achieve it. In this context, efficient testing is the only solution. You must test code that has a high probability of containing errors, and minimally test the remaining code, realizing that some in which one is relatively confident may not be tested at all. Design analysis, based on past experience and baselines, is the best help in locating the critical code.

If management is truly enlightened and disciplined, they will conform to a product delivery system like the one we defined in the new paradigm. In this case, marketing windows are provided with functions based on an appropriate ranking with respect to marketing issues. The software development organization, with help from marketing, sales, support, and others, will create a project plan providing appropriate and realistic delivery dates. Often, if the complete product cannot be delivered in time, intermediate products may create appropriate credibility with customers or subsystems which may fill customer needs until the entire product can be delivered.

11.3.3 Minimizing the Impact of Risk

To minimize the impact of risk, you must have guidelines to make your choices intelligent and well thought out. Limited resources must be allocated to the error-prone code. There are other tools which may help. Many of these concepts are described earlier in the book, but a summary is included here so you can see how they apply not only to quality, but also to risk. The factors discussed here affect both project-related risks and test-related risks. However, because increasing testability is a huge component to minimizing risk, it is covered in its own section following this one.

Creating a Schedule An attempt should be made to identify, well in advance, just what the marketing window is that you are trying to meet. You can work backwards, based on the estimated length of time to build the product, to determine when the project should begin. You can then assemble the necessary resources and provide the necessary training to build the product in an appropriate period of time. Some tools which can help you schedule the project are described below.

Stable Specification   If time is taken early on to create a complete specification based on research in the user community, competitive analysis, and upcoming technology, a stable specification can be created. The value of a stable specification is that it allows you to manage the architecture and manpower in such a manner as to keep the product in sync with the schedule. This specification should be as complete as possible—especially in terms of the user interface or user profile and it must maintain the same look and feel as earlier versions, and its outputs should be backward and forward compatible. The specification with its accompanying software architecture should be maintained on-line, preferably in an appropriate CASE tool. This will allow for it to be maintained across the life cycle of the product.

Configuration Management   No matter how careful the systems analysis team creating the specification is, the product will change across its life cycle. If a product does not change across its life cycle, it often is unmarketable when it finally reaches the marketplace. In order to keep everything in sync, a Configuration Control Board should be established to review proposed changes to the product. An impact assessment statement created by each group impacted by the change allows for effective decision-making.

Typically, a change to the product can invalidate as many as several thousand test cases, scores of pages of documentation, as well as marketing and education documents. But allowing for such changes and keeping everything current pays for itself by keeping everything parallel. Everyone works against a complete, stable, updated specification and accompanying software architecture.

Parallel Life Cycle   It is well worth the effort to create and maintain a complete, stable specification and to keep all phases parallel. This is a fundamental part of the product delivery system. If various parts of the software development process such as training, delivery, support, documentation, and testing are required to wait until all the programming is completed, then the schedule goes out of control and is extended greatly. When the specification is kept current, the test cases are created using automated tools, and the product development documentation on-line, during a nine-month development cycle, at least eight months of testing may take place, and the three to five months necessary for creating the documentation takes place during the same time period as well. When you lose control of the specification, you must wait until the product is built to test, usually limiting the testing to one or two months—an inadequate length of time for doing appropriate testing. This almost always leads to quality problems, and little chance to apply design analysis to the testing process.

Also, since in the new paradigm almost all the testing (as opposed to audits) is related to behavior, having complete subsystems, which were designed so specific behavior could be tested early, is extremely important. If these relatively complete products are lost to the design being compromised and the specification needing to be discarded as no longer appropriate, then behavioral testing cannot be performed early. Likely, you will also be forced to attempt functional testing at the end just to see what you have. As a worst case, your testing may be reduced to merely running the program to see if it crashes and if it does not, then you release it.

Project Plan   The project plan is the basic tool which helps the product be delivered on schedule and minimizes the risks of delays. A typical project plan will provide for deliverables every two weeks. An effective project plan will provide for subsystems to begin to be delivered to the system test organization very early in the life cycle. Project plans are living documents, being modified as necessary to allow for changes approved by the Configuration Control Board.

Personnel Allocation   If projects are planned two to three years in advance and it is recognized that many changes will occur to those plans, an organization can characterize its personnel on the basis of skills mix and training and minimize the risk of having inadequate personnel on hand since programmers are not needed across all projects all the time. Thus, personnel needs can be planned for as a part of the project plan by indicating just when each component of a software product will be built so that personnel can be allocated to several projects across a one- to three-year period. This makes for effective use of personnel.

Defining Users   The time spent creating a complete, stable specification with an accompanying high-quality product architecture pays for itself many times over. The largest risk at this point is not identifying or characterizing the appropriate users. When there is a potential for several million users, this is a very difficult assessment to make. Identifying classes of users to whom the product will be sold and creating a specification for a product which will focus on each of those classes of users minimizes the risk of not identifying the target users for whom the product should be being built. Users will not buy a product that does not meet their needs, is difficult to learn or install in their environment, or requires substantial training of their personnel before it can be used effectively.

Regional/Application Users Groups   One way to identify appropriate users is to create and support regional and application-based users groups. Questionnaires and group visits to the company headquarters ensure that software specifications developers interact with these key people. Screen prototypes and new technology prototypes should be created as part of the planning process and demonstrated to as many of these potential users as possible. The impact of competitors' products on these key users should also be assessed and the product redesigned to reflect such competitor impact. This process should be on-going and during the software development process this should be the source of many of the requests for changes in the software product being built. Note that this is an important part of our marketing requirements definition filter (see Section 4.2.2).

Customer Site Visits Software Developers—including marketers, development engineers, test engineers, and documentation personnel—should be trained in the process of making meaningful, efficient site visits to customers. During such visits, not only are customer ideas observed, but also, in the actual customer environment, those responsible for designing and building the product see exactly how that product is being used. This "environment" cannot be effectively conveyed by description, only by observation.

Questionnaires/Phone Calls Where it is impractical to make customer site visits or bring customers in to company headquarters, information can be gleaned from questionnaires and from phone calls to current and prospective customers. Although this is not as effective as actual visits, it cannot be ignored as a method of gaining information.

Minimizing Creeping Featurism While Remaining Tuned to a Changing Environment

This topic has been partially addressed in several of the earlier sections. The challenge here, in terms of managing risk, is knowing how to keep changes under control while allowing them to occur. In the PC, Macintosh, and workstation environments, new products are expected every three to six months. Customers tend to be very poorly trained in computer technology and are very naive about what to expect. But this is another part of the industry that is changing. As we have repeatedly mentioned, customers are coming more and more to expect quality in the software products they purchase. In the past, software vendors could bully the customer into accepting whatever they sold. This is becoming less and less true. Now, potential customers are not exceptionally loyal to a particular vendor. The field is changing almost daily and potential customers are bombarded with new technology. This means that a vendor must keep current in the new technology and have a marketing plan that is based on taking advantage of these new technologies. This also means that software developers must adjust to building to a moving target.

The way to minimize this risk is to put a Configuration Control Board in place to evaluate changes. Proposal of changes should be encouraged, not discouraged, if the product is to be marketable when it ships. But these changes should be carefully managed. It should be recognized that while many of the changes come from users and others come from marketing and marketing studies, a large number come from the developers themselves as they work closely with the product and its technology. These proposals should not be discouraged; they should be rewarded and managed.

Minimizing the Risk of Implementing New Technology

Typically, new technology is the area with the most potential to cause a schedule to slip. To minimize this risk, developers should be trained in the new technology by attending classes and provide access to the technology as soon as it becomes available. The parts of the software product which are based on the technology should be built first. This uncertainty should be built into the project plan so that its potential negative impact to the schedule can be assessed early and adapted for. The code with the most certain dates of completion should be built last, with the old features being added at the point where their impact is most certain.

Minimizing Risk through Error Tracking The filtering process is a system. that should be modified and fixed where a filter is broken. At each phase of the life cycle, errors detected that should have been found at an earlier phase are logged, and the filter is reevaluated to see why the error got through. This minimizes the risk of these errors occurring again. Any customer-detected errors are especially critical.

Some sort of automated error-tracking software must be put in place to allow the progress of fixing the error and fixing the filter process to be performed. Some sort of management sign-off against the error log and review/inspection process must be done. This should be reviewed at least monthly to make certain that the error tracking process is working. Without management sign-off and periodic review, this entire process tends to be neglected as people go on to other tasks.

Minimizing Risk through "Root-Cause" Analysis Root-cause analysis is an attempt to determine just how an error got out into the field. It is the process employed by the test organization and the development organization to refine and update the filter process and minimize the risk of future errors. It should be included in the management sign-off process. Periodically, those responsible should make presentations to developers and test engineers to keep them posted on the effectiveness of the filters and to help them modify checklists and other devices for improving the error detection process.

Both error tracking and root-cause analysis should gradually disappear from your process if you are using the new paradigm and your filters are working. As we have mentioned elsewhere, if errors are getting through to the customer, more than 18 filters are broken simultaneously. If that is true, your product delivery process is seriously out of control. This means you need to completely reinstall the process on a new—perhaps smaller—product and revalidate it.

Minimizing Risk through Automated Tools For any traditionally oriented testing to be effective, it must be automated—from unit test through system test. Initially, any organization should examine the off-the-shelf tools provided by vendors in the industry. Those judged to be most appropriate and effective should be chosen and implemented in the development/test organizations. These can later be "fine-tuned" by adding internally developed subroutines to customize the commercial tools to the development/test environment and to the software house's products. We talked about this earlier, where we characterized some of the tools and how to evaluate them. You should note that all the automated tools we are aware of are related to functional rather than behavioral testing. The major reason is that most behavioral testing, in terms of what we defined in Chapter 5, is too hard to define generically, whereas functionality is not.

Changing the Corporate Culture   Many companies know that attempting to install software development methodologies, specification standards, software system standards, coding standards, and filtering processes related to reviews and inspections and testing is sometimes a challenge. Some programmers would rather quit than conform. This may be too severe a price for a company to pay to install these practices which propose to eliminate or at least minimize risk. Often developers are very undisciplined. They do not feel that they are doing a bad job. Errors are simply "anomalies" which occurred just by chance. They may feel that their very "undisciplined" approach is a characteristic of their "creativity." They tend to build highly innovative products, but they fail to recognize that they continue to use the same old development techniques time after time. Thus, they improve the product without improving the process.

As you attempt to implement these risk-cutting strategies, you must face this corporate culture. It is best to attempt this—unless the company is in crisis mode and must change at once—on a project by project basis, gradually adding more and more to the process until it is completely installed. Feedback must be given to the entire company.

One approach to changing the corporate culture is to create slogans which represent the company's view of life, the competition, and the real world. The best approach is to take a simple slogan that everyone can recognize, build the corporate reward system around it, and start building support for the program. At Novell, they had several slogans they lived by. One of these was, "We build innovative products!" We changed this to "We build innovative products innovatively." We then began to concentrate on the parts of the strategy a little at a time.

Holding Project Postmortems   Another valuable tool to help evaluate and fix the delivery process is the project postmortem. This is usually hard to sell to companies, but it is almost mandatory in the continuous improvement process according to Deming's quality issues. When the project has reached the stage of first customer ship, there should be a final "winding down" or "act of completion" carried out. It must be well planned, or it will fail. At the postmortem, the development team gets together to "evaluate" the entire software development process—as it pertains to their project. You should ask several questions. What went right? What went wrong? If we had time to do something over, what would it be? Where were the holes in our filter? How effective were our attempts to minimize risk? How can we improve the risk-taking process?

At Digital Technology, postmortems occur at several points. We have found that there needs to be a "formal handoff" from development to maintenance, maintenance to customer release, customer release to install-train-audit-support. This enables us to evaluate how the entire release mechanism—including final testing of user profiles and making sure the software product(s) match the sales contracts. A postmortem at each of these points has helped deliver a high quality product on time and within budget at minimum risk. Extra time building filters and checklists—and then training our people in how to use them—has really paid off.

Product Postmortems should be documented as a part of the product history and maintained in a special file with other completed projects. It might, under some circumstances, be published and made available to various members of the development team to give them insight toward improving future projects. At least, one copy should be kept in the corporate library. A side effect of this activity—with the accompanying report—is that in case of a lawsuit, it can be shown that the software house took great pains to manage the quality of the product and provided adequate testing—within the framework of the risks they felt obligated to take. It can also make it easier for you to qualify for ISO 9000 registration and other types of quality initiatives.

Refining the Process   The product delivery process does not work if it is not refined. The filtering mechanism, "root-cause analysis," and the project postmortems each provides information to make the process better. Results—both positive and negative—in a healthy environment of improvement and rewards, rather than criticism and punishment—should be used to continually improve the process. Wherever meaningful metrics can be determined, they should be maintained and used for process improvement. All these activities help your company to minimize your risk in meeting the quality goals you have set. This is especially true when you view this in terms of the Deming chain of Figure 11-1.

It should be noted that all the activities, concepts, strategies, and processes, will not work exactly the same for each organization. Some parts of this book can be used directly; other parts will need to be adapted to your organization. The process should be taken on a little at a time; one should not attempt to do everything at once. One of the most important parts is getting a good specification. This activity, usually conducted by a systems analysis team, should be started out on small projects, and as the team gains experience, it should be gradually expanded to fit more and more of the life cycle and more and more of the company's projects.

11.3.4 Minimizing Risk through Increasing Testability

Earlier, we addressed risk in terms of nontestability. Now we will address how to make software testable, hopefully in such a manner as to reduce the risk involved with developing and releasing a software product. If the issue of testability is to be addressed appropriately, it must be addressed in the framework of a software development life cycle and also in the framework of a formal, stable specification. Remember that in terms of our product delivery process, the specification comes several major stages into the process, after it has been filtered for marketing and sales input and a marketing context created for it. If you do not understand the significance of this, you should look back at the marketing requirements filter. Most companies address specifications as being only informal statements of what functions are to be included. Interfaces are "assumed" to be "programmable at the appropriate point by knowledgeable programmers" based on their innate knowledge of what the user wants. Other companies write specifications but conclude that the ongoing changes related to programming to a "moving target" make the specification a "throw-away document" as it soon loses its relevance.

It was stated by a participant at a testing conference several years ago that CASE tools and software development methodologies were ineffective in a "real-life" type of software development environment. They had used the structured analysis and design methodology, along with a particular CASE tool. The comment was that they had to make so many changes to the product during its development that the specification, maintained in the CASE tool, got out of sync with the product and the modular structure of the software architecture degraded as to be unrecognizable. The conclusion was that doing a systems analysis, keeping it in a CASE tool, building a software architecture, keeping it in the CASE tool, was all a waste of time, as the specification was constantly changing during the development of the product. Spending all that time on a systems analysis and software architecture was a waste of time, as it all was going to change anyway. The basic problem was in not managing the changes to the software system in a manner such as has been described above. We never said it was easy; we said it was necessary to minimize risk. Obviously, if the specification is maintained in a CASE environment, it is easier to maintain. If you have neither a specification nor an architecture, the project schedule is meaningless and your programmers will work until they "think" they are finished and someone will test until you run out of time. Further, software integration will be a nightmare. Neither of these situations leads to quality software, nor to the ability to ship at a pre-specified time.

Writing Testable Specifications   The question of writing testable specifications is one of going beyond writing functional definitions and defining the behavior of that function as well. One of the risks associated with testability is that of having specifications which you do not understand. If only a definition is provided, it is difficult to know what the function is to do. This is not just a question of behavioral testing; it is also an issue of being able to show the function works, regardless of whether you test it with an audit or test data. Remember that an audit shows whether the function is correct, of appropriate quality, and complete. After that, in the new paradigm, we test the behavior. In traditional testing, how do you show the function is correct? You must show that for appropriate inputs and expected outputs, you get correct outputs. As we mentioned in Chapter 5, this may involve either white box or black box testing, and for many testing experts this act of testing is a behavioral test. As we mentioned, we will not quibble over definitions; functionality is both static and dynamic. We tend to view behavioral testing somewhat differently, i.e., showing how the function works as part of the system it inhabits. This is why behavioral testing is so important once you know the basic function is correct.

Below is an example of a specification we once tested, which was stated as: "The Product will have a Screen Refreshing Algorithm." It then went on to define the algorithm. There was no attempt to indicate how it would work in the program environment, its performance, what would trigger it, how many characters would be stored in the input buffer while the screen was being refreshed, and so forth.

Basically, a testable specification is one which defines the behavior of the function in testable terms. If you continually ask of the specification: "How can this be tested? What are the input conditions? What are the output conditions? What is the expected behavior?" the specification will become testable. The developer should look at this from the unit test perspective or code audit and the test engineer from the integration and system test perspective. Both groups should agree on the specification component's testability. With a little experience doing this, along with feedback from later testing based on the filters, both developers and test engineers become very proficient at doing this.

Event Lists versus Assertions A useful approach to testable specifications is to define for the entire product an event list. Through this approach—which comes from essential systems analysis—the complete software development organization becomes familiar with the behavior characteristics of the product. You then define each of the triggers—the activities or conditions which will cause the event to execute and the response each event makes to the trigger. If this is fairly complete for the entire product, it serves to form a fairly reliable set of acceptance test criteria on which the final filter can be based to be used at the end of the project to assert the completeness and correctness of the software product.

As an alternative to this, specifications can also be made more testable by stating them as assertions. When you make an assertion, you can usually come up with a testable view of the specification. In either case, you are attempting to change a general statement of what a function is into one which not only addresses what it is, but how it behaves, as well. Both of these approaches have proven very successful in companies which have implemented them.

Reviews of Specifications Just as there are design reviews and code inspections—or our newer concept of "audits"—for looking at the software architecture and other designs and for assessing the correctness of the code, there is also the activity of reviewing the specification. This is the first point in the software development process where you can begin to assess and control for risk. Minimally, the specification should be reviewed by the software development team, made up of marketers, development engineers, test engineers, documentation personnel, and human interface personnel. Ideally, prechosen users, application developers (who are concerned that the APIs do not break their software), people from education, sales, upper-level management, etc. should also be involved. In this review activity all these individuals would see an overview of the entire product. Where screen prototypes have been created—especially to show new technology and interfaces—these should be shown. If other technologically based prototypes have already been done, they can either be demonstrated or described. Obviously, this takes a lot of effort upfront, but if even a part of this is done, it can have a positive impact on the entire development cycle. Feedback at this point is the least expensive to correct for.

Reviewing the specification against a filter, rather than using a traditional inspection, is extremely powerful. Basically you are looking at the specification in the context of the marketing requirements document and the basic structure of the filter. Both of these lead to a higher-quality specification than traditional reviews. This is especially true as your product development process, with its accompanying deliverables and filters, matures within your company. This process is also heavily impacted by the training and experience your personnel gain across the development of several software products.

Maintenance of Specifications   In order for specifications to remain current with the existing product, they must be maintained in some automated form. Someone should be assigned to keep all or a part of them up to date, and there should be management sign-off relating to the Configuration Control Board to see that changes are not made and adjusted for—unless they have also been modified in the specification. For most specifications, a CASE tool is a good place to start. Without some sort of checklist associated with the impact of each change, this sort of update will not happen. A completed checklist, signed by the responsible individuals, should, when complete, be signed off by a designated person on the Configuration Control Board. This should always happen.

We have found this to be extremely effective at Digital Technology. Without a checklist and sign-off, something always goes wrong, or someone goes around the system "for efficiency's sake" or "just to get the job done." In other companies we have found personnel involved in the creative process to be extremely undisciplined. They tend to go around the system due to impatience more than anything else. Going around the system almost always breaks it, especially in our new product delivery process. As soon as checklists and sign-offs are mandated and enforced, it takes very little effort to keep things under control. We found this to be extremely easy to implement at DT, and it should be at your company as well.

There is an excellent paper by Antonia Bertolino and Lorenzo Strigini in the February 1996 issue of *IEEE Transactions on Software Engineering* that discusses the use of testability measures for dependability assessment. This paper gives an excellent alternative view to what we have been discussing in terms of testability and dependability. It is at a moderate mathematical level, but the discussion and conclusions are easy to follow even if you miss some of the math (see Bertolino and Strigini, 1996). Their basic conclusion is that you cannot quantify testability but the mathematical reasoning involved can provide direction. Our thrust in this chapter is not with measuring testability but rather with using techniques for increasing testability to reduce risk.

Creating Testable Software Architectures   Before a product is built, there should be a preliminary view of how the entire product should look including answers to such questions as: Which modules call which other modules? Which executive modules are drivers to which subsystems? What data are passed among which modules? How is transaction processing modeled and implemented? What data structures and control information come in from the external interfaces? How is interrupt processing handled?

An attempt should be made to create a software architecture that is not only efficient based on past experience but in which all components are relatively independent of each other. This is especially true of subsystems. As was mentioned earlier, modules should not access any information or data they do not need to perform their functions. Both the structured analysis and design paradigm and the object-oriented analysis design programming paradigm lend themselves to this approach. It is important to identify and remove intermodule dependencies, or at least minimize their impact. The more independent the subsystems and modules within subsystems become, the more easily they can be tested. You would expect that the object-oriented paradigm would meet all the quality conditions, but surprisingly, it does not. The concept of inheritance is in direct contradiction to independence and executive modules.

Defining System Quality Standards A set of standards, dating back to 1975 and before (Myers, 1978) can form a basis for defining system quality standards. See also Crandall (1987). The two most important were defined above in terms of independence, minimal data access, and elimination of intermodule dependencies. Myers's standards, while dated, still have not been replaced by any more appropriate standards. As we mentioned in Chapter 8, in Briand et al. (1996), software engineering measurement criteria are characterized mathematically rather than descriptively. One set of them relates to the architectural qualities defined below. Defining and manipulating modules based on these definitions play more of a role in our new paradigm than you might expect. Due to space limitations, we are not able to explain everything about the new paradigm in this book.

Below are our versions of the definitions of these levels of quality rather than those of Myers. Myers defined module strength—or module cohesiveness—as progressing from weakest to strongest in terms of positive impact on the software systems. This is defined in terms of "maintenance," but it is just as appropriate for "testability." The various levels of quality in terms of cohesiveness are:

- Coincidental Strength—modules which are contained inside of other modules and thus have access to the code without going through a module interface. Inheritance implies this condition and thus violates a major quality standard in our paradigm.

- Logical Strength—modules which contain functions or partial functions which are packaged together because of some sort of logical relationship. Each one is accessed through the interface, but only one of them is processed for a given access.

- Classical (Temporal) Strength—modules which contain functions or partial functions which are related in time, meaning that for any one call, all of the functions or partial functions are accessed.

- Communicational Strength—modules which contain functions or partial functions which are related by the fact that they each process the same data or data structure.

- Sequential Strength—modules which contain functions or partial functions for which the output of one is the input to the next.

- Informational Strength—modules which contain functions which are packaged together because of their knowledge of either a data structure or a common function, or some other "knowledge element." The major difference between this and a logical strength module is that while only one function is accessed per evocation, with informational strength modules, the access is through external entry points. Informational strength modules are basic to our new paradigm.

- Functional Strength—modules which contain only one function, or for which all the code is related to the processing of one function. These modules are the basis of fan-in in the new paradigm, but we also consider modules which contain only partial functions (considered by Myers to be coincidental strength) to also be valid, provided their purpose is to provide independence through fanning into "knowledge elements" which eliminate existing dependencies.

In Myers's view, coincidental strength is the worst and functional strength is the best in terms of contribution to quality, i.e., maintainability and testability. Modules, in a design review or architectural audit, should be characterized according to their strength and/or contribution to independence, and an attempt made to "fix" them so they are either functional or informational strength or so that they make a positive contribution independence.

In this context, the strong "cohesion" or "packaging" should lead to modules where the functionality is contained in one place, thus making the traditional testing of that function easier. In some cases, this can lead to "functional primitives," which lend themselves to the creation of reusable test suites, as well as reusable functions. The farther you deviate from the "ideal," the more you must cross module boundaries to test a given function. This complicates the creation of test cases both at the unit and integration testing stages, as a decrease in functionality usually is accompanied by an increase in intermodule dependencies, as described below.

Module coupling is defined to be the degree of relationship between two modules. It can be classified as follows:

- Content Coupling—code inside one module calls or makes reference to or modifies code inside of another module without passing through the external interface.

- Common Coupling—one module is related to another by their accessing common global data structures.

- External Coupling—one module is related to another by their accessing common global data elements.

- Control Coupling—one module is related to another by the fact that one module knows and controls code inside the other module.

- Stamp Coupling—one module is related to another by the fact that one module explicitly passes a data structure to the other module.

- Data Coupling—one module is related to another by the fact that one module explicitly passes only the necessary data elements to the other module.

Content coupling is the worst type of coupling because the dependencies are almost impossible to eliminate, and data coupling is the best. Of all of these, common coupling is one of the most common violations of good software design and one of the most insidious in terms of its impact on maintenance and testing. Yet it is insisted on by programmers who should know better—it is part of the "tradition" of certain products such as compilers and operating systems. Data elements should be passed explicitly to provide a visible interface to the software designers and maintenance engineers.

Creating a minimal, visible interface makes it easier to perform integration testing. One important consideration is the elimination of "intermodule dependencies" where a decision, wired-in value, or data element or structure is "linked" in some way across a module boundary. Note that this goes further than just data relationships, which is what Myers considers. We are looking at any knowledge relationship that goes across the module boundaries. In dependency analysis, this may also be related to "state dependencies" which are invisible across module boundaries. But the quality standards based on coupling play an extremely important role in our new paradigm.

Module boundaries must also be tested at integration. Often this involves drawing directed graphs of the two modules in question and defining paths which cross the module boundaries through the interface. For very obscure dependencies, this may not be obvious nor easy to do. Worse, obscure dependencies may be missed and not tested at all! A discussion of an approach to this is given by Harrold and Soffa (1989).

There are other design objectives Myers defines, which also play an important role in our new paradigm. They will not be defined or explained here, mainly because they are design strategies rather than quality measures. These measures of good modularity are defined in Myers (1978, 1979a) and Yourdon and Constantine (1979) and the impact is described in Peters (1987). A description of what causes different module strengths and couplings to occur, what their impact is on maintenance and testing, and what can be done to fix them, is given in Crandall (1987).

Other than these measures, little is given to help systems designers find measures of software quality, but these measures have a great impact on the product. Further, they help guide developers into effective software development thought processes. Ideas such as the use of tables to hide error messages or to hide the "meaning of data" can be of great value—especially when building national language versions of the products. Successively refining a product using informational strength modules to enhance packaging and functional decomposition to increase localization of functionality and to isolate the software from its environment can make products which will run relatively independent of their operating environments—an especially valuable concept when providing products which run on multiple platforms. As a consequence, they will be easier to test; test coverage will be easier to attain. This can also have a positive impact on the time to market reduction that the software organization is attempting to achieve.

High quality in terms of these measures will minimize the risk of parts of the software not being evaluated when changes are made, due to decisions made by the Configuration Control Board. Characteristics which are not visible are often missed both in terms of redesign and in terms of testing. Ideally, in this context, all the code which is impacted by an executive module—or any other module—should fall below it in the software hierarchy. While this explanation may have appeared lengthy, these quality issues are among the most important risk reduction issues you can consider. And as we have stated, they play an important role in our new paradigm.

Reviews of Software Architectures   Once the software organization has understood and "internalized" the above mentioned measures of software system quality, they are prepared to hold effective design reviews—with a set of examination rules based on the above measurements. As an alternative, as part of the new paradigm, filters could be created and used in audits, rather than following the review process.

Creating Testable Code   Most programming texts concentrate on the syntax of a programming language. While they may stress structured programming, they rarely stress the programming thought process or code quality. When viewing code in terms of low-level, detailed design, one recognizes that a different thought-process from what is usually presented in a programming text is necessary (Crandall, 1990). There is a "mini-life cycle" which takes place. It consists of:

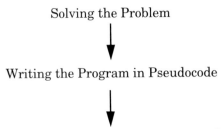

Solving the Problem

Writing the Program in Pseudocode

Converting the Pseudocode Program into Code in a Target Language

Imposing these levels of abstraction on the programming process makes it easier to convert from one target language to another—and our experience at Novell has shown that there is little time lost when programming takes place in pseudocode (which is reviewed during a code inspection) which then is converted to the target language. This has proven even more successful at Digital Technology as we have moved to 4GLs and event-driven high-level languages in the Mac environment. When this process is integrated into the entire software development process and related to high-level design, products can be created which are relatively error free and the entire development process is actually shortened. For more information on providing measures of code quality, see Crandall (1987). As explained in our chapter on quality standards, there are measures of code quality and testability which are effective. We will not repeat them here.

As has been stressed before, intramodule dependencies and intermodule dependencies cause the most trouble to maintenance programmers and test engineers. Yet they are the least understood and least recognized of all the conditions which occur in software development. The rule of thumb with respect to segment dependencies is to eliminate them, or package them together, if that is not possible. As was mentioned before, intermodule dependencies are not always eliminated by minimizing module coupling; often they are more obscure than that. But it is beyond the scope of this book to further comment on these areas.

It should be noted that this is one of the most neglected areas of software development, but it has the potential of causing a great deal of difficulty to maintenance programmers and test engineers. If it can be shown that these dependencies do not exist, then minimal numbers of test cases can be run with a high degree of test coverage. Otherwise, one is not obtaining the coverage one expects. Worse, if their existence is detected, it may increase the number of test cases from hundreds to tens of thousands to test the impact of these dependencies.

At the programming level, much of the risk associated with the need to do a large amount of testing to obtain satisfaction with and confidence in the software can be eliminated with a little effort to eliminate these sources of problems.

Setting Quality Standards There are no actual metrics associated with the aspects of software and code design other than error rates and complexity metrics. Much of what has been discussed above relates to everyone's accepting and "buying on" to the design issues. Inspection rules and checklists can be adapted to include examining the impact of these measures on the particular part of the software system under observation and under test. If everyone "buys on" to these issues, and if every effort is made to conform, this effort (which costs little in terms of time) can actually go a long way toward minimizing the risk of shipping error-prone, hard-to-maintain-and-test code and software systems.

Dealing with "Old Wives' Tales" For many programmers, there exist basic assumptions as to what is efficient and inefficient in implementing subsystems and in implementing code. Their arguments are related to the fact that performance is an important quality issue in software development and that that is what the issue really is. Originally, there was some reason why code was written a certain way, but now it is part of the organization's "culture." The best programmers are extremely self-confident and feel that they have demonstrated the quality of their code over a great many projects. Concepts which were proven years ago are now accepted as being correct "by definition." It is difficult in this type environment to begin to impose "new" standards.

The point at which this code is brought into question is the point at which the risk can be minimized most easily. Since it is worth the effort, the battle should be fought as early in the life cycle as possible. It is worth a little bit of time at this early stage to write the code both ways and then see which actually runs faster (or in other ways meets the performance criteria). If it does run faster in this particular instance, then you have demonstrated that there is a need for performance issues to violate quality standards. It should be noted that this is an exception to the rules, and it is allowed specifically because performance is at issue. But everyone should note that in the name of "performance" the team has decided to increase the risk. This means that this particular piece of code will be flagged at all phases of the life cycle as having the potential of a large number of errors. In this manner, one has not alienated certain programmers by being too dogmatic.

The big issue here is how many test cases are the equivalent of a code audit. If programmers conform to the coding standards we have proposed, then you can pattern match in an audit to determine correctness. This is mainly because of the small number of correct patterns you create using the standards. Once you give in to programmers in terms of allowing alternatives, you are back in the old paradigm and the risk is extremely great that errors will get through because the number of possible patterns against the number of correct patterns is too great to assure correctness.

One solution is to tell programmers that if they insist on violating the code quality standards in the name of efficiency or creativity or whatever, then they will be required to run test cases to a required level of coverage—either in terms of white box or black box coverage—before their code will be released to integration. If this is enforced, it does not take long for them to be converted to the standards. If this is imposed in a realistic manner, programmers usually recognize that if, for efficiency's sake, they must violate standards, then it is realistic to test to that level simply to minimize the risk of error. It is risk management, not punishment.

Recognizing Intermodule and Intramodule Dependencies and Programmer Assumptions   While we have called attention to inter- and intramodule dependencies, we have not addressed how to recognize them in this section. Rather, it is described in Chapter 2. At the system level, often inter-module dependencies can be found by walking transactions or data through the various modules of the system and attempting to observe—while looking at the big picture—where such dependencies might exist.

Holding Code Inspections   Code inspections pay for themselves many times over. There are several good books on the market relating to how to conduct inspections, such as Freeman and Weinburg (1977), Yourdon (1985), and a new book by Dorothy Graham and Tom Gilb (1995). In addition, there are several commercial courses available—from such experts as Michael Fagan, Tom Gilb, and others.

Code inspections are usually easy to get programmers to attend, as the most confident of them tend to want their code visible (and it is a good learning environment for new programmers). But it is harder to get programmers to agree to the "rules" (similar to ones based on the discussion above). Often a good code inspection can be the equivalent of 30,000 test cases because of the attempt to achieve a correct pattern—without dependencies. Intramodule dependencies are easy to see in an inspection (if you are looking for them), but they are incredibly difficult to test for—or to recognize their existence simply by examining the results of test cases. But you should note that "looking for errors" or "error detection" is not as effective as matching a small number of patterns to show an algorithm or software subsystem is correct.

As we discussed earlier, Arthur (1993) mentions that often even with inspections, over 50 percent of a product's development time can be devoted to finding and fixing bugs. As we further stated, a much more efficient approach is to design the errors out and guarantee their absence through audits, rather than inspections. The effectiveness of this approach must be developed and perfected over time and is not instantaneous.

Refining the Filters An effective test program is best viewed as a series of filters. At the earliest point, a design review—or audit—should call attention to marketing sales requirements and specification errors. At this point in the life cycle, it might cost only $10–$15 per error to eliminate them, whereas if they are not found until the product is shipped and the error found by a user, the same error may cause 100,000 lines of code to be rewritten, the product recalled, and then completely retested and redocumented; the cost would be enormous, perhaps several million dollars. "Ideally," we should detect 100 percent of the specification errors, and failure to do so is a failure of our filter, review, and feedback process to be sensitive to the type of error allowed through the process.

In terms of the new paradigm, filters have a more subtle significance. If a deliverable is built correctly, there should be no errors in it. The purpose of a filter is, as we have stated many times, to show accuracy, completeness, and quality. When an audit is held at any point in the product delivery process using a filter, it should quickly become obvious if there is a deficiency in the deliverable in terms of any of the three characteristics of the filter. At this point, the error is not in the filter, it is in the deliverable and the filter has caught it. If on the other hand the error or deficiency is not in this deliverable but an earlier one, then the error is in the earlier filter as well as the earlier deliverable, and both should be fixed. This provides for very rapid feedback and the ability to fix the process many times during one development cycle. Also, it is often very useful to run any software products still in a product delivery process against the broken filters, if they are applicable to the other product(s). The cost savings explained below will be true regardless of whether the new paradigm is used or if traditional testing is used.

If the software architecture is reviewed—and evaluated against the measures of system quality described above—it may cost only $30 or $40 to fix the error. On the other hand, if such designs containing poor structure are allowed to get through, it may result in large parts of the system tested to 100 percent statement coverage (giving an unrealistic sense of security) with the errors not being tested, because they are in relationships rather than in logic. It is almost impossible to test for poor systems design, but it can be observed much more easily in a design review of the software architecture. Again, this is viewed as a filter (coding errors cannot be found, as the coding has not as yet taken place). We would hope to catch 100 percent of the design errors, and any specification errors which may have gotten through.

If the code in each module is reviewed in a code inspection, we would expect to find most of the errors by "pattern matching" the module against the specification for that module. Normally an attempt is made to "paraphrase" the code rather than "reading it verbatim" or giving statement numbers. Code should be reviewed by colleagues, with at least one "expert" on the area being inspected. Similarly, someone from the test organization should be present, attempting to find errors but also attempting to visualize just how the module will be tested. Ideally, code should be reviewed after the programmer has decided that it has passed its "first successful compile." Prior to that coding errors are not recorded or maintained; after that—in both the inspection and the unit test—errors should be logged.

While inspections tend to take place—as defined in the previous paragraph—they are not as effective as audits, but you should note that audits are merely a variation on inspections, yet they are in a different paradigm. We are showing that quality, completeness, and accuracy are present—not that errors are present and need to be removed. But if errors are present, it means that we have problems with our design and programmer training and perhaps we need to fix the way we build software as well as adhere to standards.

After the code passes the code inspection, it is promoted to unit test. This may be done by the developer, by the test engineer assigned to the project, or by a special unit test team, organized to test the critical code (i.e., that which is determined to have "high risk"). A test plan for the module should be written by either the developer or a test engineer and reviewed by that, or a different, test engineer. Based on the "time available to test," a risk analysis should be performed by the developer and the test engineer; if there is any question, it might be reviewed by others from the development organization and from the test organization. Sometimes a design review should be held for the test plan, test strategy, and risk analysis. Ideally, all coding errors should have been caught and eliminated at this point. If not, then there was a problem with our filter, which must be corrected. Code that needs to be actually executed to demonstrate correctness comes from a deviation from your "comfort level." Normally this is related to your ability to filter, not to the failure of the code to conform. Again, you should note that we are not talking about a function's behavior; we are talking about its correctness.

Integration follows the same pattern. Again, this may be done by developers or test engineers. If the entire software development process is working correctly, the modules are created in a particular order, established by the project plan. When the modules making up the appropriate subsystem have been completed, the integration testing of the subsystem is done. This usually allows for some of the system characteristics or behavior to be tested, as well as the module interfaces. This process is viewed as a filter. It should not identify errors that should have been caught at code inspection or the unit test, as they should have been caught earlier; it should only catch interface errors. This may lead to a re-visit to the software architecture with certain errors which could not be detected until the subsystem had been built being caught at this time.

As the various subsystems are completed and tested, the test organization begins running the previously developed automated test suites against the system. As we have repeatedly stated, these refer to user profiles and other tests of software behavior, not functional correctness. Because at this point, you begin integration of larger and larger subsystems, more and more testing of the system characteristics can occur. Eventually, the entire system is available for testing. Ideally, this should only take about a month or less—after the development team has finished their last coding and testing. But it should be noted that system testing has been going on for almost the entire development time. This means that the risk of not being able to test adequately has been virtually eliminated.

To this point, we have progressed through unit to integration to subsystem to system testing. We have mentioned that this process is followed whether or not we are using the new paradigm. The major differences are related to pattern matching to determine functional correctness or actually running test cases to determine functional correctness. With the new paradigm, we put much more emphasis on behavioral testing in terms of how the entire system behaves. We emphasized earlier in terms of testability that the functional specification is more testable if it is defined in terms of behavior.

The last type of testing to be performed before the acceptance test and release of the product is beta testing. Alpha testing, which usually refers to testing "in house," and beta testing are used in the traditional testing environment as "ad hoc" testing strategies. In our opinion, they are effective, but tend to be very wasteful—both of the company's resources and the customer's resources. It is better if, when the system becomes available, customers are selected to test the system for environments expensive or difficult to create in the software house's environment. Ideally, automated test suites are provided to each beta test site, and they do exhaustive testing of the product under the direction of the software test organization. If specific user profiles are to be tested manually, they should be carefully supervised to show they have been followed correctly and the usability and the accuracy and completeness of the product(s) have been assessed.

Ideally, if the product has passed all the filters, there should be no need for "alpha testing." As part of the release process, perform several prespecified tests of user profiles before installing the product for beta testing at a user's site. If the error detection filters have functioned effectively and the final part of the product release process is followed, no errors should remain in the product sent to the customers.

11.3.5 Building a First-Rate Testing Organization

It should be obvious that this risk minimizing process is based on a high-quality, well-trained test organization. How should one be built? First of all, learning the testing strategies for unit testing is extremely simple. They can be described in an afternoon. But they are, for all their simplicity, very difficult to implement. It is easy to require 100 percent statement coverage on a module, but it may be very difficult to achieve. It is even more difficult to achieve basis path coverage, or even a small amount of coverage with data flow testing. Black box testing is also easy to learn, but it is hard to implement with any type of reasonable interface coverage if there are dependencies present.

System testing is even more difficult. It often requires hundreds of thousands of well thought-out test cases. Some types of testing—such as usability testing—are very difficult to quantify, let alone determine what is a usability error. Some companies spend millions of dollars creating usability labs, which have a positive impact on their products. Smaller companies cannot afford such a "luxury." In our experience, simply by defining user profiles and providing highly modifiable interfaces using tools such as FaceSpan™ and others, it is easy to define highly usable interfaces with minimum training and ease of use.

Still, a software testing organization pays for itself over and over. You should start with as high a ratio of test engineers to development engineers as possible. The best ratio is around 2:1 (one test engineer for every two development engineers). You may not be able to achieve that initially. With a 10:1 ratio, test engineers can be little more than policemen and coaches. With 5:1, they can begin playing a stronger role. Some of the test organization should be assigned to development teams; others are assigned to program/build the test harnesses which will come into play when the software product reaches the system test. Initially, there may be much more risk involved than the company feels comfortable with. All that can be done is to focus on the most risk-prone areas (especially in terms of customer impact) and do your best.

Remember that in terms of the new paradigm, you do not eliminate testing; you simply shift the focus in two ways:

- You design out errors rather than inspect or test them out
- Your testing emphasis—both automated and manual—is to test the behavior of the system.

Programming Skills versus Testing Skills   Test engineers are not technicians. The best test engineers are programmers who are devoting a stage of their career to testing. A danger is that they will lose their programming skills by only working on inspections and test plans or audits. To be fair to them, the careers of test engineers should be managed in such a way that they can spend 25 percent to 30 percent of their time in programming activities. Fortunately, if they are given the chance to build the automated tools necessary to system test each company product, there should be adequate programming involvement. If this does not happen, test engineers will use the test organization as a stepping stone to programming and you will be faced with a staff doing everything possible to transfer out. This is both dangerous and expensive for the test organization.

11.4 SUMMARY AND CONCLUSIONS

It can be seen that the risk associated with software products and getting them to market is not a "roll of the dice" operation. There are several areas for which "risk" can be defined. Once one has identified the areas of risk, one can begin to take steps to minimize the risk in each area. Some of these activities must be done at the management level; others are done at the project management level; still others are done at the software design level and the software architectural level. At the coding, testing, and system test levels, often the corporate culture needs to change before risk can be adequately addressed.

In each of the areas we have discussed, decisions must be made. In some cases these decisions are very painful to address, as they change the way the corporation has done business (i.e., getting software products to market). If what is being done currently (albeit, with very high risk) seems to be working, people do not want to change. That is as much a part of the risk minimization process as anything else.

You should not begin by taking on the entire corporation's efforts all at once (unless the corporation is in danger of going bankrupt, based on the current set of projects). The ideas presented here should be viewed as a new technology and should be implemented as such. Its impact should be assessed early in the life cycle. It should be tried on small, nonessential projects at first to determine how it is going to work in your organization. Most of what we have presented will work immediately; other concepts will take time and training to make them work. Patience should be maintained as you try and adapt what is presented here to the culture of your organization.

The same holds true of the quality movement and TQM. As you have seen in the first part of this chapter, there are a lot of practices that companies can perform to start a quality initiative. Unfortunately, if companies start from a typical QA approach, namely creating a QA organization, pushing for quality initiatives, starting a test organization, and attempting to decrease the number of errors (or defects or "opportunities") through Six Sigma and other approaches, it will take years to achieve the goal and millions of dollars worth of investment (although there have been some notable exceptions). The concepts of flat management and employee empowerment, customer-oriented products, and continuous improvement will not work unless there is an underlying, initial process.

As we have tried to present throughout the book, our new paradigm is based upon a market-driven, quality-oriented product delivery process. This is very much in the spirit of Deming and follows closely the concepts of TQM. It is also very easy to install in a company, though defining and developing the deliverables and the filters—and then adapting them to reality—takes time. Being patient to continually "fix" the filters based on feedback and allowing the employees time to "mature" in the process and technology is also important. The new paradigm is not only easier to implement, it also provides a more efficient software development life cycle. We have shown you ways to consider life cycle efficiency.

In addition, we have encouraged you to measure what you do and put in place a corporate measurement program. But at the same time, we have cautioned you to be careful what you measure and how you use it. You should be especially careful about using statistical quality control, as often there is not a direct carry-over from hardware strategies to software strategies. Deming encourages the use of case studies over statistical inference. Excellent statistical inference is based on good measurement strategies, effective sampling, and reduction of the error of the estimate. This is practically impossible to achieve in software development for the reasons we stated in Chapter 8.

We hope this book has opened your eyes to some extremely effective, new approaches to software quality which can help you reach the corporate quality goals you need to achieve competitive advantage based on quality products delivered on time and within budget to happily satisfied customers.

Checklists and Templates

The following is a set of sample checklists and templates you might find useful.

A.1 TEST CASE FORM

Date: _____   Tested by:_____

System: _____   Environment:_____

Function: _____   Screen: _____

Version: _____

Condition to Test:

_____

_____

_____

Data/Steps to Perform:

_____

_____

_____

Expected Results:

_____

_____

_____

Actual Results:

1. _____

2. _____

A.2 CHECKLIST FOR A VENDOR-DEVELOPED PACKAGE

Project Name:

Project Manager:

Start and End Dates:

Testing Analyst:

1.0 Vendor Selection:

1.1   Does the vendor have an effective organization evidenced by   [   ]
formal organization charts with clearly defined roles and
responsibilities?

1.2   Does the vendor have effective management information and   [   ]
monitoring systems which provide adequate and timely
information to management on the status of the project?

1.3   Are project expenses periodically monitored to ensure actual   [   ]
expenses are well documented and controlled and are within
budget guidelines?

1.4   Does the vendor have a documentation librarian for all project-   [   ]
related material and is this kept current?

1.5   Does the vendor have a plan for ongoing communication between   [   ]
project members to ensure the development effort is effective
and efficient?

2.0 Project Proposal:

2.1   Does the vendor have a Requirements Document?   [   ]

2.2   Does the vendor have a Test Plan?   [   ]

2.3   Does the vendor have Test Cases?   [   ]

2.4   Does the vendor have inputs and outputs of the Test Cases?   [   ]

2.5   Will the vendor share the Test Cases with us?   [   ]

2.6   Have you decided on the delivery time and cost estimates?   [   ]

2.7   Have you decided on a method of communication (via letters/   [   ]
telephone, etc.)?

2.8   Have you prepared your own business requirements inventory?   [   ]

2.9   Will the vendor allow you to interview their testers for   [   ]
additional information you may need?

A.3 DEVELOPMENT LIFE CYCLE CHECKLIST

1.1   Identify and obtain Project Leader   [   ]

1.2   Identify and obtain Project Resources   [   ]

Business Requirements Definition

2.1   Define Current Business Organization   [   ]

2.2   Refine understanding of Business Problem   [   ]

2.3   Identify Project Objectives   [   ]

2.4   Identify Current Systems Processes, Interfaces, and Costs   [   ]

2.5   Identify Current Business Processes, Interfaces, and Costs   [   ]

2.6   Using Requirement acquisition, identify new business   [   ]
           requirements and consolidate into an itemized list of
           requirements

2.7   Identify strategic business issues related to the project   [   ]

2.8   Identify specific business functions and organizations that will   [   ]
           be impacted

2.9   Develop Business Cost Benefit Analysis   [   ]

2.10   Present Business Requirements, Business Cost/Benefit Analysis   [   ]
           Proposal to customer and obtain approval

2.11   Create initial system solution overviews. Include Scope,   [   ]
           Objectives, Dependencies, Opportunities, Contingencies,
           Feasibility, Assumptions, Risks, and Degree of Computerization

2.12   Identify system performance objectives: Include Data Access,   [   ]
           Transaction Volume, Frequency, and Peak-Period Requirements

2.13   Analyze system growth potential and identify key growth   [   ]
           indicators

2.14   Identify changes in the current environment due to the new   [   ]
           system

2.15   Compare and document data model with existing models and   [   ]
           physical database

2.16   For each overview estimate: Staff Months, Development Costs,   [   ]
           and Support Costs

2.17   Do Cost Comparison Analysis for proposed system solutions   [   ]

2.18   Obtain Approval or Declination of system solution   [   ]

2.19   Data dictionary loaded with all current information   [   ]

2.20   Data flow diagram updated   [   ]

A.4 CONCEPTUAL DESIGN CHECKLIST

1.1	Select tasks, activities, and resources required	[ ]
1.2	Translate Requirements to Functional Specification	[ ]
1.3	Define overall system framework	[ ]
1.4	Update Functional Model (decomposition should be complete)	[ ]
1.5	Define Coding Structures involved	[ ]
1.6	Define Processing Rules	[ ]
1.7	Define Sequential Processing Logic	[ ]
1.8	ID Hardware and Control Software	[ ]
1.9	Obtain Transaction Estimates	[ ]
1.10	Establish Backup and Recovery Procedures for new system	[ ]
1.11	Prepare plan for Change Control Management: procedures, forms, etc., for new system	[ ]
1.12	Create Project Data Model from Conceptual Data Model	[ ]
1.13	Update Data Dictionary	[ ]
1.14	Update Functional Model with Transaction Estimates	[ ]
1.15	Conduct Walk-through, set Acceptance Criteria, and Obtain Sign-off	[ ]
1.16	Do Data Reconciliation; compare and document Data Model with existing models and physical database models and physical databases	[ ]

A.5 DETAIL DESIGN CHECKLIST

1.1	First cut physical database; new physical names	[ ]
1.2	Review any existing prototype designs	[ ]
1.3	Define Data Elements	[ ]
1.4	Describe Transactions	[ ]
1.5	Design Output Formats	[ ]
1.6	Design Edits, Error Message Correction Procedures	[ ]
1.7	Design Input Formats	[ ]
1.8	Design interfaces to existing external systems and between application systems, subsystems, and module	[ ]
1.9	Update Project Data Model, Data Flow Diagrams, and Data Dictionary	[ ]
1.10	Validate Logical Views of Transactions	[ ]
1.11	Physical Database fully denormalized	[ ]
1.12	Design Processing Structure: Module relationships and process flows	[ ]
1.13	Update Frequency and Volume Estimates	[ ]
1.14	Identify Preventative Controls to ensure data integrity	[ ]
1.15	Prepare System Specs: Specify routines, modules, and subsystems	[ ]
1.16	Create Operations Specifications: Work flows, procedures, recovery processes, and security	[ ]
1.17	Validate Access Requirements against Database Design	[ ]
1.18	Finalize Detail Design: Create Design Report	[ ]
1.19	Finalize System Specifications including Cost, Schedules, Resources, and Scope for development phase	[ ]
1.20	Physical database schema complete	[ ]
1.21	Obtain Sign-off from customer and IS Manager	[ ]

A.6 SYSTEMS DEVELOPMENT CHECKLIST

1.1   Prepare plan for change control management: Procedures,   [   ]
      forms, etc., for development objects

1.2   Set up Programming Environment   [   ]

1.3   Create bug tracking system   [   ]

1.4   Start System Maintenance Phase   [   ]

1.5   Identify productivity aids and establish procedures for their use   [   ]

1.6   Update data dictionary   [   ]

1.7   Obtain passwords, libraries   [   ]

1.8   Establish backup and recovery procedures for development   [   ]
      objects

1.9   Code and Compile Applications Software   [   ]

2.0   Create Technical Turnover Plan   [   ]

2.1   Conduct module and integration testing   [   ]

2.2   Update data dictionary   [   ]

2.3   Create documents that link functions to specific programs, then   [   ]
      show file updates and flow charts for the programs

2.4   Schedule technical walk-through and on-line demo with   [   ]
      manager of Maintenance and Enhancements

A.7 TRAINING AND IMPLEMENTATION CHECKLIST

1.1	Create Training Approach	[ ]
1.2	Determine tasks, dependencies, and contingency plans	[ ]
1.3	Estimate time frames	[ ]
1.4	Determine staffing needs and availability	[ ]
1.5	Develop training materials	[ ]
1.6	Obtain training facilities	[ ]
1.7	Train Users	[ ]
1.8	Create Implementation Plan	[ ]
1.9	Determine tasks, dependencies, and contingency plans	[ ]
1.10	Coordinate involvement of data center and field support	[ ]
1.11	Estimate time frames	[ ]
1.12	Determine staffing needs and availability	[ ]
1.13	Obtain sign-off from customer, data center, and support sites	[ ]
1.14	Install Hardware and Communications	[ ]
1.15	Prepare Conversion Requirements	[ ]
1.16	Create Data Conversion Plan Cut over procedures, controls, and special one-time processes	[ ]
1.17	Design and Code conversion programs	[ ]
1.18	Create conversion test plan	[ ]
1.19	Run conversion test on test machine	[ ]
1.20	Verify conversion output	[ ]
1.21	Obtain sign-off from customer and finance	[ ]
1.22	Load and verify special system or edit tables for conversion	[ ]
1.23	Execute conversion programs	[ ]
1.24	Verify converted data	[ ]
1.25	Obtain sign-off from customer and finance	[ ]

A.8 SUPPORT AND OPERATIONS CHECKLIST

1.1	Determine support training needs	[ ]
1.2	Identify support analysts for project; Include Hotline support	[ ]
1.3	Review staffing requirements in light of system impact	[ ]
1.4	Obtain copies of functional design	[ ]
1.5	Do an operational analysis of project for support issues	[ ]
1.6	Determine involvement in documentation creation/auditing	[ ]
1.7	Determine depth of test planning involvement	[ ]
1.8	Get agreement from project leader on warranty period	[ ]
1.9	Conduct turnover interview	[ ]
1.10	Participate in system and acceptance testing	[ ]
1.11	Begin Operations planning	[ ]
1.12	Create organizational procedures	[ ]
1.13	Publish and review procedures	[ ]

A.9 TESTING CHECKLIST

1.1	Create System and Acceptance Tests	[ ]
1.2	Start Acceptance test creation	[ ]
1.3	Identify test team	[ ]
1.4	Create workplan	[ ]
1.5	Create Test Approach	[ ]
1.6	Link Acceptance Criteria and Requirements to form the basis of acceptance test	[ ]
1.7	Use subset of system test cases to form requirements portion of acceptance test	[ ]
1.8	Create scripts for use by the customer to demonstrate that the system meets requirements	[ ]
1.9	Create test schedule; Include people and all other resources	[ ]
1.10	Conduct Acceptance Test	[ ]
1.11	Start System Test creation	[ ]
1.12	Identify test team members	[ ]
1.13	Create workplan	[ ]
1.14	Determine resource requirements	[ ]
1.15	Identify productivity tools for testing	[ ]
1.16	Determine data requirements	[ ]
1.17	Reach agreement with data center	[ ]

1.18	Create Test Approach	[ ]
1.19	Identify any facilities that are needed	[ ]
1.20	Obtain and review existing test material	[ ]
1.21	Create inventory of test items	[ ]
1.22	Identify Design states, conditions, processes, and procedures	[ ]
1.23	Determine the need for code-based (white box) testing; Identify conditions	[ ]
1.24	Identify all functional requirements	[ ]
1.25	End inventory creation	[ ]
1.26	Start test case creation	[ ]
1.27	Create test cases based on inventory of test items	[ ]
1.28	Identify logical groups of business function for new system	[ ]
1.29	Divide test cases into functional groups traced to test item inventory	[ ]
1.30	Design data sets to correspond to test cases	[ ]
1.31	End test case creation	[ ]
1.32	Review business functions, test cases, and data sets with users	[ ]
1.33	Get sign-off on test design from project leader and QA	[ ]
1.34	End Test Design	[ ]
1.35	Begin Test Preparation	[ ]
1.36	Obtain test support resources	[ ]
1.37	Outline expected results for each test case	[ ]
1.38	Obtain test data; Validate and trace to test cases	[ ]
1.39	Prepare detailed test scripts for each test case	[ ]
1.40	Prepare and document environmental setup procedures; Include backup and recovery plans	[ ]
1.41	End Test Preparation phase	[ ]
1.42	Conduct System Test	[ ]
1.43	Execute test scripts	[ ]
1.44	Compare actual result to expected	[ ]
1.45	Document discrepancies and create problem report	[ ]
1.46	Prepare maintenance phase input	[ ]
1.47	Reexecute test group after problem repairs	[ ]
1.48	Create final test report; include known bugs list	[ ]
1.49	Obtain formal sign-off	[ ]

A.10 DOCUMENTATION CHECKLIST

1.1	Consult with Documentation Services for Document Planning	[ ]
1.2	Begin Documentation Approach	[ ]
1.3	Do audience research and rough design	[ ]
1.4	Review Staffing Plan	[ ]
1.5	Review approved budget	[ ]
1.6	Establish Review Team	[ ]
1.7	Create preliminary schedule	[ ]
1.8	Identify all issues with audience research and rough design	[ ]
1.9	Conduct Review meeting for approval of approach and budget	[ ]
1.10	Complete Document Design with Table of Contents	[ ]
1.11	Revise Schedule and Budget	[ ]
1.12	Locate Contractors	[ ]
1.13	Review and approve Design, Schedule, and Budget	[ ]
1.14	End Documentation approach	[ ]
1.15	Begin Alpha Test	[ ]
1.16	Create test approach and acceptance criteria; Establish test team	[ ]
1.17	Conduct Test	[ ]
1.18	Conduct Feedback and Review	[ ]
1.19	Complete Rewrites	[ ]
1.20	End Alpha Test	[ ]
1.21	Start Beta Test	[ ]
1.22	Conduct Beta test with rewrites	[ ]
1.23	Publish and distribute Documentation	[ ]

A.11 SYSTEM MAINTENANCE CHECKLIST

1.1	Begin Enhancement Cycle	[ ]
1.2	Update System Documentation	[ ]
1.3	Support system operations; address reported problems	[ ]
1.4	Monitor and support production system	[ ]
1.5	Provide consultation on future enhancements	[ ]
1.6	Evaluate system performance: Network, Database, Interactive, and Batch	[ ]
1.7	Update data dictionary	[ ]

A.12 VENDOR SELECTION CHECKLIST

1.	Does the vendor have experience in developing similar systems?	[ ]
2.	Have you contacted all the references given by the vendor?	[ ]
3.	Are all the references favorable?	[ ]
4.	Has the vendor demonstrated that he has adequate qualified resources to develop the requested system?	[ ]
5.	Is the vendor prepared to submit a "Proposal"?	[ ]
6.	Are there detailed product requirements or specifications?	[ ]
9.	Is the definition of performance level required and is it clear to the vendor?	[ ]
10.	Has the vendor given cost estimates?	[ ]
11.	Is there definition of the quality level required and is it relayed to the vendor?	[ ]
12.	Has the schedule with target dates for deliverables been given to the vendor?	[ ]
13.	Does the vendor agree to the schedule?	[ ]
14.	Has the vendor signed confidentiality statement?	[ ]
15.	Are all the procedures of vendor test identified and agreed upon by you and the vendor?	[ ]
16.	Has the specification of acceptance or rejection criteria been identified and relayed to the vendor?	[ ]
17.	Have you identified the final approval authority of the acceptance of the product?	[ ]
18.	Is there a signed contract between the vendor and you?	[ ]

A.13 REVIEW CHECKLIST

Select the questions applicable to your review needs based on the type of review you are conducting (Technical Review, Code Review, or Documentation Review). (DD = Detail Design; TP = Test Plan)

1. Is the scope of the project identified and clear?
2. Is the terminology clear?
3. Is there adequate budget allocated to the project?
4. Are all the resources allocated?
5. Is the Project Plan developed?
6. Are all the activities included in the Project Plan?
7. Have the data from pervious projects been utilized to reconcile the estimate?
8. Is the Development Plan complete and signed off by all involved parties?
9. Does it include adequate requirements and operation concept verification?
10. Were end users directly involved?
11. Are the Requirements clear and testable?
12. Are the system interfaces clearly identified?
13. Are the human interface requirements identified?
14. Are the capacity requirement identified?
15. Is the performance requirements clearly articulated?
16. Are requirements consistent with allocated resources, schedule, and budget?
17. Are steps taken to ensure everyone understands the functional requirements?
18. Have the users signed off on the Requirements Document?
19. Have the users developed acceptance criteria?
20. Are all the external and internal interfaces properly identified and documented?
21. Is there a Problem and Opportunity Statement in the Marketing Requirement?
22. Does Requirement cover proposed approach and alternatives?
23. Are the business and technical risks identified?
24. Were appropriate steps taken to validate the requirements and operational concept?
25. Does any item conflict with another item in the Requirements Document?
26. Can each function be mapped from the Requirements Document to the Design Document?
27. Does the Design Document give a complete process of each function?
28. Is the algorithm according to the desired function? (DD)
29. Has error handling been identified and specified? (DD)

30. Are all the interfaces consistent with the architecture of the system? (DD)

31. Will it be possible to determine whether a function works according to the requirements during Unit Test

32. Are all interdependencies identified?

33. Are there any other dependencies?

34. Does the Design Document contain a list of external interface dependencies?

35. Are the designs cost-effective?

36. Does the development of the code comply with the existing code standards?

37. Have all the functions from the design been translated into code?

38. Are the coding standards for comments or language style adhered to?

39. How easy is the system to use?

40. Are all the identified errors resolved?

41. Are there any misinterpretations of a process in the models?

42. What things are in the design models because we've always done it that way? (Use space provided on the last page.) Can this be improved?

43. Is there anything in the models that can be explained in a better way?

44. Are all the design documents clean, clear, and concise when taken as a whole?

45. Within the design documents, are the Process descriptions meaningful to all the readers?

46. Are any processes repeated?

47. Were all the activities defined in the Quality Assurance Plan implemented?

48. Was adequate training provided to the users?

49. Does everyone within the project know about the predefined standards?

50. Are there redundant operations shown on the design for which there is no cost/productivity benefit?

51. Are all interfaces between program units completely, correctly, and clearly described?

52. How costly and difficult would it be to modify present recommendation?

53. In the code, are comments included for major functional areas?

54. In the code, are the comments meaningful and clear?

55. In the code, are comments included in such a way that they do not interfere with the program's readability?

56. In the code, does each module implement a single, clearly defined function?

57. In the code, does each module clearly document its own functionality?

58. In the code, does each loop execute the correct number of times?

59. In the code, if a loop is exited prematurely, is any cleanup required and performed?

60. Has system security been adequately addressed?

61. Is there provision for user feedback?

62. Are all the major functions identified in the Test Plan? (TP)

63. Has traceability matrix between requirements and test cases developed?

64. Are resources and tools identified for testing?

65. Is the test schedule consistent with the overall project schedule?

66. Are there test cases for security tests?

67. Are there test cases for performance tests?

68. Are there test cases for response time?

69. Are all the test cases accompanied with the expected results?

70. Are there test cases to test the logic paths?

71. Are there test cases for error handling?

72. Is there provision for making changes?

73. Will changes in the system cause difficult or expensive changes to the documentation?

74. Is there adequate provision for distribution of the documents?

75. Are all essential topics complete?

76. Is terminology consistent throughout all documents?

77. Are the definitions clear and correct?

A.14 PRODUCT ASSURANCE CHECKLIST

1. Determine product acceptability: Will the product function correctly? Will the product consist of all the functions mentioned in the Requirements Document?

2. Analyze product's attributes: Will the product meet quality attributes?

3. Analyze operational aspect: Will the product fit into the current operational environment? Will the response time be adequate?

4. Verify legal compliance: Will the product meet legal requirements (i.e., Federal, State, Department of Defense, etc.)?

5. Verify standards adherence: Will the product meet established standards and procedures?

A.15 TEST PLAN TEMPLATE

(Name of the Product)

The purpose is to prescribe the scope, approach, resources, and schedule of the testing activities: to identify the items being tested, the features to be tested, the testing tasks to be performed, the personnel responsible for each task, and the risks associated with this plan.

Prepared by:

(Names of preparers)

(Date)

TABLE OF CONTENTS

1.0 INTRODUCTION

A brief summary of the purpose of this document, e.g., This Test Plan outlines the activities which will be conducted during the testing process and it documents other related topics which contribute toward the quality and productivity of the project.

2.0 OBJECTIVES AND TASKS

2.1 Objectives

Describe the objectives supported by the Master Test Plan, e.g., This Test Plan will define tasks and responsibilities and will be used as a vehicle for communication. It will be used as a service level agreement, etc.

2.2 Tasks

List all tasks identified by this Test Plan, i.e., development of test cases, test execution, post-testing meeting, problem reporting, etc.

3.0 SCOPE

This section describes what is being tested, such as all the functions of a specific product, its existing interfaces, integration of all functions, error messages, stress testing of all functions, etc.

4.0 TESTING STRATEGY

Describe the overall approach to testing. For each major group of features or feature combinations, specify the approach which will ensure that these feature groups are adequately tested. Specify the major activities and techniques which will be used to test the designated groups of features.

The approach should be described in sufficient detail to permit identification of the major testing tasks, e.g.,

1. **Performance (Functional) Testing:** A process of testing to verify that the functions of a system are present as specified in the Requirements Document.
2. **Unit Testing:** Testing conducted to ensure that the lowest levels of code are ready to assemble into the final system and that all necessary logic is present and works properly.
3. **System and Integration Testing:** Testing the system to ensure that the program of system components passes information and functions together correctly according to the function specifications. The software and/or hardware elements will be combined and tested until the entire system has been correctly integrated.

4. **User Acceptance Testing:** Testing conducted by the users to make sure that the system is built according to the requirements and that all functions operate properly.

For each high-level category, mentioned above, describe the definition of the testing, participants, and methodology

4.1 Performance (Functional) Testing

Definition: List what is your understanding of Performance Testing for your project. (Performance Testing: To test the system to determine if performance meets the requirements as stated in the User Requirement.)

Participants: Who will be conducting Performance Testing on your project. List the individuals who will be responsible for this activity.

Methodology: Describe how Performance Testing will be conducted. Who will write the test scripts for the testing, what high-level performance tests will be conducted; how each part of this test will be executed.

4.2 Unit Testing

Definition: List what is your understanding of Unit Testing for your project. (Unit testing is a process of testing the individual subprograms, subroutines, or procedures in a program.)

Participants: List the names of individuals/departments who will be responsible for Unit Testing

Methodology: Describe the type of test data being used; how it will be tracked; who will write the test scripts for the Unit Testing; what would be sequence of events of Unit Testing; what high-level tests will be conducted and how each part of this test will be executed.

4.3 System and Integration Testing

Definition: List what is your understanding of System and Integration Testing for your project.

System Testing: System Testing is a series of different tests whose primary purpose is to fully exercise the system to uncover its limitations and measure its full capabilities. The objective of the System Test is to test the integrated system to verify that it meets specified requirements.

Integration Testing: Integration Testing is an orderly progression of testing in which software and/or hardware elements are combined and tested until the entire system has been integrated. The purpose is to measure the correctness of each program unit's behavior once the program has been combined with other programs.

Participants: Who will be conducting System and Integration Testing on your project. List the individuals who will be responsible for this activity.

Methodology: Describe how System and Integration testing will be conducted. Who will write the test scripts for the System and Integration testing, what high-level system and integration tests will be conducted; how each part of this test will be executed.

4.4 Stress Testing

Definition: List what is your understanding of Stress Testing for your project. (Stress Testing is a data value that corresponds to a minimum or maximum input, internal or output value specified for a system. Example: Testing will be conducted to evaluate the system beyond the limits of its specified requirements.)

Participants: Who will be conducting Stress Testing on your project. List the individuals who will be responsible for this activity.

Methodology: Describe how Stress Testing will be conducted. Who will write the test scripts for the testing, what high-level stress tests will be conducted; how each part of this test will be executed.

4.5 User Acceptance Testing

Definition: List what is your understanding of User Acceptance Testing for your project. (The purpose of Acceptance Testing is to confirm that the system is ready for operational use. During Acceptance Test, end users (customers) of the system compare the system to its initial requirements.)

Participants: Who will be conducting User Acceptance Testing on your project. List the individuals who will be responsible for this activity.

Methodology: Describe how the User Acceptance testing will be conducted. Who will write the test scripts for the testing, what high-level acceptance tests will be conducted; how each part of this test will be executed.

4.6 Regression Testing

Definition: List what is your understanding of Regression Testing for your project. (Regression Testing is the selective retesting of a system or component to verify that modifications have not caused unintended effects and that the system or component still works as specified in the Requirements.)

Participants: Who will be conducting Regression Testing on your project. List the individuals who will be responsible for this activity.

Methodology: Describe how Regression Testing will be conducted; which previously developed test cases will be selected for retesting and how proper test coverage will be ensured to test all affected functions.

5.0 HARDWARE REQUIREMENTS

- Computers: List the hardware that you are going to be using to conduct your testing.
- Modems: If you are going to use modems, list the numbers and manufacturer.

6.0 ENVIRONMENT REQUIREMENTS

6.1 Mainframe

Specify both the necessary and desired properties of the test environment. The specification should contain the physical characteristics of the facilities including the hardware, the communications and system software, the mode of usage (for example, stand-alone), and any other software or supplies needed to support the test. Also specify the level of security which must be provided for the test facility, system software, and_proprietary components such as software, data, and hardware.

6.2 Workstation

List if any of the testing is going to be conducted on the workstations. Specify how the workstations should be configured.

7.0 TEST SCHEDULE

State specific test tasks, responsibilities, target start and end dates, and actual start and end dates. Also state how often the test schedule will be reviewed and by whom.

7.1 Major Deliverables

Identify the project deliverable. For example,
- Test Plan
- Test Cases
- Test Incident Reports
- Test Summary Report

7.2 Post-Testing Meeting

Indicate if a post-testing meeting will be scheduled and if so, when. What would be the agenda of the meeting. Normally this meeting is held at the end of the testing phase to inform the entire project team of the status of the testing activities, i.e., how many problems were encountered, how many were fixed, and how many are still open. Also in this meeting, discussion of when and how the open problem will be resolved takes place.

8.0 CONTROL PROCEDURES

8.1 Problem Reporting

Document the procedures for recording problems encountered during testing. If a standard form is going to be used, attach a blank copy as an "Appendix" to the Test Plan. In the event you are using an automated incident logging system, write those procedures in this section. Specify how the problems are going to be prioritized.

8.2 Change Requests

Specify the procedures that will be followed for changes. Identify the individuals who have the authority to make the decision regarding the inclusion of the change in the product and also the individuals who have the authority to approve these changes.

9.0 FUNCTIONS NOT TO BE TESTED

If there are any functions that are not going to be tested, list them, along with the reason, i.e., time constraint and low risk, code reused and was previously tested with 100 percent satisfaction, etc.

10.0 RESOURCES/ROLES AND RESPONSIBILITIES

Specify the staff members who are involved in the testing and what their roles are going to be (e.g., Mary Brown/ User/ develop Test Cases for Acceptance Testing). Identify groups responsible for managing, designing, preparing, executing, and resolving the test activities as well as related issues. Also identify groups responsible for providing the test environment. These groups may include developers, testers, operations staff, etc.

11.0 SIGNIFICANTLY IMPACTED DEPARTMENTS (SIDs)

Identify and list all the internal departments that will be impacted by this product.

12.0 DEPENDENCIES

Identify dependencies, such as code availability, testing resource availability, and test tools availability.

13.0 RISKS/ASSUMPTIONS

List the risks associated with the project, i.e., if the unit tested code is not turned over for systems testing on the predetermined date, the entire schedule will slip; indicate any assumptions, i.e., it is assumed that the product will be unit tested prior to system testing.

14.0 TOOLS

Indicate if you are planning to use any automated tools for testing.

15.0 APPROVALS

Specify the names and titles of all persons who must approve this plan. Provide space for the signatures and dates.

Name (In Capital Letters)	Signature	Date
1.		
2.		
3.		
4.		

A.16 WHERE TO OBTAIN GUIDELINES/STANDARDS

ISO Information

In the United States, the copies of ISO 9000 standards and other information can be obtained from American National Standards Institute, 11 West 42nd Street, 13th Floor, New York, NY 10036. The standards and regulation information can be obtained from National Center of Standards and Certification Information, National Institute of Standards and Technology, TRF Building, Room A163, Gaithersburg, MD 20899. For information on RAB accreditation and other topics, American Society of Quality Control, 611 E.Wisconsin Avenue, Milwaukee, WI 53202.

Standards, Processes, and Continuous Improvement Sources

1. ANSI, American National Standards Institute: U.S. standards on systems quality and related topics New York, NY—(212) 642-4900.
2. ASQC, American Society for Quality Control: Active software associations, Milwaukee, WI—(414) 272-8575.
3. IEEE Computer Society: Publications, software engineering standards, conferences, Washington, DC—(202) 371-1013.
4. IFPUG, International Function Point Users Group: Publishes tenders for function points, conducts conferences, Westerville, OH—(614) 895-7130.
5. SEI, Software Engineering Institute: Provides CMM and related training, Pittsburgh, PA—(412) 268-6874.

A.17 DESCRIPTIONS OF FRONTEND FILTERS FOR THE PRODUCT DELIVERY PROCESS

PRODUCT DEVELOPMENT CHECKLIST

The purpose of this checklist is to identify and enforce the use of the filters necessary to build a high-quality product. This covers the area from marketing through sales through marketing requirements, software specifications, software architecture, project plan, and code development, and implementation. Every document must be created and filtered, though not all documents are equally important to all products—and for some, only a small number are relevant.

Remember that a filter is made up of three concepts:

- Completeness
- Quality
- Accuracy (versus Precision)

A filter can be an outline, a template, a prototype document or product, or a checklist. Sometimes, all that is necessary is to use the filter to assure that all the components of the deliverable have been considered.

Product Name:_____

Table A-1

Department	Development Step Document	Date Completed	Initials
Administration	3-Year Marketing Analysis [Initial Anticipated Leverage (Sales / Cost of Building the Product)]		
Marketing	Product Description/ Positioning		
Marketing	Product Plan		
Marketing	Interim Products		
Sales	Preliminary Sales Plan [Adjusted Anticipated Leverage (1)]		
Sales/Marketing	Preliminary Budget		
Marketing	Requirements Definitions		
Development	Software Specification		
Development	Software Architecture		

Table A-1 (Continued)

Department	Development Step Document	Date Completed	Initials
Development	Project Plan		
Development	Product Development		
Development	Software Audit (Module Level)		
Development	Behavioral Testing		
Operations	User Profile Testing (Work Flow/Task/Products)		
Documentation	Documentation Development		
Development	Handoff to Operations [Adjusted Anticipated Leverage (2)]		
Operations	Certification and Delivery		

THREE-YEAR MARKETING ANALYSIS

This document should only be filled out once—and then updated as necessary as new opportunities present themselves. There is much more that can be added to this plan. The plan should also include such things as new technologies we must master and new platforms we should consider.

1.0 What Is Our Marketing Plan for the Next Three Years?

This should involve such things as:

- What do our customers want?
- From our corporate mission statement and our corporate vision, what additional functions/products can we provide our customers—especially if we can build and leverage them for little or no additional cost?
- What do our noncustomers want?
- What would it take to convert noncustomers into customers?

In a more general sense, what is our marketing direction?

2.0 What Markets Should We Be In and Dominate?

This should be based on the fact that we have knowledge and expertise in our specific field. The fact that we have a strong, stable customer base and strong inroads into some other markets should allow us to maintain financial stability while moving into more "off-the-shelf"-type products.

3.0 What Sequence of Products Will Get Us There?

As we develop products, we should design a sequence of products that will accomplish two things:

- Allow us to use an iteration of technology so we will be prepared for new markets as we enter them in the future.
- Allow us to deliberately build interim products which can be used as a base as we move into new markets.

If we design our software architectures to make use of the Open Doc technology, we can supplement our own interim products with third-party products from other vendors.

We also look at other platforms on which our software should reside, i.e., we implement our software so it can run equally well in a Mac or PC environment.

4.0 Against What Competing Products Should We Position Ourselves?

As a part of our marketing analysis, we must perform a competitive analysis. Without a competitive analysis, we have no idea how to position our products in such a manner as to make it easy for our salespeople to show why our products are superior in functionality, ability to solve user problems, cost-effectiveness, and ease of use.

As we create the sequence of products to get us to our three-year goal(s), we must also create a marketing presence and visibility in each of the areas we wish to compete in. A lot of the marketing effectiveness in this area depends on the creation of a perception of product quality. This is especially true as we position ourselves against the competition. Our marketing strategy must show immediately—in terms of three-dimensional words and images that instantly create a context and positioning for our products—that our products are high quality, and higher quality than the competition. (Most computer advertisements fail to provide any focus on what their products are, how they are positioned against the competition, or what the quality of their products is or how it can be measured and evaluated. Three-dimensional words and images can also provide instant recognition of our advertisements without potential customers needing to read every word.)

The following types of comparisons should always be made for each competitor's product:

4.1.1. Competitors:
4.1.1.1. Product:
Competitor #1: xxxxxxxxxxxxxxxxxxxx:
(1) What are their strengths?
(2) What are their weaknesses?
(3) What are the differences in functionality between our company and this competitor? How does this impact our ability to compete (both positively and negatively)?

(4) How does our company interface with competitors' products and what additional functionality can we provide—if the competitors' product is already installed (i.e., can we get a foot in the door by providing extended functionality through an interim product?)

Our company:

(1) What are our strengths against this competitor?

(2) What are our weaknesses against this competitor?

Competitor #2: xxxxxxxxxxxxxxxxxxxx:

Etc.

4.1.1.2. Product:

Etc.

5.0 What New Technologies Do We Need to Master?

6.0 What Perceptions Are There about Our Company that We Need to Foster? How?

7.0 What Perceptions Do We Need to Change? How?

_____INITIAL ANTICIPATED LEVERAGE (SALES + COST OF BUILDING THE PRODUCT)

PRODUCT DESCRIPTION/POSITIONING

This document is basically a "vision" of what our product should be. It shows how this product fits with the rest of our product line and—very importantly—how we intend to differentiate our product from those of the competition to maximize our competitive positioning in the market.

- Strengths (of our product—against each competitive product)
- Functionality
- Usability
- Installability
- Trainability (training cost overhead to the customer)
- (Other Quality Measures)

Note that it is at this point that we have a good feel for the quality issues of the product. Quality is not the number of errors per thousand (or million) lines of code—quality is what the users must see, feel, and be able to use when they purchase the product. These are all defined in terms of the *user profiles* and *behavioral testing* we evaluate as a part of our "product release" mechanism. But it is at *this* point in *this* document where the quality issues are defined and evaluated.

We should—at this point—have a pretty good idea of the GUI interfaces, functionality of the product, and selling strategy. We should also have an idea what the preliminary leverage should be. The marketing strategy may impact the "look/feel" of our product, i.e., Microsoft's Windows® 95 start button with the clouds was a good marketing strategy.

This differs from the three-year marketing plan document in that it only addresses the competition for this particular product.

1.0 General Description of Product

This should only constitute a general description—in enough detail that a Sales/Marketing person can understand it enough to sell it.

2.0 Positioning of Current Product

This is where we describe where and how we intend to sell the product. We further define it in terms of its functionality and delivery time-table.

2.1 What is the marketing environment?
This can be defined in terms of the competition and the needs of our customers and potential customers.

2.2 What is the marketing window?
This is where we define the dates during which we can sell our product—in terms of both our customers and the competition—and what the risks are of our missing the end dates, and perhaps some intermediate dates.

2.3 What functionality will allow us to effectively position our product?
   (1) What functionality must be there?
   (2) What functionality should be there?
   (3) What functionality would be nice to be there?
   (4) Must this product be backward-compatible?
   (5) With what third-party software must this product interface? Is this an Open Doc interface? If not, what do we need to do?
   (6) On what platforms must this product run?
   (7) Against which GUI standards must this product interface?
   (8) With which succeeding (follow-on) products must this product interface?
   (9) Can this product be repackaged and marketed in other markets?
   (10) What have we learned from our competitive analysis?

This is an important document, as it provides the necessary information for the product marketing plan and—just as importantly—the sales plan. It further indicates the relative risk of not reaching the marketplace with the appropriate functionality.

PRODUCT MARKETING PLAN

Through this document, we attempt to define the strategy we will use to market the product. Some of this is only of importance to the sales organization, while other parts are important to development, as well. To the software development organization, this allows for intelligent partitioning of the product into components to help the sales and marketing organizations meet their goals. This also gives the development organization more insight into what they are building to help them do a more intelligent job of designing and developing it.

1.0 How Early Should the Product Be Announced?

(1) Does our strategy allow our customers to have available in a timely manner the new features/technology we are continually adding to our product line?

(2) Especially for our "off-the-shelf" products, do we announce them early enough to offset the competition, yet late enough that the announcement will not stop "current sales"?

We need to make sure that we evaluate all our actions in terms of the impact on the competition—especially with respect to products such as FaceSpan where our success will spawn a lot of competition if we don't actively promote and expand it.

2.0 To Whom Should the Announcement/Publicity Be Addressed?

Do we announce this in a news conference? Do we do it in a newsletter to existing customers—with a discount for early purchase? Etc.

3.0 Should There Be Preliminary Announcements? To Whom? With Nondisclosure?

The idea here is that often, we should send out beta versions to allow key users to help us evaluate software quality and user profiles. Under these conditions, we can often build credibility in new products and our ability to deliver them on time.

4.0 What Should Brochures Look Like?

(1) How many different types of brochures should be provided?

(2) Should their be recognizable logos/patterns, etc., to generate product/company recognition? (How are these reflected in our title screens and GUI interfaces?)

It is important to maintain our look/feel, but also, we should be aware that new looks, reflecting three-dimensional words and new uses/versions of our product should also be seriously considered. This means that if we are entering several different markets, our brochures may need to be market-specific.

5.0 How Should Demand for Our Product Be Created?

(1) News releases?

(2) Direct mail?

(3) Trade shows (sales)?

(4) Demonstrations (sales)?

This should be coordinated with the announcement(s), but the reason it should be considered separately is so a budget can be created for it well in advance—and as a part of the preliminary budget—which follows shortly.

6.0 What Does Software Development Need to Do to Support the Marketing Strategies in This Deliverable/Filter?

Demo Disks? Subproducts (Interim Products)? Nonoperational Demo(s)? Intermediate Versions?

It is important for software development to know what they need to provide and when they need to do so, so they can schedule manpower and take these issues into account as they construct the software specification and the software architecture. Without this, it is difficult to come up with a realistic project plan.

7.0 Who Are the Potential Customers? (What Customer Needs Are We Attempting to Fill?)

What percentage of these customers do we feel we can win this (next) year?

This is a preliminary attempt to identify specific customers who we feel will be interested in buying this new version of our product. The sales organization will need to be directly involved in consulting with the marketing organization to make these estimates realistic.

8.0 For Each Type of Customer, How Do We Create— or Re-Create—a Need for This Product?

This has a tremendous impact on how we design our product. At this point we may need to rethink our customer needs (after we have reevaluated things from the sales point of view).

9.0 How Do We Make Our Products Cost-Effective Per Customer Need?

(1) What are the different pricing strategies?

(2) Do these strategies allow the various types of users to achieve a cost-effective solution to their problems?

(3) Do we provide differing hardware/software configurations which allow users to obtain a solution which is cost-effective and realistic to each type of potential user?

Not only must these pricing strategies be matched to user needs, they must be evaluated in terms of hardware costs as well. In terms of our earlier comments on quality issues, the cost of training and installation must also be taken into account—both in terms of our ability to make money and the customer's ability to save (or make) money. We should have a fairly good set of estimates of cost/benefit tables for our different classes of potential users—based on various scenarios.

10.0 Do the Solutions Provided by Our Product Line—Especially as Related to This Product—Allow a Large Enough Set of Cost-Effective Solutions to Meet All the Needs of Our Potential Customers?

Is this true when compared against our competitors' products?

(1) Do we provide a path for a potential customer to get to a solution based on our product line?

(2) If a competitor's product line is already being used by a potential customer, do we have a way of integrating our products around those of the competitor—without requiring a costly replacement or updating solution (i.e., do we provide an effective systems solution path)?

(3) Do we have a solution which runs on a potential customer's existing hardware?

(4) Have we provided a solution which allows for easy upgrading to new commercial hardware and software—as it becomes available?

We need to make it easy for our salespeople to acquire new customers. The sales organization should have great input into this part of our software proposal. This is especially true when the salesperson is in the position of attempting to win—or win back—a customer. It is important to remember that one of the costs involved relates to training and upgrading our system.

It also costs a lot more to get a former customer back than it does to keep him/her. This is why the checklists of our release process are so important.

INTERIM PRODUCTS

Many times, large products can be made up of systems of smaller products. This is easy to design into a product when the general context is known. It is especially easy through the use of executive modules, massage modules, and fan-in—based on the concepts of dependency analysis. As we gain more experience with the Open Doc technology, this will become even easier—especially as we use third-party products.

What interim products can be easily created or derived from the product we are building to allow us to maintain a cash flow until the main (or major) product is completed?

PRELIMINARY SALES PLAN

This document—along with its implementation—provides the "dose of reality" to the product delivery system. It is here that we get a relatively good feel for the "top value" of our "leverage estimate." ("Leverage" is the "times earnings" we will get for the product, i.e., if it costs us $1 million to build the product, what are our chances of making $20 million on the product?) We need to have a feel for the time to

- Sell
- Install
- Train
- Support

Without realistic estimates of these issues, we can fall on our face. The development organization has a strong impact on these issues through how we design the user profiles and make the usability/installability/trainability issues relatively small and simple. The sales organization must give us very specific feedback in these areas, and development must provide products that are easy for the salespeople to sell.

1.0 What Methods of Selling Will Be Used?

(1) Direct sales, resellers, distributors, etc.?
   (a) On what basis will they be selected (i.e., how do they qualify?)?
   (b) How will they be compensated?
   (c) What incentives will be offered?
(2) What is the specific sales procedure for each method to be used?
   (a) What training will be needed for the sales staff? Where does it appear in the budget?
   (b) How long will the sales process take?
   (c) How will the follow-up and tracking of leads be handled?
   (d) What will be the customer's major concerns in regards to purchasing the product?
      (i) How do we overcome these objections?
      (ii) Is there anything the software organization can do to have a positive impact in this area?

This will be especially important to consider if we market an off-the-shelf series of products.

2.0 What Are Our Best Estimates of:

(1) Time to complete a sale.
(2) Time to install a product.
(3) Time to train the users on the product.
(4) Amount of support necessary (time and money).

This is important both as we create our preliminary budget and figure out training and support costs—as well as whether or not we need to hire/train more people—or whether we can use alternative sales and marketing strategies.

3.0 What Are the Best Forecasts of:

(1) Size of customer base.

(2) % of customer base expected to purchase product.

(3) Income per month or quarter.

(4) Additional personnel needs in which areas, i.e., sales, support, training, etc.

This is also important in setting up our preliminary budget.

4.0 What Sales Tools Will Be Needed?

(1) What is the estimated cost of these materials?

(2) What special collateral, presentations, or demonstrations will be needed? Estimated cost?

This is also important in setting up our preliminary budget.

5.0 What Sales Budget Will Be Required to Meet Our Sales Forecast?

This sales information will be most useful when we are selling new products or are moving into new sales areas or environments. If this is done right, we should be getting a fairly "precise" figure for the "numerator" of our "leverage estimate." This is also important in setting up our preliminary budget.

PRELIMINARY BUDGET

In the context of "leverage," we need to have a preliminary budget. By itemizing the projected expenses, we can get a more realistic (accurate)—though not "precise"—estimate of what it will cost to build, release, and support the product.

(YOU NEED TO MAKE UP A MORE REALISTIC FORMAT FOR THE PRELIMINARY BUDGET.)

_____ADJUSTED ANTICIPATED LEVERAGE (I—MORE PRECISE SALES FORECAST)

MARKETING REQUIREMENTS DEFINITION

In terms of impact on the software development organization, the marketing requirements definition document is by far the most important. It creates the context for the product being built. It is similar to pre-reading a book before actually starting to study it. It is in this deliverable that the actual functionality is defined—and rated in terms of sales leverage. It also lets the developers understand the constraints that will be placed on the product—and project. The budget is made more precise, and the time constraints on the project are spelled out more realistically. Risk—in terms of the functions that may need to be left out, or held for a future release, are identified.

1.0 Introduction

1.1. General Context for Product.
- (1) What is the justification for the product?
  - (a) Why should it be created?
  - (b) How does this help our customers?
  - (c) What is the leverage of the product (i.e., expected costs against anticipated sales, refined by the sales document)?
- (2) What marketing window(s) must we reach?
  - (a) What is the earliest date we should try for?
  - (b) What is the latest date we can meet and still be within the window?
  - (c) What is the anticipated impact/risk if we miss it?
    (See discussion of functionality for what can be eliminated, if necessary.)
- (3) What is the impact on current products?
  - (a) Which products does this replace?
  - (b) If this is a complete replacement of an existing product, at what point will we stop supporting it?
  - (c) With which products must this product interface?
  - (d) What alternatives for how this product interacts with other current products are possible?
  - (e) In what ways will this product impact the user profile(s)?
  - (f) In what ways will this product impact the current products with which it interfaces/interacts?
- (4) To what level of user is this product directed?
  - (a) How does this level of experience impact the interface?
  - (b) With what interface standards will the users be familiar (i.e., Macintosh, Windows, etc.)?
  - (c) What impacts are expected on their work flows, paradigms of use, ability to master use of product without additional training, need for additional training, etc.?
    - (i) What patterns should we attempt to capture or reproduce?
    - (ii) At what level should user's manuals and training courses be pitched? What format should they be in?
    - (iii) Will purchasers/users require additional training from us? How should it be provided (i.e., CD-ROM, Apple guide, Web page, on-site courses, public courses, on-line documentation/help, etc.)?

1.2. How Will This Product Be Used?

(1) Description of how it will be used.

    (a) Work flow.

    (b) Work organization.

(2) Description of products it can produce.

(3) Description of problems it will solve.

(4) Will it be retro-fitted into existing, automated products?

    (a) Ours?

    (b) Competitors (interoperability)?

    (c) Ancillary products they will need to purchase to extend usability (interoperability)?

(5) Must it be backward-compatible with earlier products or databases?

(6) Is this part of a sequence of products described in the three-year plan?

    (a) How and where does it fit in the three-year plan?

    (b) How does the technology involved help us evolve toward future products?

        (i) What are the technologies involved?

        (ii) What training is it anticipated we will need?

        (iii) Where and how can it be obtained? Do we need to include it in the budget? Is it already in the budget?

2.0 Platforms and Device Interfaces

2.1. Upon which platforms must this product be operable?

2.2. What type(s) of hardware configuration(s) will be required?

(1) Should this run in a client/server environment?

(2) What types of configurations should be supported?

(3) Toward what types of parameters should this be directed (i.e., number of users, hardware requirements, network requirements, performance, etc.)?

2.3. With what types of devices should this product interface?

(1) Competing devices.

(2) Vendors.

(3) Type of support available/needed (i.e., us, them, VAR's third-party maintenance, third-party consulting, etc.).

In this latter area especially we should be certain that we have evaluated all vendors, suppliers, and support/training/consultant providers. Then we should either make a recommendation or be prepared to step in if third parties foul up our customers. This seems to always be a high-risk area.

3.0 Functionality

This is an iterative list of functions. It is usually a good idea to group the functions into sets of absolutely necessary, valuable, and nice to have. This makes it easier to evaluate what to include and exclude if there are problems. For each, the following outline might be used.

(1) Name of function.

(2) Description of function.

(3) Problem solved by function (justification).

(4) Relative importance of function to marketability of the product (associated risk analysis).

(5) Data required.

(6) Data produced.

(7) Function is a part of which:

    (a) User profiles.

    (b) Tasks.

    (c) Events.

    (d) Screens and menus.

(8) Constraints.

As stated above, this iterates through the entire set of functions expected to be implemented in this product. If the functions are already a part of another product with which this product interfaces, then this should be indicated—but the details can be left out here. The major idea to consider here is that if the functions are the same, there is no problem, but if they are almost the same, then care should be taken to see that they are modified correctly in the appropriate place.

This works best if the functions are divided as to their importance first and then listed. It is probably easier to list them in alphabetical order within priority for ease of locating them. In some situations, it is better to list them by user profile or by event, depending on the complexity of the system you are implementing.

4.0 Prototype Screens and Other Interfaces

(1) Interface standards.

(2) Relationship(s) to user profiles.

(3) Relationship(s) to events—usually found within user profiles.

(4) Examples (with protocols and "transaction sequences").

Sometimes these screens are given in great detail; other times only a superficial view is given. With the availability of FaceSpan, it is possible to create fairly "realistic" screens for demonstrations. With the additional availability of Apple scripts, these "prototype screens" can be made even more realistic.

5.0 Preliminary Financial Considerations

(1) Budget.

(2) Hardware requirements (for programmers/trainers/documentation personnel/support personnel, etc.).

(3) Manpower requirements (assigned as per project plan schedule).

(4) Training requirements (in necessary technology—mainly programmers and technical support personnel).

This should be planned for way in advance through the "needs analysis" of the three-year marketing plan. It should also be included in the company budget for the appropriate year.

SOFTWARE SPECIFICATION

If the software specification has been completed accurately, it should be very stable and able to be managed fairly easily through configuration management. This makes it possible for documentation, training, support, sales, and marketing to build and implement their programs in a parallel fashion, without waiting for development to finish the product (at which point everyone knows what it is!). This document does not merely "relist" the functions; it also defines them in terms of their "behavior." It also shows their relationship to the user profile and other interfaces. While the term "event list" tends to be misleading in the Apple event environment, the concept is extremely important. The idea is that the occurrence of the "event" of a function—caused by a trigger—produces the same result (response) regardless of where it occurs in the software system. This provides for a massive reduction in the number of states the system can take on.

The use of an information model—regardless of what it is—allows developers to create a software architecture with traceability back to the software specification. This is an important issue of software development. Other parts of the software specification are related to further definitions of the software system and ways of maintaining quality during development and implementation. A major part of this relates to the data model (usually expressed as an entity/relationship diagram), database model, and data dictionary.

1.0 Information Model

(1) Process-oriented (or object-oriented) model.

(2) Event list (assertions).

(3) Entity/attribute/relationship model.

(4) Database model (may need to be optimized).

(5) Data dictionary.

There are hundreds of "information modeling techniques" in the software industry. There are those who "proclaim" that "only the object-oriented paradigm is correct." This is not true; there are many problem-solving techniques that will work. The object-oriented paradigm has several inherent weaknesses.

- As a methodology, it is complex to train and implement, thus leading to errors and "overhead" in its initial stages of implementation.
- "Objects"—per se—are not stable. Not everyone perceives something as an object in the same way as everyone else. You may have a different view of the same object yourself later on.
- If your "class" is big enough, you can do "sequential binding" after you implement the system, but if your class is too small, there is nothing to do but start over.
- Inheritance always causes dependencies! These can be eliminated through fancy footwork, but the question is: "Why bother?"
- Deliberately designing in dependencies can often provide gains in performance, e.g., Informix has stated that by including the dependency of "Time" in their "Time Series" data blade, they were able to increase performance by a factor of 8.
- There is always trade-off between dependencies and performance; you must decide if it is worth it and just how you intend to manage the "fallout" from any designed-in dependencies. This issue is involved at both the code level and at the system architecture level.

Any software development methodology will work, as long as it provides

- Traceability from the specification to the software architecture.
- The ability to insert executive modules and perform dependency analysis.
- The ability to isolate individual transactions and allow for minimization of the number of states in the software system.

2.0 Functional Specification

(1) User profiles.

(2) External interface specification.

(3) User interfaces.

(4) Usability design (pattern matching, paradigm shift, function access).

(5) Interface standards (Macintosh, X/Open, Windows, Common User Access [CUA], etc.).

(6) Third-party software interfaces and data compatibility (interoperability).

(7) Hardware interfaces.

(8) Database interfaces (massage modules, industry standard interfaces, etc.)

The concepts in this section are new to the software development area—especially those relating to user profiles and usability design. Using FaceSpan and Apple events, we can provide user interfaces and user profiles that are easy to change, and we can allow the users to experiment until they find the most efficient version of the user profile to perform their tasks. We must attempt to define user profiles in terms of the ability to create products, according to some prespecified work flow. In addition, however, we must attempt to change the perception of user profile from "driving a rental car around San Francisco" to "driving a rental car (in general)."

Most of the remaining terms are fairly standard in the industry, and we must only be careful to design and implement them correctly.

3.0 Constraint Document

The purpose of the constraint document is to define issues which impact the software system. These might involve:

- Performance.
- Efficiency (the ability to perform large calculations in a relatively small amount of memory or time).
- Memory or device constraints.
- Platform constraints.
- Trainability.
- Etc.

4.0 Performance Criteria Document

Some parts of the performance criteria might be considered under [3.0], while more complete, specific criteria might be found here. This could be related to response time for

- Screen manipulations.
- Searches.
- Etc.

5.0 Hardware Specification

6.0 Adjusted Preliminary Budget

7.0 Preliminary Project Plan

At this point the project plan is mainly a high-level schedule of the highlights of completion dates.

8.0 Preliminary Manpower Allocation

This is a high-level estimate of the number of personnel (along with the requisite skills and training needed).

9.0 Standards Document

This typically defines programming standards, system architectural standards, and the documentation standards which relate to the inside and the outside of the code. It may also relate to project histories, error histories, filter breakdowns, scheduling anomalies, etc.

10.0 Quality Plan

This is specifically a description of how you intend to create a quality process and product (for a given product, type, or class of product). It should provide a definition of all the deliverables and filters involved, with their associated quality measurements.

11.0 Test Plan

This relates to how the product will be tested. It involves whether or not "code audits" (pattern matching) will be used, what testing resources in terms of hardware, software, and personnel will be needed; which user profiles are most appropriate to test; if on-site beta testing will be necessary to realistically test some of the profiles; and which software quality standards will apply (from the product description/positioning document) and how they will be tested. It also involves the time allocated to the testing schedule and how it fits with the rest of the project plan.

12.0 Documentation Plan and Schedule

13.0 Preliminary Product Release Plan

Since some products are complex and require substantial customer "hand holding" during installation, and others are simple "off-the-shelf" types, the release plan must be realistically developed and evaluated. Many times, "installation checklists" must be created and verified. Sales audits must be created and validated to assure that customers have the right hardware and network configurations to support the products. Appropriate training materials (in the appropriate format for the product being released) must be created and validated. The same is true for training and installation manuals created for the customers. The release plans for differing types of products are often radically different from product to product.

SOFTWARE ARCHITECTURE

The major key to the success—and the quality, schedule predictability, deliverability, and maintainability—of a product is based on its architecture. There is no single architecture that is completely correct, but any valid strategy or methodology should produce traceability back to the original specification from the architecture.

Whether you are in an Open Doc environment or an object-oriented environment or whatever else, there are some considerations that will always be true:

- All subsystems should be managed—if possible—through use of Executive modules.

    Massage modules.

    High fan-in leading to

        High module and subsystem reuse.

        Minimal dependencies.

    State processors leading to a minimal number of highly independent states of the system.

- All subsystems should be managed—if possible—to minimize risk.

Resulting subsystems should be small, independent, and capable of "reuse." They should be able to be "integrated" using a "little-bang" concept. Traceability should always be possible back to the original specification. At the lowest level, the modules and subsystems making up the architecture should be able to be built and implemented in less than two weeks each.

PROJECT PLAN

The project plan is the first point in the product delivery process where a precise schedule and budget can be established. If the architecture has been appropriately designed, and risk analysis has been performed on a function-by-function and subsystem-by-subsystem basis, a "low-risk" development strategy can be put in place using small, independent subsystems and the "little-bang" concept. In addition, executive modules, fan-in to eliminate dependencies, massage modules, and informational strength modules can be used to create a development strategy that quickly establishes "credibility" with customers and upper-level management. The schedule can be easily managed in the context, and personnel can be moved back and forth among projects to keep critical paths on schedule.

At this point, all the remaining development activities become "parallel" in nature:

- Software development and implementation.
- Documentation.
- Course preparation for training.
- Support training.
- Preparation for marketing.
- Preparation for sales.
- Preliminary stages of delivery system put in place and validated:

    User profiles.

    Checklists.

    "Dry runs" of installation process.

The product development strategy—with personnel, product/subsystem/ schedule in place—should be placed in a Gantt chart and managed (in parallel) with the other release activities.

SOFTWARE DEVELOPMENT

Software, regardless of the implementation language, should be planned and developed in English (using Pseudo code) and then converted to the target language. Once the code has been implemented, it should be documented with:

- Module Preamble or Prolog
- Inputs and Outputs to Modules
- Calling Sequences (Jackson Hierarchies and 1/0 Tables)
- Data Dictionaries and Data Typing

This software should be built using well-defined coding standards minimizing the number of structures, eliminating dependencies, and minimizing the number of states the system can take on. The software is the "filtered" against these standards with the emphasis outlined in the definition of a filter. (Completeness, Quality, and Accuracy are a fundamental part of this definition.) This process is referred to as a "Code Audit" and is based on "pattern matching" rather than "error detection."

Functional Testing can be performed, but it is best tied to the behavior of the function in the context of a User Profile or an Event. This is what is called *behavioral testing*, rather than "black box" testing. White box testing does not really seem productive in this context.

Once an entire product has been completed, then it passes through another filter which allows it to be released to maintenance, where it must pass a *further* filter. These filters involve installation checklists, site hardware/software/network audits (depending on the product), person responsible for maintenance, availability of automated test suites (tied to functions, user profiles, or events), availability of accurate documentation, hardware/software requirements, etc.

At this point, it is handed off to Operations for extensive User Profile Testing—against the quality standards expressed in the original Product Description/Positioning Document and Product Marketing Plan. When it has passed their criteria ß-testing may take place, *but only with contract-based users who are required to perform certain tests against User Profiles in environments impossible to create or duplicate in the Development environment*. A product should NEVER be released publicly in a "beta version" as it accomplishes nothing positive and creates a feeling of "lack of quality" or "lack of testing" on the part of users. It also sends a message of "lack of confidence" in the product on the part of the Software Development Organization. The Release Filter might also relate to the "certification" of the people on the "help desk," "trainers," "implementers," and others.

The rest of the Product Release Process should be based on check-lists or other types of filters, which are "certified" after use and both the product, process, and individual using them to install/train/sell a product evaluated and corrected or modified based on the feedback the filters provide.

A.18 DESCRIPTION OF PROCESS FOR CONFIGURATION CONTROL BOARD IMPACT ASSESSMENT DOCUMENT CHANGES TO FROZEN APPLICATIONS

This document (which follows) is used as a filter by a company or organization to help them maintain a strong, effective Configuration Management Organization. This can be used to make changes to the Product Delivery Process at any point, but usually the deliverables are in a state of flux until they reach the Software Specification Filter. Once a company begins the Software Architecture and Project Plan—the specification (of the application) is frozen. From this point on, all code created comes under "configuration control," and they manage it on that basis.

At the top of the document record the "CCB Number," which is ultimately logged in a database and tracked through their Quality System. The rest of the header is placed at the top to make it easier to file and recover later on should one need to. Once the Configuration Control Board Contact Person has hand-carried it through the system and it has been signed-off, it is given to the Manager of Software Maintenance, who takes responsibility for following-through with appropriate action and making sure it is not mis-placed or delayed. Once everything is completed, the form is filed for historical purposes. Should a change not be approved but rather held for a later release, then it is stored in a future release file and considered later on by the marketing organization, as new releases are planned. If the change is not approved as "too risky," "having too large an impact," or "being too frivolous," it is rejected and the reasons conveyed to the Change Owner (though the form is still retained for the records).

As you examine this document you see that there is a sequence in which it is "hand-carried" to each participant. When they sent multiple copies in electronic form over E-mail, it would tend to get lost somewhere and most people did not know what the issues were and did not know whether or not to sign. The document would still get lost when they sent an electronic version in sequence. It turned out best to have the Configuration Control Board Contact Person hand carry it to each participant in sequence. The order begins with the Change Owner, who fills out the form. It then goes to a programmer for a software-oriented description. Often changes have a more severe impact than expected, once the actual change is understood. Many other times, simple automation of an interface or installation procedure solves the problem, without changes to the code or software architecture.

At this point, the form is taken in sequence to someone from each organization involved to obtain an "impact assessment." Most often, this begins with Marketing, as this is usually where the first "judgement call" should be made. Usually a change will almost always have a positive impact on marketing. From there it goes to Sales. Usually there is a positive impact here, as well. But the

Sales Organization needs to know about all changes so they can modify their sales approaches based upon how these changes impact them.

Then the CCB form is taken to the Support Organization. Almost always the support organization needs to make some changes to how they answer the phone and what they tell customers who call in. In extreme cases, it can mean that a small training session for those manning the support desk needs to be held—or a technical update document needs to be given to them. *Sometimes their perception of customer complaints and other issues helps everyone else to understand the severity of the need for the change. Many times the CCB form is submitted by individuals at the Help Desks, based on their interaction with the customers. But anyone in the company can submit a CCB: Programmers, Salespeople, Marketing, Support, Training, or anyone else.*

Often, training materials created by the Training Organization need to be updated, especially if there is a change to an interface or to a work flow within a User Profile.

Software Development, who usually needs to make the change must assess its impact—especially if there are dependencies involved. The impact on the User Validation (User Profile) Testing group must be assessed. Usually this involves their scheduling time and resources to completely test the product (if it has been released) based on the change. Once "little bang" integration has occurred, the subsystem is turned over to the Maintenance Organization, and changes are made there. The impact either here or in development is assessed and another "judgement call" is made. Often all these changes have a negative impact on Software Development and Maintenance, usually because of the need to allocate manpower in unscheduled ways.

If the CCB progresses this far, then the Documentation Organization provides its impact assessment. This usually involves "already printed" manuals and so addenda need to be provided and new versions of the manuals up-dated. At this point, the entire management staff reads the document in sequence—from the CEO, President, Product Manager, Senior Programmer, to the Vice President of Software Development. This last individual manages any conflicts surfaced by the document and calls for a meeting of the entire Configuration Control Board, should this prove necessary. *It may seem unrealistic to you to have everyone on the management team from the CEO down sign off—and it may be unrealistic in your company—but some companies have found that this is merely a part of the responsibilities of a highly committed, highly disciplined, quality-oriented management team!*

The reason the filters are re-evaluated by each of the signatories is because *every organization* is managed through use of the filters. In some cases, an error has gotten through because a filter is broken at some point; in other cases, the problem is that the change affects how the filter is used, or will be used in the future. *This is a fundamental part of the quality control program, as a part of the Product Development Process under the new paradigm.*

Once a change has been approved, the change is made and a revised product, with revised documentation of all parts—including appropriate release notes, filtered and processed by the appropriate parts of the release organization.

(The term "cut to dev" is one company's expression for meeting the appropriate quality conditions and completeness criteria and being placed in our code library. It goes successively from the Product Folder to the Testing Folder to the Release Folder, each of which has filters and sign-offs. The automated test scripts are updated and re-run against the Product(s) in the Product Folder on a routine, timely basis. Using the CCB form, User Profiles, Documentation, Training Materials, etc., are updated and validated against the new version—based on the "documented impact assessments" from the CCB form and any other considerations which have surfaced while the version was being created.) Often this involves new versions released to customers, resellers, and licensees. Some companies have found that if this is managed correctly, they do not end up with "one-off" versions nor with different versions at different customer sites. These minor versions are managed in terms of creation dates such as 3/10/96, 5/25/96, etc., and are shipped to all their customers if the reasons are strong enough. Usually the new version has little impact on the customer, since a company should ship it with automated installation tools which are relatively transparent to them. Sometimes other numbers are used to help tie this to their change database, which allows the creation of any version of their product—to the nearest week— whether it is a newly developed product or a legacy product.

As the company releases major versions of their product line, they *do* have customers who remain on old versions. But this means a large customer base remains on (say) Version 3.1, another customer base on Version 4.1, and an advanced set of customers on the newest release, Version 4.2. How this is managed is mainly a marketing consideration, based on keeping a healthy cash flow based on their marketing base of customers. Supporting older versions depends on what type of product it is. Usually off-the-shelf versions are maintained only for 18 months to 2 years, while marketing concerns and maintenance contracts usually govern the rules for larger products.

FILTER FOR CONFIGURATION CONTROL BOARD IMPACT ASSESSMENT DOCUMENT CHANGES TO FROZEN APPLICATIONS

CCB No. _____

Issue (Error/Feature):

Name: _____

Final Resolution: Date: _____

Fix by: _____   Signature: _____
               Date   Manager Responsible

Deferred to: _____   Signature: _____
               Date   Manager Responsible

Rejected: _____   Signature: _____
               Date   Manager Responsible

Future Wish: _____ | _____   Signature: _____
          Priority   Software Release   Manager Responsible

FINAL OWNER OF ISSUE (ERROR/FEATURE): _____

SIGNATURE: _____

Purpose: This form is to be used when the code in an application which has been frozen is to be modified (i.e., new feature, bug fix, etc.). This code can be:

1. A product which has shipped.
2. A product under development based on a signed-off specification to which a new feature is to be added or to which a major modification is proposed.
3. A subsystem that has been tested and frozen in the "read-only library."
4. A module or code segment that has been tested and frozen in the "read-only library."

When this form has been filled out and signed by the appropriate individuals and then signed by the Configuration Control Board it is authorization for the change/feature addition/modification to be made. When the appropriate changes have been made, the remainder of the form, signed by appropriate individuals, shows that the change/feature addition/modification has been appropriately designed, programmed, tested, and documented and can be cut to dev and the updated code given to the Software Release Organization.

Distribution: This form should be submitted to the Configuration Control Board Contact Person who will hand-carry it to each department/individual listed on the form. When this is completed, it will be given to Maintenance who will call for the Configuration Control Board Meeting and follow through on the last half of the form.

ISSUE (PROBLEM/PROPOSED FIX)
(FEATURE/PROPOSED IMPLEMENTATION)

(to be filled out by person submitting request)

Date: _____   Issues Database ID #: _____

New Feature ID #

Application and Version: _____

Preliminary Error Severity/Priority: _____

Submitter: _____

Sales: ___ Marketing: ___ Technical Support: ___ Customer: ___ Development: ___ Maintenance: ___

Testing: ___ Management: ___

Address: _____

Phone: _____

Signature of Issue "Owner": _____

Description of Issue: _____

_____

_____

_____

Justification for Change: _____

_____

_____

_____

Issue Relationship to User Profile: _____

_____

_____

_____

Could Automation Eliminate This Problem: _____

_____

_____

_____

SOFTWARE-ORIENTED DESCRIPTION

(to be filled out by a designated engineer)

Technical Description of Change: _____

_____

_____

_____

Applications that Will Be Affected: _____

_____

_____

Folders and Files that Will Be Affected: _____

_____

_____

Risk of Causing Other Bugs: _____

_____

_____

Estimated Schedule to Completion: _____

_____

_____

Programmer: _____ Date: _____

_____

_____

IMPACT ASSESSMENT

   MARKETING: _____

_____

_____

Submitter: _____ Date: _____

Approve (for Version): _____ Disapprove: _____

Comments: _____

_____

Manager: _____ Date: _____

Filters, Checklists, and Other Products Affected: _____

_____

_____

_____

SALES: _____

_____

_____

Submitter: _____   Date: _____

Approve (for Version): _____   Disapprove: _____

Comments: _____

_____

Manager: _____   Date: _____

Filters, Checklists, and Other Products Affected: _____

_____

_____

_____

SUPPORT: _____

_____

_____

Submitter: _____   Date: _____

Approve (for Version): _____   Disapprove: _____

Comments: _____

_____

Manager: _____   Date: _____

Filters, Checklists, and Other Products Affected: _____

_____

_____

_____

TRAINING: _____

_____

_____

Submitter: _____   Date: _____

Approve (for Version): _____   Disapprove: _____

Comments: _____

_____

Manager: _____   Date: _____

Filters, Checklists, and Other Products Affected: _____

_____

_____

_____

SOFTWARE DEVELOPMENT: _____

_____

_____

Programmer: _____ Date: _____

Schedule: _____

Approve (for Version): _____ Disapprove: _____

Comments: _____

_____

Manager: _____ Date: _____

Filters, Checklists, and Other Products Affected: _____

_____

_____

_____

USER VALIDATION (User Profile) TESTING: _____

_____

_____

Implementer: _____ Date: _____

Schedule: _____

Approve (for Version): _____ Disapprove: _____

Comments: _____

_____

Manager: _____ Date: _____

Filters, Checklists, and Other Products Affected: _____

_____

_____

_____

MAINTENANCE: _____

_____

_____

Programmer: _____   Date: _____

Schedule: _____

Approve (for Version):_____   Disapprove: _____

Comments: _____

_____

Manager: _____   Date: _____

Filters, Checklists, and Other Products Affected: _____

_____

_____

_____

DOCUMENTATION: _____

_____

_____

Documentation Expert: _____   Date: _____

Schedule: _____

Approve (for Version):_____   Disapprove: _____

Comments: _____

_____

Manager: _____   Date: _____

Filters, Checklists, and Other Products Affected: _____

_____

_____

_____

Management Signatures:

Chairman & CEO: _____

Approve (for Version):_____Disapprove: _____

Comments: _____

_____

President: _____

Approve (for Version):_____Disapprove: _____

Comments: _____

_____

Product Manager: _____

Approve (for Version):_____Disapprove: _____

Comments: _____

_____

Sr. Programmer: _____

Approve (for Version):_____Disapprove: _____

Comments: _____

_____

Vice President of Software Development: _____

Approve (for Version):_____Disapprove: _____

Comments: _____

_____

Does this need a meeting of the CCB?   YES: _____ NO: _____

_____

_____

(Note that the following information should be kept but will no longer be a part of the CCB form. Instead, it will be kept electronically by the Code Librarian and the appropriate parts released as technical notes. Other parts will help us evaluate our code-level, system-level, and design-level filters. *It should be part of the Release Checklist.*)

IMPLEMENTATION/TESTING

To be completed by individuals responsible for the programming, testing, library updating, and release of the product and fix. It should be returned to the Configuration Control Board Contact Person to start the release process.

MAINTENANCE:

Description of Fix: _____

_____

_____

Impact of Fix: _____

_____

_____

Re-Evaluation of Risk Analysis: _____

_____

_____

Strategy to Make Fix: _____

_____

_____

Module(s) Affected: _____

_____

_____

Changes Made: _____

_____

_____

Lines of Code Changed: _____

_____

_____

Logged:

    Bug Data Base: _____

    Code Preamble: _____

    Module Dependency Analysis: _____

    Module History: _____

Programmer: _____ Date: _____

Manager: _____ Date: _____

DEPENDENCY ANALYSIS:

Directed Graph: _____

Dependency Analysis: _____

Risk Analysis: _____

_____

_____

SYSTEM TESTING: _____

_____

_____

_____

Programmer: _____ Date: _____

Comments: _____

_____

_____

Manager: _____ Date: _____

CUT TO NEW RELEASE _____

_____

Code Librarian: _____ Date: _____

RELEASE OF FIX: _____

_____

Fix Owner (Support/Sales Support, etc.): _____

_____

CUSTOMERS TO WHOM FIX IS DISTRIBUTED:

_____

_____

_____

_____

RELEASE NUMBER: _____

Person Responsible for Release: _____ Date: _____

VP: Development: _____ Date: _____

Manager: Operations: _____ Date: _____

A.19 STRATEGY FOR MINIMIZING THE NUMBER OF CORRECT SOLUTIONS IN A MODULE

Introduction. In order for us to create an effective filter for our Code Audits, it is necessary for us to minimize the number of correct solutions. We have talked about this several times in terms of the Structure Theorem, i.e., *if the process* P *is a proper program, then it can be equivalently written using only the 3 canonical forms*. A proper program is one which meets the following criteria:

- It has a *single entry* and a *single exit*.
- It contains no *eternal loops*.
- It contains no *dead code*.

The three canonical forms are:

- Simple Sequences.
- Branches [IF THEN, IF THEN ELSE, and CASE or SELECT/CASE].
- Loops [DO WHILE (pre-test loop), REPEAT UNTIL (post-test loop), and FOR (counting loops)].

If we are to minimize the number of correct structures, we must limit which of the above variants on the basic canonical forms we will allow. We must also limit the number of patterns for beginning and ending structures, etc. This means that we will begin with a set of standards closely based on a coding example that each programmer has. Note that the reasons for imposing standards are related to our ability to *restrict* the number of correct patterns to a small number which are easy to "pattern match" against. Thus, we will only allow:

Simple Sequences in which the logic is broken out in a form making it easy to understand at a glance, without needing to "re-read" the logic.

- Complex assignment statements should be broken into logical components, rather than building one complex statement, possibly continued across several lines.
- No nested function calls. The first function call would be defined as a variable, which would be used in the second function call, etc.
- Function calls requiring many variables should be broken into:
  - A set of *input* variables.
  - A set of *output* variables.
  - A possible set of variables which are used for both *input and output*. (This should be avoided wherever possible.)

If a function call is more complex than this, the variables might be broken into *one per line* with a comment following it as to its meaning.

- Variable definitions should be broken out *one per line*, with a comment following each as to its meaning. This way, they become the *data dictionary* for the module.

- Boolean expressions—regardless of the structure in which they are found—should meet the following conditions:

  - They must not contain function calls. Function calls should be defined previous to the structure in which they are used as a variable using an assignment statement—with a meaningful variable name.

  - If there are nestings of boolean relationships, they should be broken out through parentheses to make them easier to read and listed on multiple lines to make them easier to pattern match against.

  - Variables in either boolean expressions or argument lists of function calls must not be incremented or decremented. *V++* must be incremented in an assignment statement *following* the boolean expression or function. *++V* must be incremented in an assignment statement *before* the boolean expression or function, etc. The "++" and "--" notation of "C" should never be used. Always use *variable = variable + 1* at the point in the logic structure where it should be! *They are too error-prone to be of any value.*

Loops should all be *pre-test loops*. This means that *only the DO WHILE structure will be used*. Since all loops have the same logic structure, regardless of the *initialization, boolean expression in the WHILE statement, end,* or *incremental conditions*, they will *all* be implemented using the WHILE structure. (I.e., FOR-LOOPS are out—regardless of the implementation language.) There is no logical difference between counts from 1 to 10, counts from 1 to N, loops to sentinel values, loops to EOF, or loops to "a value less than e," or whatever else delimits it. All loops are made up of:

- Initialization section (including such things as *SUM = 0, SUMSQ = 0,* in addition to *I = 0* as a loop variable). To eliminate dependencies, *all* variables that impact the initialization of the while loop should be gathered into an *initialization section*—or as close to it as possible.

- Boolean expression of WHILE LOOP should meet the conditions of boolean expressions as defined above. In a WHILE LOOP, complex boolean expressions usually will indicate an error in thought-process.

- Update section should come just before ENDWHILE structure and should contain all the update conditions on which the boolean expression of the WHILE LOOP is based (usually just one). The corresponding statements to those above, i.e., *SUM = SUM + X,* and *SUMSQ = SUMSQ + X**2* can come anywhere, but usually they, plus *I = I + 1* would be the only values calculated inside the loop. (Usually, other logic or processing should be irrelevant to calculating sums and sums of squares (such as transformations on the x variable, or whatever).)

- END WHILE, which should be a comment following the "}" or "END" statements, depending on the language. (Consistency of structure—including indenting and labelling—is a tremendous aid in spotting errors in logic.

Branches should all reduce to a CASE or SELECT/CASE statement. Depending on the language, CASE statements deal with numbers (1, 2, 3, ...), characters (a, b, c, ...), or strings (red, blue, green, ...), or in the case of "C" just the first two. Interval data and complex boolean expressions are implemented using the SELECT structure. Its structure does not exist in most programming languages but is created by using a comment: SELECT, followed by a sequence of IF statements whose boolean expressions create the various CASE segments. (In languages with a "BEGIN/END"-type structure, it is possible to simply put the code in a segment following each IF. We should use the CASE/SWITCH structure in "C" and "PASCAL" until we find the other is better.

Dependencies and States should also be considered. We want to make each segment independent from any other segment and from any control structure. Similarly, the independence should go the other way as well. In addition, each control structure should be made independent of any other control structure. When creating a boolean expression, the entire set of possible conditions defined by the TRUE or FALSE condition, whether based only on true or false or on various values, or the existence of values within ranges, i.e., $x > 0$ or $0 \leq x \leq 100$ or whatever else. But it must be *evaluated* in terms of the *entire set of possibilities*.

Independence usually decreases the number of states from a multiplicative factor to an additive factor. I.e., our example of 100 interdependent functions produced 100! or 10^{154} possible states, whereas if they are designed to be mutually independent, then this reduces to 100 or only 10^2 possible states. The maintainability created and the reduction in "error proneness" could be worth several months' design effort.

In addition, whenever loops are considered, if a loop executes 1,000 times, and the processing is "loop invariant," then the loop has only one state; however, if each time the loop processes, its processing logic changes—or some other conditions modifies the state, based on the loop variable or condition, then there are 1,000 (or more) states.

You can see that the reduction is non-trivial; *it is massive!*

In terms of User Profiles, there are two benefits. In a "usability-oriented design," there is a close relationship between the profile and the actual code that implements it—sometimes approaching "one-to-one." When an Event List is used to create the specification, and it is designed to provide the *same solution* each time it is "triggered," regardless of the environment in which it is triggered, then we again have minimized the number of states and made the software more user-friendly. But in addition, we have minimized the states and made the software more maintainable and less error prone.

In legacy software that may be full of dependencies, maintenance usually leads to the "push-and-pop" syndrome. This is where the removal of one error causes another one somewhere else. *Regression Testing rarely catches this.* That is why it is usually worthless to do it. Often the errors are considered "random," i.e., they only occur once every 100 or 1,000 times. Actually the software is "deterministic," i.e., for a given input, it **always** produces the same output. This means the User Profile is random, not the error. Each time the User Profile runs, it causes the error. There is only a finite number of user profiles—regardless of the number and effect of the dependencies. For this reason, you do not need to duplicate the error; you need to locate the offending User Profile. The bug can be tracked through the various states the system takes on. The more you know about the offending User Profile, the fewer you need to examine to find the error.

In a similar manner, new features can be attached to a program by designing them into the code, while designing out the effects of associated dependencies. While our New Paradigm is oriented toward how to design error-free software, its concepts can be used to make it easier to debug and modify, as the same principles apply. Often, by examining the states, with their dependencies, you can fix *other* User Profiles which might cause the error in the "rare event" that they execute. This helps eliminate the "push-and-pop" syndrome which has for so many years been a maintenance nightmare.

But the main goal of this communication is to show that in terms of correct "real world" problem-solving, the concept of minimizing the number of correct solutions by *constraints* is extremely effective and is *mathematically correct.*

A.20 CRITERIA FOR CODE AUDITS

The purpose of this communication is to lay some groundwork for our Code Audits. It will constitute a preliminary filter. As you know, filters cover three concepts:

- Completeness (checklists, prototypes, forms, etc.)
- Quality (conformance to standards, ease of reading/use, appropriateness, etc.)
- Accuracy (error-free, lack of "error-proneness," independence, minimal # of states, etc.)

Filters change as we find more appropriate ways to use them—and they can change relatively quickly. In "event-driven" languages, we may need to establish "standard structures" to make things easier for us to pattern match against.

In "Code Inspections," the standard *speed* for inspecting code is between 200 and 400 lines of code per hour. Our approach should be around 200 to 400 lines of code per 10 to 15 minutes. It should be *much more efficient* because we are not attempting to "speed through" nor to "find errors." Our goal is to prove correctness through pattern matching against a small number of "correct patterns"—usually only one or two!

Peer programmers should make sure that those individuals whose code we audit learn to use the "entire" thought-process; not just go as fast as they can. They should proceed at a rate they feel comfortable with—and still cover all the issues, challenging them as they proceed through the code.

This *especially* pertains to concepts like:

- Correct, Complete Documentation:
  - Code Preambles or Prologs
  - Inputs and Outputs to Module(s)
  - Calling sequences (Jackson Hierarchies and I/O Tables)
  - Data Dictionaries and Variable Typing
- Correct Structures:
  - Proper Indentation
  - Proper "documentation" of code segments and structures
  - Proper naming conventions for variables, arguments, subroutine calls, etc.
  - NO SUBPROGRAM CALLS INSIDE OF SUBPROGRAM VARIABLE LISTS, BOOLEAN EXPRESSIONS, etc.
  - Labeling *all* END WHILE, END CASE, AND END IF THEN ELSE's, regardless of what the delimiter is in the target language
  - WHILE-Loops only (no FOR-Loops are *ever valid*—regardless of the language). In "C" the fact that it is so "versatile" makes for unreadable code. For "code audits," code must be clear enough to be pattern-matched within 2–3 seconds! It is hard to tell if a new language has implemented the FOR-loop as a DO WHILE or a REPEAT UNTIL. ("FOR I = 1, N" evaluated for N = 0 could execute "once" or "never," without your knowing which, from the context.)
  - NO use of I++, ++I, or I+ = in "C" or other languages using such constructs. Mathematically, they are "implicit," rather than "explicit," and do not immediately indicate what is being done—though it can be learned. Use I = I + 1 instead. Even experienced programmers have difficulty figuring out what ++I means!
  - Complete boolean expression(s) for the SELECT/CASE structure should be used to evaluate *all* states *before* converting them to nested IF THEN ELSE's (if necessary).
  - Decompose all non-mutually exclusive sets of boolean expressions into mutually exclusive sets by defining all their intersections as mutually exclusive subsets.
  - Make sure all the components of a particular logic structure are gathered in the appropriate place, i.e., *initialization section, WHILE statement, update section,* and *END WHILE statement.*

- Code inside logic structures:
  - Make sure the code in each segment makes no assumptions about its environment nor rules imposed by code in other parts of the system.
  - All code segments should be invariant, no matter where they are executed, i.e., *inside loops, code related by function / subprogram calls,* and *code related to one or more logic structures.*
  - Make sure that each segment or segment relationship—-whether related to loops, branches, or subprogram calls—is reduced to the smallest number of invariant states. (In multi-programming, this means that "Executive Modules" should be used to keep track of states during "interrupt-handling" rather than imbedding the interrupt logic in one of the two modules that are in contention.)
  - States can be further stabilized and reduced by defining *entities* in the code and analyzing their *attributes*. Normally, this is done by defining the relationships among the attributes, i.e., mutually exclusive or non-mutually exclusive, and then processing them at WHILE loops or CASE statements, as appropriate.
- Independence and State-invariance are concepts similar to one another. State Invariance is related to the concepts in the Product Specification which we call *events*. An event (non-Apple definition) is a small collection of functions that operate together to create a mini User Profile. Each event is activated by a *trigger* and the software system provides a *response. This response must be the same regardless of which of the one-or-many environments it is activated in.*

As is discussed elsewhere, dependencies can exist among code segments, between code segments and logic structures, and from logic structure to logic structure.

Programmers should learn to "coach" each other until everyone becomes proficient.

A.21 THOUGHTS ON THE THEORY BEHIND THE NEW PRODUCT DEVELOPMENT PROCESS AND A PROPOSED CODE AUDIT FILTER

Over the past few weeks we have been thinking about the *underlying mathematical theory* behind the various parts of the new paradigm contained in the Product Delivery Process. Some individuals have commented on this process as being "theory"—to which we have responded: "It is *not* a theory; it is a practical product development strategy." While this is true, it does not mean that it is not "mathematically provable." Below follows an outline of the underlying mathematical theory behind our process. No formal proofs will be shown—and a description of what the mathematics are, and how they apply, will be given later on, as we have the time.

The Product Delivery Process: Contrary to the approach taken by the various Software Development Life Cycle Models, our process is more broad. It involves the *entire delivery* of a product, from a market driven requirements document through the actual delivery and installation of the product. To learn to use the entire process, we must understand that the *maturity* is based on successive learning experiences, much like learning to play tennis. If we don't hit the ball every time, we must just keep practicing. This applies to the front-end filters as well as those based on the checklists used at the "product hand- off" phases and "product release" and "customer installation" phases.

As we have previously stated, an organization may be at an SEI CMM level 5 in terms of *capability*, but in terms of *maturity*, they may vary from a "one" or a "two"on most current projects to a few projects that are around a "four." We have come to believe that an entire company should not be evaluated as to CMM; it should be on a project-by-project basis, as the maturity depends on the experience of the programmer(s) and the complexity of the product being created. Further, the CMM model does not measure "quality," it measures "manageability." Just as in playing tennis, we must practice until we are mature and competent— but we have to *start* somewhere.

Everyone—from upper level management on down to middle and low-level management—should keep trying to improve the process (and the documents and filters involved) each time you define a new product. For this Product Delivery Process to work, *every phase* must have a:

- Plan
- Strategy
- Schedule

Based on:

- Deliverables (products)
- Filters

For this process to work, the filters must be used with feedback to continuously improve the process. *Creativity* is entirely possible, but just as with the use of a compiler, *creativity is within the discipline imposed by the environment!*

Often, there are those who would like to argue "best approaches" or "best solutions" in the abstract. This is *not productive!* You should take the approach the company has decided upon and *improve it through use of the filters*. Most of you recall, that management was very willing to let you attempt to come up with "counter-examples" for the REPEAT UNTIL structure. If we need to start—and stage—a product and you feel it cannot be isolated from the "unknowns," if you can draw us a valid design, then we will consider your point-of-view. But the solution to the problem is what we are after, not an argument as to who is right. You must show us the problem so we can solve it, rather than arguing in the "abstract."

The power of this is that, rather than forming committees to achieve "buy-on" and to "implement change," we insert filters that measure quality at an appropriate point in the process. *Everyone begins today to create software that meets quality criteria—as we have defined it. If we are wrong, the filter will catch it and we will change the filter. THAT IS THE PURPOSE OF A FEEDBACK- ORIENTED PROCESS.* In many companies where object-oriented methodologies or "clean room" methodologies have been "installed," it has taken 4 - 5 years—and then has ended in failure. With the filter-oriented approach, the entire process, with code and architectural quality in place, can begin and can be enforced in a matter of days! *If a programmer or other "key employee" resists the standards, he or she is told: "Any deliberate violation of the standard will be caught by the filter and the product (code) will be rejected. Any attempt to deliberately circumvent the process will be considered a DELIBERATE ATTEMPT TO SABOTAGE THE COMPANY and you will be fired! However, if you use the filter used to capture the standards and find a counter- example, the filter will be immediately modified to reflect the 'error.'"* This tends to reflect the concept of "capability" (in terms of the CMM) in terms of "creating quality" rather than "managing and measuring 'process.'" This is a major change in perception. Since the process can be immediately implemented, the capability should be instantaneous. In addition, the process, with its filters, can be instantly managed. You are no longer trying to implement management and control, you are trying to implement effectiveness of using the process. It is like trying to become a good tennis player. The correct process is assumed. The emphasis is on learning to play effectively to win (zero defects) and coaching and feedback to make the process work. In our new paradigm, when we are unsure of how something is working, we practice by "walking a product through the appropriate process and its filters over and over again until we feel we have mastered it and our product and filters are correct." This means the emphasis in on delivering a product with *zero defects*, rather than one with *six sigma, or 3.4 errors per million lines of code.* In our paradigm, effective, error-free *delivery of the product*, or a *quality software release process* is just as much a quality goal and is just as achievable as "zero defect software."

A View of the Mathematics Involved: Here then is a list of the various mathematical models and/or proofs for all our Product Delivery Process—even the part about filtering code rather than testing it.

By restricting the logic to 3 structures (DO WHILE loops, SELECT/CASE statements, and SIMPLE SEQUENCES), enforcing dependency analysis, and using "state reduction," it is almost always possible to come up with only one solution that is correct. If you use set theory and force all sets and their intersections to be *mutually exclusive*, then you can visualize and validate every state the program can take on, and the code inside each segment is "state invariant" and independent of the code in every other segment by definition. This minimizes the number of states a loop or subprogram can take on to "one." Since all these strategies pertain to the *structure of the logic* rather than to the logic itself, it is very easy to transfer the approach from one code segment to another—and it is independent of the programming language, whether it be a 4GL or assembly language.

The other parts of the process are easy to show mathematically as well. They involve:

- General Systems Theory.
- Formal Logic (Linear Algebra).
- Set Theory.
- State Modeling.
- Combinatorics.
- Entity/Relationship/Attribute Modeling (modeling logic, rather than data).
- Logic Structure (Dependency Analysis and Information Hiding).
- Pattern Matching.
- General Problem-Solving.
  - The generation of alternative *problem-statements* with reduction to an "ideal" through imposition of constraints.
  - The generation of alternative *solutions* with reduction to an "ideal" through imposition of constraints.
  - The generation of alternative *implementation strategies* with reduction to an "ideal" through imposition of constraints.

The constraints we are able to impose on the program logic are what make it possible to reduce the number of solutions from a potentially infinite number to potentially only one. State invariance and dependency analysis allow us to decrease the number of states by dividing the "original" number of states by the number of invariant states that can be created. (The number of states becomes *additive*, rather than *multiplicative*!) Using the concept of *entities*, with their accompanying *attributes*, helps reduce the number of states. If the attributes are mutually exclusive, they can be implemented through a CASE structure; if they are not, then they can be implemented through a DO WHILE structure.

[We were reviewing with a beginning programmer (a part time high school employee) some of his code using this approach, and we found a User Profile that was very rare and obscure (if you were viewing it from the outside). The programmer was truncating file names to conform to HTML. We told him it was "dead code," because HTML forces you to only use 31 characters and does not allow more. It turns out that software we were attaching allows more than 31 characters, so if someone uses a user created file and names it XXX...XX1 (with 32+ characters) and gives another file the same name with a "2" instead of a "1," when the new program truncates the file name, it will overwrite the original file. This would probably occur rarely, but when it does, it would appear that the file did not write correctly and you would probably look for the error in the wrong code. This is a serious error because the program runs automatically rather than manually (with an "eternal" WHILE loop), so files could be corrupted and not observed until significant damage had occurred. Finding this with test cases would be almost impossible, unless they uncovered the error by chance. We found it in less than 30 seconds by looking at the states of the code.]

The Proposed Code Audit Filter: The reason why it is possible to *design out errors* rather than design tests to see if they are present is due to the fact that we can—through the imposition of *constraints*—reduce the number of patterns that are correct. By adding analysis strategies relating to *dependency analysis* and *state reduction through "state invariance,"* we can go further in *guaranteeing* correctness. These strategies are similar to those discussed in Section A.19, but the approach is slightly different.

Introduction. In order for us to create an effective filter for our Code Audits, it is necessary for us to minimize the number of correct solutions. We have talked about this several times in terms of the Structure Theorem, i.e., *if the process* P *is a proper program, then it can be equivalently written using only the 3 canonical forms.* A proper program is one which meets the following criteria:

- It has a *single entry* and a *single exit*.
- It contains no *eternal loops*.
- It contains no *dead code*.

The three canonical forms are:

- Simple Sequences.
- Branches [IF THEN, IF THEN ELSE, and CASE or SELECT/CASE].
- Loops [DO WHILE (pre-test loop), REPEAT UNTIL (post-test loop), and FOR (counting loops)].

If we are to minimize the number of correct structures, we must limit which of the above variants on the basic canonical forms we will allow. We must also limit the number of patterns for beginning and ending structures, etc. This means that we will begin with a set of standards closely based on the coding example that several of you have proposed. Note that the reasons for imposing standards are related to our ability to *restrict* the number of correct patterns to a small number which are easy to "pattern match" against. Thus, we will only allow:

Simple Sequences in which the logic is broken out in a form making it easy to understand at a glance, without needing to "re-read" the logic.

- Complex assignment statements should be broken into logical components, rather than building one complex statement, possibly continued across several lines.
- No nested function calls. The first function call would be defined as a variable, which would be used in the second function call, etc.

- Function calls requiring many variables should be broken into:
  - A set of *input* variables.
  - A set of *output* variables.
  - A possible set of variables which are used for both *input and output*. (This should be avoided wherever possible.)

  If a function call is more complex than this, the variables might be broken into *one per line* with a comment following it as to its meaning.

- Variable definitions should be broken out *one per line*, with a comment following each as to its meaning. This way, they become the *data dictionary* for the module. Their names should be *unique, meaningful,* and *not confusing.*

- Boolean expressions—regardless of the structure in which they are found—should meet the following conditions:
  - They must not contain function calls. Function calls should be defined previous to the structure in which they are used as a variable using an assignment statement—with a meaningful variable name.
  - If there are nestings of boolean relationships, they should be broken out through parentheses to make them easier to read and listed on multiple lines to make them easier to pattern match against.
  - Variables in either boolean expressions or argument lists of function calls must not be incremented or decremented. *V++* must be incremented in an assignment statement *following* the boolean expression or function. *++V* must be incremented in an assignment statement *before* the boolean expression or function, etc. The "++" and "--" notation of "C" should never be used. Always use *variable = variable + 1* at the point in the logic structure where it should be! *They are too error-prone to be of any value.*

Loops should all be *pre-test loops*. This means that *only the DO WHILE structure will be used*. Since all loops have the same logic structure, regardless of the *initialization, boolean expression in the WHILE statement, end,* or *incremental conditions*, they will *all* be implemented using the WHILE structure. (I.e., FOR-LOOPS are out—regardless of the implementation language. It is not instantaneously obvious in a given language whether it is evaluated as a DO WHILE loop or a REPEAT UNTIL loop.) There is no logical difference between counts from 1 to 10, counts from 1 to N, loops to sentinel values, loops to EOF, or loops to "a value less than e," or whatever else delimits it. All loops are made up of:

- Initialization section (including such things as *SUM = 0, SUMSQ = 0*, in addition to *I = 0* as a loop variable). To eliminate dependencies, *all* variables that impact the initialization of the while loop should be gathered into an *initialization section*—or as close to it as possible.

- Boolean expression of WHILE LOOP should meet the conditions of boolean expressions as defined above. In a WHILE LOOP, complex boolean expressions usually will indicate an error in thought-process.
- Update section should come just before END WHILE structure and should contain all the update conditions on which the boolean expression of the WHILE LOOP is based (usually just one). The corresponding statements to those above, i.e., $SUM = SUM + X$, and $SUMSQ = SUMSQ + X^{**}2$ can come anywhere, but usually they, plus $I = I + 1$ would be the only values calculated inside the loop. [Usually, other logic or processing should be irrelevant to calculating sums and sums of squares (such as transformations on the x variable, or whatever).]
- END WHILE, which should be a comment following the "}" or "END" statements, depending on the language. (Consistency of structure— including indenting and labeling—is a tremendous aid in spotting errors in logic.)

Branches should all reduce to a CASE or SELECT/CASE statement. Depending on the language, CASE statements deal with numbers (1, 2, 3, …), characters (a, b, c, …), or strings (red, blue, green, …), or in the case of "C" just the first two. Interval data and complex boolean expressions are implemented using the SELECT structure. Its structure does not exist in most programming languages but is created by using a comment: SELECT, followed by a sequence of IF statements whose boolean expressions create the various CASE segments. In languages with a "BEGIN/END"-type structure, it is possible to simply put the code in a segment following each IF. I would like us to use the CASE/SWITCH structure in "C" and the similar structure in "PASCAL" until we find the other is better.

To *assure* the complete analysis of the possible states, we should think in terms of sets. If the sets are mutually exclusive, then the CASE statements can be defined to cover all possible sets (and the code contained therein is independent). If the sets are not mutually exclusive, then all possible intersections must be defined. They *will* be mutually exclusive.

Logic should always be independent of its environment. If a "rule" applies to a third-party product or to another part of the current product's code, the "rule" should be *enforced* at this point as well, rather than assuming that the third-party product will take care of it. On the other hand, if this logic runs the same (correctly) regardless of the third-party-software-based "rule," then duplicating it here would cause a dependency. Indentation rules should be based upon the standardized coding example our senior programmers have provided us with.

Any time that a call is made to a particular subprogram, the argument list should be validated against the parameter list to make sure there are:

- No inter-module dependencies.
- Consistent and accurate use of the arguments and parameters in *both* sets of code.
- No change of state possible in *either* set of code.

Code should be made *self-documenting* through meaningful variable names—and understandable assignment statements, boolean expressions, and control structures. Logic segments should be compared to adjacent logic segments and logic structures to make sure no dependencies are present.

When the code logic is being created, it is helpful to think in terms of *entities* being processed and their *attributes*. Can these entities be reduced to sub-entities which are more "state invariant" and thus more re-usable. As was mentioned earlier:

- If attributes for a given entity are *mutually exclusive*, then the appropriate ones should be processed either as a *simple sequence* or as a CASE statement. Their use should be validated in each instance.

- If attributes for a given entity are *not* mutually exclusive they should be processed either as a *simple sequence* or as a DO WHILE structure.

Since the employment of this approach constitutes a *filter*, its feedback mechanism will allow us to fix it if it is wrong. If you can show a counter-example, this will *also* be considered. Since the concepts discussed above deal with:

- A small number of correct patterns.
- Independent code structures and segments (and subprograms).
- Minimizing the number of invariant states.

It is possible that there will be *performance hits*. These must be analyzed on a case-by-case basis and violations of the programming standards handled—and documented—for each particular case. There are also some specialized "error-handing" activities and other systems environment-related processes we must conduct. For this to provide a single solution, we must agree on one ideal answer and all of us use it. This way, there will only be one pattern to observe. Any violation will be a difference and considered an "error," even if it runs correctly. This allows us to "constrain" our solution to only one correct pattern (of all those providing us with a right answer).

A.22 THOUGHTS ON THE DIFFERENCE BETWEEN ADVERTISING, SALES, AND MARKETING

Introduction: Often people think that *marketing, advertising,* and *selling* are basically the same thing. We thought that as a company begins to market "shrink-wrapped" products rather than large, vertical market-oriented software, it might provoke some meaningful discussion to publish our views on each of these areas of interest. Although a company might be relatively experienced in marketing to large individual customers and chains, these concepts *still* apply.

Marketing is related to how to create *instant recognition* for a product and its trademarks and quality. The "golden arches" indicate McDonald's in any language or culture. They also indicate quality and "sameness" anywhere in the world. This is because McDonald's has created an image related to *three-dimen-*

sional symbols. *Three-dimensional words* are also effective, though they tend not to cross language barriers the way symbols do.

Marketing has basically the following goals:

- *What is it?* (Product recognition.) This comes from creating a "context" for the product and its positioning in the marketplace.

- *What does it do?* (Perception of use.) Marketing should provide an instant perception of how the product can be used. This should apply to each of the ways in which the product can be used. Often, this is different for each market or collection of users.

- *Why is it better?* (Instant perception of quality.) This is not easy to do in a marketing campaign. Images used to convey quality must be part of the "look/feel" of the product—or the images used to identify the product.

- *Who uses it?* (Prestige and credibility of existing users.) This can be accomplished through use of testimonials, joint packaging with ancillary or compatible products, joint advertising, etc.

- *How do customers use it?* Advertisements can be created to show a sequence—through successive advertisements—of ways the product can be used. This is usually through instantly identifiable situations.

Aggressive marketing strategies should be aimed at different markets or groups of users. Often, one can identify and "sell" individuals in each marketplace who evaluate products and publish their findings in regular columns in magazines aimed at various "niches" of product users.

A Marketing Plan outlines a strategy—based on steps; timing, (marketing windows); and achievable, measurable goals. It should have a formal beginning and end. It should provide adequate lead time to allow for high quality products to be delivered on time.

Sales: Selling differs from marketing in the sense that it is the *validation* of the marketing plan. Marketing goals are often difficult to recognize and measure; sales goals are easy to identify and measure. Some considerations are:

- *How do we create a need on the part of a potential customer?* Good salespeople effectively and efficiently identify and "gain access" to potential customers. They quickly recognize how to convince a potential customer that a particular product is cost-effective in solving a potential customer's problem. They also can show how—regardless of what product or approach the customer is using—the customer can switch over to the proposed product without major inconvenience or training.

- *How do we position the product?* Can a customer add it to their existing work flow? Is it something that makes their work flow more efficient? Is it part of an identifiable set of solutions to customer needs? (If it is *too* radical a solution, we might lose credibility. If it is too *new* a technology, we might be too far ahead for the customer to perceive a need—or that the solution will provide stability and continuity to the customer's product or work-process.)

- *Who are our competitors?* We not only must show that our product is better than the competitions; we must make certain that it is easy for the sales personnel to show *exactly how* our product is better. This must be done, feature-by-feature, against *each* competitor's product(s).
- *What are the various environments in which our product(s) can be used?* Can we show that we provide a cost- effective solution in each case?

A selling strategy involves:

- Finding out who the potential customers are.
- Gaining access to the potential customers.
- Maximizing the percentage of sales per number of contacts.
- Time to complete a sale.
- Cost of making a sale.
- Cost of installation.
- Cost of training.
- Ease of moving someone from potential customer to customer.
- Convincing existing customers to upgrade to newer products or versions of products.
- Maintaining old or current customers against the competition.

A Sales Plan should define exactly which customers or potential customers will be identified and contacted *each week*. Sales projections should be based on achievable, specifically defined sales goals. A good salesperson knows exactly who he/she will contact each week and how likely the potential customer is to purchase the product. This requires *focus* and *measurability*.

Advertising is an aggressive strategy for making a product, its quality, and its uses visible to the potential customers. Good advertisements provide for an immediately identifiable set of three-dimensional words or images to create:

- Recognition
- Quality
- Need (or use)

Within two to three *seconds* of reading an advertisement. If the advertisement is obscure, misleading, or hard to understand, then its cost is wasted. Advertisements should create a *fun, active interest* in the product. The emphasis is on action and three-dimensional words and images rather than just information.

An Advertising Plan has a strategy, a set of stages, and a set of measurable goals. It should be viewed as an integral part of a marketing plan and a sales plan—and it should be evaluated in terms of its ability to help a company achieve its marketing and sales goals. Its main access is to help a company gain access to potential customer bases.

A Software Glossary with Commentary

Ad Hoc Teams: Teams that are called together from throughout an organization, having different skills and perspectives, to help create and evaluate (filter) a deliverable. This is different from standing committees which take up a lot of time and accomplish little. Sometimes ad hoc teams can operate through e-mail or a few short meetings with individual assignments made and reviewed in a follow-up meeting.

Behavioral Testing: Testing how the system actually behaves, rather than whether the functions work, either at the system level or at the module level. Different behaviors of a software system may relate to installability, usability, serviceability, reliability, etc. These also turn out to be measures of software quality. Many testing experts believe that black box testing is also behavioral testing, but we think this confuses the issue. Most software behavior issues should be addressed in terms of the customer or user, not the software developer.

In various places in the book, we have addressed software testability in terms of specifying functions as either assertions or events with associated triggers and system responses. This allows for measurable responses as to the behavior of the function in various contexts, rather than the traditional test case + output = expected output, which we do not consider to be a behavior-based test. In large automated test systems, you need an oracle to specify all the expected outputs. Most of the time, this is not a trivial task. We feel our approach is better.

Competitive Advantage: Almost every organization competes in some way with other organizations, whether they are profit or nonprofit, government or commercial, large or small, etc. Competitive advantage can be getting a product to market early in a marketing window; providing customer services to access and gain a larger customer base through use of an internal software system; using Management Information Systems (MIS) to know the status of your company and its ability to compete effectively; and the ability to bid for certain requests for proposal with the knowledge you can come through within budget, on schedule, and with the appropriate quality.

Cycle Time Reduction: This is a part of the quality program used by Motorola, Texas Instruments, IBM, and others to win the Malcolm Baldrige National

Award for Quality. It is related to making the development cycle more efficient by breaking it into small, repeatable parts, which can then be optimized. Other parts of the process are related to "empowered," effective, and accountable ad hoc teams; "Six Sigma;" "university-type" employee education curriculums; and a six-step, customer-oriented continuous process improvement program.

Dependency Analysis: Dependency analysis is a process for removing dependencies from logic structures and code segments at the module (code) level or intermodule relationships at the system level. A by-product of this approach is that you no longer need to perform regression testing or unit-level functional testing.

At the code level, this is related to packaging all segments of code which contain dependencies (or "segments of knowledge") into the same or adjacent control structures. Attempts should be made to eliminate dependencies from the relationships among the control structures and the code segments contained within them.

At the system level, dependencies can be removed by effective use of

- Executive Modules: These are modules in which high-level logic is packaged, making it possible for direct traceability back to the original specification. Because they create independence, you can repackage small or large subsystems many different ways to achieve various results or goals, without losing the basic traceability or functionality. If you use data flow diagrams from structured analysis and design, any time there are two or more bubbles on an arc (or path), you link them together with an executive module rather than "factoring" down the various paths in order to convert from the data flow paradigm into the module or "tree" structure paradigm.

- Dependency-Oriented "Fan-in": Normally, "fan-in," i.e., having multiple modules call a single, particular module, is used for module "reuse" and for building libraries of reusable functions. In the new paradigm, the product delivery process, "fan-in" is not only used in this manner, it is also used when dependencies have been identified across various pieces of code. This code is extracted from the modules in which it appears and fan-in is used to "package" the dependency in one place. This essentially eliminates it from the other modules, thus eliminating the dependency.

- Massage Modules: These modules are used when you attempt to use fan-in either to isolate a "common" function or a dependency and the modules containing the condition(s) are not quite the same. Massage modules allow you to convert the way the calling modules perceive the module to be fanned into so they perceive it the same way. For example, modules needing a row by column within level, row within column, and row by level within column sort routine, respectively, are converted by massage modules into modules requiring only one one-dimensional sort routine.

- Informational Strength Modules: If the dependencies (or "knowledge") within a set of modules are so different they cannot be related by fan-in or massage modules, they can always be "packaged" in informational strength modules. These modules have multiple interfaces and multiple entry points allowing each dependency to be considered as a separate program but considered with the rest of the set should anything triggering (or affecting) the dependency occur. This also works in the same way for any piece of "knowledge" but ordinarily this "knowledge" indicates a dependency.

- Transaction Processors: Many times it is necessary to change the "state" of a system. Usually this is done through various loops and data accesses, but other times, it is accomplished by menus either "pull-down," "button-oriented," or whatever. When these are "modeled" by state-transition models, you gain a mathematically elegant approach. Unfortunately they get complex very fast and do not protect you from dependencies. Transaction processors use the menu to identify the desired state and then transfer the system to that state, defining it as an independent subsystem. If any part of the rest of the system is needed, it is fanned into, as we described above. This allows these systems based on transactions to be built as individual, independent systems which can be easily integrated into the rest of the system. Each transaction system has its own set of independent states, which makes it easy to be evaluated through pattern matching.

Feedback Mechanisms: All effective processes contain a feedback mechanism. Measurements and metrics are types of feedback mechanisms. The type we use is called a filter. Most measurement- and metric-oriented feedback mechanisms have a delay of anywhere from several months (within a project) to a substantial length of time after it is completed. Filters, on the other hand, give instantaneous feedback, allowing for them to be "fixed" many times during the product delivery process should they "break."

Filters: Filters are analogous to "coffee filters." Rather than reaching in and extracting a coffee ground, one pours the coffee through a filter. The basic concept in our paradigm is that

- an ad hoc team creates a deliverable against its predefined standard of quality
- the deliverable is passed through a filter which can be defined as a checklist, an outline, a prototype document, or a quality standard (especially useful in programming). The filter measures

  completeness

  accuracy

  quality

  (Note that accuracy might be an approximate leverage, date, etc., while precision is the most exact value possible for that preliminary value or estimate.)

In this context, not only are grounds (errors) filtered out; quality is introduced through the filtering process. If an error is found later in the process, the error means that a deliverable had an error in it and the filter was broken and did not catch it. Not only is the deliverable fixed; the filter is fixed as well. Other products in the system are also refiltered at the same time to see if the filters allowed errors to pass through for them as well at that particular stage.

Functional Testing: Functional testing can be defined in terms of black box testing (involving inputs and outputs usually involving domain testing, cause-and-effect graphing, truth tables, equivalence class testing, etc.) and white box testing (involving the actual structure of the module under test usually involving a coverage measure such as segment coverage, branch coverage, basis path, or path coverage). White box testing is always involved at the unit level, while black box can be used at the unit, integration, or system level.

Independence-Based Software Architectures: All software development methodologies lead to some sort of software architecture. Some are object-oriented analysis and design, structured analysis and design, Jackson systems programming, Warnier's logical construction of systems, Orr's data structured systems design, etc. Our software development methodology is closely related to structured analysis and design, but it goes further in guaranteeing that there is traceability back to the original specification and that all the modules and subsystems are independent of each other. If two functions or subsystems are independent of each other, there is no way that a maintenance fix to one can cause an error in the other. This is why you no longer need to perform regression testing if you do a good job of designing out the dependencies.

Further, if the modules and subsystems are independent of each other, integration becomes a trivial task and takes a minimal amount of time. Rather than top-down, bottom-up, threaded, or big-bang integration, with associated drivers, stubs, and other problems, you get what we call "little-bang" integration, which involves bringing small, independent subsystems together with executive modules taking the place of drivers and no need for stubs.

Inspections versus Testing: Many people consider such inspection techniques as code inspections, code walk-throughs, or design reviews to be more cost-effective than testing. Inspections involve a multidisciplinary team performing error-detection strategies with a moderator, scribe, author, and various experts taking part. This differs from our filtering strategy in that we are pattern matching against a small number of quality-based patterns for correctness (accuracy), completeness, and quality, rather than finding errors (at the code level). But there are many more filters (18+) in our product delivery process than the stages in the traditional life cycle where inspections are used. In our paradigm, unit-level testing is replaced by "code audits," which involve the pattern-matching filters mentioned above. Traditional testing, as compared to code audits and inspections, involves actually running live test cases against parts of the code.

ISO-9000: A quality standard that makes it easier to market internationally. It does not guarantee the quality of a product; only the fact that you are using a quality process and are documenting it to a level where it can be audited. This allows for ISO-9000 registration.

Life Cycle Approach to Software Development: Life cycles are a traditional method for building software, though there are many organizations that do not use them. They vary from IBM's "snail curve" and the "waterfall" life cycle model, which are sequential in nature, to the spiral life cycle and others that are "component-oriented" or "iterative" in nature. Each of these leaves testing to the very end of the entire development cycle. There are some parallel life cycle models, but they tend not to be very popular.

Our product development process contains within it a parallel life cycle model. While there are those who criticize it as being risky when everything is brought together, they do not understand that when it is integrated with a "little-bang" approach, you are doing "build a little, integrate a little, and test a little." This is a very risk-free process and conforms very closely to Deming's approach to quality.

Logic—From a Functional Point of View: One reason why our "code audit" filter approach works so well is that functions reflect an active and passive view of logic. In order for a function to work, it must contain the proper logic. The logic must be specific to the function being implemented. But no matter what the logic is, it can be represented with only three logic structures. Further, with a disciplined use of these three logic structures, eliminating dependencies, only a small number of patterns are "correct" and only a small number of patterns are "incorrect." This is a powerful observation.

Logic—From a Structural Point of View: If you view logic from a structural point of view, an even more amazing observation occurs. That is that the same logic structures can represent many different functions. An example is a WHILE loop. It has the same four components whether it is a count from 1 to 10, a count from 1 to N, a loop until a sentinel value is reached, a loop until an "end of file" is reached, or a loop until two values get within a certain range of each other. Logic structure dependencies will be the same regardless of the function in which they occur.

This observation, with the accompanying view of functional logic, provides a powerful reason why the new paradigm can be used to eliminate the need for traditional functional testing. The same thing holds true at the system level for regression testing. If there is no dependency between two components, there is no way changing one can cause an error in the other.

Managing against "Leverage": Most companies that have been forced to downsize in the past several years have suffered from poor management and leadership. They have not had effective, visionary marketing plans. Good management must be as highly disciplined as good programmers and other software developers. Flat management also contributed to the personal disasters in the lives of employees due to downsizing.

Effective, disciplined management requires not only an accurate view into the future of their business; it also requires middle-level management (and "empowered" ad hoc teams working under them) who are disciplined enough to manage each employee based on "leverage." Leverage is how many times you can market an employee's salary, either in terms of products, corporate advantage, or customer service or whatever else helps a company meet its strategic goals.

Marketing Organization: Any company, to succeed, must have a corporate mission statement and a five-year plan for how to achieve it. (Some executives feel more comfortable with a three-year plan. If you can convince them to create a three-year plan, it is better than no plan, or one in which they have no confidence and will not use.) The steps must be specific and measurable. If you are building commercial software, this is tied to a strong, competent marketing organization. Such an organization must keep in touch with the customer base, know their wants and needs, and have a vision of what can be provided in addition. As outlined in our marketing requirements definition document, this also shows a competitive analysis and how to move customers painlessly from the competition to your product base, as well as how to keep them. Some companies where we have worked or consulted who have had a far superior product than the competition have lost their market share through poor marketing practices.

Number of Correct Solutions to a Processing Problem Can Be Reduced to Three or Four: It can be shown through the structure theorem of structured programming that all processes can be implemented using only three basic logic structures (whether the processes are a cookie recipe or a computer program). Further, if these logic structures are restricted to those which do not encourage dependencies, for any software process, there are only three or four logic structures that provide correct solutions and a similar few structures that can be wrong. This makes it easy to detect correct solutions through pattern matching rather than traditional testing.

These patterns are:

- DO WHILE loops (test before entering the loop).
- SELECT/CASE (sequence of CASE structures, i.e., CASE 1 (with its logic), CASE 2 (with its logic), etc. The SELECT part is how you implement interval data, i.e., $0 < x < 25$, rather than ordinal data such as 1, 2, 3; or set-type data such as male, female, etc.).
- SIMPLE SEQUENCES of statements or commands.

"Off-the-Shelf"-type Software: Software such as Microsoft Word, Lotus Notes, etc., which is sold commercially and not customized for a particular user. It is supported by staff manning telephones, faxes, WANs, bulletin boards, etc.

Product Delivery Process (System): We have tried to show the difference between this type of approach and the traditional life cycle approach to software development. This approach begins with the customer (through marketing and sales) and ends with a product release process, which is also customer-oriented (through training, support, and installation). (There are many QA people who understand and preach this type of approach, but it is hard to get most organizations to understand why all these are necessary.)

The attributes are:

- Market-driven: Triggered by marketing concerns. These, to be effective, should be tied to a five-year marketing plan which truly anticipates market directions, even if (especially if) they are constantly changing.

- Deliverables-Oriented: Oriented to actual products, semiproducts, or other "entities" that can be identified, processed, and measured. Most projects fail because they may be "schedule-driven," but they do not have identifiable deliverables which, when completed, will show progress toward the end of the project. These must be accompanied by a "strategy" for building the software system.

- Based on Successive, "Measurable" Milestones: For a delivery process or any process to succeed, it must be based on a succession of measurable milestones. These milestones should show who is to do what and under what conditions and in what time frame they will be completed. Deliverables are effective demonstrations of achieving a milestone. Almost any project can be managed effectively and predictably if the project plan is based on these considerations.

- Based on Parallel Development: Parallel development works for several reasons. If you have many people working on things in parallel and then bringing system components containing dependencies and poorly defined interfaces and functionality together in a "big-bang" integration, you are doomed to fail. But if you use the "little-bang" integration we propose, along with independent subsystems with well-defined interfaces, this works exceedingly well.

- Based on "Leverage-Oriented" Metrics: If software projects and all aspects of a corporation are managed correctly and with discipline, it is possible to maximize the effectiveness of all participants in a product delivery process in terms of their contribution to the financial returns of the company. Metrics should be emphasized which make it possible to reach this goal.

Project Plans: Project plans are effective and highly predictive if they are carried out with discipline and appropriate feedback. They must be planned and managed around things that actually happen and can be measured, for example, modules or subsystems completed which can be evaluated or tested.

Through effective use of a Gantt chart or other tools, it is possible to put the least competent programmers on the critical path, saving the most proficient programmers for the critical code, or that requiring special expertise. If the project gets in trouble schedule-wise due to missing dates because of overoptimism or additional features, there are three things you can do

- Increase the Schedule: In some cases, the only thing you can do is negotiate and increase the schedule, even though this is what you are trying to avoid.

- Remove Noncritical Functionality: If it is possible, there may be some functionality that can be held for a later release or simply removed with minimal effect. This is often a good solution, and the most practical.

- Add Manpower: Add programmers (and others) to the project to help get it back on schedule. Many people feel that because of communication problems, this is not a good solution. This is only true if those added to the project are new hires or those unfamiliar with the project or the technology. (It may also be true if there are a lot of dependencies involved.) But if these are your best, most competent programmers who have been working on the critical code, it is possible to catch up with very little impact. Since these key programmers are not on the critical path, pulling them off their part of the project has little impact on their part of the schedule and great positive impact on the critical path.

Return on Investment: All quality initiatives relating to quality assurance, test organizations, or even measurement programs must be justified to upper-level management through "return on investment." Each of these costs the company money and resources and must be justified as being valuable. Software products should also be justified in a similar manner.

Six Sigma: Six Sigma is part of a quality initiative employed by Motorola, Texas Instruments, IBM, and others in an attempt to achieve a reduction in error rate from (say) 65,000 errors per million lines of code to 3.4 errors per million lines of code. While many measure this in terms of all errors, you need to have a clear picture as to what is involved. Should it be only errors that reach the customer? What about errors that individual programmers encounter while compiling their code? There are six steps involved in this process including identifying the customer, identifying the supplier, and continuous process improvement, but the approach gives you very little help in figuring out exactly how to do it. The other steps will not be covered in this definition.

Software States: The states of a software system are merely the condition the system is in after a piece or set of data has executed, a button has been pushed, a menu item selected, one iteration of a loop executed, or something similar. Usually, the system has moved from one state to another and in testing, you test or evaluate the system to make sure it has made the transition to the correct state under the proper conditions. While this is a simple concept, incorrect software implementations can lead to hundreds of millions of states and any kind of testing, automated or manual, provides such a small amount of coverage as to be worthless.

Test through Pattern Matching: One of the major breakthroughs of the new paradigm is that much testing can be accomplished through pattern matching rather than running "live" test cases. While this may seem "unrealistic," everyone does it. We pattern match to get from the airport to the hotel. If we read a mathematical formula in a statistics book, such as that of the arithmetic mean, we pattern match against the "summation sign," the "subscripts," and the other algebraic symbols. No one would think of "verifying" the equation by running 2,000 data elements through it to see if it is correct. A WHILE loop and a summation symbol are logically equivalent and the algebraic equation that follows the summation sign is the same as what you implement through a series of "assignment statements" in C or COBOL.

Traditional Testing: Traditional testing involves running live test cases against a product, or a module or subsystem within a product and verifying the results against a test oracle to see that they are correct. People argue against pattern matching by saying that the software may be so complex that you cannot understand how it works. They also feel that there may be so many states that the system takes on it is impossible to analyze all of them manually. Our response is that if you do not understand what the program is doing, how do you find valid test cases to run against it or test oracles to show your results are correct? The same is true with exceedingly large numbers of states. If you have too many states, how do you find adequate test cases to cover them all? If you only select a few, on what basis do you select them? Test cases rarely uncover dependencies. Only in regression testing are they effective, and then, only when you happen to cover the two parts of the code between which the dependency exists, assuming fixing one has broken the other.

Validation: This is an attempt to show if the correct software product is being built. It involves testing the software against its specification at the end of the project to ensure that it meets its requirements, i.e., that it does what it is supposed to do.

Verification: This is an attempt to show if the product has been built correctly. This verification takes place after each phase of the software development process against a set of predetermined standards.

References and Additional Reading

Apte, Kishor, and Meena S. Iyer. 1995. "Beyond ISO 9000: The First Step." *The Journal of the Quality Assurance Institute*, Vol. 9, No. 3, July 1995, pp. 7–17.

Arthur, Lowell Jay. 1993. *Improving Software Quality: An Insider's Guide to TQM*. New York: John Wiley & Sons, Inc.

Beizer, Boris. 1984. *Software System Testing and Quality Assurance*. New York: Van Nostrand- Reinhold Company.

Beizer, Boris. 1991. *Software Testing Techniques*, Second Edition. New York: Van Nostrand- Reinhold Company.

Beizer, Boris. 1995. *Black-Box Testing: Techniques for Functional Testing of Software and Systems*. New York: John Wiley & Sons.

Beizer, Boris. 1996. Personal communication with one of the authors, April 1996.

Bertolino, A., and A. L. Strigini. 1996. "On the Use of Testability Measures for Dependability Assessment." *IEEE Transactions on Software Engineering*, pp. 97–108, Vol. 22, No. 2, February 1996.

Boardman, T. J. 1994. "The Statistician Who Changed the World, W. Edwards Deming, 1900–1993." *The American Statistician*, Vol. 48, pp. 179–187.

Boehm, Barry W. 1976. "Software Engineering." *IEEE Transactions on Computers*, December 1976, pp. 1226–1241.

Boehm, Barry W. 1981. *Software Engineering Economics*. Englewood Cliffs, NJ: Prentice-Hall.

Boehm, Barry. 1988. "Industrial Software Metrics Top 10 List." *Quality Time, IEEE Software*.

Bohm, C., and G. Jacopini. "Flow Diagrams, Turing Machines and Languages with Only Two Formation Rules." *Communications of the ACM*, Vol. 9, No. 5:366–71.

Booch, Grady. 1994. *Object-Oriented Analysis and Design: With Applications*, Second Edition. Redwood City, CA: Benjamin Cummings.

Briand, Lionel C., Sandro Morasca, and Victor R. Basili. 1996. "Property-based Software Engineering Measures." *IEEE Transactions on Software Engineering*, Vol. 22, No. 1, January 1996, pp. 68–86.

Brooks, Frederick P., Jr. 1995. *The Mythical Man-Month*, Anniversary Edition. Reading, MA: Addison-Wesley Publishing Company.

Bruce, Phillip, and Sam M. Pederson. 1982. *The Software Development Project: Planning and Management*. New York: John Wiley and Sons.

Buckley, Fletcher J. 1989. *Implementing Software Engineering Practices*. New York: Wiley Series in Software Engineering Practice.

Cameron, John. 1989. *JSP & JSD: The Jackson Approach to Software Development*, Second Edition. Washington, DC: IEEE Computer Society Press.

Caplan, Frank. 1980. *The Quality System*, Second Edition. Philadelphia: Chilton Book.

Card, David N., with Robert L. Glass. 1990. *Measuring Software Design Quality*. Englewood Cliffs, NJ: Prentice Hall.

Charette, Robert N. 1990. *Applications Strategies for Risk Analysis*. New York: McGraw Hill.

Chen, Peter. 1977. *The Entity-Relationship Approach to Logical Data Base Design*. New York: Q. E. D. Information Sciences.

Chen, T. Y., and Y. T. Yu. 1996. "On the Extended Number of Failures Detected by Subdomain Testing and Random Testing." *IEEE Transactions on Software Engineering*, pp. 109–119, Vol. 22, No. 2, February, 1996.

Cho, C. K. 1980. *An Introduction to Software Quality Control*. New York: Wiley Interscience.

Cho, C. K. 1987. *Quality Programming: Developing and Testing Software with Statistical Quality Control*. New York: John Wiley & Sons.

Coad, Peter, and Edward Yourdon. 1991a. *Object-Oriented Analysis*, Second Edition. Englewood Cliffs, NJ: Yourdon Press.

Coad, Peter, and Edward Yourdon. 1991b. *Object-Oriented Design*. Englewood Cliffs, NJ: Yourdon Press.

Coleman, Derek, et al. 1994. *Object-Oriented Development: The Fusion Method*. Englewood Cliffs, NJ: Prentice Hall.

Crandall, Vern J. 1987. Computer Science 427: Software Design and Implementation, Lecture Notes, Alexander's Print Stop, Provo, UT.

Crandall, Vern J. 1989a. "Testing in a Local Area Network Environment." *Quality Week*, May 16–19, 1989, San Francisco, California.

Crandall, Vern J. 1989b. "The Development of an Industry-Education Relationship in the Test Environment: The Novell-Brigham Young University Experience." Sixth International Conference on Testing Computer Software, May 22–24, 1989, Washington, D.C.

Crandall, Vern J. 1989c. "Installing a Methodology in an Organization." Eighth International Enterprise-Wide Information Management Conference, St. Louis, Missouri, September 6 - 8, 1989.

Crandall, Vern J. 1990a. "Product-Oriented Development Methods." Software Development `90, February 6–9, 1990, Oakland, California. [Also presented the following year as "Getting Your Software Products to Market," Software Development `91, February 1991, Santa Clara, California (1991) and Software Development `93, February 1993, Santa Clara, California (1993).]

Crandall, Vern J. 1990b. "Building Testable Software: Building Test Awareness into Software Development." Second International Software Testing Methods, Tools, and Techniques Conference, February 28–March 2, 1990, Orlando, Florida.

Crandall, Vern J. 1993. "The Cost-Effectiveness of Software Testing: Making a Case to Management." *The Journal of the Quality Assurance Institute*, October 1993, pp. 8–20. (Chosen Best Paper of 1993.)

Crandall, Vern J. 1994a. "Handling Risk in Software Development Part 1: Identifying and Managing Risk." *The Journal of the Quality Assurance Institute,* January 1994, pp. 21–25.

Crandall, Vern J. 1994b. "Handling Risk in Software Development Part 2: Minimizing the Impact of Risk." *The Journal of the Quality Assurance Institute,* April 1994, pp. 28–41. (This two-part paper was chosen Best Paper of 1994.)

Crandall, Vern J. 1995. "The Software Product Development Life Cycle." *Proceedings of the 1995 International Information Technology Quality Conference,* Orlando, Florida, April 6, 1995.

Creech, Bill. 1994. *The Five Pillars of TQM.* New York: Truman Valley Books/Dutton.

Davis, Alan M. 1990. *Software Requirements: Analysis and Specification.* Englewood Cliffs, NJ: Prentice Hall.

DeCarlo, Neil J., and W. Kent Sterett. 1990. "History of the Malcolm Baldrige National Quality Award." *Quality Progress,* March 1990, pp. 21–27.

DeMarco, Tom. 1979. *Structured Analysis and System Specification.* Englewood Cliffs, NJ: Prentice Hall.

DeMarco, Tom. 1982. *Controlling Software Projects: Management, Measurement, and Estimation.* Englewood Cliffs, NJ: Yourdon Press.

Deming, W. E. 1986. *Out of the Crisis.* Cambridge MA: Massachusetts Institute of Technology, Center for Advanced Engineering Study.

Dickensen, Brian. 1980. *Developing Structured Systems.* Englewood Cliffs, NJ: Yourdon Press.

Dijkstra, Edsgar. 1968. "Go To Statement Considered Harmful." *Communications of the ACM,* Vol. 11, No. 3: 147–178.

Fagan, Michael E. 1976. "Design and code inspections to reduce errors in program development." *IBM Systems Journal,* Vol. 15, No. 3, pp. 182–211.

Fagan, Michael E. 1986. "Advances in Software Inspections." *IEEE Transactions on Software Engineering,* July 1986, pp. 744–751.

Flavin, Matt. 1981. *Fundamental Concepts of Information Modeling.* Englewood Cliffs, NJ: Yourdon Press.

Forse, Thomas. 1989. *Qualimétrie Des Systêmes Complexes: Mesure de la qualitÉ du logiciel.* Paris: Les èditions D'Organisation.

Francisco, Andrea, editor. 1992. "Street-wise Systems." *Information Week,* March 23, 1992, p. 66.

Freedman, Daniel, and Gerald Weinberg. 1977. *Technical Inspections and Reviews.* Boston, MA: Little, Brown and Company.

Gane, Chris, and Trish Sarson. 1979. *Structured Systems Analysis: Tools and Techniques.* Englewood Cliffs, NJ: Prentice Hall.

Gilb, Tom. 1977. *Software Metrics.* New York: Winthrop.

Gilb, Tom. 1988. *Principles of Software Engineering Management.* Reading, MA: Addison-Wesley Publishing Company.

Gilb, Tom. 1991. "Software Metrics: Practical Approaches to Control Software Projects." Paper presented at YSG Conference, Cardiff, Wales. April 1991.

Gill, Patricia. 1995. "The Power to Be Your Best: Transforming Self and Organization." 15th International Software Testing Conference, Orlando, Florida, November 13–17,

1995. (Cited article by Wysockl, Bernard. "Corporate Anorexia." *The Wall Street Journal,* July 5, 1995.)

Glass, Robert L. 1992. *Building Quality Software.* Englewood Cliffs, NJ: Prentice Hall.

Goethert, Wolfhart. 1992. *Software Effort Measurement: An Architecture for Counting Staff-hour and Reporting Schedule Information.* (CMU/SEI-92-TR-22) Pittsburgh, PA: SEI, Carnegie-Mellon University.

Grady, Robert B. 1989. "Dissecting Software Failures." *HP Journal.* April 1989: 57–63.

Grady, Robert B. 1992. *Practical Software Metrics for Project Management and Process Improvement.* Englewood Cliffs, NJ: Prentice Hall.

Grady, Robert B., and Deborah L. Caswell. 1987. *Software Metrics: Establishing a Company-Wide Program.* Englewood Cliffs, NJ: Prentice Hall.

Hahn, Gerald J. 1995. "Deming's Impact on Industrial Statistics: Some Reflections." *The American Statistician,* Vol. 49, No. 4, November 1995, pp. 336–341.

Halstead, M. 1977. *Elements of Software Science.* New York: Elsevier.

Hansen, Kirk. 1983. *Data Structured Program Design.* Topeka, KS: Ken Orr and Associates.

Harrold, Mary Jean, and Mary Lou Soffa. 1989. "Interprocedural Data Flow Testing." Proceedings of the ACM SIGSOFT `89 Third Symposium on Software Testing, Analysis, and Verification, December 13–15, 1989, Key West, Florida.

Hatley, Derek J., and Imtiaz Pirbhai. 1987. *Strategies for Real-Time System Specification.* New York: Dorset House.

Hayes, William F. 1995. "The Baldrige Process." In Ken M. Shelton, editor, *In Search of Quality: A Manager's Perspective.* Provo, UT: Executive Excellence, Inc., Chapter 14, pp. 101–104.

Hetzel, Bill. 1988. *The Complete Guide to Software Testing,* Second Edition. Wellesly, MA: QED Information Sciences, Inc.

Hetzel, Bill. 1993. *Making Software Measurement Work: Building an Effective Measurement Program.* Wellesly, MA: QED Publishing Group.

Higgins, David. 1979. *Program Design and Construction.* Englewood Cliffs, NJ: Prentice Hall.

Higgins, David. 1983. *Designing Structured Programs.* Englewood Cliffs, NJ: Prentice Hall.

Hoffman, Daniel, and Paul Strooper. 1995. *Software Design, Automated Testing and Maintenance.* Boston, MA: International Thomson Computer Press.

Hollocker, Charles P. 1990. *Software Reviews and Audits Hand Book.* New York: John Wiley & Sons.

Humphrey, Watts S. 1989. *Managing the Software Process.* Reading, MA: Addison-Wesley Publishing Company.

Humphrey, Watts S. 1995. *A Discipline for Software Engineering.* Reading, MA: Addison-Wesley.

IBM. 1978. Managing the Application Development Process, IBM Independent Study Course, IBM Corporation.

"IBM's Rochester Facility Strives for 'a Perfect 10'." 1990. *Electronic Business,* October 15, 1990.

IEEE 982. 1988. "Standard for Measures to Produce Reliable Software."

IEEE Standard for Software Verification and Validation Plans. 1986. Washington, DC: IEEE, Std. 1012-1986 (R1992).

IEEE Standard Glossary of Software Engineering Terminology. 1990. Washington, DC: IEEE Std. 610.12-1990.

Ingevaldsson, Leif. 1979. *JSP: A Practical Method of Program Design*. London: Chartwell-Bratt Ltd.

Jackson, M. A. 1975. *Principles of Program Design*. New York: Academic Press.

Jackson, M. A. 1983. *System Development* Englewood Cliffs, NJ: Prentice Hall.

Jacobson, I., M. Christerson, P. Jonsson, and G. Overgaard. 1992. *Object-Oriented Software Engineering*. Reading, MA: Addison-Wesley Publishing Company.

Jarvis, Alka S. 1988. "How to Establish a Successful Test Plan." EDP Quality Assurance Conference, Washington, DC, November 14–17, 1988.

Jarvis, Alka S. 1989. "Letters & Science: Test Plan," Lecture Notes, Zebra Copy, Cupertino, California.

Jarvis, Alka S. 1992. "Disaster Recovery." *The Journal of the Quality Assurance Institute*, April 1992, pp. 36–38.

Jarvis, Alka S. 1993. "Improvement Process Based on Metrics." 3rd Annual Software Quality Conference, Milpitas, California, May 24, 1993.

Jarvis, Alka S. 1994. "Applying Software Quality." The Seventh International Software Quality Week, San Francisco, California, May 17–20, 1994.

Jarvis, Alka S. 1995a. "Applying Metrics." First World Congress for Software Quality Conference, San Francisco, California, June 20–22, 1995.

Jarvis, Alka S. 1995b. "Exploring the Needs of a Developer and Tester." Quality Conference 95, Santa Clara, California, April 4–7, 1995.

Jones, T. Capers. 1986. *Programming Productivity*. New York: McGraw-Hill.

Jones, T. Capers. 1991. *Applied Software Management: Assuring Productivity and Quality*. New York: McGraw-Hill.

Kaner, Cem, Jack Falk, and Hung Quoc Nguyen. 1993. *Testing Computer Software*, Second Edition. New York: Van Nostrand-Reinhold.

Kehoe, Ray, and Alka S. Jarvis. 1995. *ISO 9000-3*. New York: Springer-Verlag.

Kerzner, Harold. 1979. *Project Management: A Systems Approach to Planning, Scheduling, and Controlling*. New York: Van Nostrand Reinhold.

King, David. 1988. *Creating Effective Software: Computer Program Design Using the Jackson Methodology*. Englewood Cliffs, NJ: Yourdon Press.

Kowal, James A. 1994. *Behavioral Models: Specifying Users' Expectations*. Englewood Cliffs, NJ: Prentice Hall.

Linger, R. C., H. D. Mills, and B. I. Witt. 1979. *Structured Programming: Theory and Practice*. Reading, MA: Addison-Wesley.

Maples, Mike. 1995. Interview. *Information Week*.

Marca, David A., and Clement L. Mcgowan. 1988. *SADT: Structured Analysis and Design Technique*. New York: McGraw-Hill.

Marciniak, J. 1994. *Encyclopedia of Software Engineering*. New York: John Wiley & Sons, Inc.

Martin, James. 1989. *Information Engineering, Book I: Introduction*. Englewood Cliffs, NJ: Prentice Hall.

Martin, James. 1990a. *Information Engineering, Book II: Planning & Analysis*. Englewood Cliffs, NJ: Prentice Hall.

Martin, James. 1990b. *Information Engineering, Book III: Design & Construction*. Englewood Cliffs, NJ: Prentice Hall.

Martin, James, Kathleen Kavanagh Chapman, and Joe Leben. 1991. *Systems Application Architecture: Common User Access*. Englewood Cliffs, NJ: Prentice Hall.

Mascot, Version 3.1, The Official Handbook of. June 1987. London, England: Crown Copyright.

McCabe, J. J., and C. W. Butler. 1989. "Design Complexity Measurement and Testing." *Communications of the ACM*, Vol. 32, No. 12, December 1989, pp. 1415–1424.

McCabe, T. J. 1976. "A Complexity Measure." *IEEE Transactions on Software Engineering*, SE-2 (4), December 1976, pp. 308–320.

McCabe, Thomas J. 1982. "Structured Testing: A Software Testing Methodology Using the Cyclomatic Complexity Metric." National Bureau of Standards Special Publication, December 1982: 500–599.

McClure, Carma. 1996. "Making Object Technology and Re-use Inseparable Partners." International Information Technology Conference, Orlando, Florida, April 16–19, 1996.

McConnell, Steve. 1993. *Code Complete: A Practical Handbook of Software Construction*. Redmond, WA: Microsoft Press.

McMenamin, Stephen M., and John F. Palmer. 1984. *Essential Systems Analysis*. Englewood Cliffs, NJ: Yourdon Press.

Metzger, Phillip W. 1981. *Managing a Programming Project*, Second Edition. Englewood Cliffs, NJ: Prentice Hall.

Metzger, Philip W. 1987. *Managing Programming People: A Personal View*. Englewood Cliffs, NJ: Prentice Hall.

Meyer, Bertrand. 1988. *Object-Oriented Software Construction*. Englewood Cliffs, NJ: Prentice Hall.

Mills, Harlan D. 1983. *Software Productivity*. Boston, MA: Little, Brown and Company.

Mills, H. D., R. C. Linger, and A. R. Hevner. 1986. *Principles of Information Systems Analysis and Design*. New York: Academic Press.

Murine, Gerald E. 1988. "Integrating Software Quality Metrics With Software QA." *Quality Progress*, November 1988: 38–43.

Musa, J. D., A. Iannino, and K. Okumoto. 1987. *Software Reliability: Measurement, Prediction, Application*. New York: McGraw-Hill.

Myers, Glenford J. 1976. *Software Reliability Principles & Practices*. New York: John Wiley & Sons.

Myers, Glenford J. 1978. *Composite / Structured Design*. New York: Van Nostrand-Reinhold.

Myers, Glenford J. 1979a. *Reliable Software Through Composite Design*. New York: Van Nostrand-Reinhold.

Myers, Glenford J. 1979b. *The Art of Software Testing*. New York: John Wiley & Sons.

Orr, Ken. 1981. *Structured Requirements Definition*. Topeka, KS: Ken Orr and Associates.

Page-Jones, Meilir. 1988. *Practical Guide to Structured Systems Design*, Second Edition. Englewood Cliffs, NJ: Yourdon Press.

Page-Jones, Meilir. 1985. *Practical Project Management: Restoring Quality to DP Projects and Systems*. New York: Dorset House Publishing,

Parnas, D. L. 1972. "On the Criteria to Be Used in Decomposing Systems into Modules." *Communications of the ACM*, December 1972, pp. 1053–1058.

Perry, William E. 1986. *How to Test Software Packages: A Step-by-Step Guide to Assuring They Do What You Want*. New York: John Wiley & Sons.

Peters, Lawrence. 1987. *Advanced Structured Analysis and Design*. Englewood Cliffs, NJ: Prentice Hall.

Peters, Tom. 1995. "The Peters Principles: Still Leadership." *ASAP*, October 9, 1995.

Pressman, Roger S. 1988. *Making Software Engineering Happen: A Guide to Instituting the Technology*. Englewood Cliffs, NJ: Prentice Hall.

Pressman, Roger S. 1992. *Software Engineering: A Practitioner's Approach,* Third Edition. New York: McGraw-Hill.

Putnam, L. H. 1978. "A General Empirical Solution to the Macro Software Sizing and Estimating Problem." *IEEE Transactions on Software Engineering,* July 1978: 345–361.

Putnam, L. H. 1980. "A Tutorial on Software Cost Estimating and Life-Cycle Control: Getting the Software Numbers." IEEE No. EHO: 168–5.

Radice, R. A., N. K. Roth, A. C. O'Hara, Jr., and W. A. Ciarfella. 1985a. "A Programming Process Architecture." *IBM Systems Journal,* Vol. 24, No. 2, pp. 79–90.

Radice, R. A., J. T. Harding, P. E. Munnis, and R. W. Phillips. 1985b. "A Programming Process Study." *IBM Systems Journal*, Vol. 24, No. 2, pp. 91–101.

Radice, Ronald A., and Richard W. Phillips. 1988. *Software Engineering: An Industrial Approach, Volume I*. Englewood Cliffs, NJ: Prentice Hall.

Raysman, Richard. 1992. "The Software Development Contract:." In Hancock (Ed.), *Corporate Counsel's Guide to Software Transactions*. Chesterland, OH: Business Laws Inc., pp. 4.001–4.023.

Ross, D. T. 1985. "Applications and Extensions of SADT." *IEEE Computer Magazine*, Vol. 18, No. 4, April 1985, pp. 25–34.

Ross, D. T., and K. E. Schoman. 1977. "Structured Analysis for Requirements Definition." *IEEE Transactions on Software Engineering*, Vol. SE-3, No. 1, January 1977, pp. 6–15.

Rumbaugh, James, Michael Blaha, William Premerlani, Frederick Eddy, and William Lorensen. 1991. *Object-Oriented Modeling and Design* Englewood Cliffs, NJ: Prentice Hall.

Shlaer, Sally, and Steve Mellor. 1988. *Object-Oriented Systems Analysis: Modeling the World in Data*. Englewood Cliffs, NJ: Yourdon Press.

Shlaer, Sally, and Steve Mellor. 1992. *Object Lifecycles: Modeling the World in States*. Englewood Cliffs, NJ: Yourdon Press.

Schulmeyer, G. Gordon. 1990. *Zero Defect Software*. New York: McGraw-Hill.

Sommerville, I. 1985. *Software Engineering,* Second Edition, Reading, MA: Addison-Wesley Publishing Company.

Spendolini, Michael J. 1992. *The Benchmarking Book*. New York: AMACOM: The American Management Association.

Stevens, Roger T. 1979. *Operational Test & Evaluation: A Systems Engineering Process*. New York: Wiley-Interscience.

Stevens, Wayne P. 1981. *Using Structured Design: How to Make Programs Simple, Changeable, Flexible, and Reusable*. New York: Wiley-Interscience.

Stevens, Wayne, Larry Constantine, and Glenford Myers. 1974. "Structured Design." *IBM Systems Journal*, Vol. 13, No. 2: 115–139.

Teichroew, D., and E. A. Hershey. 1977. "PSL/PSA: A Computer Aided Technique for Structured Documentation and Analysis of Information Processing Systems." *IEEE Transactions on Software Engineering*, Vol. SE-12, No. 1, January 1977, pp. 41–48.

Ward, Paul T., and Stephen J. Mellor. 1985a. *Structured Development for Real Time Systems. Volume 1: Introduction and Tools.* Englewood Cliffs, NJ: Yourdon Press.

Ward, Paul T., and Stephen J. Mellor. 1985b. *Structured Development for Real Time Systems. Volume 2: Essential Modeling Techniques.* Englewood Cliffs, NJ: Yourdon Press.

Ward, Paul T., and Stephen J. Mellor. 1986. *Structured Development for Real Time Systems. Volume 3: Implementation Modeling Techniques.* Englewood Cliffs, NJ: Yourdon Press.

Ward, William T. 1989. "Software Defect Prevention Using McCabe's Complexity Metric." *HP Journal*, April 1989: 64–68.

Warnier, Jean-Dominique. 1974a. *Entraînement â la Programmation: Tome 1: Construction des programmes.* Paris: Les èditions D'Organisation.

Warnier, Jean-Dominique. 1974b. *Logical Construction of Programs,* Third Edition. New York: Van Nostrand Reinhold.

Warnier, Jean-Dominique. 1979a. *Guide des utilisateurs du systême informatique.* Paris: Les èditions D'Organisation.

Warnier, Jean-Dominique. 1979b. *Précis de Logique Informatique: La Transformation des Programmes, LCP.* Paris: Les èditions D'Organisation.

Warnier, Jean-Dominique. 1979c. *Précis de Logique Informatique: Les Procédures de traitement et leurs données, LCP.* Paris: Les èditions D'Organisation.

Warnier, Jean-Dominique. 1979d. *Précis de Logique Informatique: Pratique de l'organisation des données d'un systême, LCS.* Paris: Les èditions D'Organisation.

Warnier, Jean-Dominique. 1981. *Logical Construction of Systems.* New York: Van Nostrand Reinhold.

Warnier, Jean-Dominique. 1982. *Entraînement â la Programmation: Tome 2: Exploitation des données.* Paris: Les èditions D'Organisation.

Warnier, Jean-Dominique. 1985a. *Entraînement â la Programmation: LCP: Tome 1: Notions Fondamentales.* Paris: Les èditions D'Organisation.

Warnier, Jean-Dominique. 1985b. *Entraînement â la Programmation: LCP: Tome 2: DÉveloppements.* Paris: Les èditions D'Organisation.

Weinberg, Gerald M. 1975. *An Introduction to General Systems Thinking.* New York: Wiley-Interscience.

Weinberg, Gerald M. 1992. *Software Quality Management: Vol. 1: Systems Thinking.* New York: Dorset House Publishing.

Weinberg, Gerald M. 1993. *Software Quality Management: Vol. 2: First-Order Measurement.* New York: Dorset House Publishing.

Weinberg, Gerald M., and Daniela Weinberg. 1979. *On the Design of Stable Systems.* New York: Wiley-Interscience.

Weinberg, Victor. 1978. *Structured Analysis.* Englewood Cliffs, NJ: Yourdon Press.

Welker, Kurt D., and Paul W. Oman. 1995. "Software Maintainability Metrics Models in Practice." *Crosstalk*, November/December 1995.

Wilson, Peter. 1995. "Testable Requirements—An Alternative Sizing Measure." *The Journal of the Quality Assurance Institute,* October 1995.

Wysockl, Bernard. 1995. "Corporate Anorexia." *The Wall Street Journal*, July 5, 1995.

Yourdon, Edward. 1975. *Techniques of Program Structure and Design.* Englewood Cliffs, NJ: Prentice Hall.

Yourdon, Edward. 1985. *Structured Walkthroughs*, Third Edition. Englewood Cliffs, NJ: Yourdon Press.

Yourdon, Edward. 1989. *Modern Structured Analysis.* Englewood Cliffs, NJ: Yourdon Press.

Yourdon, Edward, and Larry L. Constantine. 1979. *Structured Design: Fundamentals of a Discipline of Computer Program and Systems Design.* Englewood Cliffs, NJ: Prentice Hall.

Zachman, John. 1987. "A Framework for Information Systems Architecture." *IBM Systems Journal,* Vol. 26, No. 3. 1987.

Index

LICENSE AGREEMENT AND LIMITED WARRANTY

READ THE FOLLOWING TERMS AND CONDITIONS CAREFULLY BEFORE OPENING THIS DISK PACKAGE. THIS LEGAL DOCUMENT IS AN AGREEMENT BETWEEN YOU AND PRENTICE-HALL, INC. (THE "COMPANY"). BY OPENING THIS SEALED DISK PACKAGE, YOU ARE AGREEING TO BE BOUND BY THESE TERMS AND CONDITIONS. IF YOU DO NOT AGREE WITH THESE TERMS AND CONDITIONS, DO NOT OPEN THE DISK PACKAGE. PROMPTLY RETURN THE UNOPENED DISK PACKAGE AND ALL ACCOMPANYING ITEMS TO THE PLACE YOU OBTAINED THEM FOR A FULL REFUND OF ANY SUMS YOU HAVE PAID.

1. **GRANT OF LICENSE:** In consideration of your payment of the license fee, which is part of the price you paid for this product, and your agreement to abide by the terms and conditions of this Agreement, the Company grants to you a nonexclusive right to use and display the copy of the enclosed software program (hereinafter the "SOFTWARE") on a single computer (i.e., with a single CPU) at a single location so long as you comply with the terms of this Agreement. The Company reserves all rights not expressly granted to you under this Agreement.

2. **OWNERSHIP OF SOFTWARE:** You own only the magnetic or physical media (the enclosed disk) on which the SOFTWARE is recorded or fixed, but the Company retains all the rights, title, and ownership to the SOFTWARE recorded on the original disk copy(ies) and all subsequent copies of the SOFTWARE, regardless of the form or media on which the original or other copies may exist. This license is not a sale of the original SOFTWARE or any copy to you.

3. **COPY RESTRICTIONS:** This SOFTWARE and the accompanying printed materials and user manual (the "Documentation") are the subject of copyright. You may not copy the Documentation or the SOFTWARE, except that you may make a single copy of the SOFTWARE for backup or archival purposes only. You may be held legally responsible for any copying or copyright infringement which is caused or encouraged by your failure to abide by the terms of this restriction.

4. **USE RESTRICTIONS:** You may not network the SOFTWARE or otherwise use it on more than one computer or computer terminal at the same time. You may physically transfer the SOFTWARE from one computer to another provided that the SOFTWARE is used on only one computer at a time. You may not distribute copies of the SOFTWARE or Documentation to others. You may not reverse engineer, disassemble, decompile, modify, adapt, translate, or create derivative works based on the SOFTWARE or the Documentation without the prior written consent of the Company.

5. **TRANSFER RESTRICTIONS:** The enclosed SOFTWARE is licensed only to you and may not be transferred to any one else without the prior written consent of the Company. Any unauthorized transfer of the SOFTWARE shall result in the immediate termination of this Agreement.

6. **TERMINATION:** This license is effective until terminated. This license will terminate automatically without notice from the Company and become null and void if you fail to comply with any provisions or limitations of this license. Upon termination, you shall destroy the Documentation and all copies of the SOFTWARE. All provisions of this Agreement as to warranties, limitation of liability, remedies or damages, and our ownership rights shall survive termination.

7. **MISCELLANEOUS:** This Agreement shall be construed in accordance with the laws of the United States of America and the State of New York and shall benefit the Company, its affiliates, and assignees.

8. **LIMITED WARRANTY AND DISCLAIMER OF WARRANTY:** The Company warrants that the SOFTWARE, when properly used in accordance with the Documentation, will operate in substantial conformity with the description of the SOFTWARE set forth in the Documentation. The Company does not warrant that the SOFTWARE will meet your requirements or that the operation of the SOFTWARE will be uninterrupted or error-free. The Company warrants that the

media on which the SOFTWARE is delivered shall be free from defects in materials and workmanship under normal use for a period of thirty (30) days from the date of your purchase. Your only remedy and the Company's only obligation under these limited warranties is, at the Company's option, return of the warranted item for a refund of any amounts paid by you or replacement of the item. Any replacement of SOFTWARE or media under the warranties shall not extend the original warranty period. The limited warranty set forth above shall not apply to any SOFTWARE which the Company determines in good faith has been subject to misuse, neglect, improper installation, repair, alteration, or damage by you. EXCEPT FOR THE EXPRESSED WARRANTIES SET FORTH ABOVE, THE COMPANY DISCLAIMS ALL WARRANTIES, EXPRESS OR IMPLIED, INCLUDING WITHOUT LIMITATION, THE IMPLIED WARRANTIES OF MERCHANTABILITY AND FITNESS FOR A PARTICULAR PURPOSE. EXCEPT FOR THE EXPRESS WARRANTY SET FORTH ABOVE, THE COMPANY DOES NOT WARRANT, GUARANTEE, OR MAKE ANY REPRESENTATION REGARDING THE USE OR THE RESULTS OF THE USE OF THE SOFTWARE IN TERMS OF ITS CORRECTNESS, ACCURACY, RELIABILITY, CURRENTNESS, OR OTHERWISE.

IN NO EVENT, SHALL THE COMPANY OR ITS EMPLOYEES, AGENTS, SUPPLIERS, OR CONTRACTORS BE LIABLE FOR ANY INCIDENTAL, INDIRECT, SPECIAL, OR CONSEQUENTIAL DAMAGES ARISING OUT OF OR IN CONNECTION WITH THE LICENSE GRANTED UNDER THIS AGREEMENT, OR FOR LOSS OF USE, LOSS OF DATA, LOSS OF INCOME OR PROFIT, OR OTHER LOSSES, SUSTAINED AS A RESULT OF INJURY TO ANY PERSON, OR LOSS OF OR DAMAGE TO PROPERTY, OR CLAIMS OF THIRD PARTIES, EVEN IF THE COMPANY OR AN AUTHORIZED REPRESENTATIVE OF THE COMPANY HAS BEEN ADVISED OF THE POSSIBILITY OF SUCH DAMAGES. IN NO EVENT SHALL LIABILITY OF THE COMPANY FOR DAMAGES WITH RESPECT TO THE SOFTWARE EXCEED THE AMOUNTS ACTUALLY PAID BY YOU, IF ANY, FOR THE SOFTWARE.

SOME JURISDICTIONS DO NOT ALLOW THE LIMITATION OF IMPLIED WARRANTIES OR LIABILITY FOR INCIDENTAL, INDIRECT, SPECIAL, OR CONSEQUENTIAL DAMAGES, SO THE ABOVE LIMITATIONS MAY NOT ALWAYS APPLY. THE WARRANTIES IN THIS AGREEMENT GIVE YOU SPECIFIC LEGAL RIGHTS AND YOU MAY ALSO HAVE OTHER RIGHTS WHICH VARY IN ACCORDANCE WITH LOCAL LAW.

ACKNOWLEDGMENT

YOU ACKNOWLEDGE THAT YOU HAVE READ THIS AGREEMENT, UNDERSTAND IT, AND AGREE TO BE BOUND BY ITS TERMS AND CONDITIONS. YOU ALSO AGREE THAT THIS AGREEMENT IS THE COMPLETE AND EXCLUSIVE STATEMENT OF THE AGREEMENT BETWEEN YOU AND THE COMPANY AND SUPERSEDES ALL PROPOSALS OR PRIOR AGREEMENTS, ORAL, OR WRITTEN, AND ANY OTHER COMMUNICATIONS BETWEEN YOU AND THE COMPANY OR ANY REPRESENTATIVE OF THE COMPANY RELATING TO THE SUBJECT MATTER OF THIS AGREEMENT.

Should you have any questions concerning this Agreement or if you wish to contact the Company for any reason, please contact in writing at the address below.

Robin Short
Prentice Hall PTR
One Lake Street
Upper Saddle River, New Jersey 07458